THE SCREENWRITER'S SOURCEBOOK

A COMPREHENSIVE MARKETING GUIDE
for SCREEN and TELEVISION WRITERS

■ MICHAEL HADDAD

CHICAGO
REVIEW
PRESS

Library of Congress Cataloging-in-Publication Data

Haddad, Michael.
    The screenwriter's sourcebook : a comprehensive marketing guide for screen and television writers / Michael Haddad.— 1st ed.
        p. cm.
    Includes index.
    ISBN 1-55652-550-8
    1. Motion picture authorship—United States—Marketing—Directories. 2. Television authorship—United States—Marketing—Directories. 3. Motion picture authorship—United States—Vocational guidance. 4. Television authorship—United States—Vocational guidance. I. Title.
    PN1996.H255 2005
    808.2´3´0688—dc22

2004011483

We have endeavored to make all the information contained in this book accurate at the time of publication. However, all things are subject to change so please verify names, addresses, and so forth before sending out any materials.

Cover and interior design: Monica Baziuk

Published by Chicago Review Press, Incorporated
814 North Franklin Street
Chicago, Illinois 60610
ISBN 1-55652-550-8
Printed in the United States of America
5 4 3 2 1

The artist must be a prophet, not in the sense that he foretells things to come, but that he tells the audience, at the risk of their displeasure, the secrets of their own hearts.

— SAUL BELLOW

CONTENTS

ACT ③ RESOURCES 257

ACKNOWLEDGMENTS

THE BEST THING about the entertainment business is the people you meet along the way. Of course it's also true that the worst thing about the entertainment business is the people you meet along the way (but we won't go there). Robin Harris, Carl Donahue, Bruce Fisher, Edward Rogers, Sam Kearns, and Randy Irwin have all lent assistance, wisdom, inspiration, goodwill, and common sense throughout this endeavor. Without them it would have been impossible.

Gina Reed, Michael Aury Marks, Owen Stacy, Linda Verns, Robin Meyer, and Lenny Ross have all taken time out of busy schedules to help me track down leads, deadlines, names, credits, facts, and elements I may have neglected, forgotten, or ignored. Pejman Partiveli, Liz Glotzer, Edgar Bravo, John Banner, and Dean Simone have offered suggestions, input, and encouraging words.

Cynthia Sherry had the faith to make it happen.

Lisa Rosenthal scanned, probed, corrected, deleted, and edited text with an unerring eye and constant support. Her creative editing, feedback, and suggestions made all the difference.

Sharon Mahoney has been my inspiration, sounding board, and guiding light throughout.

Linda McDonald has provided counsel, advice, enthusiasm, and encouragement, all of which proved invaluable.

And finally, to the ones who continue to light the path: Preston Sturges, Paddy Chayefsky, Joel and Ethan Coen, Elia Kazan, Julius and Philip Epstein, Billy Wilder, Ernest Lehman, Charlie Kaufman, Ernst Lubitsch, Jean Renoir, Sergio Leone, Ingmar Bergman, and Philip Barry.

INTRODUCTION

YOU FINISHED YOUR SCRIPT. That's great! Now what?

In Hollywood it's often said that everyone writes but no one reads. Agents, managers, and even the most powerful producers seem to have story ideas they're working on, but getting them to read *your* script is one of the most difficult tasks you will face as a writer. When I first started working as a script analyst I was told that I was recommending too many scripts. I liked fewer than 5 percent! They didn't *want* to see a recommendation because it meant they were going to have to do something. This gives you an idea of what you're up against. Not only do they *not* want to read your script, they're also praying *they won't like it*. Liking it would require getting involved, and getting involved means getting it made, which is an uphill battle—even for a successful producer.

Yet producers, agents, managers, and executives will tell you without fail, they're *desperately* looking for a good story. Every weekend they drag home piles of scripts searching for the one that makes them feel passionate, only to be disappointed time and again. As talented as many professional screenwriters are, they also tend to be formulaic. They've

---

▌ SCRIPT APPEAL ▌ Before you start sending out scripts, whether for a contest or to a contact in the industry, make sure your script is properly formatted. No sky blue paper, no colored ink, no fancy typeface. Use black Courier 12-point type on plain white paper with solid brass fasteners (not the cheap brass-coated ones) and plain card-stock cover. If you want to be inventive and try something new, do it in the writing, not the presentation. Make sure there are no typos. Don't give them a reason to toss your script.

learned the shortcuts and they know what works, so they rely on this bag of tricks in creating their scripts. Unfortunately the formula approach will never create a great script, the kind that people can't get out of their heads. There is simply no replacement for inspiration, and that often comes from the most unlikely places. So why doesn't Hollywood go out and seek material from nonprofessionals? Because Hollywood knows most amateur scripts are bad. They might have to review a thousand to find the one truly original, inspired script that might be next year's hit, and they just don't have the time or patience to search it out.

As a result, studios don't review scripts. Instead, they rely on producers to bring them quality material. This winnows down the number of submissions to a manageable level, and they know they won't have to look at scripts that are technically deficient. So how do you get to a producer? You don't. They have the same problem—they don't want to be deluged with scripts so they rely on literary agents to bring them quality material. If a good literary agency likes a writer enough to take him or her on, that's a badge of approval that impresses producers. So how do you get to an agent? You don't. The best agents aren't interested in unproduced writers. They only make money if *you're* making money. If all you've got is a nice smile and a few good lines, they're not going to get paid. So how does a new writer *become* a produced writer? That's the conundrum every writer faces, and there's no simple answer.

The truth is Hollywood is devoted to shutting people out. You can't really blame them; the number of people interested in breaking into the movie business is staggering. There has always been, and probably always will be, something about the movie business that captures the collective imagination. We reserve a special awe for the movies, and even the biggest names in television, sports, and music—people already at the peak of their profession—yearn for success in the movie business as though it's the truest measure of success.

As dire as this may seem, somewhere in Hollywood right now there's a writer with no more experience than you inking a $400,000 deal for his or her first script. People do succeed; people do break through the defenses. The studios don't want a thousand writers; they just want the two or three good ones. To get there you're going to have to beat out the 998 others. If you're not good enough, you'll fail. If you don't have faith in your script, you'll stumble. But if your script is good and you know it so you're persistent, then you'll find opportunities. Just keep reminding yourself that Hollywood *needs* new material; they *hunger* for it. The whole industry is devoted to what's new and fresh. They can't afford to ignore you forever.

You need a champion.

Have you ever heard the phrase "It's all who you know"? It's a cliché in Hollywood but it's absolutely dead-on. If you were a Hollywood insider and were forced to close the doors to the multitude of wannabes but still needed to look for material, where would you go? To people you know. People whose opinion you trust. People to whom you owe a favor, or people who helped you get where you are. You reduce the scope of what you have to review by limiting it to your field of influence, your own web of friends and contacts. But how does a writer break into this web of friends and contacts?

Until your script finds someone who loves it, *someone in a circle of influence,* it's just going to end up in the recycling bin no matter how good it is. This book is your guide to getting it to those people. What can you do to improve your chances? Be realistic. This process requires persistence, salesmanship, and passion. Hollywood's not going to come to you, so you'd better learn how to handle the word *no* (you'll hear a lot of it) and be sure this is what you want. And if you follow the guidelines laid out in this book, you'll get your work read, and that's the key to getting it made.

First and foremost you need to believe in your work. Then you need to put on your salesman's hat and tell people *why* they must read it. Don't stop there. When they get back to you and tell you why they didn't like it, you have to tell them why they're *wrong*. Yes, that's the way the business

---

▌ There are software programs such as Final Draft and Movie Magic that format your script for you. With a few minutes of practice you'll be able to write a screenplay without worrying about the formatting details. (See "Online Resources— Screenwriting Software" for information about these programs.) If you don't want to buy the software, check out scripts on the Internet and use them as a formatting guide. (See "Online Resources—Script Libraries" for a list of script sites.)

▌ **TIP:** Don't rely on printed scripts you might find at the bookstore as a formatting guide, as these often do not adhere to industry standards.

works. A thick skin and unshakable self-confidence will be your greatest allies on the journey ahead.

This book is organized as follows: "Act I: Contests," "Act II: Career Opportunities," and "Act III: Resources." These are road maps that will serve you well on this journey.

"Act I: Contests" includes screenplay contests, fellowships, grants, and development opportunities. If your script is solid and you don't have any Hollywood contacts, this is the place to start. Simply speaking, a contest win will get you an agent, an agent will get you a producer, and a pro-

---

▌ **THE RELEASE:** I know a few talented writers with scripts sitting on the shelf because they're scared someone will steal their idea. Do people really steal script ideas? Sure, but it doesn't happen as often as you think. There are a lot of great ideas out there; there's even a good chance someone else has had *yours,* but the devil is in the details. It's the *execution* of an idea that makes a great script, not the idea itself. If the writing is strong and the idea is unique, your script is ahead of the game. Besides, if you're an unknown, your script will be cheap. That veteran writer they hire to rip off your idea has a Beverly Hills mortgage to pay. So copyright your work (see "Copyright and Script Registration" to find out how) and forget about it. You need to get it into as many hands as you can, and that won't happen if you're worried about losing it.

And while we're on the subject, be prepared to sign a release. Some companies insist on this before they will read your work. It's a one-page document with room to enter the title of the script, its length in pages, your name, address, date, and signature. It's a legal document that promises them you won't sue them no matter what they do, even if they rip you off. Obviously, this is for their protection and not yours, and you generally have little choice but to comply. It's easy to understand their concern; they've been sued by amateurs that have sent scripts with a similar storyline to something the company had already committed to making. This is why an unsolicited script will be returned to you *unopened.* Opening it proves they had access to your material. Most of these cases were groundless but nonetheless expensive to defend. So are you signing away your rights? Probably not. Even though signing the release seems to give the company license to steal your idea, a court will likely rule that the document is unenforceable if it's clear you were ripped off. So sign it, forget it, and don't worry. You've got to get your script out there.

ducer will get it made. The most influential contests are designated with
★. Winners and finalists in any of these competitions will get the attention of top producers, agents, and managers—in other words, they'll
come to you. A win in any of the other contests will still open doors, but
you'll have to do the legwork. Your phone won't ring off the hook, but a
win may make the difference when it comes to getting a literary agent to
read your script. It becomes a selling point and you'll need as many of
those as you can get. If you put together a string of contest wins, you will
find it much easier to convince people to read your script. After all, no
matter how good a salesman you are, industry players will only be so
impressed by your assessment of your own talent. They need proof.

"Act II: Career Opportunities" includes listings of agents, managers,
and producers. If you have a contest win or you feel your salesmanship
skills are up to the task, this is the section for you. A manager isn't a strict
requirement for a screenwriter, but managers tend to be more approachable than agents, and a good one will get you a better agent than you
could get on your own. You'll pay for this service, as they take 15 percent
of your earnings (agents take another 10 percent), but when you're starting out, you need all the help you can get. It may be your manager, for
instance, who puts your script into the hands of the star or director that
gets the project made. In Hollywood it's often said you make nothing on
your first movie and make up for it on your second. Don't let money get
in your way, there's time for that later.

"Act III: Resources" includes copyright registration information (very
important); sources for emergency funds for struggling writers (difficult
to get); colonies, retreats, and residencies (getting away from it all may
help you get something inspiring down on paper); an entertainment
industry resource guide including guilds, unions, and professional associations; motion picture libraries and museums; networks and cable
channels; state arts agencies; state film commissions; and studios. It also
offers a compendium of online resources including advice and tips on
copyright and script registration, entertainment business, finding an
agent, independent filmmaking, job opportunities, legal resources, news
and publications, screenwriting courses, research, script libraries, stores,
writing groups, and more. There's a wealth of screenwriting information
available online these days, and it would be worthwhile for you to spend
a few hours checking out these twenty-four/seven resources.

A word of caution here: There are a lot of scams out there so be careful. Some folks bill themselves as Hollywood insiders and offer to represent you for a fee. Others say you need their professional analysis to get your script noticed. Not true. No one who's legit will charge you a dime. It's unfortunate that there are many people ready to cash in on the hopes and dreams of the rest of us, but with a healthy does of cynicism you can avoid them. *No one should have to pay to be a writer.*

Each section and subheading that follows has its own introduction, so don't worry if you're still not sure exactly what a producer does or what the difference is between a fellowship and a grant; it will all be explained as you go. There is also a glossary of terms at the end of the book you can turn to as needed. You will also find an index of contests catalogued by genre and a submission calendar to help you see at a glance which deadlines are approaching.

Good luck and keep writing!

CONTESTS

ACT ①

SCREENPLAY CONTESTS

SCREENPLAY CONTESTS offer everything from a first-look deal at a studio to more than $5 million in cash prizes. In recent years, more scripts have been found through contests than ever before. *Stolen Summer, Finding Forrester, The Laramie Project, Blue Car, Boys Don't Cry, Love & Basketball, Requiem for a Dream,* and *Bottle Rocket* were all made from scripts that won film contests. What is the reason for this trend?

The answer is simple. It takes one and a half to two hours to read a script and from $60 to $100 to critique it. Producers don't have time to read scripts themselves; they hire someone to do it. As a result, many Hollywood producers and entertainment companies simply don't bother with outside scripts. They already have relationships with writers, agents, and managers, so they get scripts through authorized channels. "But my script is better than those!" you cry. It may well be, but they can't afford the time and energy to read the hundred others to get to yours. Hollywood knows it can't afford to ignore new talent, so contests provide a buffer between them and the unknown writer. Contests may be the new writer's best route to getting noticed.

Pay close attention to the major contests marked with ★. These are the most influential. A win or even high placement in any of them will likely get you an agent. Of course these are also the most competitive.

Acclaim Film

Mission Statement: Our affiliated production companies will have the chance to consider the scripts of the winners, runners-up, finalists, and semifinalists for our film and TV contests. The companies already affiliated with us include Good Machine (*Crouching Tiger, Hidden Dragon*),

Recorded Picture Company (*Naked Lunch, The Last Emperor*), and the Donners' Company (*Lethal Weapon* series, *X-Men*).

Deadlines: EARLY: February 8; STANDARD: March 19; FINAL: April 23

Entry fees: EARLY: $45; STANDARD: $55; FINAL: $60

Categories: All genres

Prizes: FIRST PLACE: $1,000 cash; SECOND PLACE: Up-to-date books on writing and selling scripts. All winners and finalists may receive consideration by established production companies and agencies.

Previous Winners: FIRST PLACE: *Ghost of the Crossroads* by Michael Spohr ▌ Set in the Mississippi Delta circa 1940, it follows the friendship between a former Negro League ballplayer and a mysterious white wanderer. ▌ SECOND PLACE: *Maybe in My Next Life* by Doreen Orion ▌ To find the source of her disastrous love life, a young woman uses a forbidden artifact to travel to past lives—only to discover she's been making the same stupid mistake since time began. ▌ THIRD PLACE: *T & A* by Scott F. Butler ▌ In the summer of 1979, Billy O'Keefe, a romantic but ineffectual young man of privilege, is compelled to embark upon a bizarre odyssey to prove his manhood to his future father-in-law, an eccentric self-made billionaire.

Contact Information: 300 Central Ave., Ste. 501, St. Petersburg, FL 33701

(727) 502-9049 Phone

Web: www.acclaimtv.netfirms.com

E-mail: acclaimtv@go.com

Actors' Choice Awards

Mission Statement: Five talented attendees of the Screenwriting Symposium or Producers Seminar will receive an SCSFe (Screenwriters Conference in Santa Fe) Actors' Choice Award based on the first ten pages of their screenplays. These winning scenes will be presented in live readings by our actor-judges during the Annual Screenwriters Conference in Santa Fe. A brief critique session moderated by Karen Jones Meadows will follow each reading.

> ▌ *Writing scripts is very much like choreographing to music. There are measured scenes that go on for a certain amount of time, with a beginning, middle, and end.*
> —**JOAN TEWKESBURY**, screenwriter, *Nashville*

Deadline: April 28

Entry fee: $25 plus conference attendance

Categories: All genres; first ten pages of each script only

Prizes: Winners will receive Final Draft software and certificates of achievement from SCSFe. In addition, their winning scenes will be forwarded to the producers attending the Producers Seminar, and presented in live readings at the Actors' Choice Awards ceremony.

Previous Winners:

Drumsticks by Lyn Davis, Albuquerque, NM | *La Llorona* by Kristin Goodman, Chicago, IL | *The Faith Equations* by David Hames, Colorado Springs, CO | *Fast One* by Paul Taegel, Los Angeles, CA | *Dead Alice* by Charlie Tramontana, West Pittston, PA

Contact Information: The Screenwriting Conference in Santa Fe, P.O. Box 29762, Santa Fe, NM 87592

(866) 424-1501 Phone

(505) 424-8207 Fax

Web: www.scsfe.com

E-mail: writeon@scsfe.com

AFC Storytelling International Screenwriting Competition

Mission Statement: The mission of the African Film Commission (AFC) is to assist in the development of the African film industry. The AFC works with African governments and leaders to establish film commissions in their respective regions or countries, and promotes education, awareness, and collaboration throughout the continent of Africa.

Deadline: March 31

Entry fee: $30

Categories: Scripts with African content

Prizes: FIRST PRIZE: $5,000 plus an all-expenses-paid one-week trip to Los Angeles to collect the AFC Screenwriting Award and to be officially introduced to the Hollywood international film community; SECOND PRIZE: $3,500 along with an AFC Award; THIRD PRIZE: $2,000 along with an AFC Award

Contact Information: 8306 Wilshire Boulevard #330, Beverly Hills, CA 90211

(310) 770-6246 Phone

Web: www.africanfilmcommission.org

E-mail: info@africanfilmcommission.org

A.K.A Shriekfest Horror/Science Fiction Screewriting Contest

Mission Statement: A.K.A Shriekfest is a festival dedicated to discovering new and overlooked artists. The point of the festival is to help filmmakers by letting as many people see their films as possible, not by limiting when and where the films are shown. We want to celebrate the art of filmmaking without all the politics!

Deadlines: EARLY: March 12; STANDARD: May 28; FINAL: July 23

Entry fees: EARLY: $25 (short), $35 (feature); STANDARD: $35 (short), $45 (feature); FINAL: $45 (short), $55 (feature)

Categories: Shorts and features in the horror/thriller/sci-fi genres

Prizes: Cash, product awards, and trophies

Previous Winners: BEST FEATURE: *Bathory* by James D. Clayton | SECOND PLACE: *Gomorrah* by Phil Penningroth | THIRD PLACE: *Ark* by Alan Chan | BEST FEATURE IN THE UNDER-18 CATEGORY: *My Boyfriend's Back* by Stephanie Wood | BEST SHORT: *Dead Sober* by Stephan A. Foley | SECOND PLACE: *Eyewitness* by Gary Davidson

Contact Information: P.O. Box 920444, Sylmar, CA 91392

Web: www.shriekfest.com

E-mail: email@shriekfest.com

All Access Screenwriting Competition

Mission Statement: Welcome to the first annual All Access Screenwriting Competition, an extraordinary opportunity for talented screenwriters to open the door to Hollywood and its dealmakers. We asked writers what they really wanted from a screenwriting competition and the response was overwhelming: access to Hollywood. We've taken this a step further to give three winners an unprecedented four levels of industry exposure and access, plus some cool prizes and cash.

Deadlines: EARLY: July 31; FINAL: November 15

Entry fees: EARLY: $40; FINAL: $50

Categories: All genres

Prizes: FIRST PLACE: $250; SECOND PLACE: $150; THIRD PLACE: $100. Winning script synopses are also submitted to more than ninety participating companies including 20th Century Fox Studios, New Line Cinema, Paramount Classics, Walt Disney Pictures, Universal Pictures, Imagine

Entertainment, Samuel Goldwyn Films, ICM, and CAA. Winners' names and screenplay titles will be published in a print ad in the *Hollywood Reporter* in February or March. Publication time depends on the availability of ad space. Winners also receive a copy of that issue of the *Hollywood Reporter*. In addition, winners receive Final Draft 6 software and a *Syd Field's Screenwriting Workshop* DVD.

Contact Information: 13428 Maxella Ave. #501, Los Angeles, CA 90292

(310) 577-3181 Phone

Web: www.soyouwannasellascript.com

E-mail: questions@soyouwannasellascript.com

All Student Screenplay Contest

Mission Statement: Brown University undergraduate David Peck started the Ivy Film Festival in 2001 with classmate Justin Slosky. The idea was to create a venue for undergraduate film work on par with professional film festivals and to host events allowing emerging filmmakers to learn from industry experts. The screenwriting contest is designed to give undiscovered scriptwriters exposure and a chance to have their talent discovered. Toward this goal, representatives from various agencies, management firms, and production companies read the winning scripts from the contest.

Deadlines: STANDARD: February 1; FINAL: February 14

Entry fees: STANDARD: $20 (short); $35 (feature); FINAL: $25 (short); $45 (feature)

Categories: Feature and short scripts; all genres accepted

Prizes: The top five short and feature-length screenplays are sent to Beverly Hills where they are evaluated by agents at Genesis Literary Agency and various other management companies. The winners are announced at the festival in April at Brown University. They are also posted on the Web site.

Previous Winners: DIRECTOR'S AWARD: *The Greatest Hour* by Mani Chandy, Brown University ┃ SHORT: *Welcome to Saranac Lake* by Daniel Falcone,

---

┃ *I don't take the movies seriously, and anyone who does is in for a headache.*
  —BETTE DAVIS

Columbia University ❚ FEATURE: *All-American Boy* by Kevin Colligan, UCLA Extension

Contact Information: 75 Waterman St., Box 1930, Brown University, Providence, RI 02912

(401) 867-4977 Phone

Web: www.ivyfilmfestival.com

E-mail: screenplay@ivyfilmfestival.com

American Accolades Screenplay Competition

Mission Statement: The American Accolades Screenwriting Competition aims to create new opportunities in Hollywood for artists with fresh perspectives and is designed to provide an outlet for emerging talent and undiscovered screenplays. Finalist judges include agents, managers, and industry executives.

Deadlines: EARLY: November 14; STANDARD: December 30; FINAL: February 27

Entry fees: EARLY: $40; STANDARD: $50; FINAL: $60

Categories: Drama, thriller, comedy, sci-fi/action/adventure, other

Prizes: GRAND PRIZE WINNER: Total for winning best of best in all genres: $2,500; FIRST PLACE IN EACH SUBCATEGORY (drama, thriller, comedy, sci-fi/action/adventure, other): $500. All finalists receive a comprehensive screenplay analysis and entry into the American Accolades Hall of Fame.

Previous Winners: DRAMA: *The Paper Route* by Danny M. Howell ❚ COMEDY: *Baked Alaska* by Julie Kim and Kariné Marwood ❚ SCI-FI/ACTION/ADVENTURE: *Hannibal* by Jack Davidson ❚ THRILLER: *Inside Job* by Ryan Bradley ❚ OTHER: *Containment* by Brad Campbell

Contact Information: 2118 Wilshire Blvd., Ste. 160B, Santa Monica, CA 90403

Web: www.americanaccolades.com/accoladesTV.htm

E-mail: info@amercianaccolades.com

❚ *I had to be my own best salesman. I had to know everything that was going on in Hollywood, who might or might not be interested in my piece, and guide my agent in those directions, even if he disagreed.*

—**TOM SCHULMAN**, screenwriter, *Dead Poets Society*

American Accolades TV & Shorts Competition

Mission Statement: This competition is geared toward discovering budding artists and breaking them into Hollywood. Like its big brother, the American Accolades Screenwriting Competition, the American Accolades TV & Shorts Competition aims to create new opportunities in Hollywood for artists with fresh perspectives.

Deadline: November 13

Entry fee: $55

Categories: Television spec script, pilot, MOW, miniseries, short script

Prizes: GRAND PRIZE: $1,000 ($500 Grand Prize, plus $500 for winning a competition category); FIRST PLACE IN EACH CATEGORY (half-hour spec, half-hour pilot, one-hour spec, one-hour pilot, MOW, short script): $500. Finalists receive professional feedback from The Academy Writers Clinic and entry into the American Accolades TV & Shorts Hall of Fame.

Previous Winners: ONE-HOUR SPEC: *The West Wing:* "Farewell to Tuvalu" by Doug Molitor ∎ SHORT SCRIPT: *The Anniversary* by Ham Tran ∎ HALF-HOUR SPEC: *Sex and the City:* "The Need for Speed" by David Rosen and Stacy Van Heusen

Contact Information: 2118 Wilshire Blvd., Ste. 160B, Santa Monica, CA 90403

Web: www.americanaccolades.com/accoladesTV.htm

E-mail: info@amercianaccolades.com

American Cinema Foundation Screenwriting Competition

Mission Statement: Feature films and television influence the way the vast majority of Americans view their lives, providing the most widely seen entertainment and information. The ACF Screenwriting Competition seeks new voices that will contribute positively to the richness and complexity of the stories in the media. The American Cinema Foundation was founded to nurture and reward television and feature film projects that address fundamental social values, support and strengthen the concepts of the common good and common culture, and promote democratic pluralism.

Deadline: March 31

Entry fee: $30

Categories: All genres

Prizes: The winning first place script will receive a cash award. The American Cinema Foundation may increase or decrease the number of prizes awarded at its sole discretion. For scripts written by more than one author, the authors will arrange the division of any award.

Previous Winners: 2001: *Father Eight* by Douglas J. Augustin I 2000: *Hi-Hat Hattie* by Larry Parry I 1999: *Out of the Night* by William S.E. Coleman

Contact Information: American Cinema Foundation, 9911 W. Pico Blvd., Ste. 510, Los Angeles, CA 90035

(310) 286-9420 Phone

(310) 286-7914 Fax

Web: www.cinemafoundation.com

E-mail: acinema@cinemafoundation.com

American Screenwriters Association/Writers Digest International Screenplay Competition

Mission Statement: The American Screenwriters Association (ASA) is organized for educational purposes, including the promotion and encouragement of the art of screenwriting. We welcome interested individuals from around the world who are pursuing the writing of documentaries, educational films, feature films, television, radio, and large-screen format films. Today, the American Screenwriters Association has an international membership of more than 1,200 members located throughout the United States, Europe, the Pacific, and the Middle East in twenty-seven countries and 901 cities.

Deadlines: EARLY: August 15; STANDARD: October 15

Entry fees: EARLY: $40 ASA members, $50 nonmembers; STANDARD: $45 ASA members, $55 nonmembers

Categories: All genres

Prizes: GRAND PRIZE: $5,000 and a trip to the ASA International Screenwriters Conference, Mick Caswell Award for Screenplay Excellence awarded during the Screenwriting Hall of Fame Awards, free conference registration, travel, and accommodations; SECOND PLACE: $2,500; THIRD PLACE: $1,000; FOURTH PLACE: $500; FIFTH PLACE: $250; SIXTH PLACE: $100 cash

Previous Winners: *Death Watch* by Marlo Brawer, Toluca Lake, CA I *Curtain of Iron* by Inis Clubs, Colorado Springs, CO I *Safe Harbor* by Susan Demasi, Greenlawn, NY I *Middle America* by Stuart Ross Fink, New York,

NY | *Jayne Foole* by David Sanger and David Lipton, Studio City, CA | *Birds & Bees* by Suzanne Stavinoha, Austin, TX
Contact Information: 269 S. Beverly Dr., Ste. 2600, Beverly Hills,
  CA 90212-3807
(866) 265-9091 Phone
(866) 265-9091 Fax
Web: www.goasa.com
E-mail: asa@goasa.com

★ American Zoetrope Screenplay Contest

Mission Statement: Throughout its thirty-year history American Zoetrope has sought new creative possibilities in technology. The purpose of this contest is to give new screenwriters industry exposure. In its first thirty years, American Zoetrope has produced some of the most important films in American cinema—films that have been recognized with fifteen Academy Awards and sixty-eight nominations. At the core of this success is a steadfast dedication to storytelling. In the words of founding director Francis Ford Coppola, who won his first Oscar for the screenplay *Patton,* "the story is the foundation upon which all else is built."
Deadlines: EARLY: August 1; FINAL: September 1
Entry fees: EARLY: $30; FINAL: $40
Categories: All genres
Prizes: $5,000 Grand Prize. The top ten screenplays will be considered for film option and development by American Zoetrope, and considered for representation by ICM, UTA, Paradigm, and The Firm.
Contact Information: 916 Kearny St., San Francisco, CA 94133
(415) 788-7500 Phone
(415) 989-7910 Fax
Web: www.zoetrope.com/contests
E-mail: contests@zoetrope.com

Usually when you have a block, it's because you've lost the motor of the story.
—AMY HOLDEN JONES, screenwriter, *Indecent Proposal* and *Mystic Pizza*

SCREENPLAY CONTESTS

America's Best Writing Competition

Mission Statement: America's Best Writing Competition is currently accepting feature-length scripts, short stories, poems, and stage plays for year-round writing competitions. The work is judged not on the basis of mass appeal or marketing opportunity, but solely on the impact of the words. All written material our judges feel merit acknowledgement can win. Writers may win based on best dialogue, creative concept, character development or any other combination of words that work wonders.

Deadline: September 23

Entry fees: SCREENPLAYS: $35; TV SCRIPTS: $25; SITCOMS: $25

Categories: Screenplays, TV dramas, TV sitcoms

Prizes: SCREENPLAY: $10,000 First Prize; TV DRAMA: $1,000 First Prize; SITCOM: $1,000 First Prize

Contact Information: 3936 S. Semoran Blvd., Ste. 368, Orlando, FL 32822

(407) 894-9001 Phone

(407) 894-5547 Fax

Web: www.writersfoundation.com

E-mail: info@writersfoundation.com

Another Sleepless Night Screenwriting Competition

Mission Statement: Our competition is designed to give writers the chance for exposure to professionals in the film industry.

Deadlines: EARLY: September 30; STANDARD: April 15

Entry fees: EARLY: $30; STANDARD: $50

Categories: All genres

Prizes: FIRST PLACE: $1,000 and submission to studio; SECOND PLACE: submission to studio; THIRD PLACE: recognition and endorsement by Sleepless Night Productions

---

Writers are vain, selfish, and lazy, and at the very bottom of their motives lies a mystery. Writing . . . is a long, exhausting struggle, like a long bout of some painful illness. One would never undertake such a thing if one were not driven by some demon one can neither resist nor understand.

—GEORGE ORWELL

Previous Winners: ❘ FIRST PLACE: *On Approved Credit* by Greg Brainerd ❘ A comedy about four college friends on a mission to bring down the credit card companies after all their belongings are repossessed for failure to pay their bills. ❘ SECOND PLACE: *5 Years* by Jason "Fuzzy" Batten ❘ A reincarnation gone wrong creates a holy war between good and evil as one man has five years (five days) to save the fate of all mankind, escape a demon hunting him down, and fulfill his destined love. ❘ THIRD PLACE: *Wide Awake* by Rob Williams ❘ A Seattle police detective battles the demons of sleep paralysis while tracking a serial killer who is closer than he knows.

Contact Information: c/o Marisa Sommerville, 256 S. Robertson Blvd.
#405, Beverly Hills, CA 90211
(858) 829-6394 Phone
Web: www.anothersleeplessnight.com
E-mail: anothersleeplessnight@hotmail.com

Applause Screenwriting Competition

Mission Statement: All Applause Screenwriting Competition judges are well-known screenwriting instructors and/or Hollywood industry professionals. The first, second, and third place winners will have their scripts sent to production companies, managers, and agents.

Deadlines: EARLY: July 31; STANDARD: January 31

Entry fees: EARLY: $50; STANDARD: $55

Categories: All genres

Prizes: FIRST PLACE: $1,000; SECOND PLACE: $500; THIRD PLACE: $250 ❘ Other prizes include exposure package by The Insiders System; Lets-Do-Lunch with Hollywood execs; promotion packages by So You Wanna Sell a Script and InkTip.com; Action/Cut Filmmaking Seminar; script critiques by James Mercurio and Michael Thunder; tickets to Hollywood by the Bay screenwriting festival; books from Michael Wiese Productions; *Spec Screenplay Sales Directory, Absolute Markets* Premium Edition; *The Hero's 2 Journeys* DVD; software including Power Structure, StoryCraft, and Final Draft; and *Scr(i)pt* magazine subscription.

Previous Winners: Doug Hundley of Calpella, CA, won the Grand Prize of $1,000 in the 2002 Applause Screenwriting Competition and the Gold Country/Lake Tahoe Regional Award of $1,000. Hundley's script *Finn Again* chronicles the continuing adventures of Huck Finn in his twenties.

Syrie James of Los Angeles took the Second Prize of $500 for her high-concept script *Up*. After a construction accident, a man's inability to sleep changes his attitudes toward time, success in business, and what's important in a mate. Scott Lipanovich of Santa Rosa, CA, took the Third Prize of $250 for his youth-market script *Running Through Stone,* which follows a circle of high school friends whose football rivalry with another school gets fatally out of hand.

Contact Information: P.O. Box 3098, Rocklin, CA 95677
(916) 435-9862 Phone
Web: www.applause4you.com
E-mail: applause4you@bvunet.net

Arizona Screenplay Search

Mission Statement: Sponsored by the Arizona Screenwriters Association, Final Draft screenwriting software, and Inktip.com, the Arizona Screenplay Search seeks unproduced feature-length screenplays for two competitions: One for screenplays that take place outside the state of Arizona, another for screenplays that take place in Arizona.

Deadline: March 1

Entry fee: $30

Categories: All genres

Prizes: There are two grand prizes for each competition. Each Grand Prize winner receives $200 in cash and two VIP passes to the 2004 Phoenix Film Festival (retail $650). Second Place in each competition wins two full festival passes to the 2004 Phoenix Film Festival (retail $250). The top five finalists in each competition will have their screenplays listed on the Phoenix Film Festival Web site; they will also receive filmmaker discounts to the 2004 Phoenix Film Festival and will be included in the press information for the Arizona Screenplay Search.

TIP: Be sure to research any screenplay competition not listed in this book before sending your money; some of them aren't legitimate. Do a Google search and check to see if the contest has been mentioned in any respected periodicals. An even easier test: does the Web site look professionally designed?

Contact Information: 2345 E. Thomas Rd., Ste. 100, Phoenix, AZ 85016

(602) 955-6444 Phone

Web: www.phxfilm.com

E-mail: festival@phxfilm.com

AudioScript CD Contest

Mission Statement: Do you believe your screenplay would make a perfect audio CD? Five winners will be chosen to have their feature-length screenplays adapted to an AudioScript CD.

Deadline: January 31

Entry fee: $25

Categories: All genres

Prizes: AudioScript CD of screenplay (retail value $600), 60 days free revision CDs (retail value $300), 10 percent discount on future AudioScript CD order (retail value $60), Cinepunkstudios logo T-shirt (retail value $20), feedback on the winning script (retail value $50)

Contact Information: 1614 Hawthorne Dr., Unit Left, State College, PA 16801

Web: www.cinepunkstudios.com

E-mail: info@cinepunkstudios.com

★ Austin Film Festival and Heart of Film Screenplay Competition

Mission Statement: Austin Heart of Film Screenplay Competition is dedicated to rewarding talented writers with the opportunity to have their work read by production companies.

Deadlines: SCREENPLAYS: May 7; TELEPLAYS: June 1

Entry fees: Screeplays: $40; TELEPLAYS: $30

Categories: SCREENPLAY: adult/family, comedy; TELEVISION: sitcom, drama

Prizes: SCREENPLAY: ADULT/FAMILY CATEGORY: $5,000 cash, reimbursement of round-trip airfare (up to $500, excluding frequent flyer miles), hotel compensation while at the festival (up to $500), and the AFF Bronze Typewriter award; COMEDY CATEGORY: $5,000 cash, reimbursement of roundtrip airfare (up to $500, excluding frequent flyer miles), hotel compensation while at the festival (up to $500), and the AFF Bronze Typewriter Award. The winners will also have their screenplays read in Los Angeles at a staged reading with professional actors. All finalists receive a complimentary Producer's Badge (value: $650) to the Film Festival and Heart of Film Screenwriters Conference. All semifinalists may purchase a Producer's Pass for $130 (value: $650).

TELEVISION: $1,000 for each category winner. Airfare compensation up to $500, excluding frequent flyer miles, hotel compensation up to $500, and the AFF Bronze Typewriter Award for each category winner. All awards will be presented at the Austin Film Festival Awards Luncheon.

Success Stories: *Excess Baggage,* winner in the Adult category, written by Max Adams, was optioned by Columbia. The movie stars Alicia Silverstone and Benicio del Torro. *Goodbye Lover,* winner in the Adult category, written by Ron Peer, was picked up by Gotham Entertainment. The movie stars Patricia Arquette, Don Johnson, and Ellen DeGeneres. *Natural Selection,* a semifinalist in the Adult category, written by B. J. Burrow and Allen Odom, was optioned by 24/36 Productions. The movie, starring David Carradine, Michael Bowen, Darren Burrows, Stephen Root, and Bob Balaban, aired on Showtime. Available on DVD. *Miracle in Lane Two,* a finalist in the Family category, written by Donald Yost and Joel Kauffmann, was optioned by Disney and aired on the Disney Channel. *Happy Hour,* written by Richard Levine, was optioned and made into a film, starring Anthony Lapaglia, Eric Stoltz, Caroleen Freeny, and Robert Vaughn. It was directed by Mike Bencivenga.

Contact Information: 1604 Nueces, Austin, TX 78701
(512) 478-4795 Phone
(512) 478-6205 Fax
Web: www.austinfilmfestival.com
E-mail: info@austinfilmfestival.com

TIP: Paperclip your check to your application, don't leave it loose in the envelope. If you pay by money order, make sure your name is on it.

Every great film should seem new every time you see it.
—ROGER EBERT

BEA National Juried Faculty Script Writing Competition

Mission Statement: The Broadcast Education Association National Juried Faculty Script Writing Competition is designed to promote and recognize outstanding faculty scripts determined in a peer-juried evaluation of creative work. Each entrant must be a member of the faculty of a U.S. university, college, or community/technical college, or of any BEA academic member institution anywhere in the world.

Deadline: January 10

Entry fee: $35

Categories: Short script on a selected theme (2004 theme was "Hope," 2005 theme is "Honor")

Prizes: FIRST PLACE: $200 from the BEA; Screenwriter software from Screenplay Systems, Inc.; $100 Sage Publications gift certificate; a free book of choice from Focal Press; the book *Screen & Stage Marketing Secrets* from James Russell Publishing; and professional coverage of the winning script by Peter Mellencamp, noted Hollywood script consultant and analyst. SECOND PLACE: check for $100 from the BEA; Screenwriter software from Screenplay Systems, Inc.; $75 Sage Publications gift certificate; book of choice from Focal Press; and *Screen & Stage Marketing Secrets*. THIRD PLACE: Screenwriter software from Screenplay Systems, Inc.; $50 Sage Publications gift certificate; book of choice from Focal Press; and *Screen & Stage Marketing Secrets*.

Contact Information: Fred G. Thorne, Cal State University-Chico, Communication Design, Chico, CA 95929

(530) 893-4800 Phone

Web: www.marquette.edu/bea/write/faccompann.html

E-mail: fthorne@csuchico.edu

Best in the West Screenwriting Competition

Mission Statement: This contest is designed to promote both the beauty and uniqueness of the American West and the talent of new unproduced writers. We are in the process of reorganizing the Best in the West Screenwriting Competition. New categories will be added and a new deadline announced as soon as possible. We also hope to obtain some additional sponsors and prizes.

Deadline: November 30

Entry fees: $40 for first submission, $35 for each additional script

Categories: Old West and New West

Prizes: In addition to a small Western-motif prize awarded to our first- and second-place winners in each category, winners will have their scripts posted on the Writers Script Network Web site.

Previous Winners: OLD WEST: FIRST PLACE: *Shooting Starr* by Dave Pearce, Rancho Palos Verdes, CA | Headstrong U.S. Marshal Dunn abducts feisty Maybelle, whom he mistakes for the infamous frontier outlaw Belle Starr. He's hell-bent on escorting her to stand trial as satire, escape, rescue, and brutal marauders blend with an unexpected danger—love. **NEW WEST:** FIRST PLACE: *Wyld Widows* by Tom Lavagnino, Los Angeles, CA | A woman who wishes to become pregnant by her incarcerated husband is denied a conjugal visit, so she teams with two friends to break into the prison to facilitate her desperation- and biological clock–driven agenda.

Contact Information: P.O. Box 520750, Salt Lake City, UT 84152-0750

(801) 487-1842 Phone

Web: www.bestinthewest.com

E-mail: bestinwestscript@bigplanet.com

Big Bear Lake Screenwriting Competition

Mission Statement: The Big Bear Lake International Film Festival is a non-profit organization dedicated to showcasing emerging film talent and independent films. Our goal is to bring up-and-coming filmmakers and industry professionals together in the Big Bear Lake community. The festival screens independent feature films, short films, student films, documentaries, animation, and family films. Each year there is a special sidebar cultural showcase—2004 will showcase African American films.

Deadlines: EARLY: March 1; STANDARD: April 15

Entry fees: EARLY: $30; STANDARD: $40 ($25 for local residents)

Categories: All genres

> An audience will forgive you almost anything at the beginning of a picture, but almost nothing at the end.
>
> —ROBERT TOWNE, screenwriter, *Chinatown*

Prizes: Script submission to a list of agents, producers, and managers; film festival pass; David Freeman's "Beyond Structure" workshop; Final Draft software; script consultation by Story InSight Script Consulting

Previous Winners: FIRST PLACE: *Lavender Blue* by Norman Lapidus and L. Lee Lapidus I SECOND PLACE: *Stalag America* by Daniel C. Hall and Jonathan R. Hall I THIRD PLACE: *The Proteus Mandate* by Jane C. Turville

Contact Information: P.O. Box 1981, Big Bear Lake, CA 92315-1981

(909) 866-3433 Phone

Web: www.bigbearlakefilmfestival.com

E-mail: woodduck@pineknot.com

Breakthrough with a Scream Screenwriting Contest

Mission Statement: Our purpose is to expose new science fiction and horror writers to industry professionals.

Deadlines: EARLY: September 30; STANDARD: April 15

Entry fees: EARLY: $30; STANDARD: $50

Categories: Horror and science fiction

Prizes: First Place winners receive $1,000 and submission to studio. Second Place winners receive submission to studio. Third Place winners receive recognition and endorsement by Sleepless Night Productions.

Previous Winners: FIRST PLACE: *Flash* by Jamie Cogburn I A man experiences flashes of horrifying scenes of brutality and is terrified to learn these flashes are coming true. He desperately attempts to stop the events from happening, but reality is blurred when he is no longer sure if he is the savior or the cause. I SECOND PLACE: *Gendercide* by Kris Hall I Fifty years in the future, two New York City cops battle villains who have created biological weapons that target specific races and genders. I THIRD PLACE: *The Guardians* by L. C. Cruell I They are everywhere. A timid young woman with superhuman powers uncovers a secret scientific society that has manipulated mankind from behind the scenes for a hundred years, is now ready to emerge, and has only thing standing in their way: her.

Contact Information: c/o Marisa Sommerville, 256 S. Robertson Blvd.

#405, Beverly Hills, CA 90211

(858) 829-6394 Phone

Web: www.anothersleeplessnight.com

E-mail: anothersleeplessnight@hotmail.com

SCREENPLAY CONTESTS

Burris-Hulett Literary Management Monthly Screenwriter Discovery Awards

Mission Statement: Most screenwriters believe their stories have the elements to go all the way to the big-time, if only an industry buyer would pay attention! With about 50,000 new screenplays registered with the WGA each year, the hurdles get higher and the barriers tougher for a well-crafted screenplay to receive meaningful recognition of merit. Burris-Hulett has connections with established buyers of screenplays in New York and Hollywood, as well as with independents across the United States. As we open more doors for screenwriters, we seek exceptional screenwriters with outstanding stories to tell.

Deadline: Last day of the month

Entry fee: $25

Categories: All genres

Prizes: Up to two awards each month: Best Overall Award and Best of Genre Award. ▮ All genres are eligible each month for the Best Overall Award. An additional Best of Genre Award will be given each month for the best of the specific genre emphasized that month. Monthly award winners will receive recognition through publicity releases, will be considered for representation by Burris-Hulett Literary Management, and will be considered for production.

Contact Information: 5547 S. Lewis Ave., Tulsa, OK 74105

(918) 749-6335 Phone

(918) 749-5411 Fax

Web: www.hulettlawfirm.com

E-mail: hulettlawfirm@aol.com

▮ *For me the challenge is always to look inside myself and find what's really behind what I'm working on.*

  —**TOM SCHULMAN,** screenwriter, *Dead Poets Society*

▮ *I think part of being a good screenwriter is being as concise as possible.*

  —**ERIC ROTH,** screenwriter, *Forrest Gump*

Century City Film Festival Screenplay Competition

Mission Statement: The Century City Film Festival Screenplay Competition is designed to give deserving writers recognition and possibly a career boost. We are looking for fantastic scripts in any genre.

Deadlines: EARLY: March 4; STANDARD: April 30; FINAL: May 31; EXTENDED: July 1

Entry fees: EARLY: $30; STANDARD: $40; FINAL: $45; Extended $55

Categories: All genres

Prizes: A read from top management and literary companies, an All-Access Pass to the festival, invitations to exclusive filmmaker and VIP parties, personal introductions to decision-makers attending the fest, screenwriting software, packages from all of the sponsors, and a closing-night award for the First Place winner with recognition to the other nine.

Contact Information: P.O. Box 67132, Century City, CA 90067

(310) 551-1035 Phone

(310) 388-1383 Fax

Web: www.centurycityfilmfestival.com

E-mail: david@thebroadcaster.com

Christian Screenwrite

Mission Statement: The mission of Christian Screenwrite is to foster and promote Christian writers, contemporary Christian screenplays, and awareness of Christian experiences in film. Our objective is to utilize the medium of film to spread to both Christians and non-Christians the principles of forgiveness, faith, redemption, and love demonstrated and taught by Jesus Christ.

Deadline: January 30

Entry fee: $30

Categories: Submissions must meet one or more of the following criteria: 1. Scripts whose main storyline deals with or is based on biblical Christian principles, morals, values, and beliefs. For example, *A Walk to Remember.* 2. Contemporary scripts whose main character is a Christian. For example, *The Apostle.* 3. Scripts that explore the supernatural from a biblical perspective.

Prizes: FIRST PLACE: $500; SECOND PLACE: $250; THIRD PLACE: $250

Previous Winners: FIRST PLACE: Gary Miner ┃ SECOND PLACE: Mark Anthony Vashon ┃ THIRD PLACE: Kasey Phinney
Contact Information: P.O. Box 447, Bloomfield , NJ 07003
(862) 579-6064 Phone
Web: www.christianscreenwrite.com
E-mail: info@christianscreenwrite.com

Cinescape Magazine's Genre Screenwriting Competition

Mission Statement: *Cinescape*'s unique screenplay competition was established to help science fiction, fantasy, horror, and action-adventure screenwriters to be discovered by the film industry. Winners will receive cash and prizes and will be introduced to agents, managers, producers, and studios. Judges will include members of the *Cinescape* staff along with Hollywood industry professionals.
Deadlines: EARLY: May 15; STANDARD: June 30
Entry fees: EARLY: $25; STANDARD: $30
Categories: Horror, sci-fi, fantasy, action/adventure
Prizes: FIRST PLACE: $2,500; SECOND PLACE: $1,500; THIRD PLACE: $500; FOURTH PLACE: $250; FIFTH PLACE: $100 ┃ All Winners receive Final Draft screenwriting software, mention in a *Cinescape* article on winners and their scripts, and a one-year subscription to *Cinescape*.
Previous Winners: FIRST PLACE: *Dark Side of the Moon* by Tom McLaughlin ┃ While carrying out a hit for the mafia in Las Vegas, the last werewolf on Earth encounters the vampire that murdered his family twenty years earlier and all hell breaks loose as the two monsters clash in Sin City. ┃ SECOND PLACE: *DayTrippers* by Roger C. Hull ┃ A television journalist makes an alarming discovery about humanity's future when he becomes caught up in a cat-and-mouse game with aliens that take deadly thrill rides in human bodies. ┃ THIRD PLACE: *The Agent* by Edward Case ┃ A veteran agent from a covert group that secretly controls events through the subtle manipulation of time receives an execution order for a woman who might be the daughter he abandoned long ago.
Contact Information: 1223 Wilshire Blvd. #402, Santa Monica, CA 91403-5400
Web: www.cinescape.com/scriptcontest
E-mail: scriptcontest@cinescape.com

Drawn Productions Short Script Writing Contest

Mission Statement: Drawn Productions seeks out the best short scripts for cash awards and prizes.

Deadline: July 25

Entry fee: $20

Categories: Short scripts

Prize: $1,000

Previous Winners: FIRST PLACE: *Before Sean* by Xylina Rae Kinsey ▌ SECOND PLACE: *Shadow Talk* by Justin T. Ostensen ▌ THIRD PLACE: *A Change of Heart* by Anselmo Garcia, Jr.

Contact Information: P.O. Box 5662, Cary, NC 27512-5662

(919) 678-1000 Phone

(919) 677-0097 Fax

Web: www.skyleeentertainment.com

E-mail: drawnp1@aol.com

eShay.com Script Writing Competition

Mission Statement: eShay.com is an Internet showcase for independent shorts and films from the hottest new writers and directors. We have plans to carry entertainment to new levels with our revolutionary Internet and film venture. Movies are currently playing! Sign up for our newsletter so you'll know the inside scoop on the latest production.

Deadline: July 15

Entry fee: $25

Categories: All genres

Prizes: Script consultation, storyboarding software, and budgeting software.

Contact Information: 258 Harvard St., #361, Brookline, MA 02446-2904

(877) 706-8869 Phone

Web: www.eshay.com

E-mail: info@eshay.com

▌ **TIP:** Bad scripts are tossed by page 15. Make those first pages count. Keep it moving and set up a conflict that will get under the reader's skin.

SCREENPLAY CONTESTS

The Fade In Awards

Mission Statement: The Fade In Awards were established in 1996 to assist talented new writers and writer/directors in gaining recognition within the Hollywood community in order to begin a career as a working filmmaker.

Deadline: October 30

Entry fee: $40

Categories: FEATURES AND SHORTS: comedy, action-adventure, thriller, drama, film noir, family

Prizes: GRAND PRIZE: iMac computer, plus airfare and hotel accommodations (three days and two nights) to meet with top literary agents and studio executives (or cash equivalent); FIRST PRIZE (in each category): $750, script analysis by WGA-credited writer, Waterman fountain pen, and one-year *Fade In* subscription; SECOND PRIZE (in each category): $500, script analysis by WGA-credited writer, and one-year *Fade In* subscription; Third Prize (in each category): $250, script analysis by WGA-credited writer, one-year *Fade In* subscription. Winners will be listed in an upcoming issue of *Fade In, Variety,* and/or the *Hollywood Reporter.*

Success Stories: After Jon Bokenkamp entered his thriller *Preston Tylk,* we signed him with ICM, he was hired to write a feature for director William Friedkin, has since directed *Preston Tylk* and sold his documentary *After Sunset* to AMC. Now, after writing a feature for Julia Roberts and another for Halle Berry, Bokenkamp's newest project, *Taking Lives* starring Angelina Jolie, is filming in Canada. After Josh Gordin and Will Speck entered their short *Culture,* both signed with ICM. *Culture* was nominated for an Academy Award, and Gordin and Speck are directing their first feature.

Contact Information: 289 S. Robertson Blvd. #467, Beverly Hills, CA 90211
(800) 646-3896 Phone
Web: www.fadeinonline.com
E-mail: awards@fadeinonline.com

TIP: Hollywood sometimes makes movies with 160-page scripts, but a contest judge will groan if yours is anywhere near that. Do yourself a favor and stay under 120. If you can get it under 110, so much the better.

Film in Arizona Screenwriting Competition

Mission Statement: The Film in Arizona Screenwriting Competition is dedicated to helping a great script get the attention and interest of industry professionals.

Deadlines: No contest held in 2003. Check Web site for 2004 dates.

Entry fees: EARLY: $30; STANDARD: $40

Categories: Must be set in Arizona

Prizes: Foot in the Door prize package: Airfare to L.A., rental car, hotel accommodations, $1,000 cash, script evaluation, prearranged meetings with many industry professionals, and congratulatory ads in the *Hollywood Reporter* and *Variety*. Additional $1,000 award to top-scoring Arizona writer from among the finalists.

Contact Information: 3800 N. Central Ave., Bldg. D, Phoenix, AZ 85012

(602) 280-1386 Phone

Web: www.azcommerce.com/azfilmcommission.htm

Filmmakers Magazine/The Radmin Company Screenwriting Competition

Mission Statement: Filmmakers.com is currently accepting entries for the screenwriting competition, which is now in its fourth year! The Radmin Company will read the top fifty scripts, the top twenty will receive a free pass to The Screenwriting Expo, and the top ten writers receive script notes and consideration for representation. They will also get to pitch their scripts to a Hollywood producer.

Deadlines: EARLY: September 30; STANDARD: January 31

Entry fees: EARLY: $39; STANDARD: $49

Categories: All genres

Prizes: FIRST PRIZE: $5,000; SECOND PRIZE: $1,000; THIRD PRIZE: $500; FOURTH PRIZE: $250; FIFTH PRIZE: $100

Previous Winners: FIRST PLACE: *My Brother's Keeper*, Thriller, by Christian Parkes, California ❙ SECOND PLACE: *Sandman*, Drama, by John Morby, Jr., Connecticut ❙ THIRD PLACE: *When Pigs Fly*, Fantasy, by Noelle C. Nelson, California

Contact Information: Filmmakers.com, Screenplay Division, P.O. Box 54050, Irvine, CA 92619

Web: www.filmmakers.com/contests

E-mail: info@filmmakers.com

1st Act Screenplay Competition

Mission Statement: The 1st Act Screenplay Competition is dedicated to finding the next great undiscovered talent and turning his or her screenplay into a feature film.

Deadlines: EARLY: August 31; STANDARD: November 30; FINAL: December 31

Entry fees: EARLY: $30; STANDARD: $50; FINAL: $100

Categories: All genres

Prizes: FIRST PRIZE: Guaranteed production with a $2 million budget, a professional union crew, and an experienced director. In addition, our top screenwriter will receive any needed career guidance and mentoring, one-on-one, from a development executive at Marullus Productions. SECOND PRIZE: $2,000 cash; THIRD PRIZE: $1,000 cash.

Top ten finalists will receive copies of Movie Magic Screenwriter and will have their work read by producers and other industry decision-makers.

Contact Information: P.O. Box 2435, Venice, CA 90291

(310) 396-4430 Phone

Web: www.marullus.com

E-mail: info@marullus.com

First Fifteen Minutes Screenplay Competition

Mission Statement: A movie either hooks you in the first fifteen minutes or it doesn't hook you at all, which means that the first ten to fifteen pages of your script are the most crucial. You must get the reader involved quickly. The First Fifteen Minutes Screenplay Competition gives you the opportunity to measure your screenplay strictly on the merits of its hook.

Deadline: Ongoing

Entry fee: $15

Categories: All genres; first fifteen pages only

Prizes: Scenewriter software

> *I write scripts to serve as skeletons awaiting the flesh and sinew of images.*
> —INGMAR BERGMAN

Previous Winner: Based on the Internet posting of his win, Craig Clyde has an L.A. literary manager interested in his project.
Contact Information: 3110 Oliver St., Dallas, TX 75205
(214) 522-4865 Phone
Web: www.tanglewoodfilms.com
E-mail: david@tanglewoodfilms.com

Great Lakes Film Association Annual Screenplay Competition

Mission Statement: The annual screenplay competition is a way for new and veteran screenwriters to get the break they need. After our first competition numerous agencies contacted us about our winning screenplays.
Deadlines: EARLY: March 29; STANDARD: April 30;
Entry fees: EARLY: $30; STANDARD: $40
Categories: All genres
Prizes: Prizes for the winning screenplay will include $500, two nights' accommodations for you and a guest, and two passes for the 2004 Great Lakes Film Festival ($300 value), where you will be honored on awards nights.
Previous Winners: *Honor Among Thieves* by Bill Balas I *Intolerable Circumstances* by Matt Duffen I *It Is & It Isn't* by Michael Levin
Contact Information: 6851 Rt. 6N West, Edinboro, PA 16412
(814) 873-5069 Phone
Web: www.greatlakesfilmfest.com
E-mail: screenplays@greatlakesfilmfest.com

Great Plains Film Festival Screenwriting Contest

Mission Statement: The Great Plains Film Festival is a biennial regional venue for independent film and video artists working in the U.S. and Canadian heartland. We are committed to presenting work to the public as well as to potential distributors and exhibitors throughout the region and the nation. In addition to the competition screenings there will be a special selection of films and videos by, for, and about Latino people. Conceived to honor the richness of Latino culture by celebrating the strength of the Latino spirit and providing positive images of Latinos, the festival hopes to build bridges of understanding among the diverse cultures living in the Great Plains.

Deadline: June 2

Entry fees: $30

Categories: Scripts that are 85 percent filmable in Nebraska or the Great Plains

Prize: $1,500

Previous Winners: *The Motherless Nanny* by Sheila Jenca, Los Angeles, CA

Contact Information: 313 N. 13th St., P.O. Box 880253, Lincoln, NE 68588-0253

(402) 472-5353 Phone

(402) 472-2576 Fax

Web: www.rossfilmtheater.org

E-mail: help@nebraskascreenwriter.com

Hollywood Screenplay Discovery Awards

Mission Statement: The Hollywood Film Festival was created to bridge the gap between Hollywood and the global creative community. The festival comprises the Hollywood Film Conference, an intensive three-day networking event with top Hollywood professionals, and the Hollywood Film Screenings. The Hollywood Screenplay Discovery Awards (formerly the Hollywood Columbus Screenplay Discovery Awards) were created to bridge the gap between emerging screenwriters and the established industry. We provide our winners with what they need most: feedback and access to key decision-makers.

Deadline: November 30

Entry fee: $55

Categories: All genres

Prizes: First, Second, and Third Place winners receive cash prizes, and their scripts are introduced to major studios. Winners also receive two VIP passes (value $2,600) to the prestigious Hollywood Film Festival, which gives them an opportunity to network with top film industry professionals, and the Hollywood Film Awards Gala, where more than a thousand prominent Hollywood celebrities and studio executives will gather to honor major Hollywood talent and emerging filmmakers.

Previous Winners: FIRST PLACE: *Bathsheba* by Jack Brosky, California
SECOND PLACE: *Love and Larceny* by Martha A. McCoy and Carrie S.

McCoy, Massachusetts ▌ THIRD PLACE: *Blindsighted* by Leslie R. Henderson, Texas

Contact Information: 433 N. Camden Dr., Ste. 600, Beverly Hills, CA 90210

(310) 288-1882 Phone

Web: www.hollywoodawards.com

E-mail: awards@hollywoodawards.com

Hollywood Scriptwriting Contest

Mission Statement: Established in 1976, the Hollywood Scriptwriting Institute was the first screenwriting school. One of its major innovations was that it enabled students to finish their scripts as they completed the course. Partially due to HSI's efforts, independent filmmakers now provide new writers with never before available opportunities. Aspiring writers may now find recognition and gain entry into the entertainment industry more readily.

Deadline: Monthly; postmarked by 15th of each month

Entry fee: $50

Categories: All genres

Prizes: The winner will receive a one-year subscription to *Scr(i)pt,* a premiere Hollywood magazine with feature articles and the latest information on upgrading writing skills and marketing strategy. The winner also receives a brief analysis of the winning script from the Hollywood Scriptwriting Institute's contest committee. All winners receive a Screenwriting Award-Winning Certificate, which will be posted on the Internet for one month.

Previous Winners: Lifetime Honorary Screenwriting Achievement Award to *No Greater Love* by Russell Dye, Eugene, OR

Contact Information: 1605 Cahuenga Blvd., Dept. A, Hollywood,
  CA 90028-6201

(800) 727-4787 Phone

Web: www.moviewriting.com

E-mail: info@moviewriting.com

> ▌ *Cinema is the most beautiful fraud in the world.*
>   —JEAN-LUC GODARD

SCREENPLAY CONTESTS

Hollywood's Next Success Screenwriting Contest

Mission Statement: Our purpose is to recognize screenwriting talent no matter where we find it, to help advance the sale of a script, and to propel the careers of writers wanting to break in.

Deadlines: EARLY: Dec. 15; STANDARD: Feb. 14; FINAL: April 28

Entry fees: EARLY: $24; STANDARD: $34; FINAL: $48

Categories: Feature: drama, comedy, sci-fi/horror; Television: series spec, original pilot, TV movie

Prizes: Seven winners will receive promotion direct to thousands of producers, agents, managers, and studio execs. Every winner is guaranteed a minimum of five direct requests for his or her script as consideration for purchase, or for representation or the hire of the writer. The scripts of the 2002 and 2003 winners were requested by more than a hundred different industry execs. The winning writers have secured representation as a direct result.

Previous Winners: FEATURE: *The Stench of Arizona* by Vance Kotrla | *Living Together* by Wayne Niemi | *Jumpers* by Colin MacLeod | TV SCRIPTS: *Gilmore Girls:* "My Bad Boy's Back" by Brooke Purdy | *Alas Babylon* by Art Ayris | *Local News* by Paul Marx

Contact Information: 4647 Kingswell Ave. #134, Los Angeles, CA 90027

Web: www.hollywoodsnextsuccess.com

E-mail: info@hollywoodnextsuccess.com

An Impractical Venture Screenwriting Competition

Mission Statement: Impractical Ventures seeks to supplement financial support with critical support. Coverage will be provided to all entrants as well as cash prizes to the top three finishers and submission to industry professionals for the top ten finishers in the feature-length and short-script divisions.

Deadlines: STANDARD: March 31; FINAL: April 29

Entry fees: STANDARD: $25 (short), $40 (feature); FINAL: $35 (short), $50 (feature)

Categories: All genres

Prizes: FEATURE: First Place $500, Second Place $300, Third Place $200; SHORT: First Place $250, Second Place $175, Third Place $75 | In addition, the top ten finishers in each division will be referred to industry professionals with our recommendation. All twenty finalists will have their name and script title published online and in print media.

Contact Information: 333 Washington Blvd., P.O. Box 330, Marina Del Rey, CA 90292-5136

(310) 203-1345 Phone

Web: www.geocities.com/impventures/contest.html

E-mail: impventures@yahoo.com

Independent Black Film Festival Screenwriting Contest

Mission Statement: IBFF's screenwriting competition provides opportunities for screenwriters to receive feedback on their screenplays and to go before an industry jury for final evaluation. All screenplays submitted will receive reader feedback so writers can take suggestions and improve their scripts. In addition, the top ten finalists have the chance to rewrite their scripts before the final round of competition. First, Second, and Third Place winners will have their scripts read by several key producers.

Deadline: October 31

Entry fee: $45

Categories: All genres

Prizes: Final Draft software, cash prizes

Contact Information: P.O Box 18914, Atlanta, GA 31126

(770) 912-8951 Phone

Web: www.indieblackfilm.com

E-mail: screenplay@indieblackfilm.com

Indiefest Screenwriting Competition and Market

Mission Statement: Indiefest celebrates the "vision without compromise" spirit of the independent filmmaker. Indiefest sponsors include 94.7 Zone Radio (an ABC station), W Hotels, Village Entertainment, the Illinois Film Office, Chicago Community Cinema, Ticketweb, and Atom Groom Design Studio. Nearly seven thousand attendees viewed some of the best inde-

> Cinema is a matter of what's in the frame and what's out.
> —MARTIN SCORSESE

pendent films from the United States and ten other countries at the 2003 festival. The Indiefest Awards ceremony presented twelve awards, which included three writing awards sponsored by the Screenwriter's Project.

Deadlines: EARLY: March 1; STANDARD: May 1; FINAL: June 1

Entry fees: EARLY: $40; STANDARD: $50; FINAL: $60

Categories: All genres

Prizes: See the Web site for details.

Previous Winners: FIRST PLACE: *City of Nets* by Debbie Bolsky | SECOND PLACE: *A House Divided* by Michael Amato | THIRD PLACE: *Last Shot* by Jimmy O'Ready

Contact Information: P.O. Box 148849, Chicago, IL 60614-8849

(773) 665-7600 Phone

(773) 665-7660 Fax

Web: www.indiefestchicago.com

E-mail: info@indiefestchicago.com

International Family Film Festival (IFFF)

Mission Statement: The IFFF is a forum to encourage and reward writers and producers of family films. At the most recent festival, three filmmakers had their films licensed by distributors. Two screenwriters had their work optioned, and one screenplay is headed for production this fall. According to Chris Shoemaker, "It is exciting to see the beginning of a groundswell at the festival in support of these independent producers. The producer's success is, after all, the goal of the festival."

Deadline: March 10

Entry fees: $60 (features); $30(shorts)

Categories: Features and Short Scripts: drama, comedy, animation, sci-fi/adventure

Prizes: Winners will receive a plaque, and all the finalists will receive certificates at the awards ceremony. A Screenwriters Showcase will spotlight the finalists in the Feature and Short categories with a reading of one scene from each script by professional actors from the Dee Wallace Stone Actors Studio.

Previous Winners: BEST DRAMA FEATURE: *Uncommon Denominator* | BEST COMEDY FEATURE: *Sonny* | BEST SCI-FI/ADVENTURE FEATURE: *Children of the LSR Medallion* | BEST ANIMATION FEATURE: *Scotty* | BEST DRAMA SHORT: *Homefront* | BEST COMEDY SHORT: *Supermarket Squirt* | BEST ANI-

MATION SHORT: *The Adventures of Roman* ❚ BEST SCI-FI/ADVENTURE SHORT: *Way Station*
Contact Information: P.O. Box 801507, Valencia, CA 91380-1507
(661) 257-3131 Phone
(661) 257-8989 Fax
Web: www.iffilmfest.org
E-mail: ifffinfo@myexcel.com

Jury of Peers Screenwriting Contest

Mission Statement: We help screenwriters get the recognition they deserve by publicizing select screenplays in the Hollywood trades, and by making information on the selected writers and screenplays available to anyone in Hollywood who's interested. The winner of our annual contest and five finalists are recognized in print ads in *Variety* and are featured on our Web site where interested parties can read excerpts of the winning screenplays and contact the winners.
Deadline: November 15
Entry fee: $45
Categories: All genres
Prizes: GRAND PRIZE: A cash prize of $250. Each of the five finalists receives $100. In addition, the Grand Prize winner and the five finalists have their names published in two print ads in the trade publication of *Variety*.
Previous Winners:
GRAND PRIZE: *Monster Boys* by Jay Craft ❚ FINALISTS: *Class* by Jake Bauman ❚ *Trixie Seymour: The Girl with the X-Ray Eyes* by Frank Crawford-Herman
Contact Information: 2554 Lincoln Blvd., Ste. 401, Marina Del Rey, CA
  90291
(310) 428-3159 Phone
Web: www.juryofpeers.net
E-mail: info@juryofpeers.net

❚ *Even if I set out to make a film about a fillet of sole, it would be about me.*
  —FEDERICO FELLINI

Kay Snow Writing Awards

Mission Statement: The purpose of this annual contest, named in honor of Willamette Writer's founder, Kay Snow, is to help writers reach professional goals in writing in a broad array of categories.

Deadline: May 15

Entry fees: $10 for members of Willamette Writers; $15 for nonmembers; free for students

Categories: Adult fiction, adult nonfiction, poetry, juvenile short story or article, screenplay; ten-page maximum excerpt

Prizes: Adult: First Place $300, Second Place $150, Third Place $50; Student: First Place $50, Second Place $20, Third Place $10

Previous Winners: FIRST PLACE: *Legend of the Raven* by Teresa Bishop, Brush Prairie, WA | SECOND PLACE: *River Rats* by Dorine Rivers, Richland, WA | THIRD PLACE: *The Sacrifice of Isaac* by Stacy Coffey, Portland, OR

Contact Information: Willamette Writers, 9045 SW Barbur Blvd., Ste. 5A, Portland, OR 97219-4027

(503) 452-1592 Phone

(503) 452-0372 Fax

Web: www.willamettewriters.com

E-mail: wilwrite@teleport.com

Key West IndieFest

Mission Statement: Key West IndieFest is an international event that accepts entries from all over the world.

Deadline: January 31

Entry fees: 61–120 pages $90; 31–60 pages $80; 11–30 pages $70; 1–10 pages $60

Categories: All genres

Prizes: Winning scripts will be showcased at the Key West IndieFest.

Contact Information: 1107 Key Plaza #136, Key West, FL 33040

(305) 293-7698 Phone

(305) 292-4178 Fax

Web: www.keywestindiefest.com

E-mail: mc@quesoproductions.com

L.A. International Short Film Festival
Screenwriting Competition

Mission Statement: The mission of Filmmakers United, the presenting organizers of the Los Angeles International Short Film Festival, is to celebrate and cultivate the art of the short film. Through fundraising, education, competition, and film appreciation, the LA Shorts Fest serves as an incubator of the short film, nurturing filmmakers and their works from development through distribution. Entering its seventh year, the LA Shorts Fest is the largest short film festival in the world and one of the few recognized by the Academy of Motion Pictures Arts and Sciences. Last year's festival garnered more than 1,100 film entries and drew more than 10,000 moviegoers, filmmakers, and entertainment executives. Since its inception, sixteen festival participants have gone on to earn Academy Award nominations and three have won the Oscar for their films. In 2003, five films that premiered at the 2002 LA Shorts Fest were nominated for an Oscar. We are excited to announce that we will now offer screenwriters the opportunity to submit completed full-length feature scripts.

Deadline: July 1

Entry fee: $30

Categories: All genres

Prizes: Winners receive representation at LA Short Film Festival and the opportunity to have the winning screenplays read in Los Angeles at a staged reading with professional actors.

Previous Winner: *A Vicious Circle* by Spencer Beglarian

Contact Information: LA Shorts Fest, 12930 Ventura Blvd. #915, Studio City, CA 91604

(323) 851-9100 Phone

Web: www.lashortsfest.com

E-mail: info@lashortsfest.com

Mania Fest

Mission Statement: ManiaFest is a genre film festival celebrating the work of science fiction, fantasy, and horror screenwriters and filmmakers. This four-day event applauds the efforts and imaginations of those who push the boundaries between reality and fiction—whether with nightmarish visions or views of other worlds. Produced by Mania Entertainment in association with *Cinescape* magazine, festival events include panels such as "Masters of Horror" and "Comics to Films" with leading industry genre filmmakers. In addition, there is a screenplay, feature, and short film competition with $12,000 in cash and prizes. As Steven Spielberg remarked in his acceptance speech at Mania's 2002 Saturn Awards, nine of the top ten highest-grossing films of all time are from the science-fiction, fantasy, or horror genre.

Deadlines: EARLY: May 31; STANDARD: June 30; FINAL: August 16

Entry fees: EARLY: $35; STANDARD: $40; FINAL: $45

Categories: Sci-fi, fantasy, horror

Prizes: FIRST PLACE: $2,000; SECOND PLACE: $1,000; THIRD PLACE: $500; FOURTH PLACE: $250; FIFTH PLACE: $100

Contact Information: P.O. Box 807, Santa Monica, CA 90403-5400

(310) 399-2622 Fax

Web: www.maniafest.com

E-mail: festivaldirect@mania.com

Minute Movies Short Script Competition

Mission Statement: Our intention is to bring exposure to exceptional screenplay writers.

Deadline: December 31

Entry fee: $20

Categories: Short scripts

Prizes: Winners receive a copy of Dramatica Pro Writing and Screenwriter 2003 software and inclusion in the book *A Few More Minute Movies* with paid royalties.

The length of a film should be directly related to the endurance of the human bladder.

—ALFRED HITCHCOCK

Film spectators are quiet vampires.

—JIM MORRISON

Previous Winners: *Women are from Seattle, Men are from New York* by Jan C. Bot ▌ *A Blessing. Umm Hmm. Yes* by Rhonda Lombardo ▌ *Dreams Deferred* by Jason W. Camp

Contact Information: 5815 E. La Palma Ave. #33, Anaheim, CA 92807

(714) 693-3327 Phone

(714) 693-1377 Fax

Web: www.minutemovies.bsplive.com

E-mail: minutemovies@bsplive.com

Moondance International Film Festival

Mission Statement: The objective of the Moondance International Film Festival is to promote and encourage screenwriters and independent film-makers, and find the best work in stage plays, radio plays, TV scripts, musical scores, lyrics, librettos, musical videos, puppetry theater, and short stories. Moondance provides a forum in which those creative, talented, and dedicated artists have the opportunity for their work to be viewed and accepted by the powers that be within the international film community.

Deadline: March 15

Entry fees: SCREENPLAY: Feature $75; Short $50 ▌ TELEVISION: Pilot $75; spec (half-hour) $50; spec (hour) $75; movie of the week (MOW) or Miniseries: $75

Categories: Feature, short, TV pilot, TV spec, TV MOW, or miniseries

Prizes: Spirit of Moondance; the Columbine Awards; the Dolphin Awards

Success Stories: Francis Ford Coppola recently optioned a Moondance screenplay. Jodie Foster requested the 2001 finalists' screenplays for consideration. One winner was invited to screen her film at Cannes, got a three-picture deal, and is now in Australia doing the films. Other films were purchased or previewed by Sesame Street Productions, Lifetime Television, Oxygen Media (Oprah's cable channel). Five were bought by a Singapore channel. More than a dozen Moondance films were recently purchased by KQED-TV, San Francisco, Canal Plus, the Sundance Channel, and the Independent Film Channel.

Contact Information: 970 Ninth St., Boulder, CO 80302

(303) 545-0202 Phone

Web: www.moondancefilmfestival.com

E-mail: info@moondancefilmfestival.com

National Screenwriting Competition

Mission Statement: We are one of the few competitions that provide feedback on your entry. Just drop us an e-mail after the finalists are announced. We can't release readers' notes, but we always provide general feedback on your script when requested, i.e., ratings in the areas of storyline, characterization, and dialogue. All scripts will be evaluated based upon concept, structure, character, cinematic quality, and quality of the writing.

Deadline: November 29

Entry fee: $45

Categories: All genres

Prizes: FIRST PLACE: $2,500 and possible option; SECOND PLACE: $500 and possible option; THIRD PLACE: $250 and possible option

Previous Winners: FIRST PLACE: *Post-Traumatic Shakespeare,* comedy, by Toni Hood and Tyrone J. Neuhauser, Las Vegas, NV I SECOND PLACE: *Voices,* comedy/drama, by Marvin C. Krueger, North Hollywood, CA I THIRD PLACE: *The Mirror Man,* suspense, by Delray K. Dvoracek, Fargo, ND

Contact Information: 150A Morristown Rd., Matawan, NJ 07747

(732) 583-2211 Phone

(732) 583-4123 Fax

Web: www.nationalscreenwriting.com

E-mail: director@skyweb.net

Ohio Independent Screenplay Awards

Mission Statement: Independent Pictures (IP) is the proud sponsor of Script Mill, Ohio Independent Screenplay Awards, Ohio Independent Film Festival, Independent Film School, Film Production Training Program, regional AIVF Salons, Fiscal Agent Sponsorship Program, Speakers Bureau, and a variety of curatorial programs. Established in 1997, the Ohio Independent Screenplay Awards is a competition for screenwriters with unproduced work. Submitted screenplays are judged by Independent Pictures' readers who select six finalists to be judged by several Hollywood and New York producers. One award-winning screenplay is presented at Script Mill (professionally acted and directed unstaged screenplay reading program), which kicks off the Ohio Independent Film Festival.

Deadlines: EARLY: June 1; STANDARD: July 1

Entry fees: EARLY: $40; STANDARD: $60

Categories: All genres

Prizes: The Ohio Independent Screenplay Awards features three different awards: Best Screenplay Award; Best Northcoast Screenplay Award (majority of the screenplay set in Northern Ohio), created to encourage filmmaking in Ohio; and Best Voice of Color Screenplay Award (story that reflects people of color and/or is written by a person of color). Awards for each winning screenplay: $500 and submission to feature film producers in Hollywood and New York City.

Contact Information: 1392 W. 65th St., Cleveland, OH 44102

(216) 651-7315 Phone

(216) 651-7317 Fax

Web: www.ohiofilms.com

E-mail: ohioindiefilmfest@juno.com

Organization of Black Screenwriters Script Competition

Mission Statement: The Organization of Black Screenwriters, Inc. (OBS), began in 1988 as a forum to address the lack of black writers in the entertainment industry. Our primary function is to assist screenwriters in the creation of works for film and television and to help them present their work to the industry. As a result of our efforts and the continued growth of the organization, we have developed a powerful network, which includes the Writers Guild of America and many agents, producers, directors, and studios.

Deadline: August 31

Entry fee: $30

Categories: Comedy, drama

Prizes: Winning pilot scripts are read by major production companies and top talent agencies (UTA, Edmonds Entertainment, UPN, Disney, Fox TV), and winners in each genre will receive a cash prize and a professional table reading.

Film lovers are sick people.
—FRANCOIS TRUFFAUT

SCREENPLAY CONTESTS

Previous Winners: COMEDY: *She's My Dad* by Bonita Alford ❙ DRAMA: *Sanctuary* by Lemar Fooks

Contact Information: 1968 W. Adams Blvd., Los Angeles, CA 90018

(323) 735-2050 Phone

(323) 735-2051 Fax

Web: www.obswriter.com

E-mail: obswriter@sbcglobal.net

Oshun55 Productions Features

Mission Statement: Oshun55 Productions is a production company dedicated to breathing diversity and consciousness into the film and television industry. We are committed to helping develop and promote emerging writers and are focused on developing and producing film, television, music, Internet projects that reflect and appeal to a diverse audience.

Deadlines: EARLY: March 15; STANDARD: June 30

Entry fees: EARLY: $25; STANDARD: $30

Categories: Short, feature

Prizes: GRAND PRIZE IN EACH CATEGORY: $500 cash. Top three winners receive Screenwriting Expo admission, one-year subscription to *Creative Screenwriting* magazine, Sophocles screenplay software, *Scr(i)pt* screenplay coverage, script consultation from On The Page, and a $50 gift certificate for Amazon.com.

Previous Winners: First Place Feature: *I Love You Dolores Cullapick* by Walter Williams ❙ Second Place Feature: *The Wolf's Lair* by Michael Penhallow ❙ First Place Short: *The Moor* by Caerthan Banks ❙ Second Place Short: *Clown Camp* by Dan Borengasser

Contact Information: P.O. Box 291043, Los Angeles, CA 90029

(310) 358-2970 Phone

Web: www.oshun55.com

E-mail: info@oshun55.com

❙ *A film is never really good unless the camera is an eye in the head of a poet.*
   —ORSON WELLES

Pacific Northwest Writers Conference Literary Contest

Mission Statement: Established in 1956, Pacific Northwest Writers Association (PNWA) was founded by a group of writers who wanted to connect to other writers, publishers, agents, and editors across the country. The dedication of the Pacific Northwest Writers Association, a nonprofit organization, to Northwest writers encompasses the development of writing talent from pen to publication through education, accessibility to the publishing industry, and participation in an interactive writing community. The organization's overall goals are to provide professional development for writers, to establish and maintain a relationship with the publishing industry, and to create and sustain partnerships with other arts and service organizations.

Deadline: February 17

Entry fees: PNWC members $35, nonmembers $45

Categories: All genres

Prizes: FIRST PLACE: $600 and the Zola Award; Second Place $300; Third Place $150

Previous Winners: FIRST PLACE: *Not Just Over the Rainbow* by Mitzi Miles-Kubota, Ashland, OR ▌ SECOND PLACE: *Amazing Days* by Ute Muegge-Lauterbach, Wiesbaden, Germany ▌ THIRD PLACE: *Sapphire* by Russell Post, Olga, WA

Contact Information: P.O. Box 2016, Edmonds, WA 98020-9516

(425) 673-2665 Phone

Web: www.pnwa.org

E-mail: pnwa@pnwa.org

PEN Center USA West Literary Awards

Mission Statement: Since 1982 PEN Center USA, a literary and human rights organization affiliated with International PEN, has sponsored a unique regional literary competition to recognize outstanding works published or produced by writers who live in the western United States. There are winners in ten categories—including, fiction, poetry, drama, journalism, screenplay, and nonfiction—celebrating the written word in all its forms. Winners are chosen by panels of judges composed of writers, editors, critics, and booksellers. Previous winners include Barbara Kingsolver, Nicholas Kazan, Maxine Hong Kingston, Richard Reeves, Callie

Khouri, Pete Dexter, Michelle Carter, Robert Schenkkan, Cameron Crow, Cyrus Nowrasteh, Charles Fuller, Cherrie Moraga, and Michael Tolkin.
Deadline: January 31
Entry fee: $25
Categories: Only scripts for films completed during the current year are eligible; submit final shooting script.
Prizes: Each winner receives a $1,000 cash prize and is honored at a ceremony in Los Angeles. The winning play will be published by Dramatic Publishing Company, which will thereafter license productions and send the author royalties.
Previous Winners: TELEPLAY: *10,000 Black Men Named George* by Cyrus Nowrasteh ▌ SCREENPLAY: *Adaptation* by Charlie and Donald Kaufman
Contact Information: 672 S. Lafayette Park Pl. #42, Los Angeles, CA 90057
(213) 365-8500 Phone
(213) 365-9616 Fax
Web: www.penusa.org
E-mail: pen@penusa.org

Producers Outreach Program–Scriptwriters Network

Mission Statement: Founded in 1986, The Scriptwriters Network is a nonprofit, volunteer-based organization created by writers for writers. The network serves its members by enhancing their awareness of the realities of the business, providing access and opportunity through alliances with industry professionals, and furthering the cause and quality of writing in the entertainment industry.
Deadline: Quarterly
Entry fees: $30 for Scriptwriters Network members, $60 for WGA members
Categories: All genres

▌ *Roger Corman taught me a very valuable lesson. He said you could make a movie about just about anything as long as it had a hook to hang the advertising on.*

—**AMY HOLDEN JONES**, screenwriter, *Indecent Proposal* and *Mystic Pizza*

Prizes: Every entrant in the Producers Outreach Program receives a minimum of two but as many as eight professional-level evaluations from peer writers. Roughly one-third of the scripts that have successfully passed through this program have been optioned or sold.

Contact Information: 11684 Ventura Blvd., Ste. 508, Studio City, CA 91604

(323) 848-9477 Phone

Web: www.scriptwritersnetwork.com/prodrech.html

E-mail: info@scriptwritersnetwork.org

Rhode Island International Film Festival Screenplay Competition

Mission Statement: The Rhode Island International Film Festival (RIIFF) is one of only three broadly focused, independent festivals in New England accepting works of any type (dramatic, documentary, experimental), on any subject matter and in any genre. Screenplays will be judged by a panel of distinguished industry professionals, educators, peers, and film fans.

Deadline: June 1

Entry fee: $35

Categories: All genres

Prizes: The Grand Prize winner will have segments of the work produced during Take 1-2-3: Filmmaking with the Pros, RIIFF's annual master class on production, which features the participation of a noted director. The winner will also receive cash and prizes valued at over $10,000, including Final Draft software.

Previous Winners: GRAND PRIZE: *The Imperfect Cell* by Lance Hammer, Los Angeles, CA | FIRST PRIZE: *Bach Double* by Barbara Marshall, Austin, TX | SECOND PRIZE: *The End of Grace* by Nicholas Katsapetses, San Francisco, CA | THIRD PRIZE: *Rebels and Roses* by Ellen Maria Gavin, Venice, CA

Success Stories: Dana Biscotti Myskowski, winner in 2002, is negotiating with Renegade Effects Studio in North Hollywood for production of her script, *Princess & the Pirate,* with a $43 million production budget.

Contact Information: P.O. Box 162, Newport, RI 02840

(401) 861-4445 Phone

(401) 847-7590 Fax

Web: www.film-festival.org

E-mail: flicksart@aol.com

★ Samuel Goldwyn Writing Awards Competition

Mission Statement: The Samuel Goldwyn Writing Awards Competition is dedicated to supporting student screenwriters at any campus of the University of California.

Deadline: May 30

Entry fee: None

Categories: All genres; students of University of California system only

Prizes: First Place is $10,000; Second Place is $5,000; Third Place is $3,000; and Honorable Mentions receive $2,000 and $1,000.

Previous Winners: FIRST PLACE: *Brown Widow* by Beverly Neufeld | SECOND PLACE: *Road To Redemption* by Leslie Dallas | THIRD PLACE: *Delilah County* by Chad Nyerges

Contact Information: Awards Coordinator, UCLA School of Theater, Film and Television, 103 E. Melnitz Hall Box 951622, Los Angeles, CA 90095-1622

(310) 206-6154 Phone

E-mail: chernand@tft.ucla.edu

San Diego Screenwriting Contest

Mission Statement: The San Diego Film Foundation produces the annual San Diego Film Festival and the San Diego Screenwriting Contest, and hosts many other year-round, cinema-related events to foster and promote the film community in San Diego. Its mission is to bring about a greater knowledge and appreciation of cinema through question-and-answer sessions with filmmakers and their casts, guest appearances by nationally recognized film artists, nightly receptions with the filmmakers, an Opening Night Premiere Party, an exclusive Actor's Ball and Award Ceremony, as well as a closing night Wrap Party.

Deadline: April 15

Entry fee: $50

Categories: All genres

Prize: Recognition at the San Diego Film Festival

Previous Winners: *Bachelorman* by Rodney Lee Conover, Jeffrey Hause, and David Hines

Contact Information: San Diego Film Foundation Screenplay Contest, P.O. Box 16396, Beverly Hills, CA 90209

(619) 582-2368 Phone
(619) 286-8384 Fax
Web: www.sdff.org
E-mail: info@sdff.org

Screen Arts Foundation $5,000 Prize for Screenwriting

Mission Statement: The Screen Arts Foundation Prize recognizes three winning writers and their feature-length screenplays. Last year's winning scripts were requested by Warner Brothers, United Artists, United Talent Agency, and HBO Films.

Deadline: November 5

Entry fees: $32 for one script or $42 for two

Categories: Drama, comedy, sci-fi/horror/fantasy

Prizes: Two winners receive $1,000 each; the Grand Prize winner receives $3,000.

Success Stories: *"My script,* The Paper Route, *won the Grand Prize in January 2002, and in my experience, the contest delivered what it promised and more. They paid me promptly and immediately publicized the results. They generated twenty requests for my script—that's twenty more than I received from publicity over the script's December 2002 First Place finish in* Scr(i)pt *Magazine's Open Door Contest, and more than the script received in total from ten other contests it placed in (including Nicholl quarterfinalist in 2001). The requests came mostly from studios, established producers, and respected agents or agencies."* —Previous winner, DANNY HOWELL

Contact Information: 419 N. Larchmont Blvd., Ste. 89, Los Angeles, CA 90004

Web: www.screenartsfoundation.org

▌ **TIP:** Apply early. It's often cheaper and your script stands a better chance of standing out. Two months before the deadline yours may be the only script that comes in that day. The day of the deadline, you could be one of a thousand.

▌ *Listen carefully, shake your head thoughtfully, then leave them in the dark . . .*
   —JACK B. SOWARDS, screenwriter, *Star Trek: The Wrath of Khan*

SCREENPLAY CONTESTS

Screenplay Festival

Mission Statement: Screenplay Festival was established to solve two major problems. First, it is simply too difficult for talented but unconnected writers to gain recognition and get their material read by legitimate agents, producers, directors, and investors. Second, agents, producers, directors, and investors complain that they cannot find great material, but they generally refuse to accept unsolicited material. This means that unless the script comes from a source that is known to them, they will not read it. Screenplay Festival seeks to eliminate this chicken-or-egg problem. By accepting all submitted screenplays and judging them based upon their quality, Screenplay Festival tries to give undiscovered screenwriters an opportunity to rise above the crowd.

Deadlines: EARLY: July 1; FINAL: September 1

Entry fees: EARLY: $35; FINAL: $50

Categories: All genres

Prizes: In each of five categories, a $1,000 prize will be awarded.

Previous Winners: GRAND PRIZE WINNER: *King of The Castle* by Debra Johnson

Contact Information: 11693 San Vicente Blvd., Ste. 806, Los Angeles, CA 90049

(310) 801-7896 Phone

(310) 820-2303 Fax

Web: www.screenplayfestival.com

E-mail: info@screenplayfestival.com

Screenwriters Forum Annual Screenplay Contest

Mission Statement: It is our goal at the Screenwriters Forum to recognize, reward, and encourage new screenwriting talent. We strive to promote aspiring screenwriters by providing them with much-needed exposure to the industry. Each of our contest winners is announced to our entire database of agents and producers. Notification to industry professionals will include a personalized logline that describes the story.

> *There are just two stories: going on a journey and a stranger comes to town.*
> **—JOHN GARDNER**

Deadline: September 30

Entry fee: $30

Categories: All genres

Prizes: First Place is $1,000. The top three winners also receive a special personalized announcement that is sent to each of the agents and producers in our database. Winner also receives complete script-evaluation package including coverage scores and our in-depth analysis package.

Contact Information: P.O. 16604, Tampa, FL 33687-6604

(813) 416-0427 Phone

Web: www.screenwritersforum.com

E-mail: contact@screenwritersforum.com

Scriptapalooza Screenwriting Competition

Mission Statement: The Scriptapalooza Screenwriting Competition's mission is to put new writers on the path to a promising career. Since the competition began in 1998, winners have been able to land agent interviews and get meetings with production companies and directors. Past participants included Jim Henson Co., Samuel Goldwyn Films, and Edmonds Entertainment. A complete list of participants is on Scriptapalooza's Web site.

Deadline: EARLY: January 5; STANDARD: March 5; FINAL: April 15

Entry fees: EARLY: $40; STANDARD: $45; FINAL: $50

Categories: All genres

Prizes: First Place is $10,000. Second Place, Third Place, and ten runners-up receive a software package from Writer's Studio (Storyview, Screenwriter 2000 and Dramatica Pro). In addition, all winners receive consideration from established production companies and literary representatives.

Previous Winners: FIRST PLACE: *Reckless Endangerment* by Howard Sklora | SECOND PLACE: *The Conspiracy* by Robert C. Fleet | THIRD PLACE: *Dining with Dinah* by Theresa Shaw

Success Stories: A former Second Place winner, *Falling Over Venus* by Andrea Bailey, is in pre-production at Universal Studios with Mary Stuart Masterson attached to direct.

Contact Information: 7775 Sunset Blvd. #200, Hollywood, CA 90046

(323) 654-5809 Phone

Web: www.scriptapalooza.com

E-mail: info@scriptapalooza.com

Scriptapalooza TV Competition

Mission Statement: The Scriptapalooza TV Competition is dedicated to discovering new talent and showing them the path to a promising career. Past winners have been able to land interviews with agents and get meetings with production companies and directors. Past participants have included Jim Henson Co., Samuel Goldwyn Films, and Edmonds Entertainment. A complete list of participants is on Scriptapalooza's Web site.

Deadlines: May 15 and November 15

Entry fee: $40

Categories: Television: pilot, half-hour spec, and one-hour spec

Prizes: First Prize in each category is $500, Second Prize in each category is $200, and Third Prize in each category is $100. All winners also receive consideration from established production companies and literary representatives.

Previous Winners: PILOT ▐ FIRST PRIZE: *Lam* by Mickey Levy ▐ SECOND PRIZE: *Sundays at 7* by Paul Kiernan and Cid Stoll ▐ THIRD PRIZE: *Starborn* by Nancy Brauer ▐ **HALF-HOUR SPEC** ▐ FIRST PRIZE: *Malcolm in the Middle*, "Cruel and Unusual" by Alex Sabeti ▐ SECOND PRIZE: *Curb Your Enthusiasm,* "Shirts and Skins" by Aaron Blitstein ▐ THIRD PRIZE: *Will and Grace,* "Straight Outa Brooklyn" by Shannon Ryan and Steve Krueger ▐ **ONE-HOUR SPEC** ▐ FIRST PRIZE: *The West Wing,* "The Second Law of Thermodynamics" by Matthew Federman and Stephen Scala ▐ SECOND PRIZE: *Alias,* "The Package" by Jared Romero ▐ THIRD PRIZE: *The Dead Zone,* "True Self" by Frederick Kim

Success Stories: Scott Gray, a Scriptapalooza winner, and Barbara Schwartz, a Scriptapalooza finalist, both won 2003 Daytime Emmys for Outstanding Children's Animated Program for the TV series *Rugrats*.

Contact Information: 7775 Sunset Blvd. #200, Hollywood, CA 90046

(323) 654-5809 Phone

Web: www.scriptapalooza.com

E-mail: info@scriptapalooza.com

▌ *A film is—or should be—more like music than like fiction. It should be a progression of moods and feelings. The theme, what's behind the emotion, the meaning, all that comes later.*

—STANLEY KUBRICK

Scr(i)pt Magazine Open Door Contest

Mission Statement: The Open Door Contest is designed to help launch an aspiring screenwriter's career. The contest is held quarterly, and each features a cash prize and is sponsored by an accredited agent, manager, or producer interested in finding new talent. Winners receive a cash prize and notes and consideration for representation . Scripts may be passed along to interested agents and producers with the screenwriter's permission. Cosponsors of recent contests include The Paradigm Agency, Dimension Films, and Zide-Perry Entertainment.

Deadline: Quarterly

Entry fee: $45

Categories: All genres

Prizes: The winner receives $3,000, consideration for literary representation, Final Draft screenwriting software, a $200 gift certificate from The Writers Store, a two-year membership to Script P.I.M.P.'s Writer's Database, and a copy of "Dr. Format Answers Your Questions."

Previous Winners: FIRST PLACE: *Robbing Bingo,* action, by Jon Cellini ❙ SECOND PLACE: *Slow City,* drama, by Jonathan Herman and Laurel Almerinda ❙ THIRD PLACE: *Benny's Orgy,* comedy, by David Light and Joseph Raso

Contact Information: Open Door Contest, *Scr(i)pt* **Magazine, 5638 Sweet Air Rd., Baldwin, MD 21013**

(410) 592-3466 Phone

(410) 592-8062 Fax

Web: www.scriptmag.com

E-mail: editor@scriptmag.com

Set in Texas Screenwriting Competition/Galveston Island International Film Festival

Mission Statement: Held in conjunction with the Galveston Island International Film Festival, the Set in Texas Screenwriting Competition is open to all writers that have written specific scripts that focus of the culture and the people of Texas.

Deadlines: EARLY: July 31; STANDARD: August 31

Entry fees: EARLY: $25; STANDARD: $35

Categories: Screenplays that focus on the culture and people of Texas

Prize: FIRST PLACE: $1,500
Contact Information: P.O. Box 20222, Houston, TX 77225
(713) 527-9548 Phone
(713) 523-3976 Fax
Web: www.ancestralfilms.org
E-mail: ancestrl@ancestralfilms.org

Sidewalk Moving Picture Festival Screenplay Competition

Mission Statement: The Sidewalk Moving Picture Festival Screenplay Competition brings new films to a new audience by combining a carnival atmosphere with the traditional film festival model. With all five venues within one block of Birmingham's historic Alabama Theater, Sidewalk allows filmmakers to mingle with film lovers as they eat, drink, and listen to live music while deciding which films to see next. In its first year, Sidewalk served up more than forty films to more than 5,000 attendees during the festival weekend, including six world premieres and twelve southeast premieres.
Deadline: June 1
Entry fee: $45
Categories: Short scripts
Prizes: Award sculpture designed by local artist (valued at more than $750), copy of Movie Magic Screenwriter 2000 screenwriting software, and a one-year subscription to *Filmmaker* magazine
Contact Information: 500 23rd St., Birmingham, AL 35233
(205) 324-0888 Phone
(205) 324-2499 Fax
Web: www.sidewalkfest.org
E-mail: info@sidewalkfest.org

Slamdance Screenplay Competition

Mission Statement: Slamdance began in January 1995 when a group of first-time directors screened their films as an alternative to the Sundance Film Festival. Its objective is to recognize and support new filmmakers and screenwriters on an ongoing basis. Each year the screenplay competition accepts both feature-length and short scripts. Submissions are scored on character development, story, dialogue, structure, and originality.

Deadlines: EARLY: April 19; STANDARD: June 20

Entry fees: Feature: $70 (Students $60); Short Script: $50

Categories: Drama, comedy, action, romance, period epic, coming-of-age

Prizes: FIRST PLACE: $3,000; SECOND PLACE: $1,000; THIRD PLACE: $500

In addition, ten finalists receive a $600 prize package that includes a Slamdance Festival Pass that affords entry into all Slamdance screenings and parties at the festival in Park City, Utah. The top ten also have the opportunity to become members of the WGAw Independent Writers Caucus.

Previous Winners: FIRST PLACE: *Song of Silence* by Miranda Kwok | SECOND PLACE: *The Parachute Factory* by Tanya Steele | THIRD PLACE: *Wizard of Genoa* by Gary L. Miner

Success Stories: The 2001 First Prize winner, *The Woodsman* by Steven Fetcher and Nicole Kassell, is currently in production at Paramount Classics with Lee Daniels.

Contact Information: Slamdance, 5634 Melrose Ave., Los Angeles, CA
  90038

(323) 466-1786 Phone

(323) 466-1784 Fax

Web: www.slamdance.com

E-mail: screenplay@slamdance.com

Slam Fi Screenplay Competition

Mission Statement: Slamdance Film Festival has partnered with Xeolux Entertainment to create this unique genre-specific competition looking for sci-fi or science/technology-related short and full-length screenplays and short stories. The finalists will be read by a distinguished panel of judges, composed of award-winning novelists and filmmakers in the sci-fi genre. Winners will receive cash prizes and introductions to production companies, managers, and agencies. The Slam Fi Competition is dedicated to supporting innovative writers in producing powerful, fresh stories inspired by science, technology, and the future.

Film as dream, film as music. No art passes our conscience in the way film does, and goes directly to our feelings, deep down into the dark rooms of our souls.
  —INGMAR BERGMAN

SCREENPLAY CONTESTS

Deadlines: EARLY: April 1; FINAL: May 9

Entry fees: EARLY: $20 (short), $40 (feature): $40; STANDARD: $35 (short), $55 (feature)

Categories: Sci-fi or science/technology

Prizes: FIRST PRIZE: $2,000; SECOND PRIZE: $1,000; THIRD PRIZE: $500

Previous Winners: ▌ FIRST PRIZE: *Toy Robots* by Daniel Kwak ▌ When a fourth-grader discovers that a toy ray gun can actually enlarge objects to colossal dimensions, he endeavors to save the town from the school bully using enlarged toy robots to battle him. ▌ SECOND PRIZE: *Homemaker 3000* by Jeremy Carr ▌ A lonely bachelor purchases a robotic housewife, but when he cheats on her he gets more than he bargained for. ▌ THIRD PRIZE: *Second Coming* by Joseph Calabrese ▌ Joshua, a clone created from the remains of Jesus Christ, is prepared to become the new savior, but when it's discovered that the original DNA was not that of the Messiah, he hides at a New York City soup kitchen run by a pastor and her ten-year-old son.

Contact Information: Slamdance/Slam Fi, 5634 Melrose Ave., Los Angeles, CA 90038

(323) 466-1786 Phone

(323) 466-1784 Fax

Web: www.slamfi.com

E-mail: slamfi@xeolux.com

SoCal International Film Festival and Screenwriting Competition

Mission Statement: The First Annual SoCal International Film Festival and Screenwriting Competition (SIFFSC) was formed to showcase exceptional filmmakers and screenwriters from around the world, and to exhibit their talent against the beautiful backdrop of San Diego, California. The competitive, independent nature of SIFFSC is designed to draw films from all genres that will not only intrigue us as filmmakers, but will compel us as film viewers.

Deadline: May 1

Entry fees: Feature $40; Short Scripts $30; Student $20

Categories: All genres

Prizes: FEATURES ▌ FIRST PLACE: $5,000; SECOND PLACE: $2,500 ▌ **SHORT SCRIPTS** ▌ FIRST PLACE: $2,000; SECOND PLACE: $1,000

Contact Information: P.O. Box 851, Escondido, CA 92033-0851

(760) 899-3178 Phone

Web: www.socalfilmfestival.com

E-mail: submissions@socalfilmfestival.com

Southwest Writers Workshop

Mission Statement: The purpose of the Southwest Writers contest is to encourage, recognize, and honor distinctiveness in writing. The festival received more than 600 entries from around the country last year. Editors and agents judged all entries and critiqued the top three in each category. In addition, all entries were critiqued by a qualified professional.

Deadline: June 1

Entry fees: $25 members; $45 nonmembers

Categories: All genres

Prizes: STORYTELLER AWARD: $1,000; FIRST PLACE: $150; SECOND PLACE: $100; THIRD PLACE: $75

Previous Winners: FIRST PLACE: *Four Women and a Horse* by Nina Knapp, Albuquerque, NM ⦚ SECOND PLACE: *Chartres* by Karen Albright Lin and Janet Fogg, Longmont, CO ⦚ THIRD PLACE: *Sisters* by Kim Campbell, Amarillo, TX

Contact Information: 3721 Morris N.E., Albuquerque, NM 87111

(505) 265-9485 Phone

(505) 265-9483 Fax

Web: www.southwestwriters.com

E-mail: contactus@southwestwriters.com

Storybay Screenwriting Competition

Mission Statement: Storybay is an innovative, membership-based, distance learning and mentoring program created by top industry executives, producers, and editors within the literary community. Each program is individually tailored to help educate, mentor, and develop a writer's skills while providing insight into the entertainment industry.

Deadlines: EARLY: October 31; STANDARD: December 15; FINAL: April 30

Entry fees: EARLY: $35; STANDARD: $45; FINAL: $60

Categories: All genres

Prizes: GRAND PRIZE: $5,000 and membership in Storybay; FIRST RUNNER-UP: $500 and membership in Storybay; SECOND RUNNER-UP: $500 and membership in Storybay

Previous Winners: *Beneath the Darkness* by Bruce Wilkinson ▌ After the death of his best friend, a fifteen-year-old boy struggles to expose the grim secrets surrounding a haunted house.

Contact Information: 269 S. Beverly Dr. #808, Beverly Hills, CA 90212

(800) 433-7211 Phone

Web: www.storybayacademy.com

E-mail: competition@storybayacademy.com

★ Telluride IndieFest

Mission Statement: Telluride IndieFest is dedicated to the spirit and advancement of independent filmmaking and showcases the best independent films and screenplays in the world.

Deadlines: STANDARD: April 30; FINAL: May 31; EXTENDED: June 30

Entry fees: STANDARD: (61–120 pages) $55, (31–60 pages) $50, (11–30 pages) $45, (1–10 pages) $40; FINAL: add $10

Categories: All genres

Prizes: All selected artists will have their entries presented during the Telluride Film Festival to some of Hollywood's most respected talent agencies, production companies, and film distributors.

Previous Winners: Lisa Kirazian, 2002 winner (Screenplay division) for *Cassatt and Degas:* "Telluride IndieFest was a great honor and learning experience. Fielding questions about my screenplay *Cassatt and Degas* in the live Q and A was the best training. Right now I have several producers interested in my screenplays—and a potential book deal—as a result of my winning at Telluride IndieFest 2002! Thank you!" ▌ David L. Brown, 2000 winner (Documentary division) for *Surfing for Life:* "When *Surfing for Life* screened at Telluride IndieFest, Jenny Jones saw it there, was very impressed and decided to launch a series of Jenny Jones shows on documentary filmmaking. After the first show, I was asked to consult with the show's producers on other appropriate documentaries." ▌ Stu Pollard, 1999 winner (Feature Film division) for *Nice Guys Sleep Alone:* "The enthusiastic audience response *Nice Guys Sleep Alone* received at Telluride IndieFest bolstered our confidence as we searched for distribution. We ultimately sold the film to HBO, enjoyed an exclusive run at Hollywood Video, and continue to be one of the most popular indie films at Net-flix.com." ▌ Craig Clyde, 1998 winner (Screenplay division) for *Sparrow on the Roof:* "Because of *Sparrow on the Roof* doing so well at Telluride, it was requested over and over. I finally optioned it to a European company. That makes two options and one sale for me this year and Telluride was a big part of that beginning. After a few years of trying, I might add. Many thanks. Good programs like yours really help the writers on the outside of the Hollywood fence make it to through the gate."

Contact Information: 398 W. Colorado Ave., Suite 217, Telluride, CO 81435

(970) 708-1529 Phone

(970) 728-8128 Fax

Web: www.tellurideindiefest.com

E-mail: festival@tellurideindiefest.com

Tennessee Screenwriting Association Script Competition

Mission Statement: The TSA is a professionally oriented organization, constantly striving to develop more avenues to help our members and community prepare for the real world of the entertainment business.

Deadline: August 1

Entry fee: $30

Categories: All genres

Prizes: FIRST PLACE: $1,000 plus an all-access pass to the film festival, including seminars hosted by the Tennessee Screenwriting Association; SECOND PLACE: $500; THIRD PLACE: $250

Previous Winners: FIRST PLACE: *Lucky Teeter* by Jason Allen, Nashville, TN ▌ A lonely bait shop employee is struck by lightning for the third time, resulting in a strange phenomenon—everyone he touches becomes instantly attracted to him. ▌ SECOND PLACE: *Bird Brain* by Pete Kremer, Nashville, TN ▌ It's up to lab assistant Jerry to save all creatures great and small when a diabolical animal rights activist steals his super-genius grandmother's nuclear fuel–eating, gold-pooping goose. ▌ THIRD PLACE: *Bloodline: The Legacy of Paine* by Jim O'Rear, Mt. Juliet, TN ▌ A band of Civil War vampires threaten the bloodline of an innocent child who holds the key to their world domination.

Contact Information: P.O. Box 40194, Nashville, TN 37204-0194

(615) 316-9448 Phone

Web: www.tennscreen.com

E-mail: info@tennscreen.com

Thunderbird Films Screenplay Competition

Mission Statement: Thunderbird Films is an independent film company located in New York City. Founded in 1997, we are dedicated to producing innovative and socially aware films of artistic excellence. All entries will be read by industry professionals and all finalists will be judged by an independent literary agent.

Deadline: March 3

Entry fee: $40

Categories: All genres

Prizes: FIRST PLACE: $2,000 and possible option by Thunderbird Films

Contact Information: 214 Riverside Dr., Ste. 112, New York, NY 10025

(212) 352-4498 Phone

Web: home.att.net/~thunderbirdfilms/contest.htm

E-mail: estannard@dekker.com

▌ *Hollywood is the only town where you cannot fail. You can only quit trying.*
  —**DENNIS FOLEY**, television writer, *MacGyver*

TVwriter.com Spec Scriptacular

Mission Statement: The basic fact about the television business is that in order to get into it you, the writer, must have at least three great spec episodes written for existing shows. These episodes are your calling cards. They demonstrate that you have what it takes to write on spec. In other words, they show that your writing can meet the demands of a show's individual style. As more writers work on spec scripts, the competition for industry attention increases. TVwriter.com aims to help you get your spec episodes, pilots, and even MOWs read by those who can buy them or hire you—by giving your work the next best thing to having been professionally produced.

Deadline: December 1

Entry fee: $40

Categories: Original scripts for television: sitcom, action/drama, pilot/MOW

Prizes: GRAND PRIZE: $500, representation for one year by the Terry Porter Agency, free admission to the next TV Writer.Com Summer Intensive Seminar (a $350 value), free admission to the next Guy Magar Action/Cut Film-Making Seminar (a $350 value), a copy of the latest version of Final Draft screenplay formatting software (a $225 value), and a free coverage on your next script from HollywoodLitSales.Com (a $149 value); FIRST PLACE: $100, free admission to the Guy Magar Action/Cut Film-Making Seminar of your choice, a copy of the latest version of Final Draft screenplay formatting software (a $225 value), and a free "Killer Coverage" on your next script from HollywoodLitSales.Com

Previous Winners: SITCOM: *Becker,* "Locking Out The Law" by Samantha Lavin ∥ *Everybody Loves Raymond,* "The Old Photo" by Regan Lee ∥ *Everybody Loves Raymond,* "Rise and Shine" by Kevin Miles ∥ ACTION/DRAMA: *Angel,* "If I Could Die All Over Again" by Kevin Emerson ∥ *Gilmore Girls,* "Insurance, Kale, and Feathers" by Mark Ozdoba ∥ *Law & Order,* "The

---

∥ *One of the big things you have to learn is who to listen to and when; and you can't listen to everybody.*

—AMY HOLDEN JONES, screenwriter, *Indecent Proposal* and *Mystic Pizza*

Good Wife" by Carla Robinson | PILOT/MOW: *Cable Ready,* "He Pist Me Off" by Millie Trachtenberg

Contact Information: Cloud Creek Institute for the Arts, Cloud Creek
  Ranch, 3767 MC 5026, St. Joe, AZ 72675

(805) 495-3659 Phone

Web: www.specscriptacular.com

E-mail: info@specscriptacular.com

20/20 Screenwriting Contest

Mission Statement: 20/20's purpose is to discover great screenplays and to get them placed with WGA signatory agents and into the hands of producers. If a screenplay hasn't established itself by page 20, it is unlikely that it ever will. Let's-Do-Lunch/Screenbrokers' screenplay analysts, all rated highly by *Creative Screenwriting* magazine, will read twenty pages of each entry. A twenty-point criteria checklist of "musts" for a production-ready script will determine who will be entered in the second round for reading of the entire script. All twenty criteria must be met in both rounds.

Deadline: August 20

Entry fee: $20

Categories: All genres; twenty-page excerpt from script

Prizes: WGA signatory agent representation is guaranteed for all winning scripts, plus twenty pages of the winning scripts will be read by professional actors in front of an audience of production executives.

Previous Winners: *Sticks and Stones* by Kathryn Sheard | *Moon* by Dennis Capps | *Alone* by Stephen Dudycha

Contact Information: 3639 Malibu Vista Dr., Malibu, CA 90265

(310) 454-0971 Phone

(310) 573-3868 Fax

Web: www.lets-do-lunch.com

E-mail: info@lets-do-lunch.com

★ UCLA Extension/Diane Thomas Screenwriting Awards

Mission Statement: Over the years, the Diane Thomas Screenwriting Awards have proven to be a strong starting point for successful screenwriting careers. Michael Douglas served as a judge for 2003's competition. So did Steven Spielberg; producer Kathleen Kennedy; producer Cathleen Summers of Summers Productions; agent Norman Kurland of Broder, Kurland, Webb, and Uffner; and Deborah Newmyer, former president of creative affairs at Arnold Kopelson Productions. A special perk for each year's finalists is that they are paired with individual industry mentors to take their entries to final draft. Among the mentors this year are Michael Tolkin (*The Player*), Greg Widen (*Highlander, Backdraft*), J. T. Allen (*The Preacher's Wife*), Todd Robinson (*White Squall*), and Alexandra Seros (*The Specialist, Point of No Return*).

Deadline: January 23

Entry fee: None

Categories: All genres

Prizes: Cash awards and ceremony

Success Stories: Of the 140 finalists of the award since its founding in 1987, eighteen have received "written by" credit for feature films, seven for television movies, and ten have written episodes for thirty-eight different television series. A case in point is Randi Mayem Singer, who won the first Diane Thomas Award with her script, *A 22-Cent Romance.* A bidding war broke out for the script, and it eventually sold to Orion Pictures for $350,000. Her next script, *Adam and Eve on a Raft,* was optioned by Hollywood Pictures and, from there, Fox hired her to write the screenplay adaptation of the children's book *Alias Madame Doubtfire,* now known as the hit film *Mrs. Doubtfire.* More recently, brothers David and Peter Griffiths sold their winning script, *Blood Relative,* for nearly $1 million to Mike Medavoy's Phoenix Pictures.

Contact Information: Brandon Gannon/Writers' Program, 10995 Le Conte Ave., Ste. 440, Los Angeles, CA 90024-2883

(310) 825-9415 Phone

Web: www.uclaextension.org/writers

E-mail: writers@uclaextension.edu.

> *You sell a screenplay like you sell a car. If somebody drives it off a cliff, that's it.*
> —RITA MAE BROWN, screenwriter and novelist, *Rubyfruit Jungle* and *Riding Shotgun*

Virginia Governor's Screenwriting Competition

Mission Statement: The Governor's Screenwriting Competition was created to celebrate the accomplishments of Virginia writers, as well as to promote the future of filmmaking in Virginia. It provides screenwriters with a forum for their work and an opportunity to present their scripts to decision-makers in the film industry. Each writer submits a full-length screenplay or television script to be evaluated by a panel of Virginia judges. Finalists from the first round of judging are then sent on to a second panel made up of active professionals in the film or television industry.

Deadline: June 7

Entry fee: None

Categories: Virginia writers only; majority of the script must take place in Virginia or locations that could reasonably be found in Virginia

Prizes: Three $1,000 cash awards

Previous Winners: The Virginia Film Office announced the four winners of the twelfth Governor's Screenwriting Competition. ▌ *The Six Court Martials of Uriah Levy* by Robert Davenport, Alexandria ▌ *Lost Time* by Eugene Harris, Richmond ▌ *Sunshine Cleaning* by Megan Holley, Richmond ▌ *Civilized Men* by Ivor Noel-Hume, Williamsburg ▌ Eighty-five screenplays were submitted to the competition and twelve finalists were selected to go to the second round of judging.

Contact Information: 901 E. Byrd St., Richmond, VA 23219-4048

(804) 371-8204 Phone

(800) 854-6233 Toll Free

(800) 641-0810 Recorded Message

▌ **TIP:** Most contests now use the Internet to contact applicants, so make sure you print your e-mail address clearly. If they misread even one letter, you may never hear from them.

▌ *A story should have a beginning, a middle, and an end . . . but not necessarily in that order.*

—JEAN-LUC GODARD

(804) 371-8177 Fax
Web: www.film.virginia.org
E-mail: vafilm@virginia.org

Winfemme Monthlies

Mission Statement: Women's Image Network, the producer of the annual Winfemme Film Festival and the Winfemme Monthlies, accepts three distinct categories of films, videos, and scripts: short, documentary, and/or feature. Both men and women filmmakers and/or screenwriters are encouraged to apply. Scripts may be TV specs, TV movies, feature film scripts, theater plays, and/or novellas.
Deadline: Last day of each month
Entry fee: $50
Categories: Screenplays or television scripts that feature female protagonists or are written by a woman
Prize: Festival award
Contact Information: 2118 Wilshire Blvd., Ste. 144, Santa Monica, CA 90403
(310) 229-5365 Phone
Web: www.winfemme.com
E-mail: info@winfemme.com

Winner Take All Screenwriting Competition

Mission Statement: The Winner Take All Screenwriting Competition's rules favor talent, not arbitrary opinions. The winning screenplay will go through three levels of scoring before the final numbers are tallied.
Deadlines: EARLY: May 15; STANDARD: June 30; FINAL: August 15; EXTENDED: February 16
Entry fees: EARLY: $40; STANDARD: $45; FINAL: $50; EXTENDED: $55
Categories: All genres
Prizes: The winner of the competition will receive a total of $3,000 to be distributed in ten equal payments of $300 on the first day of each month beginning in August. In addition, the winner will receive a complete screenwriter's package from Screenplay Systems, which includes Dramatica Pro, Storyview, and Movie Magic Screenwriter 2000; the most current printing of the producers edition of the *Hollywood Creative Directory;*

a one-year subscription to the online edition of *Variety;* and a $50 gift certificate to The Writers Store.

Previous Winners: Winners Kris Johnson and James Seda each obtained representation almost immediately following our announcement that they had won the WTA screenwriting competition. Kris and James are now pitching their ideas to Hollywood.

Contact Information: 531-A North Hollywood Way, Ste. 277, Burbank, CA 91505

Web: www.winner-takeall.com

E-mail: questions@winner-takeall.com

WriteMovies.com

Mission Statement: Since 1999, dozens of writers have found representation and had their books and scripts optioned as a result of participating in the WriteMovies.com contest.

Deadlines: EARLY: July 4; STANDARD: August 3; FINAL: September 3

Entry fees: EARLY: $25; STANDARD: $35; FINAL: $45; BOOKS: $49

Categories: Scripts, books, plays, short stories, articles

Prizes: FIRST PRIZE: $3,000 in cash, free travel and accommodation in Los Angeles so that the winner can attend a reception at the studio and meet with several producers, agents, directors, and managers. The top projects are submitted to the production companies and studios, and the winner is guaranteed representation.

Previous Winners: A previous winner, *The List,* is due to go into production this January (we just signed one of the hottest new directors in town), and our latest contest winner, *Living Together,* has already received thirty-five reading requests from agencies, studios, and production companies.

Contact Information: 1484½ Robertson Blvd., Los Angeles, CA 90035

(310) 276-5160 Phone

What's all this business of being a writer? It's just putting one word after another.

—IRVING THALBERG

(310) 276-5134 Fax
Web: www.writemovies.com
E-mail: admin@writemovies.com

The Writers Network Screenplay and Fiction Competition

Mission Statement: The Writers Network Screenplay and Fiction Competition is co-sponsored by WGA Signatory Literary Agencies in Los Angeles and New York and is designed to give new and talented writers across the country the chance to pursue a career in film or television.

Deadline: May 29

Entry fee: $35

Categories: All genres; fiction/nonfiction, plays, screenplays

Prizes: Up to ten winners in each category are chosen each year by our panel of judges (this year including agents from Innovative, ICM, Metropolitan, Endeavor, William Morris, Bondesen/Graup, and UTA). Each winner receives $1,000 cash and literary representation for up to two projects during the course of one year. Winning screenplays, half-hour teleplays, or plays will be distributed to the motion picture industry's top producers, directors, and production companies, and manuscripts will be sent to top publishers. Throughout the year, The Writers Network panel of credited writers will assist winners with polishing projects prior to their being submitted.

Success Stories: Matt Healy's winning script *Clay Pigeons* debuted in theaters nationwide in 1998. The film was produced by Ridley Scott and distributed by Gramercy. It starred Vince Vaughn, Joaquin Phoenix, and Janeane Garofalo. Since we signed Healy with ICM, he's finished two writing assignments (one for Richard Donner), and he landed a two-picture deal with Warner Brothers. Mike Walsh optioned two of his projects after we signed him with Ken Sherman. Jon Bokenkamp sold his winning script *Preston Tylk* after we signed him with ICM. Then he landed a two-picture deal and a writing assignment with director William Friedkin. Haven Turleygood sold his pitch to Joel Silver and landed a writing assignment with Arnold Kopelson at Fox after we signed him with Endeavor.

Contact Information: 287 S. Robertson Blvd., #467, Beverly Hills, CA 90211

(800) 646-3896 Phone

Web: www.fadeinonline.com

E-mail: writersnet@aol.com

WriteSafe Present-A-Thon

Mission Statement: The WriteSafe Group was created by Jesse Laverne Manns in 1999 and is dedicated to safeguarding the creative rights of artists in all media. The WriteSafe Present-A-Thon is a quarterly competition for all material registered with WriteSafe for public view.

Deadlines: March 31, June 30, September 30, December 31

Entry fee: Free with WriteSafe registration ($10 or two for $15)

Categories: All genres

Prizes: First Prize is consideration for publication, production, or representation by a panel of entertainment industry experts. If the work meets the standards of any one member of the panel, the winner will have an offer that could lead to a deal.

Previous Winners: FIRST PRIZE: *Return to Manila* by Joselito Seldera ▮ SECOND PRIZE: *The Second* by Jorge Lomastro ▮ THIRD PRIZE: *M100/Y100: A True Origin of a Superhero* by Michael Delle Femine (short script)

Contact Information: 422 W. Carlisle Rd., Westlake Village, CA 91361

(805) 495-3659 Phone

Web: www.writesafe.com

E-mail: admin@writesafe.com

▮ *As soon as you have chosen a subject for a film, you have already made a success or a failure.*

—BILLY WILDER

FELLOWSHIPS AND GRANTS

A *fellowship* is an award that is designed to help the writer devote more of his or her time and energy to writing. Some fellowships offer financial support and others offer residencies. The writer is usually required to certify that the support is used to create new work and produce a copy of the work at the end of the fellowship period.

A *grant* is a specific monetary award earmarked for use in creating such a new work.

Fellowships are often more highly regarded than screenplay contests. The largest and most influential, the Nicholl Fellowship, is administered by the Academy of Motion Picture Arts and Sciences (home of the Academy Awards) and receives more than 4,000 applications every year. Simply making it to the semifinals will open doors. The Chesterfield Film Fellowship is allied with Paramount Pictures and offers paid internships in television and feature film writing.

Academy of Television Arts and Sciences Student Internship Program

Mission Statement: The College Student Internship Program offers thirty-five eight-week paid summer internships in twenty-nine categories of telecommunications work. The program is a national competition and has been selected as one of the top ten internship programs of any kind in the United States by the *Princeton Review*'s "America's Top Internships." All internships are served during the summer in the Los Angeles area. Each intern receives mentoring by a former intern.

The Academy Foundation Internships are designed to provide qualified full-time students (undergraduate and graduate) pursuing degrees at colleges and universities in the United States with in-depth exposure to professional television-production techniques and practices. All interns are assigned administrative and/or production duties; however, collective bargaining agreements within the industry preclude interns from hands-on experience in certain areas. Most Academy Foundation Internships are located in Los Angeles.

Deadline: March 15

Entry fee: None

Categories: 1. AGENCY. SITE: Agency for representation of actors, directors, producers, or writers. ACTIVITIES: Phones, general office, script reading, and meetings. MINIMUM REQUIREMENTS: Liberal arts/business background, writing ability, and verbal and social skills. Strong desire to enter agency or entertainment management is a plus. **2. ANIMATION–NONTRADITIONAL (COMPUTER-GENERATED, ETC.).** SITE: Production company. ACTIVITIES: Emphasis on computer-generated animation. DESIRABLE BACKGROUND: art, animated character development, computer skills, theater arts, film, writing. All applicants must submit videocassette of animation project and storyboard—preferably of the work submitted. **3. ANIMATION–TRADITIONAL.** SITE: Production company. ACTIVITIES: Emphasis on cell animation. DESIRABLE BACKGROUND: Art, theater arts, film, writing. All applicants must submit drawing portfolio, videocassette of animation projects and storyboard—emphasis is on hand drawing. **4. ART DIRECTION/PRODUCTION DESIGN.** SITE: Art department of major studio or production company. ACTIVITIES: Exposure to set design, construction, dressing, painting, graphics, and practical locations adapted for TV production. MINIMUM REQUIREMENTS: Theater set design, and/or architectural background, including drafting. All applicants must submit portfolio of executed work including set photographs, drafting, designs, renderings, sketches, or photographs of models. **5. BROADCAST ADVERTISING AND PROMOTION.** SITE: Commercial television station. ACTIVITIES: Exposure to all aspects of TV station advertising, promotion, and publicity, with emphasis on print advertising, on-air campaigns, and press information relations. MINIMUM REQUIREMENTS: Courses in broadcast advertising and promotion, advertising/marketing, and/or journalism, plus a demonstrated creative interest in broadcast promotion. **6. BUSINESS AFFAIRS.** SITE: Studio, network, or independent production company business/legal department. ACTIVITIES: Observation of and some participation in the negotiation for and acquisition of material, employment of creative personnel and license agreements (between the network and program supplier). MINIMUM REQUIREMENTS: Law or business major or TV/film major with business/management courses. **7. CASTING.** SITE: Studio casting department or office of casting director. ACTIVITIES: Exposure to the casting process including arranging readings, answering phones, doing clerical tasks. DESIRABLE BACKGROUND: Liberal arts/communications; organizational skills, excellent people skills, and knowledge of television, movies, and theater. **8. CHILDREN'S PROGRAMMING/ DEVELOPMENT.** SITE: Network/cable. ACTIVITIES: Overview of development and production of animated and live-action children's programs. Review of scripts and process of selling ideas to the networks and cable. DESIRABLE BACKGROUND: Literature arts/communications. **9. CINEMATOGRAPHY.** SITE: TV/film studio. ACTIVITIES: Exposure to film production for prime-time television and equipment handling. MINIMUM REQUIREMENTS: Strong motion picture/video/photography background. All applicants required to submit videocassette work sample. Original work can be film or tape. **10. COMMERCIAL.** SITES: Commercial agency, production house, and post-production facility. ACTIVITIES: Participation in product conception, organization, production, and postproduction of commercials. MINIMUM REQUIREMENTS: TV/film production major/minor. **11. COSTUME DESIGN.** SITE: Wardrobe departments at studios and independent companies. ACTIVITIES: Preproduction meetings; prepping show through to taping/filming; assisting designer or costumer in wardrobe purchase, rental, and made-to-order. MINIMUM REQUIREMENTS: Theater costume design and/or fashion design background. All applicants must submit a work sample (photographs of portfolio contents preferred, no more than ten examples). **12. DEVELOPMENT (TELEVISION).** SITE: Studio or production company. ACTIVITIES: Observation and participation in the evaluation of program ideas and literary materials, selection of writers, and oversight of script development. DESIRABLE BACKGROUND: Liberal arts/communications; creative writing, literature, and theater arts. **13. DOCUMENTARY/NONFICTION PRODUCTION.** SITE: Production company or cable network. ACTIVITIES: Exposure to production of documentaries and/or reality specials, segments, or series. Includes research, studio/location production, postproduction. MINIMUM REQUIREMENTS: Background in documentary production, research,

Don't be seduced into thinking that that which does not make a profit is without value.

   —ARTHUR MILLER

writing, and computer skills. Placement outside Los Angeles is possible.
| **14. EDITING.** SITE: Studio or production company. ACTIVITIES: Observe postproduction of episodic, MOW, or miniseries. Exposure to film/tape nonlinear systems. MINIMUM REQUIREMENTS: Film and tape editing courses. All applicants are required to submit sample of film editing; suggested length: ten minutes. | **15. ENTERTAINMENT NEWS.** SITE: Production facility. ACTIVITIES: Observation of and some participation in day-to-day entertainment-industry news-gathering and broadcasting activities. MINIMUM REQUIREMENTS: TV production and journalism courses, basic computer skills. | **16. EPISODIC SERIES.** SITE: Studio or production company. ACTIVITIES: Observation of production process of current series, including script development, preproduction, filming/taping, and postproduction. MINIMUM REQUIREMENTS: Commitment to career in television production. | **17. GAME SHOW.** SITE: Offices/studios in Los Angeles. area. ACTIVITIES: Assist in production and development of original programming for network. Work with programming department staff and outside producers to manage creative and production issues. MINIMUM REQUIREMENTS: Passion for and knowledge of game shows. Production and/or development experience a plus. Must be able to work long hours, multitask, be both a self-starter and a team player. | **18. INTERACTIVE MEDIA.** SITE: Network, studio, production company, interactive agency. ACTIVITIES: Emphasis on the creation and delivery of interactive content that enhances the television experience. MINIMUM REQUIREMENTS: Courses in TV/film production and/or creative writing/storytelling as well as familiarity with interactive technologies and platforms. | **19. MOVIES MADE FOR TELEVISION.** SITE: Production company. ACTIVITIES: Preproduction, production, production assistant duties. MINIMUM REQUIREMENTS: Production background, commitment to career in television production. Out-of-town placement possible. | **20. MUSIC.** SITE: Production company/studios. ACTIVITIES: Music production (electronic and orchestral), sound design, recording, editing, studio set-up, software and hardware installation. MINIMUM REQUIREMENTS: Music background, strong interest in music for TV/film, electronic aptitude and experience, familiarity with music production software. All applicants must submit five short samples of original compositions on video or audio cassette. | **21. POSTPRODUCTION.** SITE: Postproduction facility. ACTIVITIES: Exposure to all aspects of postproduction. MINIMUM REQUIREMENTS: Videotape editing course. All candidates must submit sample of videotape editing ($\frac{1}{2}$-inch VHS only); suggested length: ten minutes. | **22. PRODUCTION MANAGEMENT.** SITE: Studio or production com-

---

█ **TIP:** Always check a contest's Web site before submitting. Print out the submission guidelines and follow them to the letter. Then *proofread* your work.

---

pany. ACTIVITIES: Organizing, scheduling, and budgeting productions, some production-assistant and general office duties. MINIMUM REQUIRE-MENTS: TV/film major, computer skills. █ **23. PROGRAMMING MANAGEMENT.** SITE: Network or cable company. ACTIVITIES: Introduction to entertainment program development and current programming; attending pitch, notes, and staff meetings; view production dailies; and visit sets. MINIMUM REQUIREMENTS: Knowledge of television, liberal arts/communication/business background. Finalists required to submit script synopsis and evaluation upon notification. █ **24. PUBLIC RELATIONS AND PUBLICITY.** SITE: Public relations firm and/or entertainment company in-house public relations department. ACTIVITIES: Researching and writing news releases, assisting in contacting all media, and attending meetings and news events. MINIMUM REQUIREMENTS: Strong writing skills. Major or minor must be in public relations, journalism, communications, publicity, or English. █ **25. SOUND.** SITE: Audio postproduction facility. ACTIVITIES: Exposure to all aspects of production and postproduction sound, including editing, supervision, mixing, transfer, sound effects, music, Foley, dialogue, and studio management techniques. MINIMUM REQUIREMENTS: Some music and/or sound effects editing and mixing experience preferred. Basic understanding of electronics, sound equipment, and computers a plus. Commitment to career in audio production. █ **26. SYNDICATION/DISTRIBUTION.** SITE: Major studio. ACTIVITIES: Observe all facets of sales, marketing, promotion, and program development/production in both domestic and international markets. MINIMUM REQUIREMENTS: Strong interest in marketing, communications, research, and/or sales. █ **27. TELEVISION DIRECTING—MULTICAMERA.** SITE: TV station or production company. ACTIVITIES: Overview of directing process using multicamera videotape and/or film format. Observation on productions such as soaps, episodic, variety, specials (except news or sports). MINIMUM REQUIREMENTS: Courses in directing and editing; experience with electronic cameras. Only finalists will be required to submit a work sample on $\frac{1}{2}$-inch VHS cassette upon notification. █ **28. TELEVISION DIRECTING—SINGLE CAMERA.** SITE: Variable. Intern is paired with an MOW, miniseries, or episodic director. ACTIVITIES: Overview of directing process using multicamera videotape and/or film format.

Observation on productions such as soaps, episodic, variety, specials (except news or sports). MINIMUM REQUIREMENTS: Courses in directing and editing; experience with electronic cameras. Only finalists will be required to submit a work sample on $\frac{1}{2}$-inch VHS cassette upon notification. **29. TELEVISION SCRIPTWRITING.** SITE: TV series. ACTIVITIES: Overview of comedy or drama writing process that may include idea inception, story meetings, revisions, and production. MINIMUM REQUIREMENTS: Strong writing background. Applicants must submit an original scene (approximately four pages) from a current comedy or drama series and a logline for the scene/episode. Finalists must submit a complete original script (long-form series episode or play) upon notification.

Prizes: The Academy of Television Arts and Sciences Foundation awards $4,000 to each intern accepted into the program, which is paid in three installments. Applicable payroll deductions are made from payments.

Contact Information: Academy Foundation–Internships, 5220 Lankershim Blvd., North Hollywood, CA 91601-3109

(818) 754-2830 Phone

(818) 761-2827 Fax

Web: www.emmys.org/foundation/internships.php

E-mail: webmaster@emmys.org

Artist Trust

Mission Statement: Artist Trust is committed to supporting art at its source—the creative individual. For more than sixteen years Artist Trust has provided information to tens of thousands of artists each year and more than $2 million in direct grant support to 1,050 Washington State resident musicians, writers, visual and craft artists, playwrights, choreographers, composers, performers, and filmmakers. The grants provide support for artist-generated projects that can include (but are not limited to) the development, presentation, or completion of new work. Awards

---

It took me fifteen years to discover that I had no talent for writing, but I couldn't give it up because by that time I was too famous.

—ROBERT BENCHLEY

are based on quality of work as represented by supporting materials and on creativity and feasibility of the proposed project.

Deadline: February 27

Entry fee: None

Categories: Plays, stage music, screenplays, teleplays, and radio scripts; Washington residents only

Prize: Up to $1,400

Contact Information: 1835 12th Ave., Seattle, WA 98122-2437

(206) 467-8734 Phone

(866) 21TRUST Toll Free

(206) 467-9633 Fax

Web: www.artisttrust.org

E-mail: info@artisttrust.org

★ Chesterfield Writer's Film Project (Sponsored by Paramount Pictures)

Mission Statement: The Writer's Film Project, based at Paramount Pictures, is one of the most prestigious screenwriting fellowships in the United States. The program originated with the support of Steven Spielberg's Amblin Entertainment. The WFP writers are chosen by competition and evaluated on the basis of prose and dramatic writing samples. Selected writers form a screenwriting workshop in Los Angeles, using their storytelling skills to begin a career in film. Each year, writers from several disciplines—fiction, theater, and film—have been chosen to participate. Each year, some of these writers have been affiliated with university writing programs, and others have been unaffiliated. During the fellowship year, each writer creates two original feature-length screenplays. Throughout the program, selected film professionals and Paramount Pictures executives serve as mentors, sharing their opinions and experience with the fellows. In past years, the group of mentors and guest speakers has included David Koepp (*Spider-Man*), Stephen Gaghan (*Traffic*), Scott Frank (*Minority Report*), Steven Zaillian (*Gangs of New York*), Daniel Pyne (*Sum of All Fears*), Bruce Joel Rubin (*Ghost*), Andy Walker (*Sleepy Hollow*), Tom Schulman (*Dead Poets Society*), Harold Ramis (*Analyze This*), Warren Beatty (*Reds*), Nicholas Kazan (*Reversal of Fortune*), Buck Henry (*The Graduate*), Robin Swicord (*Little Women*), Ed Solomon (*Men In Black*), and John Briley (*Gandhi*).

Deadline: June 21

Entry fee: $39.50

Categories: All genres

Prizes: This year up to five writers will be chosen to participate, and each will receive a $20,000 stipend to cover living expenses during the fellowship year. At year's end, WFP writers are introduced to various literary agencies. Each writer has two quality screenplays to use as samples in the pursuit of writing assignments within the film industry at large. Upon graduation from the program, many WFP writers have been signed by major literary agencies including the Creative Artists Agency (CAA), the William Morris Agency, and the United Talent Agency. WFP writers have been hired for writing assignments and have had scripts acquired by Tom Hanks, Quincy Jones, Steven Spielberg, Ron Howard, Wesley Snipes, and Francis Ford Coppola, as well as various studios and production companies including Paramount Pictures, Warner Brothers, The Walt Disney Company, Universal Pictures, Sony Pictures, MGM, United Artists, New Line Cinema, American Zoetrope, Imagine Entertainment, and DreamWorks.

Previous Winners: In the past several years, fifteen films by WFP alumni have been produced, including Warner Brothers' *A Walk To Remember,* Gramercy's *The Matchmaker* (starring Janeane Garofalo), TNT's *Hope* (directed by Goldie Hawn and starring Christine Lahti and J. T. Walsh), Paramount's *Breakdown* (starring Kurt Russell; uncredited rewrite), Warner Brothers' *Free Willy 2* (produced by Richard Donner), Universal's *Julie Johnson* (starring Courtney Love), and Timothy Hutton's directorial debut, *Digging to China* (starring Kevin Bacon and Mary Stuart Masterson). The WFP may produce the best of each program year's work. For

---

Writers are only rarely likable.

—**JOAN DIDION**, screenwriter, *A Star Is Born*

The dubious privilege of a freelance writer is he's given the freedom to starve anywhere.

—**S. J. PERELMAN**, screenwriter, *Horse Feathers* and *Monkey Business* each screenplay produced, the WFP will pay its author no less than the current minimums established by the Writers Guild of America (WGA).

Contact Information: 1158 26th St. #544, Santa Monica, CA 90403

(213) 683-3977 Phone

Web: www.chesterfield-co.com

E-mail: info@chesterfield-co.com

★ Guy A. Hanks and Marvin Miller Screenwriting Program (Established by Bill and Camille Cosby)

Mission Statement: The Guy Hanks and Marvin Miller program was established by Bill and Camille Cosby in 1993 at the University of Southern California's School of Cinema-Television. It was named in honor of Camille's father, Guy Alexander Hanks, and Bill's producer, Marvin Miller. The fifteen-week intensive workshop was designed with a dual purpose: (1) to assist writers in the completion of a film or television script and (2) to deepen the participants' appreciation for and comprehension of African American history and culture.

Deadline: October 15

Entry fee: None

Categories: Feature film and television scripts

Prizes: The program meets two evenings a week for fifteen weeks starting in February. One evening focuses on lectures and discussions about African American history and culture. The second evening is devoted to writing instruction and discussion of works in progress. Attendance is mandatory at both sections. Specific days and times will be announced after participants have been selected. Although a stipend is not available, workshop participation and books will be provided free of charge. All participants must reside in the Los Angeles area while attending the workshop.

Previous Winners: Alumni are highly respected in the industry and sought after as skilled writers. Past participants have been honored by local and national organizations including the NAACP. Our television writers have written and produced for shows including *My Wife and Kids, Girlfriends, Brothers Garcia, Family Law, Soul Food, What About Your Friends, The Parkers, Gideon's Crossing, Bette, Moesha, For Your Love, Farscape, Malcolm & Eddie, The Steve Harvey Show, Living Single, Sister-Sister, Family Matters,* and *Cosby*. Feature writers have had their scripts sold and optioned;

many have been commissioned to write for production companies and studios. Other alumni have taken active roles in the creative end of the business and have gone on to work in development and production of features and television programming.

Contact Information: 850 W. 34th St., GT132, Los Angeles, CA 90089-2211

(213) 740-8194 Phone

Web: www-cntv.usc.edu/cosby/cosby-old/about.htm

E-mail: cosbyprogram@yahoo.com

★ Nicholl Fellowships in Screenwriting

Mission Statement: The Nicholl Fellowships in Screenwriting program is an international competition open to screenwriters who have not earned more than $5,000 writing for film or television. Entry scripts must be the original work of a sole author or of no more than two collaborative authors. Entries must have been written originally in English. Adaptations and translated scripts are not eligible. Up to five $30,000 fellowships are awarded each year.

Deadlines: EARLY: April 1; STANDARD: May 1

Entry fees: EARLY: $20; STANDARD: $30

Categories: All genres

Prizes: Up to five $30,000 fellowships. Since the inception of the Nicholl program in 1986, eighty-three fellowships totaling $2,025,000 have been awarded to new screenwriters.

Previous Winners: Allison Anders (1986) is the writer-director of *Gas Food Lodging, Mi Vida Loca,* and *Grace Of My Heart* and cowriter-director of *Sugartown* and *Border Radio.* She directed one segment of the compilation film *Four Rooms* and several episodes of the series *Sex and the City.* She

---

▌ **TIP:** There's no need to use padded envelopes to send scripts, a ten-by-thirteen manila will do.

▌ *A writer is a controlled schizophrenic.*
   —EDWARD ALBEE

also served as the executive producer of *Lover Girl*. Her most recent film, *Things Behind the Sun*, which she cowrote and directed, premiered at the 2001 Sundance Film Festival. Jeffrey Eugenides (1986) is the author of the novel *The Virgin Suicides*; the film version premiered at the 1999 Cannes Film Festival. His novel *Middlesex* was awarded a Pulitzer Prize in 2003. Randall McCormick (1987) is the cowriter of *Speed 2* and received story credit on *Titan A.E.* He is also the cowriter of *Psychosushi*. Warren Taylor (1987) adapted Bob Randall's novel *The Last Man on the List*, which aired on USA as *Dead Husbands* in 1998. He wrote the TV movie *In The Eyes of a Stranger*, a revised version of his Nicholl entry script, *In the Dark*. His adaptation of Joy Fielding's novel *Tell Me No Secrets* aired on ABC. Radha Bharadwaj (1989) is the writer-director of *Closet Land* (her Nicholl entry script) and of *Basil*, which she adapted from the Wilkie Collins novel. She also wrote and directed *An Unsafe World*, currently in postproduction. Mark Lowenthal (1989) is the writer-director-producer of *Where the Elephant Sits* (his Nicholl entry script), which premiered at the 1998 Berlin Film Festival. Another 1989 Fellowship recipient Jim McGlynn's Nicholl entry script, *Traveler*, was released in 1997. Deborah Pryor's 1989 Nicholl entry script, *Briar Patch*, premiered at the 2003 Slamdance Film Festival. T. C. Smith (1990) wrote the TV movie *Beverly Hills Family Robinson*, which aired on ABC in 1997. He cowrote the short film *Scream, Teen, Scream!*, which screened at the 1997 Berlin Film Festival. He also cowrote and costarred in the short film *Ernest and Bertram*, which premiered at the 2002 Sundance Film Festival. Raymond De Felitta (1991) directed his Nicholl Fellowship script, *Two Family House*, which premiered at the 2000 Sundance Film Festival. He is the writer-director of *Cafe Society* and the Oscar-nominated short film *Bronx Cheer*. He also cowrote *Shadow of Doubt*. Ronald Emmons (1991) wrote *Rendezvous*, which aired on Black Entertainment Television in 1999. Susannah Grant (1992) wrote *Erin Brockovich*, for which she received Academy Award and WGA nominations, and *28 Days*. She is the cowriter of *Pocahontas* and *Ever After: A Cinderella Story*. She also wrote and directed a number of episodes of the Fox-TV series *Party of Five*. Andrew W. Marlowe (1992) wrote *Air Force One, End of Days*, and *Hollow Man*. Ehren Kruger's 1996 Nicholl entry script, *Arlington Road*, was released in 1999. He wrote *Reindeer Games, Scream 3*, and *The Ring*, and cowrote *The Imposter* and *New World Disorder*. His most recent project, *The Brothers Grimm*, is slated for release in 2004. Karen Moncrieff (1998) directed her Nicholl entry script, *Blue Car*, which premiered in the American Spectrum section of the 2002 Sundance

Film Festival. Mike Rich's 1998 Nicholl entry script, *Finding Forrester,* was released in 2000. He also wrote *The Rookie* and *Radio.*

Contact Information: Academy Foundation–Nicholl Fellowship, 1313 N. Vine St., Hollywood, CA 90028-8107

(310) 247-3010 Phone

Web: www.oscars.org/nicholl

E-mail: nicholl@oscars.org

★ Nickelodeon Productions Writing Fellowship Program

Mission Statement: Nickelodeon Productions is continuing its search for new creative talent and is looking for writers to work full-time developing their craft at Nickelodeon. This program stems from Nickelodeon's commitment to encouraging meaningful participation from culturally and ethnically diverse new writers. We will be offering Nickelodeon fellowships in live-action and animation television.

Deadline: March 5

Entry fee: None

Categories: TV: Live-action, animation

Prize: Three-tiered $34,000 salary for one year

Contact Information: Writing Fellowship Program, 231 W. Olive Ave., Burbank, CA 91502 Attn: Karen Horne

(818) 736-3663 Phone

Web: www.nick.com/all_nick/fellowshipprogram

Pew Fellowships in the Arts

Mission Statement: Pew Fellowships in the Arts (PFA), established by the Pew Charitable Trusts in 1991, awards grants of $50,000 to artists working in a wide variety of performing, visual, and literary disciplines. The grants provide financial support directly to the artists so that they may have the opportunity to dedicate themselves exclusively to their creative pursuits. The program's aim is to provide support at the time in an artist's career when a concentration on growth and exploration is likely to have the greatest impact on his or her long-term professional development.

Deadline: December 2

Entry fee: None

Categories: Plays, stage music, screenplays; artists must live and work in the five-county Philadelphia area

Prizes: Fellows receive $50,000 divided into equal monthly payments for a period of twelve to twenty-four months. Fellows are required to begin their fellowship period within twelve months of notification. If they wish, fellows may receive up to $15,000 of the $50,000 in an initial payment regardless of when they plan to start, with the balance paid in equal monthly installments for the term of the fellowship. Up to twelve fellowships are awarded annually.

Previous Winners (2003): Kim Arrow, Tyrone Brown, Uri Caine, Andrea Cooper, Linda Cordell, Jim Hinz, Roko Kawai, Michael Olszewski, Toby Twining, Kukuli Velarde, Anna Weesner, and Jan Yager

Contact Information: 230 S. Broad St., Ste. 1003, Philadelphia, PA 19102

(215) 875-2285 Phone

(215) 875-2276 Fax

Web: www.pewarts.org

E-mail: pewarts@mindspring.com

POWER UP Movie Making Grant

Mission Statement: Our mission is to promote, encourage, and support the visibility and integration of women in the entertainment industry through career-building resources including a resume bank, networking events, roundtables, seminars, mentors, and grants for filmmaking.

Deadline: July 25

Entry fee: $35

Categories: All genres

> **TIP:** Avoid mentioning specific songs in your script. Music is the director's decision.

> **TIP:** If your application has any mistakes or omissions they won't fix it, they won't call you, and they won't return it. They'll cash your check and trash your script.

Prizes: FIRST PLACE: $2,000; SECOND PLACE: $1,000; top three winners receive Final Draft software and individual meetings with several agents and a manager

Previous Winners: FIRST PLACE: *Water* by Mary Feuer ▌ SECOND PLACE: *Foreign Affairs* by Paula Martinac and Katie Hogan ▌ THIRD PLACE: *Darling Clementine* by Gabrielle Galanter

Contact Information: 419 N. Larchmont Blvd. #283, Los Angeles, CA 90004

(323) 463-3154 Phone

(323) 467-6249 Fax

Web: www.power-up.net

E-mail: joinpowerup@aol.com

The Playwrights' Center Grant Programs

Mission Statement: JEROME FELLOWSHIP ▌ Four fellowships are awarded each year, providing emerging American writers with funds and services to aid them in the development of their craft. Each fellow receives a $9,000 stipend, and spends up to twelve months in residence in Minnesota using the Playwrights' Center's developmental services, including workshops and readings with professional actors, dramaturgs, and directors.

Mission Statement: McKNIGHT ADVANCEMENT GRANTS ▌ Annual McKnight Advancement Grants of $25,000 each are awarded to Minnesota writers whose work demonstrates exceptional artistic merit and potential. Support of individual artists has been a cornerstone of the McKnight Foundation's arts programming since it began in 1981. A fellowship can help artists set aside periods of time for study, reflection, experimentation, and exploration; take advantage of an opportunity; or work on a new project.

Deadlines: Various, see Web site

Entry fee: None

Categories: Plays, translations, stage music, screenplays

▌ *Writing is an occupation in which you have to keep proving your talent to those who have none.*

—JULES RENARD, screenwriter, *Romance Romance*

Prize: $9,000 to $25,000

Previous Winners: *Summer Moon* by John Olive | *Urgent Fury* by Allison Moore | *Ada* by Rosanna Staffa

Contact Information: 2301 Franklin Ave. E., Minneapolis, MN 55406-1099

(612) 332-7481 Phone

(612) 332-6037 Fax

Web: www.pwcenter.org

E-mail: info@pwcenter.org

Thanks Be to Grandmother Winifred Foundation

Mission Statement: The foundation offers financial support to encourage the creativity of women fifty-four years of age and older to create, develop, and implement ideas and concepts that will improve the lives of women, including activities that allow women to achieve a specific objective; produce a report; or improve a literary, artistic, or scientific skill or talent. The foundation prefers to receive requests in writing.

Deadlines: September 21 and March 21

Entry fee: None

Categories: Plays, translations, stage music, teleplays, radio scripts

Prize: $500 to $5,000

Previous Winners: Margaret (Peggy) Grove was awarded a grant of $3,750 to research female images in Australian Aboriginal rock art.

Contact Information: Box 1449, Wainscott, NY 11975-1449

(516) 725-0323 Phone

Walt Disney Studios/ABC Writers Fellowship

Mission Statement: For the fourteenth year, Walt Disney Studios/ABC Writers Fellowship is continuing the search to discover and employ creative talent and to employ culturally and ethnically diverse writers. We are looking for up to eleven writers to work full-time developing their craft at the Walt Disney Studios and ABC Entertainment. A Daytime Writing Fellowship is also offered.

Deadline: July 16

Entry fee: None

Categories: All genres

Prizes: Fellowships are in the areas of feature film and television. No previous experience is necessary; however, writing samples are required. Fellows will be provided a salary of $50,000 for a one-year period tentatively scheduled to begin in January. Fellows chosen from outside the Los Angeles area will be provided with round-trip airfare and one month's accommodations.

Previous Winners: Nelson Soler (2000–2001), was hired as coproducer for ABC's *Are You Hot?: The Search for America's Sexiest People;* Dailyn Rodriquez (2000–2001) was hired as a staff writer on ABC's *The George Lopez Show;* and John Marsh (2000–2001) wrote an episode for the Disney Channel's *Proud Family.* Other former fellows include Joan Weiss (1999–2000), coproducer for the WB's *Everwood;* Heather Hach (1999–2000), writer of the Walt Disney remake of *Freaky Friday* and *There's a Pop Diva Loose in the Cafeteria* for DreamWorks; Meghan McCarthy (1999–2000), who sold her feature script, *The Bachelorette,* to Universal Pictures; Saladin Patterson (1996–1997), now a producer on NBC's *Frasier;* Luisa Leschin (1995–1996), now an executive story editor on ABC's *The George Lopez Show;* Peter Murrieta (1994–1995), now an executive producer and creator of the WB's *Greetings from Tucson;* Jane Espenson (1992–1993), now a coexecutive producer on *Buffy the Vampire Slayer;* Malcolm Lee (1992–1993), writer/director of the film *The Best Man* and director of *Undercover Brother* for Universal Pictures; Jacquelyn C. Edmonds (1991–1992), now a coexecutive producer on UPN's *Abby;* Laurence Andries (1991–1992), now a coexecutive producer of *Boomtown;* Tony Puryear (1990–1991), who wrote the feature *Eraser;* Reggie "Rock" Bythewood (1990–1991), writer and director of *Dancing in September* for HBO and *Biker Boyz* for DreamWorks; Gary Hardwick (1990–1991), writer of the feature films *Trippin* and *Bring It On* and writer/director of *The Brothers* and *Deliver Us from Eva.*

Contact Information: 500 S. Buena Vista St., Burbank, CA 91521-4016

(818) 560-6894 Phone

Web: www.abctalentdevelopment.com

E-mail: abc.fellowships@abc.com

You can take all the sincerity in Hollywood, place it in the navel of a fruit fly and still have room enough for three caraway seeds and a producer's heart.

—**FRED ALLEN**, television host, *Your Show of Shows*

DEVELOPMENT

FOLLOWING IS A LIST of script contests and competitions that not only award prizes, but also develop winning scripts in anticipation of putting them into production. Some of the most prestigious award programs fall into this category, such as Project Greenlight and Sundance Labs. Also listed here are workshops and conferences that put on staged readings of winning scripts to help the writer elicit audience feedback and make improvements. A script often sounds different when it's read aloud. This process can point up problems in plotting or rhythm, and/or it can garner interest in the project.

Blue Sky International Film Festival's Screenplay Competition

Mission Statement: Founded in 1997, BSIFF is dedicated to the discovery and exhibition of new talent within the independent world of filmmaking. BSIFF has become the best source for independent and world cinema in Las Vegas. Every year BSIFF showcases a variety of films from such countries as the United States, Canada, Mexico, Brazil, Japan, Korea, Singapore, India, Australia, New Zealand, England, France, and Germany.

If you have someone on the set for the hair, why would you not have someone for the words?

—LOUIS MALLE, telling producers why he wanted John Guare around during the filming of *Atlantic City*

Deadline: July 31
Entry fee: $25
Categories: All genres
Prizes: The winner will receive a $1,000 cash award and a live performance of the script by the Blue Sky Players.
Contact Information: 4185 Paradise Rd., Ste. 2009, Las Vegas, NV 89109
(702) 737-3313 Phone
Web: www.bsiff.com
E-mail: info@bsiff.com

CAPE Foundation New Writer Awards

Mission Statement: The Coalition of Asian Pacifics in Entertainment (CAPE) is a nonprofit trade organization addressing the interests of Asian Pacific Americans (APAs) in the entertainment industry. CAPE was founded in 1991 in Los Angeles, and in 1995 the organization established a New York chapter. Today, CAPE reaches more than 1,000 studio and independent film executives, television and Internet executives, film and recording producers, below-the-line talent, publicists, actors, writers, directors, and more. In keeping with the goals of the CAPE Foundation, including the promotion of Asian Pacific Americans in the entertainment community, the foundation sponsors an annual writing contest in two catagories: Screenwriting and TV Writing.
Deadline: February 13
Entry fee: $35
Categories: Feature; television
Prizes: Winners receive a cash prize, writing software, and an opportunity to pitch their winning scripts to a select group of entertainment executives. They may also receive staged readings of their winning screenplays.
Previous Winners: Dennis Kao has worked in TV production for FOX and CBS and as an executive assistant to TV/film producer Bill Todman, Jr., at Warner Brothers (*X-Men, Wild Wild West*). He is currently the production manager at Time Warner Audiobooks, where he produces, directs, and supervises the production of audiobooks published by Warner Books, Little-Brown, and Talk Miramax Books. He previously optioned the screenplay *How to Make Love to a Woman,* was a finalist for the Paramount Studios children's screenwriting contest and a participant in Lode-

stone Theater's TV writing workshop, and is currently completing *Swordsmen,* an epic tale of valor and loyalty in medieval China.

Contact Information: P.O. Box 251855, Los Angeles, CA 90025

(310) 278-2313 Phone

(310) 745-8893 Fax

Web: www.capeusa.org

E-mail: info@capeusa.org

CAST Project

Mission Statement: This is a screenwriting competition with a twist—it's already cast! This is an opportunity for writers to create a one-hour episodic to be read by Los Angeles–based judges. Winners will be considered for literary representation by agents from Shapiro-Lichtman Talent Agency, Bicoastal, and the Jackson Artists Agency. In addition, the winning script will be produced as a pilot.

Deadline: June 30

Entry fee: $40

Categories: One-hour episodes

Prizes: FIRST PLACE: The winning script is produced into a pilot. Top three winners also receive a one-year subscription to *Scr(i)pt* magazine; copies of Esther Luttrell's *Tools of the Screen Writing Trade,* Bryan Michael Stoller's *Filmmaking for Dummies,* and Laura Schellhardt's *Screenwriting for Dummies;* a one-year membership at Scriptwriters Network; a gift basket from The Coffee Bean and Tea Leaf of Burbank; and consideration for representation by Michael Wise of Shapiro-Lichtman Literary, Liz Hanley of the Los Angeles–based Bicoastal Talent Agency, and Esther Luttrell, head of Jackson Artists Agency's literary department.

Previous Winners: FIRST PLACE: *Views from a Broad* by Stacey K. Black. The winning script is going into preproduction and will be produced into a pilot. SECOND PLACE: *The Tower* by Thomas Murray ‖ THIRD PLACE: *Last House on the Block* by Terri Neish and Lexy Smith

Contact Information: 9899 Santa Monica Blvd. # 610, Beverly Hills, CA 90212

(310) 840-2240 Phone

(310) 840-2240 Fax

Web: www.thecastproject.com

E-mail: info@thecastproject.com

CFIFN Sometime in October Film Festival (SIOFF) and Screenplay Competition

Mission Statement: The Cape Fear Independent Film Network (CFIFN) is dedicated to education and promotion of the arts. With three successful years behind us, we are now preparing to produce *Prodigal Son* by Irene Slater (the winning screenplay from 2003 SIOFF).

Deadlines: EARLY: May 15; STANDARD: July 15

Entry fees: EARLY: $10; STANDARD: $20

Categories: Short scripts

Prize: Production of screenplay

Previous Winner: *Prodigal Son* by Irene Slater

Contact Information: P.O. Box 81, Wilmington, NC 28402

Web: www.cfifn.org

E-mail: info@cfifn.org

CinemaSpoke Screenplay Competition

Mission Statement: Cinema St. Louis/St. Louis International Film Festival (SLIFF) are the sponsors of the CinemaSpoke Screenplay Competition. Ten screenplays will be chosen for partial public readings. The winning script, selected from the ten, will be given a full public reading and a guaranteed submission to a Los Angeles literary agency. Our artistic vision is to present cinema that offers us glimpses into the human experience around the world. When we learn about others through a myriad of expressions, cultures, and opinions, we discover much about ourselves.

Deadline: February 6

Entry fee: $25

Categories: All genres; entrants must reside within a 120-mile radius of St. Louis

Prizes: CinemaSpoke is an opportunity for local screenwriters to have their work read aloud in a public forum by professional and amateur actors and to receive feedback from a panel of film professionals experienced in screenwriting, filmmaking, development, production, and criticism.

Contact Information: 394A N. Euclid Ave., St. Louis, MO 63108-1247

(314) 454-0042 ext. 10 Phone

(314) 454-0540 Fax

Web: www.cinemastlouis.org
E-mail: andrea@sliff.org

TEN VALUABLE SCRIPT TIPS

- Make sure your synopsis captures the essence of the script.

- Create a pressing need for action in the first few pages.

- Characterization is usually the weak link in beginner scripts. Plotting makes it exciting, but characters make us care. They should feel alive and real, be full of unexpected emotions, be unpredictable, be flawed but determined, and show three-dimensions, not one. Don't try to develop more than four or they'll all suffer.

- Many beginning writers come up with a great idea and spin it for a hundred pages. But if you look at Hollywood movies, the plot turns inside out every fifteen or twenty pages. The plot you start with is never the one you end up with. Audiences will get ahead of you if you don't constantly change directions.

- Rely on theme more than plot. A good plot is a gimmick; a theme is a driving force. It allows you to constantly change your plot without losing the audience. Have one core question in mind from the beginning and answer it in the end, but have many detours along the way.

- Show, don't tell. Come up with a visual way to give us your theme and your story.

- Don't direct it. Don't overload us with parentheticals and descriptions. Keep the style simple, and put your effort into the content.

- Write with economy. If you think you need three scenes to set something up, do it in two. Audiences are quicker to grasp things than most beginning writers realize.

- Avoid static locations, e.g., police stations, offices, hotel rooms, restaurants. Try to keep your characters moving as much as possible, put them in dynamic situations.

- Avoid clichés. If you've ever seen it in a movie before, don't put it in yours. Writing isn't the creative assembly of your favorite cinematic moments; it's putting *yourself* in an extraordinary situation and seeing what *you* would do.

DEVELOPMENT

DEADlight Horror Short Script Contest

. . . .

Mission Statement: The purpose of DEADlight is to find four great short scripts to turn into an anthology horror film for video release.

Deadlines: EARLY: January 31; STANDARD: February 28

Entry fees: EARLY: $25; STANDARD: $35

Categories: Short horror scripts

Prizes: Four winners will receive a cash prize and their scripts will be filmed for video distribution.

Previous Winners: *One More Time* by Janice Withers, Maryland | *Hell on Earth* by Jacob Guine, Texas | *Flesh Peddler* by Bill Sabers, California | *Infection* by Marcus Hightower, California

Contact Information: c/o Jarrod Cooley, P.O. Box 14121, Abilene, TX 79698

(915) 721-1764 Phone

Web: www.ninepointproductions.com/deadlight.htm

E-mail: deadlight@ninepointproductions.com

Drama Garage Thursday Night Script Reading Series

. . . .

Mission Statement: Drama Garage's Screenplay Series is housed in Hollywood, and the screenplay readings are part audition, part workshop, and part industry debut. Think of it as a loft party where you get to hear a great script. Drama Garage is dedicated to finding and developing screenplays by bringing them to life via these staged readings in an industry setting. Scripts submitted to the series are read by a panel of five readers. Once a script is selected for a mainstage event, we work with the writer to build a production team by opening up our directing pool, bringing in talent, and developing a marketing campaign around the script.

Deadline: Ongoing

Entry fee: $40

Categories: All genres

Prizes: If your script is accepted, Drama Garage will provide a fully produced staged reading in Hollywood (in a performance space with 150 to 200 seats), rehearsal time and space, a reception for more than a hundred people, listings in local entertainment newspapers such as *LA Weekly, Entertainment Today, Celebrity Services, WGA Calender, Backstage/Dramalogue West,* and electronic media, and will create a feature profile on its Web site at www.dramagarage.com. Winners will also receive Final

Draft screenwriting software, Producers 411 guide, and the Agents and Managers 411 guides.

Previous Winner: *The Killers Girls Club* by Daina Manning

Contact Information: 5242 DeLongpre Ave., Los Angeles, CA 90027

(323) 993-5700 Phone

Web: www.dramagarage.com

E-mail: dramagarage@hotmail.com

Euroscript Competition

Mission Statement: Euroscript is looking for great stories in any genre for a contemporary audience. Writers submit a four-page outline that narrates the full story. They also send a ten-page sample of a previously written screenplay to help Euroscript assess the work. All applicants will be invited to attend a free London workshop called "Improving Your Outline and Treatment." Any writer whose idea is short-listed, will then send a copy of the full-length screenplay. Winning writers receive free development of their idea via a comprehensive nine-month attachment to an experienced script consultant. The script consultant will work actively with the writer to develop the treatment to a first draft. Contact between writer and script consultant can be by telephone, letters, or e-mail. The copyright for the screenplay ultimately remains with the writer, but Euroscript expects a credit should the screenplay go into production.

Deadline: April 30

Entry fee: £35

Categories: Contest open only to EU nationals.

Prizes: Euroscript selects twenty film ideas each year to develop to full script. Euroscript then helps the selected writers to develop their stories to a final draft over nine months through a remote script-development program. Euroscript accepts submissions in all EU languages from EU writers.

Previous Winners: *Dead Red* by Mike Barnes ▌ A historical Russian drama about Stalin's final days in a villa bugged by his opponents, and the nineteen-year-old maid who discovers Stalin's double. ▌ *The Boatman* by Jessie Keyt ▌ A romance about a man in his forties who lives by a lake and dreams of sailing away—too bad his boat is a wreck and the woman he loves is behind closed doors.

Contact Information: Screenwriters' Centre, Suffolk House, 1–8 Whitfield
   Place, London W1P 5SF U.K.
+44 (0)20 7387 5880 Phone
Web: www.euroscript.co.uk
E-mail: info@euroscript.co.uk

Frederick Douglass Creative Arts Center Writing Workshops

Mission Statement: With more than a dozen workshops for beginning, intermediate, and advanced students, FDCAC enrolls hundreds of adult students each year. Poetry, short story, novel, screenwriting, and freelance writing (for magazines and newspapers) are among the workshops offered. For more than a quarter of a century, the center has launched the careers of writers whose work has been published by Doubleday, Random House, Harper & Row, E. P. Dutton, Pantheon, Dial, and Harlem River Press. It has also started a number of young stage, screen, and television writers on their way.
Deadline: Ongoing
Entry fee: $200 per workshop
Categories: Plays, screenplays, television scripts
Prizes: $50 and a staged reading
Contact Information: 270 W. 96th St., New York, NY 10025
(212) 864-3375 Phone
(212) 864-3474 Fax
Web: www.fdcac.org
E-mail: fdcac@aol.com

Get Your Movie Made in South Africa

Mission Statement: Heat Productions wants writers and directors for three films scheduled for production in South Africa on a budget of $1.5 million per picture. Heat Productions will prove that any film can be made in South Africa. Much like a theater group, we are forming a team that will be exclusive to three film productions a year. Your story can be any genre. It can take place anywhere, as South Africa has the locations for any storyline that the United States, England, and even Australia might offer.

Deadline: Ongoing

Entry fee: $25

Categories: All genres

Prizes: $5,000 and round-trip tickets to the three writers of the selected screenplays

Previous Winners: We have just signed on to produce *The Great Photo Shoot* with Jim Zuckerman, which will be directed by Richard Mann in South Africa. We are also working with Dan McCarthy, director of *Irish Eyes,* on the production of Jim Thompson's thriller *The Killer Inside Me.* We are in negotiations to attach Val Kilmer as Sheriff Lou Ford.

Contact Information: P.O. Box 480859, Los Angeles, CA 90036

(323) 933-3612 Phone

Web: www.southafricanfilm.com

E-mail: heat@southafricanfilm.com

Movie Midwifing

Mission Statement: The purpose of the annual Movie Midwifing screenwriting contest and reading series is to provide an interactive experience among audience, actors, and screenwriter to breathe life into and further shape a nascent script.

Deadline: May 15

Entry fee: $25

Categories: All genres; entrants must be Texas residents

Prizes: Four winning screenplays will be cast with professional actors and performed for the public in Austin, Texas, during September and October. Winners also receive free copies of Final Draft screenwriting software, one-year subscriptions to *Scr(i)pt* magazine, a professional videotape of the performance and more. Audience Favorite of the series will be awarded a reading produced at the Manhattan Theater Source in New York City in November.

▊ ESTIMATED NUMBER OF SCREENWRITERS

More than 40,000 story ideas and scripts are registered every year with the Writers Guild of America, and that doesn't include the scripts that are copyrighted or the ones that aren't registered.

Previous Winner: *Visions of Oz* by Scott Miles, Austin ‖ SYNOPSIS: Gordon Stewart tries to ignore his voices so he can stay near his estranged daughter. But, Lana, deranged sister of Glenda the Good Witch of Oz, has other ideas.

Contact Information: P.O. Box 3440, Austin, TX 78764-3440

(512) 443-8229 Phone

(512) 443-5751 Fax

Web: www.moviemidwifing.com

E-mail: info@moviemidwifing.com

The New York International Latino Film Festival: Latino Writers Lab

The Latino Writers Lab is designed to assist up-and-coming Latino writers who aspire to work in the film and television industry but need skills development and mentoring in order to advance professionally. In partnership with the NALIP and WGA-East, the Writers Lab is a three-day event designed for producers, directors, and screenwriters who already

---

▌Q: "When they get back to you and tell you why they didn't like it, you have to tell them why they're wrong." Can you give me some guidelines regarding this?

A: This is where a reading can help you. By eliciting honest feedback from family, friends, and strangers, you'll get an idea of what criticisms people might have for your script. You'll need to know this; no one in Hollywood will ever tell you it's awesome, don't change a thing. They'll all have a list of things they didn't like about it. That's just the way it works, so be prepared. Don't get flustered and don't get defensive. Be bright-eyed and unfazed and convey total confidence. Rhino skin, they call it. Nothing gets to you, nothing shakes you, nothing dissuades you from pushing your script. If they don't like it, something's wrong with *them,* not your script. This approach works because no matter how experienced they are, they've been dead wrong before . . . and it haunts them. So listen to their criticisms, comment on them, and then go into a passionate spiel about what's great about the story, why it's better than others, why audiences are going to love it, and how you're not going to stop until you get it made. Hollywood is swayed by utter self-confidence. Especially in the beginning, it's your greatest asset.

---

have a completed script or have produced a film or video. The goal of the Lab is to expose the twenty participants to industry executives and to provide a forum for the development of existing works, new works, or works in progress. The Lab will provide a written analysis of the submitted script, seminars, one-on-one mentoring, and a pitch session. Participants receive support and sponsor-related materials upon registration.

The organizers believe Latino participants will continue to advance their projects, meet feature and television funding and hiring sources, and expand their opportunities to work within the mainstream entertainment marketplace. The Writers Lab is a national program with an open call for participants. However, this is not a Screenwriting 101 program: applicants must have completed a teleplay, series episode, pilot, or screenplay, or produced a documentary, fiction film, or video to be considered.

New York City is the independent cinema capital of the world, and a major talent pool for indie film and network daytime and primetime writers. Holding the lab in New York City has the added advantage of providing access to professionals such as network executives, agents, distributors, production companies, development executives, and television producers that can best help these writers enter a competitive marketplace.

Deadline: March 5

Entry fee(s): None (but $250 fee to attend lab if accepted)

Categories: Television and movie scripts by Latino writers.

Prizes: Top 20 winners will be invited to an intensive four-day workshop in New York City from April 22 to April 25 to critique and improve their writing, polish their pitching skills, and discuss story logic and structure.

Contact Information: 445 W. 49th Street, New York, NY 10019

(212) 265-8452 Phone

(212) 307-7445 Fax

Web: www.nylatinofilm.com

E-mail: info@nylatinofilm.com

Old Pueblo Playwrights

Mission Statement: Old Pueblo Playwrights (OPP) is a nonprofit organization dedicated to encouraging the creation of new dramatic works by Arizona authors. Its members are writers—both professional and aspiring—who meet weekly to hear readings of their work and to discuss the work critically. OPP membership is open to any interested writers of dramatic works for stage, film, radio, or television (as well as to any other artists in those disciplines).

Deadline: Ongoing

Entry fee: $36 annual dues

Categories: Plays, translations, film scripts, teleplays, and radio scripts

Prize: A public reading of your work

Previous Winner: *The Audition* by Bret Primack ❙ A full-length play that asks the age-old question: can a man find love through the personals?

Contact Information: Box 64914, Tucson, AZ 85728

(520) 743-0940 Phone

(520) 743-7245 Fax

Web: www.oldpuebloplaywrights.com

E-mail: hal.lostriver@juno.com

People's Pilot Competition

Mission Statement: With more television networks and cable channels than ever before, the market for fresh, original ideas is at an all-time high. Executives and producers are ready for new people they can count on to supply them with material. This is the dawn of an era for you, the new writer, and your unique vision. To help you sell your series, TVWriter. Com has created the People's Pilot Competition.

Deadline: December 1

Entry fee: $40

Categories: Original scripts for television

Prizes: Grand Prize is a development deal with PendleView LLC. The winner's idea will be optioned for six months at Writers Guild of America rates in a step deal beginning with the winning entry, which will serve as an official "format," and the basis for the series, and culminate (pending network or cable channel approval) with the writing of the pilot teleplay and a position as a producer/writer of the show. Top three winners will receive a copy of Final Draft screenwriting software, free admission to the Action/Cut Filmmaking Seminar of your choice and free admission to the next TVWriter.Com Summer Intensive Seminar. ❙ WHY DIDN'T I THINK OF THAT? AWARD ❙ To encourage innovative thinking and series ideas that are genuinely new and different we proudly announce the Why Didn't I Think Of That? award to be given when and if an entry is truly original and compelling. The winner or winners of the WDITOT award will receive a trip to Cloud Creek Institute of the Arts where the creator will work with the professional staff to write and shoot a five-minute DVD presentation of the idea for viewing on the Internet and distribution to networks, production companies, and agents.

Previous Winners: *Best Medicine* by David Bass, M.D. | *Castle Quest* by Dylan Brody | *Detroit Central* by Kevin C. Sielky

Contact Information: Cloud Creek Institute for the Arts, Cloud Creek Ranch, 3767 MC 5026, St. Joe, AZ 72675

(805) 495-3659 Phone

Web: www.peoplespilot.com

E-mail: info@peoplespilot.com

| *Life isn't fair. It's just fairer than death, that's all.*
    —WILLIAM GOLDMAN, screenwriter, *Butch Cassidy and The Sundance Kid*

Praxis Film Development Workshop

Mission Statement: Praxis holds two feature film script competitions and receives approximately 200 scripts a year. From each competition we select four to six scripts to be workshopped with a veteran story editor or screenwriter. Admission to the workshops is highly competitive. We are looking for feature film scripts of any genre. Each writer remains anonymous to the jury until a shortlist has been selected.

Deadlines: June 30 and December 1

Entry fee: $75

Categories: Dramatic features

Prize: Workshop participation

Previous Winners: *The Colors of Concrete* by Sabina Ansari | *A Straight Shot of Sunshine* by Debra Chesley | *Cherry Blossoms* by Zoe Hopkins | *Suicide by Cop* by Joadie Jurgova | *A Guide for the Easily Confused* by Ira Nayman

Contact Information: Ste. 3120, 515 W. Hastings St., Vancouver, BC Canada V6B 5K3

(604) 268.7880 Phone

(604) 268.7882 Fax

Web: www.praxisfilm.com

E-mail: praxis@sfu.ca

★ Project Greenlight

Mission Statement: It's the Hollywood Cinderella story. Two childhood friends share an apartment in Los Angeles; they are struggling to break into acting. Unknown after years of hard work and tired of bit parts, they write their own script and star in it. Not only do they get recognized, they become famous and win an Oscar for Best Screenplay. A dream? Hardly. It's the true story of Matt Damon and Ben Affleck. And it is this fairytale come true that inspired them to team up with *American Pie* producer Chris Moore and Miramax Film and Television to create a contest and community that would open the industry to aspiring writers who need a big break to jumpstart their dreams.

Deadline: February 28

Entry fee: $30

Categories: All genres; entries must be submitted online

Prize: Project Greenlight will choose a feature screenplay from submissions by amateur screenwriters to be produced by LivePlanet and Miramax Films.

Previous Winners: PROJECT GREENLIGHT 1: Starting with a peer-based selection process the contestants were shortlisted to 250. After each entrant submitted a short video biography, those 250 were then narrowed down to thirty. Contest sponsors read the top thirty and whittled it down to ten very excited finalists, each of whom got to shoot a scene from his or her screenplay. Those scenes decided the top three who participated in a rigorous three-day interview process with Matt, Ben, Chris, and other panel members. After a grueling four months from submission to selection, HBO caught the winning moment on their Project Greenlight series. After days of highs, lows, and much nervous waiting, Pete Jones was awarded a $1 million budget to shoot his winning script, *Stolen Summer*. Through HBO's documentary series, the country saw Pete's journey from script to screen. ▎ PROJECT GREENLIGHT 2: On January 18, 2003, Project Greenlight 2 named the winners, Erica Beeney (Screenplay contest winner) and Kyle Rankin and Efram Potelle (Director contest winners). The HBO series on the making of the film *Stolen Summer* aired beginning June 22, 2003, and the movie was released theatrically in August. ▎ PROJECT GREENLIGHT 3: On July 13, 2004, Project Greenlight 3 named the winners, Patrick Melton and Marcus Dunston (Screenplay contest winners) and John Gulager (Director contest winner). Bravo will air the series on the making of *Feast*.

Contact Information: Project Greenlight
Web: www.projectgreenlight.com
E-mail: producer@projectgreenlight.com

Rome Independent Film Festival

. . . .

Mission Statement: The screenplay award is organized and promoted by the Rome Independent Film Festival (RIFF). The intent is to offer new filmmakers an opportunity to grow professionally by developing their films and making them accessible to the public. The RIFF will select one project and will assist in its realization from development to postproduction. The RIFF Film Grant raises funding and services from industry-related companies for the development of quality projects, estimated to reach $100,000. These generous sponsors are willing to donate their profits in order to help struggling filmmakers achieve their goals.

Deadline: November 15

Entry fee: $35

Categories: All genres

Prizes: One year's subscription to *Scr(i)pt* magazine and $1,000 cash or equivalent in technical materials. The RIFF will choose a project from the screenplay competition to develop and aid in its production with funding from the RIFF Film Grant. The grant will provide for all aspects of production and postproduction for the winning screenplay. The completed feature film will be distributed domestically and abroad as a part of the award. RIFF requests a producing credit and a special thanks to all the grant donors.

Previous Winner: AWARD FOR BEST SCREENPLAY: *La Gradiva* by Nina zu Furstenberg and Francesca Fornario

---

▌ **TIP:** Look at your script as a producer would—ask yourself how much it will cost to make. If you have a large number of effects and stunts, you're limiting your script to the handful of people who can get an $80 million movie made. If you concentrate on story, limit the locations, limit the number of characters, and keep all the action rooted firmly in the real world, you greatly increase the number of producers who can get your movie made.

Contact Information: RIFF, attn: Fabrizio Ferrari, Via Po 134, Rome, RM
00198 Italy
011 39 06 45425050 Phone
011 39 06 23319206 Fax
Web: www.riff.it
E-mail: screenplay@riff.it

The Scripteasers

Mission Statement: Scripteasers, a San Diego–based playwrights development group, provides an opportunity for writers to hear their work read by actors. The group meets on biweekly Friday evenings at 7:30 to present cold readings of plays and screenplays. Each year in May, Scripteasers presents a showcase of staged readings, representing highlights from the past year and featuring the work of writers at the peak of their talent.

Deadline: Ongoing
Entry fee: None
Categories: Plays, screenplays, teleplays
Prize: Staged reading
Contact Information: 3404 Hawk St., San Diego, CA 92103-3862
(619) 295-4040 Phone
(619) 299-2084 Fax
Web: www.scripteasers.org
E-mail: info@scripteasers.org

Sundance Feature Film Program

Mission Statement: The Sundance Institute was founded by Robert Redford and other filmmakers as a place to give back: to provide emerging filmmakers with an opportunity to work and develop their projects and skills. The Sundance Institute created the Feature Film Program in 1981 to support next-generation filmmakers. At the core of this program are the Screenwriting and Filmmaking Laboratories, held each year at Sundance, Utah. Designed to offer emerging screenwriters and directors the opportunity to develop new work, the labs offer a uniquely creative environment under the concentrated guidance of veteran filmmakers.

> ▌ **TIP:** A lot of scripts skimp on descriptions. The reader needs a mental image or the script never comes off the page. This doesn't mean long blocks of descriptive paragraphs (readers will skip over them anyway), but it's essential that your characters and locales make a strong impression. Think in shorthand. "She turns to the class, revealing a towering figure of a nun—her face resembles a man, she even has a hint of a mustache above her lip." It's not poetry but it gives you an image, doesn't it? Take a look at these moments from *L.A. Confidential*: "Swigging from a pint of gin, Stensland works skinny GARCIA. Head snaps. The kid drops to his knees drooling blood." "An old black guy in a frayed, threadbare tux plays the piano. Bud, nursing a highball at the bar, steps over to a REDHEAD with too much make-up and too many miles." Or this intro to Lester Burnham in *American Beauty*: "He's forty-two, with a wide boyish face that's just beginning to droop around the edges." If you described him as "forty-two, just entering a midlife crisis" we wouldn't get as strong an image. It's a catchphrase and it's too analytical. Give us something we can visualize.

Sundance selects fifteen to twenty projects each year for one or more areas of support. We find material in several ways, including our year-round staff search/outreach. The program staff utilizes a wide-reaching national network of program alumni, creative advisors, film school faculty, film festival staff, producers, and other film professionals to solicit material and recommendations. In addition, we maintain an open submission period each spring in which people who have no contact with the program or film industry are encouraged to submit their projects.

The point of entry to the program is most typically the January Screenwriters Lab, a five-day writing workshop that takes place in January and June. The program offers ten to twelve emerging artists the opportunity to work intensively on their feature film scripts with the support of established screenwriters. Participating writers have one-on-one problem-solving story sessions with creative advisors; they engage in individual dialogues that combine life lessons in craft with practical suggestions to be explored in the next drafts. Over the years, the group of creative advisors has included such screenwriting luminaries as Frank Pierson, Richard Price, Alan Rudolph, Joan Tewkesbury, Nelson George, Aida Bortnik, Waldo Salt, Richard LaGravenese, Alice Arlen, Ron Nyswaner, Scott Frank, Callie Khouri, Charles Fuller, Walter Bernstein,

Christopher McQuarrie, Paul Attanasio, and Allison Anders. | **THE FILM-
MAKERS LAB** | The June Filmmakers Lab is a three-week hands-on workshop
for writers and directors that takes place each June at Sundance. Participants gain experience rehearsing, shooting, and editing scenes from their
screenplays on videotape under the mentorship of accomplished directors, editors, cinematographers, and actors. Directors are encouraged to
approach their work experimentally in a collaborative environment. An
ensemble of professional actors is cast with the help of casting directors.
The small crews include experienced directors of photography, editors,
and script supervisors. The workshop is intended to give the director an
opportunity to develop skills, take risks, and see and hear the script on
its feet, removed from the pressures of production. Again, creative advisors challenge, inspire, and offer practical suggestions. Creative Advisors
for this lab have included David Cronenberg, Sydney Pollack, Terry
Gilliam, James L. Brooks, Bertrand Tavernier, Sally Field, Morgan Freeman, Agnieszka Holland, Conrad Hall, Ed Harris, John Schlesinger,
Michael Caton-Jones, Alexander Payne, Allen Daviau, Kathy Bates, Al-
fonso Cuaron, Jocelyn Moorhouse, Neil LaBute, Denzel Washington, and
Gyula Gazdag. | **THE SCREENPLAY READING SERIES** | The Screenplay Reading Se-
ries of works-in-progress provides an opportunity for screenwriters to
hear their work read aloud by an ensemble of professional actors. The
readings are held approximately four times a year in Los Angeles and New
York, and have provided an enormous artistic resource to the writers sup-
ported; most of them have never had the opportunity to hear their characters come alive. The primary goal of the reading series is to give writers the chance to pinpoint areas of the screenplay that need development
and to fine-tune their work. The Screenplay Reading Series supports projects that have already been through one of our labs. Unfortunately, we are
unable to accept open submissions for the series.

Deadline: May 1
Entry fee: $30
Categories: All genres
Prize: The Sundance Institute will provide airline travel, accommodations, and food for one writer/filmmaker per project. Sundance will consider providing accommodations and meals for additional partners, and
will ask the creative team to cover travel expenses.
Success Stories: **ALL THE REAL GIRLS** | WRITER/DIRECTOR: David Gordon
Green | PRODUCER: Lisa Muskat | CAST: Paul Schneider, Zooey Deschanel,
Patricia Clarkson | DISTRIBUTOR: Sony Pictures Classics | STATUS: Pre-

miered at the 2003 Sundance Film Festival; released by Sony Classics in February 2003 **RAISING VICTOR VARGAS** WRITER/DIRECTOR: Peter Sollett PRODUCER: Robin O'Hara, Scott Macauley, and Alain de la Mata CAST: Victor Rasuk, Judy Marte DISTRIBUTOR: Samuel Goldwyn Films/Fireworks Pictures STATUS: To be released in 2002; premiered at the 2002 Cannes Film Festival. **LAUREL CANYON** WRITER/DIRECTOR: Lisa Cholodenko PRODUCER: Jeff Levy-Hinte, Mary Jane Skalski CAST: Frances McDormand, Christian Bale, Kate Beckinsale DISTRIBUTOR: Sony Pictures Classics STATUS: To be released in 2002; premiered at the 2002 Cannes Film Festival **THE LARAMIE PROJECT** WRITER/DIRECTOR: Moises Kaufman PRODUCER: Ross Katz and Good Machine CAST: Laura Linney, Peter Fonda, Janeane Garofalo, Christina Ricci, Clea DuVall, Jeremy Davies, Steve Buscemi DISTRIBUTOR: HBO Pictures STATUS: Premiered as the Opening Night Film of the 2002 Sundance Film Festival; screened on HBO in February 2002 **THE SLAUGHTER RULE** WRITER/DIRECTORS: Alex and Andrew Smith PRODUCER: Greg and Gavin O'Connor, Michael Robinson, David O. Russell CAST: David Morse, Ryan Gosling, Ben Foster STATUS: Premiered at the 2002 Sundance Film Festival **THE END OF LOVE** (formerly *Nine Scenes About Love*) WRITER/DIRECTOR: Peter Mattei PRODUCER: Southfork Pictures and Blow Up Pictures CAST: Steve Buscemi, Rosario Dawson, Jill Hennessy, Carol Kane, Alessandro Nivola, Malcolm Gets DISTRIBUTOR: ThinkFilm STATUS: To be released in 2002; premiered at the 2002 Sundance Film Festival **HEDWIG AND THE ANGRY INCH** WRITER/DIRECTOR: John Cameron Mitchell PRODUCER: Christine Vachon, Katie Roumel CAST: John Cameron Mitchell, Michael Pitts DISTRIBUTOR: Fine Line Features STATUS: Premiered at the 2001 Sundance Film Festival, winner of the Audience Award and the Directing Award; winner of the Audience Award at the San Francisco International Film Festival and the Teddy Award at the Berlin International Film Festival; released in July 2001 by Fine Line Features **REQUIEM FOR A DREAM** WRITER/DIRECTOR: Darren Aronofsky PRODUCER: Eric Watson CAST: Jared Leto, Ellen Burstyn, Marlon Wayans, Chris McDonald, Jennifer Connelly DISTRIBUTOR: Artisan Entertainment STATUS: Premiered at 2000 Cannes Film Festival; released in Fall 2000; lead actress Ellen Burstyn nominated for an Academy Award for Best Actress; released in 2001 by Artisan Entertainment **SERIES 7** WRITER/DIRECTOR: Dan Minahan PRODUCERS: Jason Kliot, Joanna Vicente, Christine Vachon CAST: Brooke Smith, Glenn Fitzgerald DISTRIBUTOR: USA Films STATUS: Premiered at the 2001 Sundance Film Festival, followed by the Berlin International Film Festival; released in March 2001 by USA Films **HAIKU TUNNEL** WRITER/DIRECTORS: Josh and Jacob Kornbluth PRODUCERS: Josh and Jacob Kornbluth, Brian Benson CAST: Josh Kornbluth, Warren Keith, June Lomena, Sarah Overman, Amy Resnick, Helen Shumaker, Brian Thorstenson DISTRIBUTOR: Sony Pictures Classics STATUS: Premiered in American Spectrum at the 2001 Sundance Film Festival; released in Fall 2001 **O** WRITER: Brad Kaaya DIRECTOR: Tim Blake Nelson PRODUCERS: Eric Gitter, Anthony Rhulen, Daniel Fried CAST: Mekhi Phifer, Julia Stiles, Josh Hartnett, Rain Phoenix, Elden Henson DISTRIBUTOR: Lions Gate Films STATUS: Winner of Best Director Award at Seattle International Film Festival; released in August 2001 by Lions Gate Films **THINGS YOU CAN TELL JUST BY LOOKING AT HER** WRITER/DIRECTOR: Rodrigo Garcia PRODUCER: Jon Avnet, Lisa Lindstrom, Marcia Oglesby CAST: Glenn Close, Holly Hunter, Cameron Diaz, Kathy Baker STATUS: Premiered at 2000 Sundance Film Festival; international premiere as the opening night of Un Certain Regard section of 2000 Cannes Film Festival; premiered on Showtime in March 2001 **BOYS DON'T CRY** WRITER/DIRECTOR: Kimberly Pierce PRODUCERS: Eva Kolodner, John Hart, Jeff Sharp EXECUTIVE PRODUCERS: Christine Vachon and Pam Koffler CAST: Chloe Sevigny, Hilary Swank, Allison Foland, Brendan Sexton III, Peter Sarsgaard DISTRIBUTOR: Fox Searchlight STATUS: Venice Film Festival, Toronto Film Festival, New York Film Festival; released by Fox Searchlight in fall 1999 **LOVE AND BASKETBALL** WRITER/DIRECTOR: Gina Prince Bythewood PRODUCERS: Spike Lee, Sam Kitt DISTRIBUTOR: New Line Cinema CAST: Omar Epps, Alfre Woodard, Sanaa Lathan STATUS: Premiered at 2000 Sundance Film Festival; released by New Line in April 2000 **HARD EIGHT** WRITER/DIRECTOR: Paul Thomas Anderson PRODUCER: John Lyons CAST: Phillip Baker Hall, Gwyneth Paltrow, John C. Reilly, Samuel L. Jackson DISTRIBUTOR: Rysher Entertainment through Samuel Goldwyn Company **WALKING AND TALKING** WRITER/DIRECTOR: Nicole Holofcener PRODUCERS: James Schamus and Ted Hope CAST: Catherine Keener, Anne Heche, Todd Field, Liev Schreiber, Kevin Corrigan DISTRIBUTOR: Miramax Films **BOTTLE ROCKET** WRITER: Owen Wilson DIRECTOR: Wes Anderson PRODUCER: Barbara Boyle CAST: Owen Wilson DISTRIBUTOR: Tri-Star Pictures **MI VIDA LOCA** WRITER/DIRECTOR: Allison Anders PRODUCER: Dan Hassid, Bill Ewitt CAST: Angel Aviles, Seidy Lopez, Jacob Vargas, Jesse Borrego DISTRIBUTOR: Sony Classics **CRUSH** WRITER/DIRECTOR: Alison Maclean PRODUCER: Bridget Ikin CAST: Marcia Gay Harden, William Zappa, Donogh Rees DISTRIBUTOR: Strand Releasing **RESERVOIR DOGS**

WRITER/DIRECTOR: Quentin Tarantino ▌PRODUCER: Lawrence Bender, Monte Hellman ▌CAST: Harvey Keitel, Steve Buscemi, Chris Penn, Michael Madsen, Tim Roth ▌DISTRIBUTOR: Miramax Films ▌**TWENTY BUCKS** ▌WRITER: Les Bohem ▌DIRECTOR: Keva Rosenfeld ▌PRODUCER: Karen Murphy ▌CAST: Elisabeth Shue, Brendan Fraser ▌DISTRIBUTOR: Triton Releasing ▌**SMOOTH TALK** ▌WRITER: Tom Coleman ▌DIRECTOR: Joyce Chopra ▌PRODUCER: Martin Rosen ▌CAST: Laura Dern, Treat Williams ▌DISTRIBUTOR: Skouras Pictures ▌**TRIP TO BOUNTIFUL** ▌WRITER: Horton Foote ▌DIRECTOR: Pete Masterson ▌PRODUCER: Sterling VanWagenen ▌CAST: Geraldine Page, John Heard, Carlin Glynn, Rebecca de Mornay ▌DISTRIBUTOR: Island Pictures ▌**BALLAD OF GREGORIO CORTEZ** ▌WRITER: Victor Villasenor ▌DIRECTOR: Robert Young ▌PRODUCER: Moctesuma Esparza, Michael Hausman ▌CAST: Tom Bower, Edward James Olmos ▌DISTRIBUTOR: Embassy Entertainment

Contact Information: Sundance Feature Film Program, 8857 W. Olympic Blvd., Beverly Hills, CA 90211

(310) 360-1981 Phone

(310) 360-1969 Fax

Web: www.sundance.org

E-mail: featurefilmprogram@sundance.org

Women of Color Productions

Mission Statement: Women of Color Productions seeks scripts for its monthly reading series and possible inclusion in the annual Through Her Eyes: Women of Color Arts Festival.

Deadline: December 1

Entry fee: $10 per reading

Categories: Plays, stage music, screenplays

Prizes: Ten guest artists receive $300 to $600 honorarium.

Contact Information: 163 E. 104th St., Ste. 4E, New York, NY 10029

(212) 501-3842 Phone

▌ **TIP:** Your logline is as important as your script. Work on it—it's got to be enticing, mysterious, sexy, and provocative. It's your script's calling card.

DEVELOPMENT

Words from Here Short Script Contest

Mission Statement: Words from Here and Group 101 Films have teamed up to create a new contest in which fifteen short scripts will be made by Group 101 Films members and showcased in a premiere outlet in Los Angeles.

Deadline: April 15

Entry fee: $10 donation to one of three charities

Categories: Short scripts

Prize: Winners have their short scripts produced.

Contact Information:

(718) 622-1098 Phone

Web: www.wordsfromhere.com

E-mail: stilesjp@wordsfromhere.com

TIP: Amateurs tend to try too hard. Don't enclose newspaper articles, pictures, drawings, or use fancy graphics. Don't bind your script or use color copies. Avoid embossed covers. Don't send it registered, certified, or overnight. These methods will not help you stand out, but they will mark you as a beginner. Professionals keep it simple.

CAREER OPPORTUNITIES

AGENTS

D ON'T EVER send a script to an agent, manager, or producer without first getting permission to do so. Otherwise you're wasting your time. Start with a query letter or a phone call.

A *query letter* details your relevant credits, if any, and offers a brief introduction to your script.

Your query letter should contain the following information:

1. A hook or attention-grabber
2. The logline of the script
3. Your credentials or credits
4. An invitation to read the script

A *hook* is the teaser you see on a movie poster that doesn't tell you what the story is, but makes you want to see the film. Here are some examples:

- "By the time he turned twenty-one he'd killed eighteen people."
- "In space no one can hear you scream."
- "What he knows could kill us. Telling us could kill him."

A hook grabs the reader quickly. This also tells the reader immediately the most important thing about your story—will it sell?

TIP: Hollywood has a notoriously short attention span. If you get someone on the phone, don't tell the story, give the person the concept: "Terrorists hijack Air Force One," "A one-night stand turns deadly," or "Monster movie on a space station."

A *logline,* on the other hand, should encapsulate your story in a single sentence. Here are some examples:

- "Two bio-engineered soldiers battle to the death until they discover a common enemy."
- "A troubled boy is haunted by an apparition that tells him the world will end in twenty-eight days."

Most writers try to give too much information in a query letter. The important thing is to keep it brief and interesting. Why is your story different? Where's the conflict? There's a saying, "If you can't state your story in one sentence, you don't know what it is."

Be sure to enclose a self-addressed stamped envelope (SASE) or a self-addressed stamped postcard (SASP) with your query letter to make it easy for the recipient to respond.

Whenever possible, personalize a query; in other words, send it to someone by name. Consider subscribing to the *Hollywood Representation Directory* (Lone Eagle Publishing, www.hcdonline.com) to help you personalize your letters. It's expensive ($64.95) but it has up-to-date information on every major agent and agency (it's published twice a year). An

---

▌ In this section, agents that have indicated to the Writer's Guild that they are willing to read query letters from new writers are followed by (Q). This doesn't mean other agents won't read query letters, however. Playing by the rules doesn't always help you in Hollywood. Let's say you managed to bypass the entire query process and talked your way up to the head honcho—he or she might be annoyed but also impressed with your chutzpah. When the head honcho tells a staff member to look at a script, that script is treated *very* differently than one that comes in cold.

You'll notice in this book that the biggest agencies are indicated with a ★, but none of these have a (Q) beside them. They're harder to get to, but they may be worth the extra effort. These agencies have employees whose sole jobs are to keep people like you from getting through to the agents. You have to be clever, persistent, and a good liar to get past these defenses. Once you actually have an agent on the phone, no matter what subterfuge you used, you will often find him or her willing to listen to a pitch. The two key lessons: (1) everyone's looking for a great story, and (2) aggressive people respect aggressive people.

online edition is also available via www.hcdonline.com for $19.95 for a one-week trial period, which may be enough time to gather the information you need.

If you decide to call instead, a receptionist will likely put you through to a voice-mail system and you'll never hear back. Don't leave a message. Instead call again later. Be nice but persistent, chatty, and disarming. If you don't live in Hollywood, use that to your advantage. Tell them where you're from, laugh about it, and try to appeal to their compassionate side. Everyone you talk to in Hollywood, from receptionists to executive assistants, wants to sell a screenplay too, so they're usually not nice to you at first because you're competition. But once you appeal to their human side, they'll soften. After all, they're in the same boat; they understand what you're going through. The key is to keep talking, make it conversational, not pushy, and get a sense of the person you're talking to. Find a way to connect to this person as you would to a friend. It's all who you know, right? Get to know this person. If you do it right, he or she will look *forward* to taking your call the next time.

In this book the best-known agencies are flagged with ★, but your chance of a response from one of these is very small. Although they have more power in the industry, they rarely consider new material unless it comes to them with a personal recommendation. (To put it more bluntly, they would prefer to steal you from a smaller agent once you've sold something.) Agents designated (WGA) are signatories to the Writer's Guild Agreement. The Writer's Guild of America is the trade union of motion picture and television writers. The WGA has negotiated terms with Hollywood's major studios and production companies to protect writers. (Check the Web site at www.wga.org Publications navigation bar for a schedule of the minimum compensation you should receive for your script.) To be covered by the WGA minimum basic agreement, you must deal exclusively with agents and producers that are WGA signatories. Before accepting employment or selling literary material, call the Guild's signatories department at (323) 782-4514 to ensure that the company or agent is still a signatory in good standing.

There are literary agents all over the country but the most powerful ones are located in Los Angeles and New York. It's very difficult to sell a script to Hollywood unless your representatives are established nearby or have regular contact with the industry players. On the other hand, there are regional production companies sprouting up everywhere and a local agent may help you gain access to them. It may be a good idea to try to get a foot in the door if you feel the films they make have a chance of capturing Hollywood's attention.

If your query is successful, someone will call or write and ask to see the material. Send the script with a short, to-the-point cover letter. Don't include anything else with it, i.e., photos, drawings, music, and so on. This letter should be addressed to the person who gave you permission to send the script. Reference the date he or she gave you permission, and then repeat your pitch or logline. Tell him or her to call you if there are any questions.

Allow at least three weeks before calling to follow up. At this point, you've moved beyond e-mail or snail mail. Calling is much more personal and makes you harder to dismiss. Whoever your contact is, try to talk to that person for as long as possible—not just about your script but about life, movies, politics, reality television, anything you can think of. Your goal is to be remembered.

Your contact may love the script and still do nothing. You have to convince him that if he doesn't snap you up, someone else will. You have to coax her into taking the next step—signing you for representation. Be sure of yourself but not pushy. Agents don't want writers who are too shy to self-promote; show them right up front that you're not scared to sell yourself. Remember as you make your initial contacts, *everyone's* looking for a great script. Convince them that yours is the one they're looking for. If you show any doubt, you give them an excuse not to read it. It doesn't matter if you have some insecurities (most writers do), just plunge in as if this is the next *Star Wars* or *Matrix* and you'll convince at least some of them that they'd better take a look. At this stage chutzpah is more important than talent, so *keep going*.

One more time, here's the key to the agency listings that follow:

. . . .

   Most influential agencies

(WGA)   Agents that are signatories to the Writer's Guild Agreement

(Q)   Agents that are willing to read a query letter from new writers

. . . .

▋ Alabama

Pamela Wray Literary Agency

1304 Dogwood Dr.
Oxford, AL 36203
(256) 835-8008 Phone
(256) 835-0094 Fax
Web: www.wrayagency.com
E-mail: pxchange@hiwaay.net
Literary agent: Pamela Wray

▋ Arizona

Creative Authors Agency
(WGA)

12212 Paradise Village Pkwy.
South #403-C
Phoenix, AZ 85032
(602) 953-0164 Phone

J. F. Glavan Agency (WGA) (Q)

10401 E. Mcdowell Mtn. Ranch Rd.,
Ste. 2-161
Scottsdale, AZ 85255
(480) 515-5157 Phone

Pucket Literary

945 N. Pasadena #80
Mesa, AZ 85201
(480) 964-4807 Phone
(480) 964-4807 Fax
E-mail: pucketlit@aol.com
Literary agents: Clarence Pucket,
Hassan Jeng

▋ California

Above The Line Agency
(WGA)

9200 Sunset Blvd. #804
West Hollywood, CA 90069
(310) 859-6115 Phone
Literary agents: Rima Bauer
Greer, Bruce Bartlett

Acme Talent & Literary Agency (WGA) (Q)

4727 Wilshire Blvd. #333
Los Angeles, CA 90010
(323) 954-2263 Phone
(323) 954-2262 Fax
Literary agents: Kevin Cleary,
Mickey Freiberg, David
McInerney, Josh Morris

The Agency (WGA)

1800 Ave. of the Stars #400
Los Angeles, CA 90067
(310) 551-3000 Phone
(310) 551-1424 Fax
E-mail: agencyone@hotmail.com
Literary agents: Jerome Zeitman,
Harry Anderson

Agency for the Performing Arts (WGA)

9200 Sunset Blvd. #900
Los Angeles, CA 90069
(310) 273-0744 Phone
(310) 888-4242 Fax
Web: www.apa-agency.com
Literary agents: Lee Dinstman,
Jim Kellem, David Saunders, Beth
Bohn, Steven Fisher, Marc
Pariser, Wes Tydlaska

Allen Talent Agency (WGA)

3832 Wilshire Blvd., 2nd Fl.
Los Angeles, CA 90010-3221
(213) 896-9372 Phone

The Alpern Group (WGA)

15645 Royal Oak Rd.
Encino, CA 91436
(818) 528-1111 Phone
(818) 528-1110 Fax
E-mail: mail@alperngroup.com
Literary agents: Jeff Alpern, Jeff
Aghassi, Liz Wise

Animanagement

245 E. Olive Ave., Ste. 400
Burbank, CA 91502
(818) 526-7600 Phone
E-mail: animgmt@aol.com

The Artists Agency

1180 S. Beverly Dr. #301
Los Angeles, CA 90035
(310) 277-7779 Phone
(310) 785-9338 Fax
Literary agents: Richard
Shepherd, Bettye McCartt,
Maggie Roiphe, Mike Wise

The Artists Group, Ltd. (WGA)

10100 Santa Monica Blvd. #2490
Los Angeles, CA 90067
(310) 552-1100 Phone
Literary agents: Robert Malcolm,
Hal Stalmaster

Avant Talent Agency

386 E. 15th St. #E
Costa Mesa, CA 92627
(949) 722-8850 Phone
(949) 203-2188 Fax
Web: www.avanttalent.com
E-mail: info@avanttalent.com
Literary agents: Susan Antonini,
Robert Kiesling

Becsey, Wisdom, Kalajian

9200 Sunset Blvd., Ste. 820
Los Angeles, CA 90069
(310) 550-0535 Phone
(310) 246-4424 Fax
Web: www.bwkliterary.com
E-mail: agencyinfo@
  bwkliterary.com
Literary agents: Laurence Becsey,
Jeffy Kalajian, Victoria Wisdom,
Leslie Conliffe

The Bennett Agency

150 S. Barrington Ave.
Los Angeles, CA 90049
(310) 471-2251 Phone
E-mail: bennettagency@
  earthlink.net
Literary agents: Carole Bennett,
Kristin Stiff

Lillie Blayze Agency, Inc.

760 N. Main St.
Los Angeles, CA 90012
(310) 281-6859 Phone
Web: www.lillieblayzeagency.com
E-mail: hollywood@lillieblayze
  agency.com
Literary agent: Taminkia Outlaw

Bonnie Black Talent & Literary Agency

5318 Wilkinson Ave.
Valley Village, CA 91607
(818) 753-5424 Phone
Literary agent: Bonnie Black

The Bohrman Agency (WGA)

8899 Beverly Blvd. #811
Los Angeles, CA 90048
(310) 550-5444 Phone
Literary agents: Caren Bohrman,
Michael Hruska

The Brandt Company

15159 Greenleaf St.
Sherman Oaks, CA 91403
(818) 783-7747 Phone
(818) 784-6012 Fax
E-mail: brandtco@aol.com
Literary agent: Geoffrey Brandt

★ Broder Webb Chervin Silbermann Agency (WGA)

9242 Beverly Blvd. #200
Beverly Hills, CA 90210
(310) 281-3400 Phone
(310) 276-3207 Fax
Literary agents: Bob Broder,
Norman Kurland, Elliot Webb,
Beth Uffner, Ted Chervin, Chris
Silbermann, Henry Capanna,
Tricia Davey, Emile Gladstone,
Ronda Gomez-Quinones, Joan
Harrison, Todd Hoffman, Josh
Hornstock, Bruce Kaufman, Janet
Carol Norton, Matt Rice, Jim

AGENTS

Rosen, Justin Silvera, Paul Alan Smith, Chris von Goetz

Bruce Brown Agency

1033 Gayley Ave., Ste. 207
Los Angeles, CA 90024
(310) 208-1835 Phone
(310) 208-2485 Fax
E-mail: bbagency@aol.com
Literary agent: Bruce Brown

Don Buchwald & Associates (WGA) (Q)

6500 Wilshire Blvd. #2200
Los Angeles, CA 90048
(323) 655-7400 Phone
(323) 655-7470 Fax
Literary agents: Deborah Deuble, Nick Holly, Neil Stearns, John Ufland

Callamaro Literary Agency

427 N. Canon Dr., Ste. 202
Beverly Hills, CA 90210
(310) 274-6783 Phone
(310) 274-6536 Fax
Literary agent: Lisa Callamaro

Suzanna Camejo & Associates

3000 W. Olympic Blvd., Bldg. 3
  #1424

Santa Monica, CA 90404
(310) 449-4064 Phone
(310) 449-4026 Fax
E-mail: scamejo@earthlink.net
Literary agent: Suzanna Camejo

William Carroll Agency

11360 Brill Dr.
Studio City, CA 91604
(818) 761-1443 Phone
(818) 769-4081 Fax
Literary agent: Gina Eggert

Career Artists International (WGA)

11030 Ventura Blvd. #3
Studio City, CA 91604
(818) 980-1315 Phone

Cavaleri & Associates (WGA)

178 S. Victory Blvd. #205
Burbank, CA 91502
(818) 955-9300 Phone
(818) 955-9399 Fax
E-mail: cavaleri@usfilm.com
Literary agent: Al Choi

CEO Creative Entertainment Office (WGA)

1801 S. Catalina Ave. #103
Redondo Beach, CA 90277
(310) 791-4494 Phone

The Chasin Agency, Inc.
(WGA)

8899 Beverly Blvd. #716
Los Angeles, CA 90048
(310) 278-7505 Phone
(310) 275-6685 Fax
E-mail: chasin@pacbell.net
Literary agent: Scott Penney

Coast To Coast Talent Group

3350 Barham Blvd.
Los Angeles, CA 90068
(323) 845-9200 Phone
(323) 845-9212 Fax
Literary agent: Anne McDermont

Contemporary Artists, Ltd.
(WGA)

610 Santa Monica Blvd. #202
Santa Monica, CA 90401
(310) 395-1800 Phone
(310) 394-3308 Fax
Literary agent: Ronnie Leif

The Coppage Company
(WGA)

5411 Camellia Ave.
North Hollywood, CA 91601
(818) 980-8806 Phone
(818) 980-8824 Fax
Literary agent: Judy Coppage

Coralie Jr. Theatrical Agency (WGA)

4789 Vineland Ave. #100
North Hollywood, CA 91602
(818) 766-9501 Phone
E-mail: coraliejr@earthlink.net
Literary agent: Gary Dean

The Cosden-Morgan Agency

129 W. Wilson St., Ste. 202
Costa Mesa, CA 92627
(949) 574-1100 Phone
(949) 574-1122 Fax
Web: www.themorganagency.com
Literary agents: Keith Lewis, Greg Salem

I draw up charts before I do a script. I endlessly chart and rechart a movie. Before I sit down to write, I have all the scenes listed, what happens in each scene, how many pages I anticipate each scene will take.
—PAUL SCHRADER

AGENTS

★ Creative Artists Agency

9830 Wilshire Blvd.
Beverly Hills, CA 90212
(310) 288-4545 Phone

Dade/Schultz Associates

6442 Coldwater Canyon Dr. #206
Valley Glen, CA 91606
(818) 760-3100 Phone
(818) 760-3125 Fax
E-mail: dadeschultz@aol.com
Literary agent: Kathleen Schultz

Diverse Talent Group, Inc.
(WGA) (Q)

1875 Century Park E. #2250
Los Angeles, CA 90067
(310) 201-6565 Phone
(310) 201-6572 Fax
Literary agents: Susan Sussman,
Sheryl Peterson

Dytman & Associates (WGA)

9200 Sunset Blvd. #809
Los Angeles, CA 90069
(310) 274-8844 Phone
Literary agents: Jack Dytman, Jeff
Holland

Ellechante Talent Agency
(WGA) (Q)

274 Spazier Ave.
Burbank, CA 91502
(818) 557-3028 Phone

★ The Endeavor Agency
(WGA) (Q)

9701 Wilshire Blvd., 10th Fl.
Beverly Hills, CA 90212
(310) 248-2000 Phone
(310) 248-2020 Fax

Epstein-Wyckoff-Corsa-Ross & Associates (WGA)

280 South Beverly Dr. #400
Beverly Hills, CA 90212
(310) 278-7222 Phone
(310) 278-4640 Fax
Literary agent: Craig Wyckoff

The ES Agency (WGA) (Q)

110 E. D St. #B
Benicia, CA 94510
(707) 748-7394 Phone

Field-Cech-Murphy Agency
(WGA)

12725 Ventura Blvd. #D
Studio City, CA 91604

(818) 980-2001 Phone
(818) 980-0754 Fax
Literary agents: Maggie Field,
David Murphy, Judy Cech, Tim
O'Neill

Film Artists Associates

13563 Ventura Blvd., 2nd Fl.
Sherman Oaks, CA 91423
(818) 386-9669 Phone
E-mail: filmart@pacbell.net
Literary agent: Cris Dennis

Film-Theater Actors Exchange (WGA) (Q)

390 28th Ave. #3
San Francisco, CA 94121
(415) 379-9308 Phone

The Barry Freed Company, Inc. (WGA) (Q)

2040 Ave. of the Stars #400
Los Angeles, CA 90067
(310) 277-1260 Phone
(310) 277-3865 Fax
E-mail: blfreed@aol.com
Literary agent: Barry L. Freed

Alice Fries Agency, Ltd. (WGA) (Q)

1927 Vista Del Mar Ave.
Los Angeles, CA 90068

(323) 464-1404 Phone
Literary agent: Alice Fries

Fusion Management

9200 Sunset Blvd.
Los Angeles, CA 90069
(310) 278-2888 Phone

The Gage Group, Inc. (WGA) (Q)

14724 Ventura Blvd., Ste. 505
Sherman Oaks, CA 91403
(818) 905-3800 Phone
E-mail: gagegroupla@yahoo.com
Literary agents: Martin Gage,
Sharon Moist, Jonathon Westover

Dale Garrick International (WGA) (Q)

8831 Sunset Blvd.
Los Angeles, CA 90069
(310) 657-2661 Phone
Literary agents: Ed Menerth, John
Shaw

Geddes Agency (WGA)

8430 Santa Monica Blvd. #200
West Hollywood, CA 90069
(323) 848-2700 Phone
Literary agents: Ann Geddes,
Beth-Ann Zeitler

AGENTS

Laya Gelff Agency (WGA) (Q)

16133 Ventura Blvd. #700
Encino, CA 91436
(818) 996-3100 Phone
Literary agent: Laya Gelff

★ Genesis (WGA)

345 N. Maple Dr. #395
Beverly Hills, CA 90210
(310) 205-5000 Phone
(310) 205-5099 Fax
Literary agents: Jeffrey Benson,
Ian Greenstein, Michael Van
Dyck, Sayun Kim, Jeff Okin,
Michael G. Margules, Lee Cohen,
Stephen Rose, Scott Henderson,
Ken Greenblatt

Paul Gerard Talent Agency (WGA)

11712 Moorpark St. #112
Studio City, CA 91604
(818) 769-7015 Phone

The Gersh Agency, Inc.

232 N. Canon Dr. #201
Beverly Hills, CA 90210

(310) 274-6611 Phone
(310) 274-3923 Fax
Literary agents: David Gersh,
Jennifer Stephenson, Frank
Wuliger, Richard Arlook, John
Bauman, Ken Neisser, Abram
Nalibotsky, Lee Keele, David
Kopple, Sandra Lucchesi, Phil
Gersh, Joe Gatta, Lynn Fimberg

Geste, Inc.

3366 Wichita Falls Ave.
Simi Valley, CA 93063
(805) 527-2680 Phone
(805) 584-8436 Fax
Web: www.gesteinc.com
E-mail: gesteinc@aol.com
Literary agent: Norma Brody

Gold/Marshak/ Liedtke Agency

3500 W. Olive Ave. #1400
Burbank, CA 91505
(818) 972-4300 Phone
Literary agent: Kimberly Wheeler

▌ **TIP:** If you introduce more than four or five characters in the first ten pages, you've already lost the reader.

The Gold/Miller Company

9200 Sunset Blvd., Ste. 515
Los Angeles, CA 90069
(310) 278-8990 Phone

Michelle Gordon & Associates (WGA) (Q)

260 South Beverly Dr. #308
Beverly Hills, CA 90212
(310) 246-9930 Phone
Literary agent: Michelle Gordon

Grant, Savic, Kopaloff and Associates

6399 Wilshire Blvd., Ste. 414
Los Angeles, CA 90048
(323) 782-1854 Phone
(323) 782-1877 Fax
E-mail: sgkassoc@pacbell.net
Literary agents: Susan Grant, Don
Kapaloff

Graup Entertainment

9350 Wilshire Blvd, Ste. 316
Beverly Hills, CA 90212
(310) 271-1234 Phone

Larry Grossman & Associates (WGA)

211 South Beverly Dr. #206
Beverly Hills, CA 90212

(310) 550-8127 Phone
(310) 550-8129 Fax
Literary agent: Larry Grossman

Charlotte Gusay Literary (WGA) (Q)

Agent/Artists Representative
10532 Blythe Ave.
Los Angeles, CA 90064
(310) 559-0831 Phone
(310) 559-2639 Fax
Web: www.mediastudio.com/gusay
E-mail: gusay1@aol.com
Literary agent: Charlotte Gusay

Reece Halsey Agency

8733 Sunset Blvd., Ste. 101
Los Angeles, CA 90069
(310) 652-2409 Phone
(310) 652-7595 Fax
Literary agent: Dorris Halsey

Mitchell J. Hamilburg Agency (WGA) (Q)

8671 Wilshire Blvd. #500
Beverly Hills, CA 90211
(310) 657-1501 Phone
(310) 657-4968 Fax
Literary agents: Joanie Kern,
Michael Hamilburg

AGENTS

Hart Literary Management (WGA) (Q)

3541 Olive St.
Santa Ynez, CA 93460
(805) 686-7912 Phone
(805) 686-7912 Fax
Web: www.hartliterary.com
E-mail: hartliteraryagency@hotmail
.com
Literary agent: Susan Hart

Beverly Hecht Agency

12001 Ventura Pl. #320
Studio City, CA 91604
(818) 505-1192 Phone
(818) 505-1590 Fax
Literary agent: Teresa Valente

Richard Herman Talent Agency (WGA) (Q)

124 Lasky Dr., 2nd Fl.
Beverly Hills, CA 90212
(310) 550-8913 Phone
(310) 550-0259 Fax
Literary agent: Richard Herman

Hohman/Maybank/Lieb (WGA)

9229 Sunset Blvd. #700
Los Angeles, CA 90069
(310) 274-4600 Phone
(310) 274-4741 Fax

Literary agents: Robert Hohman,
Bayard Maybank, Devra Lieb

Identity Talent Agency, Inc. (WGA) (Q)

2050 S. Bundy Dr. #200
West Los Angeles, CA 90025
(310) 882-6070 Phone
(310) 820-1055 Fax
E-mail: idtalent@aol.com
Literary agent: Erik DeSando

★ Innovative Artists (WGA)

1505 Tenth St.
Santa Monica, CA 90401
(310) 656-0400 Phone
(310) 656-0456 Fax
Literary agents: Jim Stein, Jack
Leighton, Richard Saito, Kimberly
Carver, Graham Kaye, Nancy
Nigrosh

★ International Creative Management

8942 Wilshire Blvd.
Beverly Hills, CA 90211
(310) 550-4000 Phone
(310) 550-4100 Fax
Literary agents: Steve Simons,
Greg Cavic, Ron Bernstein,
Robert Newman, Dianne Fraser,
Jill Holwager, Cindy Mintz,
Nancy Etz, Jadrien Steele, Dan

Norton, Steve Seidel, Ben Smith,
Nick Reed, Brian Sher, Stacey
Rosenfelt, Nicole Clemens, Patty
Detroit, Aubrey Henderson, Doug
MacLaren, Barbara Mandel,
Mason Novick, Dan Rabinow,
Shaun Redick, Catherine Brackey,
Matt Solo, Garth Friedrich

The Susan Johnson
Agency (WGA)

13321 Ventura Blvd. #C-1
Sherman Oaks, CA 91423
(818) 986-2205 Phone
(818) 464-2420 Fax
Literary agent: Susan Johnson

Leslie B. Kallen Agency

115760 Ventura Blvd. #700
Encino, CA 91436
(818) 906-2785 Phone
Web: www.lesliekallen.com
Literary agent: Leslie B. Kallen

Merrily Kane Agency

857 S. Bundy Dr.
Los Angeles, CA 90049
(310) 820-0020 Phone
(310) 820-0404 Fax
E-mail: mka.literate@verizon.net
Literary agent: Merrily Kane

The Kaplan-Stahler-Gumer
Agency (WGA)

8383 Wilshire Blvd. #923
Beverly Hills, CA 90211
(323) 653-4483 Phone
Literary agents: Marc Provissiero,
Mitch Kaplan, Elliot Stahler,
Robert Gumer, Alan Braun

William Kerwin Agency

1605 N. Cahuenga Blvd. #202
Hollywood, CA 90028
(323) 469-5155 Phone
Literary agent: Albert Woods

Tyler Kjar Agency

5144 Vineland Ave.
North Hollywood, CA 91601
(818) 760-0321 Phone
Literary agent: Tyler Kjar

Jon Klane Agency (WGA) (Q)

120 El Camino Dr. #112
Beverly Hills, CA 90212
(310) 278-0178 Phone
(310) 278-0179 Fax
Web: www.klaneagency.com
E-mail: query@klaneagency.com
Literary agent: Jon Klane

Paul Kohner, Inc. (WGA)

9300 Wilshire Blvd. #555
Beverly Hills, CA 90212
(310) 550-1060 Phone
(310) 276-1083 Fax
Literary agent: Stephen Moore,
Brian Dreyfuss, Deborah Obad

Cary Kozlov Literary Representation (WGA)

11911 San Vicente Blvd. #348
Los Angeles, CA 90049
(310) 843-2211 Phone
(310) 843-0112 Fax
E-mail: ckreps@lafn.org
Literary agent: Cary Kozlov

Kristine Krupp Talent Agency

P.O. Box 6556
San Rafael, CA 94903
(415) 479-5404 Phone
E-mail: kktalent@aol.com
Literary agent: Kristine Krupp

The Candace Lake Agency, Inc. (WGA)

9200 Sunset Blvd. #820
Los Angeles, CA 90069
(310) 247-2115 Phone
(310) 247-2116 Fax
E-mail: clagency@earthlink.net
Literary agents: Candace Lake,
Rick Ryba

Larchmont Literary Agency (WGA) (Q)

444 N. Larchmont Blvd. #200
Los Angeles, CA 90004
(323) 856-3070 Phone
E-mail: agency@larchmontlit.com
Literary agents: Joel Millner,
Lilith Berdischewsky

Leading Artists (WGA)

800 S. Robertson Blvd. #5
Los Angeles, CA 90035
(310) 855-0565 Phone
(310) 360-9972 Fax
Web: www.leadingartists
agency.com
E-mail: information@leadingartists
agency.com
Literary agents: Joshua Berman,
Aaron Weingrad

Lenhoff & Lenhoff (WGA)

830 Palm Ave.
West Hollywood, CA 90069
(310) 855-2411 Phone
(310) 855-2412 Fax

Web: www.lenhoff.com
Literary agents: Charles Lenhoff, Lisa Lenhoff

Jack Lenny Associates
(WGA)

9454 Wilshire Blvd. #600
Beverly Hills, CA 90212
(310) 271-2174 Phone
Literary agents: Jim Lenny, Kim Lang Lenny

Paul S. Levine Literary Agency

1054 Superba Ave.
Venice, CA 90291
(310) 450-6711 Phone
(310) 450-0181 Fax
E-mail: pslevine@ix.netcom.com
Literary agent: Paul S. Levine

Michael Lewis & Associates
(WGA) (Q)

2506 Fifth St. #100
Santa Monica, CA 90405
(310) 399-1999 Phone
(310) 399-9104 Fax
E-mail: lewis@godot.net
Literary agent: Michael Lewis

Lynne & Reilly Agency (WGA)

10725 Vanowen St.
North Hollywood, CA 91605-6402
(323) 850-1984 Phone

Jana Luker Talent Agency
(WGA)

1923 ½ Westwood Blvd. #3
Los Angeles, CA 90025
(310) 441-2822 Phone
Literary agents: Jana Luker, Kathy Keeley

▌ *Writing music, writing drama, or writing comedy—all have their own rhythms, their own emotional beats that build. It's also very much like the sexual act. In a play or movie, the emotional impact is this pulsating, beating thing that has a climax. Then after the climax is the emotional release.*
—NEIL SIMON

AGENTS

Major Clients Agency

345 N. Maple Dr. #395
Beverly Hills, CA 90210
(310) 205-5000 Phone

Maris Agency (WGA)

17620 Sherman Way #213
Van Nuys, CA 91406
(818) 708-2493 Phone

The Markwood Company
(WGA)

1813 Victory Blvd.
Glendale, CA 91201
(818) 401-3644 Phone

Maxine's Talent Agency

4830 Encino Ave.
Encino, CA 91316
(818) 986-2946 Phone
Literary agent: Maxine

Media Artists Group/ Capital Artists (WGA) (Q)

6404 Wilshire Blvd. #950
Los Angeles, CA 90048
(323) 658-5050 Phone
(323) 658-7871 Fax
Literary agents: Barbara
Alexander, David Stinnett

Metropolitan Talent Agency
(WGA)

4526 Wilshire Blvd.
Los Angeles, CA 90010
(323) 857-4500 Phone
(323) 857-4599 Fax
Literary agents: Christopher
Barrett, Garth Pappas, Bradley
Glenn, Dina Carlaftes

The Stuart Miller Co. (WGA)

11684 Ventura Blvd. #225
Studio City, CA 91604
(818) 506-6067 Phone
(818) 506-4079 Fax
E-mail: smmco@aol.com
Literary agent: Stuart M. Miller

Mocean Management

8205 Santa Monica Blvd. #1-444
Los Angeles, CA 90046
(323) 658-1966 Phone
Web: www.moceanpictures.net
E-mail: moceanpictures@attbi.com

Monteiro Rose Agency, Inc.

17514 Ventura Blvd., Ste. 205
Encino, CA 91316
(818) 501-1177 Phone
(818) 501-1194 Fax
Web: www.monteiro-rose.com
E-mail: monrose@monteiro-rose
 .com

Literary agents: Jason Dravis, Milissa Brockish, Candace Monteiro, Fredda Rose

Morgan Agency, Inc.
(WGA) (Q)

129 W. Wilson St. #202
Costa Mesa, CA 92627
(949) 574-1100 Phone

★ William Morris Agency

One William Morris Place
Beverly Hills, CA 90212
(310) 859-4000 Phone
(310) 859-4462 Fax
Web: www.wma.com

David Moss & Associates

733 N. Seward St., Penthouse
Hollywood, CA 90038
(323) 465-1234 Phone
(323) 465-1241 Fax
Literary agent: H. David Moss

Natural Talent, Inc.

3331 Ocean Park Blvd. #203
Santa Monica, CA 90405
(310) 450-4945 Phone
(310) 450-4140 Fax
E-mail: naturalt@earthlink.net

Literary agents: Kelly Calder, Donna Felten

The Novus Agency

2101 Sacramento St., Ste. 103
San Francisco, CA 94109
(415) 346-8700 Phone
Web: www.novusagency.com
Literary agents: Warren Cormier, Laurie Rowley

Omnipop, Inc. (WGA)

10700 Ventura Blvd., 2nd Fl.
Studio City, CA 91604
(818) 980-9267 Phone
(818) 980-9371 Fax
Web: www.omnipop.com
E-mail: omni@omnipop.com
Literary agent: Bruce Smith

The Orange Grove Group
(WGA)

12178 Ventura Blvd. #205
Studio City, CA 91604
(818) 762-7498 Phone
(818) 762-7499 Fax
Web: www.orangegrovegroup.com
E-mail: gregmayo@orangegrove
.com
Literary agent: Gregory Mayo

Original Artists (WGA)

9465 Wilshire Blvd. #840
Beverly Hills, CA 90212
(310) 275-6765 Phone
(310) 275-6725 Fax
Literary agents: Jordan Bayer,
Matt Leipzig

Panda Talent Agency (WGA)

3721 Hoen Ave.
Santa Rosa, CA 95405
(707) 576-0711 Phone

★ Paradigm

10100 Santa Monica Blvd., 25th Fl.
Los Angeles, CA 90067
(310) 277-4400 Phone
(310) 277-7820 Fax
Literary agents: Bernie
Weintraub, Debbee Klein, Lucy
Stiles, Chris Parr, Andy Patman,
Valarie Phillips, Mark Ross, Jerry
Mika, Matthew Bedrosian, Pierre
Brogan, Sean Freidin

The Barry Perelman Agency

1800 Ave. of the Stars, Ste. 1114
Los Angeles, CA 90067
(310) 551-3000 Phone
Literary agent: Barry Perelman

Lynn Pleshette Literary Agency (WGA)

2700 N. Beachwood Dr.
Hollywood, CA 90068
(323) 465-0428 Phone
Web: lynnpleshetteagency.com
E-mail: submissions@lynnpleshette
agency.com
Literary agents: Lynn Pleshette,
Heather Roy, Michael Cendejas

Preferred Artists (WGA)

16633 Ventura Blvd. #1421
Encino, CA 91436
(818) 990-0305 Phone
(818) 990-2736 Fax
Literary agent: Brad Rosenfeld

▌ *One of the reasons cameramen have much better lives than writers is because nobody says to a cameraman, "I'll fix the lighting," because nobody knows how to do it. But everybody knows words.*

— **WILLIAM GOLDMAN**, screenwriter, *Butch Cassidy and the Sundance Kid*

The Jim Preminger Agency

450 N. Roxbury Dr., PH 1050
Beverly Hills, CA 90210
(310) 860-1116 Phone
(310) 860-1117 Fax
Web: www.premingeragency.com
E-mail: general@premingeragency
.com
Literary agents: Jim Preminger,
Dean Schramm, Ryan L. Saul

Fred R. Price Literary Agency (WGA)

14044 Ventura Blvd. #201
Sherman Oaks, CA 91423
(818) 763-6365 Phone
Literary agent: Fred R. Price

Privilege Talent Agency (WGA)

14542 Ventura Blvd. #209
Sherman Oaks, CA 91403
(818) 386-2377 Phone
(818) 386-9477 Fax
Literary agent: Carol Oleesky

Qualita Dell' Arte (WGA) (Q)

5353 Topanga Canyon Rd. #220
Woodland Hills, CA 91364
(818) 598-8073 Phone

Quillco Agency (WGA)

3104 W. Cumberland Ct.
Westlake Village, CA 91362
(805) 495-8436 Phone
(805) 373-9868 Fax
E-mail: quillco2@aol.com
Literary agent: Sandy Mackey

Renaissance Literary/Talent Agency

A Division of Artist's Management
Group
9465 Wilshire Blvd.
Beverly Hills, CA 90212
(310) 860-8000 Phone
E-mail: renaissance@earthlink.net

Renegade Management

A Crystal Sky Company
1901 Ave. of the Stars, Ste. 605
Los Angeles, CA 90067
(310) 553-9895 Phone
E-mail: mail@renegademgt.com

Michael D. Robins & Associates (WGA) (Q)

23241 Ventura Blvd. #300
Woodland Hills, CA 91364
(818) 343-1755 Phone
(818) 343-7355 Fax
E-mail: md2@msn.com
Literary agent: Michael D. Robins

Maggie Roiphe Agency
(WGA)

1721 S. Garth Ave.
Los Angeles, CA 90035
(310) 876-1561 Phone

Brant Rose Agency

10537 Santa Monica Blvd #305
Los Angeles, CA 90025
(310) 470-4243 Phone
(310) 470-4384 Fax
Web: brantroseagency.com
E-mail: hub@brantroseagency.com
Literary agent: Brant Rose

The Rothman Agency

9465 Wilshire Blvd., Ste. 840
Beverly Hills, CA 90212
(310) 247-9898 Phone
(310) 247-9888 Fax
E-mail: reception@rothman
   agency.com
Literary agents: Jim Rothman,
Dan Brecher, Dennis Kim, Chris
Prince

Sanford-Gross & Associates (WGA)

1015 Gayley Ave. #301
Los Angeles, CA 90024
(310) 208-2100 Phone

(310) 208-6704 Fax
Literary agents: Geoffrey Sanford,
Brad Gross

The Sarnoff Company, Inc.
(WGA) (Q)

3500 W. Olive Ave. #300
Burbank, CA 91505
(818) 973-4555 Phone
(818) 973-4554 Fax
Literary agent: James Sarnoff

Jack Scagnetti (WGA)

5118 Vineland Ave. #102
North Hollywood, CA 91601
(818) 762-3871 Phone
Literary agent: Jack Scagnetti

The Irv Schechter Company
(WGA)

9300 Wilshire Blvd. #410
Beverly Hills, CA 90212
(310) 278-8070 Phone
(310) 278-6058 Fax
E-mail: iscagency@aol.com
Literary agents: Irv Schechter,
Tammy Felder, Susan Simons,
John Goldsmith, Boyd Hancock,
Brian Kend, Josh Schechter

The Paul Schwartzman Office

11777 San Vicente Blvd.
Los Angeles, CA 90049
(310) 828-4040 Phone
Literary agent: Paul Schwartzman

Shafer & Associates (WGA)

9000 Sunset Blvd. #808
Los Angeles, CA 90069
(310) 888-1240 Phone

David Shapira & Associates, Inc. (WGA)

15821 Ventura Blvd #235
Encino, CA 91436
(818) 906-0322 Phone
(818) 783-2562 Fax
E-mail: ds@dsa-agency.com
Literary agents: David Shapira, Matt Shapira, Diane Pinter, Donna Gaba, Alan Bursky, Harold Augenstein, Doug Warner

★ Shapiro-Lichtman, Inc. (WGA)

8827 Beverly Blvd.
Los Angeles, CA 90048
(310) 859-8877 Phone
(310) 859-7153 Fax
Literary agents: Yale Udoff, Laura Bernstein, Mark Lichtman, Sean

Davis, Michael Shlain, Susan Shapiro, Art Rutter, Peggy Patrick, Marty Shapiro

Ken Sherman & Associates (WGA)

9507 Santa Monica Blvd. #212
Beverly Hills, CA 90210
(310) 273-8840 Phone
E-mail: ksassociates@earthlink.net
Literary agent: Ken Sherman

Jerome S. Siegel Associates (WGA)

1680 N. Vine St. #617
Hollywood, CA 90028
(323) 466-0185 Phone
Literary agent: Jerome Siegel

Richard Sindell & Associates (WGA)

9301 Wilshire Blvd. #300
Beverly Hills, CA 90210
(310) 777-8277 Phone
Literary agent: Richard Sindell

The Skouras Agency

631 Wilshire Blvd., 2nd Fl., Ste. C
Santa Monica, CA 90401
(310) 395-9550 Phone
Literary agent: Spyros Skouras

AGENTS

Daniel Sladek Entertainment Corporation

8306 Wilshire Blvd. #510
Beverly Hills, CA 90211
(323) 934-9268 Phone
(323) 934-7362 Fax
Web: www.danielsladek.com

Michael Slessinger & Associates

8730 Sunset Blvd. #270
Los Angeles, CA 90069
(310) 657-7113 Phone
(310) 657-1756 Fax
E-mail: mslessing@aol.com
Literary agents: Michael Slessinger, Billy Miller, Meegan Kelso

SMA, LLC

PMB #615
9899 Santa Monica Blvd.
Beverly Hills, CA 90212
(310) 203-8787 Phone
(310) 203-8742 Fax
Web: www.smaagency.com
E-mail: agentsara@flashcom.net
Literary agent: Sara Margoshes

Gerald K. Smith & Associates (WGA)

2930 N. Keystone St.
Burbank, CA 91504
(323) 849-5388 Phone

The Susan Smith Company (WGA)

121 N. San Vicente Blvd.
Beverly Hills, CA 90211
(323) 852-4777 Phone

Camille Sorice Talent Agency (WGA) (Q)

13412 Moorpark St. #C
Sherman Oaks, CA 91423
(818) 995-1775 Phone
Literary agent: Camille Sorice

The Stars Agency (WGA) (Q)

23 Grant Ave., 4th Fl.
San Francisco, CA 94108
(415) 421-6272 Phone
(415) 421-7620 Fax
Web: www.starsagency.com
E-mail: lynnc@starsagency.com

First, cut out all the wisdom; then cut out all the adjectives.
—**PADDY CHAYEFSKY,** screenwriter of Network, Hospital, and Marty

Literary agent: Dayne Mullins

Starwil Productions (WGA)

433 N. Camden Dr., 4th Fl.
Beverly Hills, CA 90210
(323) 874-1239 Phone
(323) 874-1822 Fax
E-mail: starwil@earthlink.net
Literary agents: Starwil Reed,
Gwen Reed, Gregory Porter

The Stein Agency (WGA)

5125 Oakdale Ave.
Woodland Hills, CA 91364
(818) 594-8990 Phone
(818) 594-8998 Fax
E-mail: mail@thesteinagency.com
Literary agents: Mitchel E. Stein,
Jim Ford

Gloria Stern Agency

12535 Chandler Blvd. #3
North Hollywood, CA 91607
(818) 508-6296 Phone
E-mail: cywrite@juno.com
Literary agent: Gloria Stern

The Stone Manners Agency (WGA)

8436 W. 3rd St. #740
Los Angeles, CA 90048

(323) 655-1313 Phone
Literary agent: Tim Stone

Stronghold Entertainment

8484 Wilshire Blvd., Ste. 425
Beverly Hills, CA 90211
(323) 951-1890 Phone

Suite A Management Talent & Literary Agency

1101 S. Robertson Blvd. #210
Los Angeles, CA 90035
(310) 278-0801 Phone
(310) 278-0807 Fax
Web: www.suite-a-management.com
E-mail: suite-a@juno.com
Literary agent: Lloyd D. Robinson

Summit Talent & Literary Agency (WGA) (Q)

9454 Wilshire Blvd. #203
Beverly Hills, CA 90212
(310) 205-9730 Phone
(310) 205-9734 Fax
Literary agent: Sandy Weindberg

Talent Associates

10200 Pico Blvd. #230
Los Angeles, CA 90024
(310) 470-0001 Phone
Literary agent: Lyle Kenny

Talentscout Management

12228 Venice Blvd., Ste. 539
Los Angeles, CA 90066
(310) 281-6213 Phone
(310) 397-3695 Fax
Web: www.atalentscout.com

Tollin/Robbins Management

10960 Ventura Blvd., 2nd Fl
Studio City, CA 91604
(818) 766-5004 Phone

Triumph Literary Agency (WGA)

3000 W. Olympic Blvd. #1362
Santa Monica, CA 90404
(310) 264-3959 Phone

The Turtle Agency (WGA)

7720 B El Camino Real #125
Carlsbad, CA 92009
(760) 632-5857 Phone
(760) 632-5858 Fax

E-mail: cturtlewal@aol.com
Literary agent: Cindy Turtle

United Artists Talent Agency (WGA) (Q)

14011 Ventura Blvd. #213
Sherman Oaks, CA 91423
(818) 788-7305 Phone
(818) 788-7018 Fax
E-mail: uat@thegrid.net
Literary agent: Carol Bailey

★ United Talent Agency (WGA)

9560 Wilshire Blvd., 5th Fl.
Beverly Hills, CA 90212
(310) 273-6700 Phone
(310) 247-1111 Fax

Unlimited Management

1627 Pontius Ave., Ste. 200
Los Angeles, CA 90025
(310) 914-9171 Phone

Van Duren Agency

11684 Ventura Blvd. #235
Studio City, CA 91604
(818) 752-6000 Phone
(818) 752-6985 Fax
E-mail: avagency@pacbell.net
Literary agent: Annette van Duren

Vision Art Management
(WGA)

. . . .

9200 Sunset Blvd., Penthouse 1
Los Angeles, CA 90069
(310) 888-3288 Phone
(310) 888-2268 Fax
Literary agents: Scott Schwartz,
Matt Ochacher

Warden McKinley
Literary Agency

. . . .

1275 Fourth St. #247
Santa Rosa, CA 95404
(707) 538-9259 Phone
(707) 539-8757 Fax
E-mail: wardenmckinley@
  yahoo.com
Literary agent: Bob Warden

Warden, White &
Associates

. . . .

8444 Wilshire Blvd., 4th Fl.
Beverly Hills, CA 90211
(323) 852-1028 Phone
Literary agents: Dave Warden,
Steve White

Wardlow & Associates
(WGA) (Q)

. . . .

1501 Main St. #204
Venice, CA 90291

(310) 452-1292 Phone
(310) 452-9002 Fax
E-mail: wardslowaso@aol.com
Literary agents: David Wardlow,
Jeff Ordway

Ann Waugh Talent Agency

. . . .

4741 Laurel Canyon Blvd., Ste. 200
North Hollywood, CA 91607
(818) 980-0141 Phone
Literary agent: Larry Benedict

The Wax Agency

. . . .

120 El Camino Dr., Ste. 114
Beverly Hills, CA 90212
(310) 550-8738 Phone

Whatever . . .
Talent Agency (WGA)

. . . .

20917 Gorgonia St.
Woodland Hills, CA 91364
(818) 884-2209 Phone
(818) 884-0403 Fax
Literary agent: Lesley Lotta

Working Artists Talent
Agency (WGA) (Q)

. . . .

13525 Ventura Blvd.
Sherman Oaks, CA 91423
(818) 907-1122 Phone

AGENTS

(818) 907-1168 Fax

Web: www.workingartistsagency
.com

Literary agent: Debora Koslowsky

The Wright Concept

1612 W. Olive Ave. #205

Burbank, CA 91506

(818) 954-8943 Phone

(818) 954-9370 Fax

Web: www.wrightconcept.com

E-mail: mrwright@wrightconcept
.com

Literary agent: Marcie Wright

Marion A. Wright Agency
(WGA)

4317 Bluebell Ave.

Studio City, CA 91604

(818) 766-7307 Phone

Literary agent: Marion Wright

★ Writers & Artists Agency
(WGA)

8383 Wilshire Blvd. #550

Beverly Hills, CA 90211

(323) 866-0900 Phone

(323) 866-1899 Fax

E-mail: info@wriart.com

Literary agents: Rick Berg, Angela
Cheng, Carel Cutler, Jim Ehrich,
Richard Freeman, Dave Phillips

▮ Colorado

Carolyn Hodges Agency
(WGA)

1980 Glenwood Dr.

Boulder, CO 80304

(303) 443-4636 Phone

Literary agent: Carolyn Hodges

▮ *The only way you can effectively learn about screenwriting is to write something and then see it done as you've written it. Then you can see where you went right, and where you went wrong.*

—ROBERT TOWNE, screenwriter, *Chinatown*

Kelly McMahan Agency
(WGA)

5686 S. Crocker St. #3a
Littleton, CO 80120
(303) 703-3723 Phone
Literary agent: Kelly McMahan

Jody Rein Books, Inc.

7741 S. Ash Ct.
Littleton, CO 80122
(303) 694-4430 Phone
(303) 694-0687 Fax
Web: www.jodyreinbooks.com
E-mail: joryrein@jodyreinbooks
.com

Don Gastwirth & Associates (WGA)

265 College St. #10-N
New Haven, CT 06510
(203) 562-7600 Phone
Literary agent: Don Gastwirth

Tall Trees Development Group (WGA)

301 Old Westport Rd.
Wilton, CT 06897
(203) 762-5748 Phone

■ District of Columbia

■ Connecticut

The Gary-Paul Agency
(WGA) (Q)

84 Canaan Ct. #17
Stratford, CT 06614
(203) 336-0257 Phone
(203) 336-0257 Fax
Web: www.thegarypaulagency.com
E-mail: maynard@optonline.net
Literary agent: Garret C. Maynard

Theresa A. Gabaldon Literary Agent (WGA) (Q)

2020 Pennsylvania Ave., NW #222
Washington, DC 20006
Literary agent: Theresa Gabaldon

Leona P. Schechter Literary Agency (WGA)

3748 Huntington St., NW
Washington, DC 20015
(202) 362-9040 Phone
Literary agent: Leona P. Schecter

AGENTS

▌ Florida

Berg Agency, Inc. (WGA) (Q)

15908 Eagle River Way
Tampa, FL 33624
(813) 877-5533 Phone
Literary agent: Carol Berg

Marshall Cameron Agency (WGA) (Q)

19667 N.E. 20th Ln.
Lawtey, FL 32058
(904) 964-7013 Phone
Literary agent: Marshall Cameron

Coconut Grove Talent Agency (WGA) (Q)

3525 Vista Ct.
Coconut Grove, FL 33133
(305) 858-3002 Phone

Hurt Agency, Inc. (WGA) (Q)

400 New York Ave., N #207
Winter Park, FL 32789
(407) 740-5700 Phone

International Artists Group, Inc.

2121 N. Bayshore Dr. #1007
Miami, FL 33137
(305) 576-0001 Phone
(305) 576-0012 Fax
E-mail: meriszittman@aol.com
Literary agent: Meris Zittman

Legacies (WGA) (Q)

501 Woodstork Circle, Perico Bay
Bradenton, FL 34209
(941) 792-9159 Phone

Cheryl McCarthy Literary Agency

7641 S. Dixie Hwy. #234
West Palm Beach, FL 33405
(361) 622-9558 Phone
(361) 799-4992 Fax
Literary agent: Cheryl McCarthy

Reverie Literary Agency (WGA) (Q)

6822 22nd Ave., N #121
Saint Petersburg, FL 33710
(727) 864-2106 Phone

▌ *Don't outline everything, because it makes the writing of the play a chore.*
—JOHN VAN DRUTEN, playwright, *I Remember Mama* and *I Am a Camera*

The Rollins Agency
(WGA) (Q)

2221 N.E. 164th St. #331
North Miami Beach, FL 33160
(305) 354-7313 Phone

The Salpeter Agency
(WGA) (Q)

7461 W. Country Club Dr., N #406
Sarasota, FL 34243
(941) 359-0568 Phone

Glenda Stafford & Associates (WGA) (Q)

14953 Newport Rd. #100
Clearwater, FL 33764
(727) 535-1374 Phone
Literary agent: Glenda Stafford

Stellar Model & Talent Agency (WGA) (Q)

407 Lincoln Rd. #2K
Miami Beach, FL 33139
(305) 672-2217 Phone
Literary agent: Cindy Freed

Tel-Screen International, Inc. (WGA) (Q)

2659 Carambola Circle N, Bldg. A
 #404
Coconut Creek, FL 33066
(954) 974-2251 Phone

■ Georgia

California Artists Agency
(WGA) (Q)

3053 Centerville Rosebud Rd.
Snellville, GA 30039
(770) 982-1477 Phone

The Genesis Agency (WGA)

1465 Northside Dr. #120
Atlanta, GA 30318
(404) 350-9212 Phone

K.T. Enterprises (WGA)

2605 Ben Hill Rd.
East Point, GA 30344
(404) 346-3191 Phone

McBrayer Literary Agency
(WGA) (Q)

2483 Wawona Dr.
Atlanta, GA 30319
(404) 634-1045 Phone

Monroe-Pritchard-Monroe
(WGA) (Q)

722 Ridgecreek Dr.
Clarkston, GA 30021
(404) 296-4000 Phone
E-mail: allinline@hotmail.com

Talent Source (WGA) (Q)

107 E. Hall St.
Savannah, GA 31401
(912) 232-9390 Phone

Writerstore (WGA) (Q)

2004 Rockledge Rd., NE
Atlanta, GA 30324
(404) 874-6448 Phone
(404) 874-6330 Fax
Web: www.peoplestore.net
E-mail: writerstore@
  mindspring.com

Hawaii

Promote-It! (WGA) (Q)

501 Hahaione St. #10J
Honolulu, HI 96825
(808) 395-1613 Phone

Idaho

The Author's Agency
(WGA) (Q)

3355 N. Five Mile Rd. #332
Boise, ID 83713-3925
(208) 376-5477 Phone

Illinois

Agency Chicago (WGA) (Q)

601 South La Salle St. #600-A
Chicago, IL 60605

Marcus Bryan & Associates
(WGA) (Q)

2970 Maria Ave. #224
Northbrook, IL 60062
(847) 579-0030 Phone
Literary agent: Marcus Bryan

Kelvin C. Bulger, Attorney at Law (WGA) (Q)

11 E. Adams #604
Chicago, IL 60603

(312) 692-1002 Phone
Literary agent: Kevin C. Bulger

Shirley Hamilton, Inc. (WGA) (Q)

333 E. Ontario Ave. #302B
Chicago, IL 60611
(312) 787-4700 Phone
Literary agent: Shirley Hamilton

Susanne Johnson Talent Agency, Ltd. (WGA) (Q)

108 W. Oak St.
Chicago, IL 60610
(312) 642-8151 Phone
Literary agent: Susanne Johnson

K. P. Agency (WGA) (Q)

300 N. State St. #4526
Chicago, IL 60610
(312) 832-9777 Phone

Law Offices of Joel Weisman, P.C. (WGA) (Q)

1901 Raymond Dr. #6
Northbrook, IL 60062
(847) 400-5900 Phone

Dalia Orentas Literary Agent (WGA) (Q)

6128 N. Damen Ave.
Chicago, IL 60659
(312) 338-6392 Phone

Silver Screen Placements Inc. (WGA) (Q)

602 65th St.
Downers Grove, IL 60516
(630) 963-2124 Phone

Stewart Talent Management Corp. (WGA) (Q)

58 W. Huron St.
Chicago, IL 60610
(312) 943-3131 Phone
(312) 943-5107 Fax
E-mail: maureen@stewarttalent.com
Literary agents: Jane Stewart,
Maureen Brookman, Maryann
Kohler Drake

Whiskey Hill Entertainment (WGA)

1000 S. Williams St.
P.O. Box 606
Westmont, IL 60559-0606
(630) 852-5023 Phone

AGENTS

> ▌ **TIP:** E-mail is developing into a powerful tool to get your query directly to the person you're trying to reach. Most entertainment companies don't publish their e-mail addresses (for good reason), so you'll have to do some sleuthing. If the Web site is listed, try the following combinations: firstname@website.com, firstinitiallastname@website.com, lastname@website.com, or firstinitiallast initial@website.com. It may take some guessing, but sooner or later you'll get through. Put your hook in the subject line to grab the person's attention and keep him or her from deleting it with the spam.

▌ Indiana

International Leonards Corp. (WGA) (Q)

3612 N. Washington Blvd.
Indianapolis, IN 46205

Jez Enterprises (WGA) (Q)

227 Village Way
South Bend, IN 46619

Joint Venture Agency (WGA) (Q)

2927 Westbrook Dr. #110B
Fort Wayne, IN 46805
(219) 484-1832 Phone

▌ Kansas

Jackson Artists Corporation (WGA)

7251 Lowell Dr.
Overland Park, KS 66204
(913) 384-6688 Phone
(913) 722-4006 Fax
E-mail: jacine@birch.net
Literary agents: Dave Jackson, Barney Bergantine

▌ Maine

Michael H. Sommer Literary Agency

202 U.S. Rte. 1, Ste. 123
Falmouth, ME 04105

(207) 773-4859 Phone
(207) 773-4859 Fax
E-mail: mhsmaine@yahoo.com
Literary agent: Michael H.
Sommer

**Talesmyth Entertainment,
Inc.** (WGA) (Q)

312 St. John St. #69
Portland, ME 04102
(207) 879-0307 Phone

■ Massachusetts

Creative Career
Management (WGA) (Q)

84 Spruce Run Dr.
Brewster, MA 02631
(508) 896-9351 Phone

The Gatsby Group

P.O. Box 1127
Boston, MA 02117
(617) 847-4430 Phone
(617) 847-0050 Fax
E-mail: gatsbygrp@aol.com
Literary agents: Douglas
Weischadle, David Weischadle

The Hill & Barlow Agency

1 International Pl.
Boston, MA 02110
(617) 428-3000 Phone
(617) 428-3500 Fax
Web: www.hillbarlow.com
E-mail: erogers@hillbarlow.com
Literary agents: Elaine M. Rogers,
John Taylor Williams

M. A. Powell Literary
Agency (WGA) (Q)

56 Arrowhead Rd.
Weston, MA 02193
(781) 899-8386 Phone

■ Michigan

The Grace Company
(WGA) (Q)

829 Langdon Ct.
Rochester Hills, MI 48307
(248) 868-5994 Phone

Joseph S. Aljouny (WGA) (Q)

29205 Greening Blvd.
Farmington Hills, MI 48334-2945
(248) 932-0090 Phone

AGENTS

▌Minnesota

Otitis Media (WGA) (Q)

1926 Dupont Ave., S.
Minneapolis, MN 55403
(612) 377-4918 Phone

▌Nevada

Tahoe Sierras Agency

P.O. Box 2179
Dayton, NV 89403
(775) 241-0881 Phone
(775) 241-0413 Fax
Web: www.tahoesierras.com
E-mail: tahoesierras@aol.com
Literary agents: Ed Oversen,
Linda Heater, Deborah Oversen

Donna Wauhob Agency (WGA)

3135 Industrial Rd. #204
Las Vegas, NV 89109
(702) 733-1017 Phone
(702) 733-1215 Fax
E-mail: dwauhob@aol.com
Literary agent: Calvin Maefield

▌New Jersey

Ellen Brown Agency (WGA) (Q)

211 Clubhouse Dr.
Middletown, NJ 07748
(201) 615-0310 Phone

Regency Literary International Agency (WGA)

285 Verona Ave.
Newark, NJ 07104
(201) 485-2692 Phone

▌ *I think it's very important to remember who we were while we're being what we are.*

—**WILLIAM GOLDMAN,** screenwriter, *Butch Cassidy and the Sundance Kid*

The Starflight Agency
(WGA) (Q)

. . . .

75 Troy Dr. #C
Springfield, NJ 07081
(908) 964-9292 Phone

Abrams Artists Agency
(WGA) (Q)

. . . .

275 Seventh Ave., 26th Fl.
New York, NY 10001
(646) 486-4600 Phone
(646) 486-0100 Fax
Literary agents: Charmaine
Ferneczi, John B. Santoianni, Jack
Tantleff

Bret Adams, Ltd. (WGA)

. . . .

448 W. 44th St.
New York, NY 10036
(212) 765-5630 Phone
(212) 265-2212 Fax
E-mail: badamsltd@aol.com
Literary agents: Bret Adams, Ken
Melamed, Bruce Ostler, Margi
Rountree

★ Agency for the Performing Arts (WGA)

. . . .

888 Seventh Ave.
New York, NY 10106
(212) 582-1500 Phone

Michael Amato Agency
(WGA) (Q)

. . . .

1650 Broadway, Ste. 307
New York, NY 10019
(212) 247-4456 Phone

Amron Development, Inc.
(WGA) (Q)

. . . .

77 Horton Pl.
Syosset, NY 11791
(516) 364-0238 Phone

Marcia Amsterdam Agency
(WGA) (Q)

. . . .

41 W. 82nd St.
New York, NY 10024-5613
(212) 873-4945 Phone
Literary agent: Marcia Amsterdam

Irvin Arthur Associates, Ltd.

. . . .

P.O. Box 1358
New York, NY 10022
(212) 570-0051 Phone
Literary agent: Irvin Arthur

AGENTS

Artists Agency, Inc. (WGA)

230 W. 55th St. #29D
New York, NY 10019
(212) 245-6960 Phone

Beacon Artists Agency
(WGA)

630 Ninth Ave. #215
New York, NY 10036
(212) 765-5533 Phone

Berman, Boals & Flynn, Inc.
(WGA) (Q)

208 W. 30th St. #401
New York, NY 10001
(212) 868-1068 Phone
Literary agents: Judy Boals, Jim Flynn

Bethel Agency

311 W. 43rd St. #602
New York, NY 10036
(212) 664-0455 Phone
Literary agent: Lewis Chambers

Curtis Brown, Ltd.

10 Astor Pl.
New York, NY 10003
(212) 473-5400 Phone

Literary agents: Timothy Knowlton, Ed Wintle, Dave Barbor

Browne, Pema, Ltd.
(WGA) (Q)

Pine Rd., Box 104B
Neversink, NY 12765
(914) 985-2936 Phone

Don Buchwald and Associates (WGA) (Q)

10 E. 44th St.
New York, NY 10017
(212) 867-1070 Phone

Maria Carvainis Agency
(WGA)

1350 Ave. of the Americas #2950
New York, NY 10019
(212) 245-6365 Phone
Literary agents: Maria Carvainis, Frances M. Kuffel

Circle of Confusion, Ltd.

575 Lexington Ave., 4th Fl.
New York, NY 10022
(212) 527-7579 Phone
(718) 997-0521 Fax
E-mail: circleldt@aol.com

Dee Mura Enterprises, Inc.
(WGA) (Q)

. . . .

269 W. Shore Dr.
Massapequa, NY 11758
(516) 795-1616 Phone

Donadio & Ashworth, Inc.
(WGA)

. . . .

121 W. 27th St.
New York, NY 10001
(212) 691-8077 Phone

Duva-Flack Associates, Inc.
(WGA) (Q)

. . . .

200 W. 57th St. #1008
New York, NY 10019
(212) 957-9600 Phone

Earth Tracks Artists Agency
(WGA) (Q)

. . . .

4809 Ave., N. #286
Brooklyn, NY 11234

Ann Elmo Agency, Inc.

. . . .

60 E. 42rd St.
New York, NY 10165
(212) 661-2880 Phone

(212) 661-2883 Fax
Literary agent: Lettie Lee

Farber Literary Agency, Inc.

. . . .

14 E. 75th St.
New York, NY 10021
(212) 861-7075 Phone
(212) 861-7076 Fax
Web: www.donaldfarber.com
E-mail: farberlit@aol.com
Literary agent: Ann Farber,
Donald C. Farber

Robert A. Freedman
Dramatic Agency, Inc. (WGA)

. . . .

1501 Broadway, Ste. 2310
New York, NY 10036
(212) 840-5760 Phone
Literary agents: Robert A.
Freedman, Selma Luttinger, Robin
Kaver

The Gersh Agency, Inc.
(WGA)

. . . .

130 W. 42nd St.
New York, NY 10036
(212) 997-1818 Phone
(212) 391-8459 Fax
Literary agents: Philip Adelman,
Pete Kaiser, Steven Unger

Graham Agency

311 W. 43rd St.
New York, NY 10036
(212) 489-7730 Phone
Literary agent: Earl Graham

The Susan Gurman Agency
(WGA) (Q)

865 West End Ave. #15A
New York, NY 10025
(212) 749-4618 Phone
(212) 864-5055 Fax
E-mail:
gurmanagency@earthlink.net
Literary agent: Susan Gurman

Harden-Curtis Associates

850 Seventh Ave., Ste. 405
New York, NY 10019
(212) 977-8502 Phone
(212) 977-8420 Fax
Web: www.hardencurtis.com
Literary agents: Nancy Curtis,
Mary Harden, Michael Kirsten,
Diane Riley

Barbara Hogenson Agency,
Inc. (WGA)

165 West End Ave. #19-C
New York, NY 10023
(212) 874-8084 Phone
(212) 362-3011 Fax
Literary agent: Barbara Hogenson

The Hudson Agency (WGA)

3 Travis Ln.
Montrose, NY 10548
(914) 737-1475 Phone
(914) 736-3064 Fax
Web: www.hudsonagency.net
E-mail: hudagency@juno.com
Literary agent: Susan Giordano

Ellen Hyman

44 Parker Dr.
Pittsford, NY 14534
(716) 264-1326 Phone
E-mail: ideovideo@yahoo.com
Literary agent: Ellen Hyman

★ International Creative
Management (ICM) (WGA)

40 W. 57th St.
New York, NY 10019
(212) 556-5600 Phone
(212) 556-5665 Fax
Literary agents: Esther Newberg,
Amanda Urban, Lisa Bankoff,
Herb Cheyette, Kristine Dahl,
Mitch Douglas, Sloan Harris,
Heather Schroder, Denise
Shannon, Amy Williams

Kalliope Enterprises, Inc.
(WGA)

15 Larch Dr.
New Hyde, NY 11040
(516) 248-2963 Phone

Kerin-Goldberg Associates, Inc. (WGA) (Q)

155 E. 55th St.
New York, NY 10022
(212) 838-7373 Phone

The Joyce Ketay Agency, Inc. (WGA) (Q)

1501 Broadway #1908
New York, NY 10036
(212) 354-6825 Phone
(212) 354-6732 Fax
E-mail: jta@joyceketay.com
Literary agents: Joyce Ketay, Carl Mulert, Wendy Streeter

Archer King Ltd.

317 W. 46th St., Ste. 32A
New York, NY 10036
(212) 765-3103 Phone
(212) 765-3107 Fax
Literary agent: Archer King

Kingdom Industries Ltd.
(WGA) (Q)

118-11 195th St., P.O. Box 310
Saint Albans, NY 11412-0310
(718) 949-9804 Phone

KMA Agency (WGA) (Q)

11 Broadway, Ste. 1101
New York, NY 10004
(212) 581-4610 Phone

Otto Kozak Literary & Motion Picture Agency
(WGA) (Q)

114 Coronado St.
Atlantic Beach, NY 11509

The Lantz Office

200 W. 57th St., Ste.503
New York, NY 10019
(212) 586-0200 Phone
(212) 262-6659 Fax
E-mail: rlantz@lantzoffice.com
Literary agents: Robert Lantz, Dennis Aspland

Laserson Creative (WGA)

358 13th St.
Brooklyn, NY 11215
(718) 832-1785 Phone

AGENTS

Lionize, Inc. (WGA)

2020 Broadway #2A
New York, NY 10023
(212) 579-5414 Phone

The Literary Group
International (WGA) (Q)

270 Lafayette St. #1505
New York, NY 10012
(212) 274-1616 Phone
(212) 274-9876 Fax
Web: www.theliterarygroup.com
E-mail: litgrpfw@aol.com
Literary agents: Frank Weimann,
Andrew Stuart

The Luedtke Agency
(WGA) (Q)

1674 Broadway #7A
New York, NY 10019
(212) 765-9564 Phone

Elaine Markson Literary
Agency (WGA)

44 Greenwich Ave.
New York, NY 10011
(212) 243-8480 Phone

Harold Matson
Company, Inc.

276 Fifth Ave.
New York, NY 10001
(212) 679-4490 Phone

McIntosh and Otis, Inc.
(WGA) (Q)

353 Lexington Ave.
New York, NY 10016
(212) 687-7400 Phone
(212) 687-6894 Fax
Literary agents: Traceu Adams,
Gene Winick, Dorothy Markinko,
Sam Pinkus, Elizabeth Winick

Claudia Menza Literary
Agency

1170 Broadway, Ste. 807
New York, NY 10001
(212) 889-6850 Phone
Literary agent: Claudia Menza

Helen Merrill, Ltd.

295 Lafayette St., Ste. 915
New York, NY 10012
(212) 226-5015 Phone
(212) 226-5079 Fax
Literary agents: Patrick Herold,
Morgan Jenness, Beth Blickers

> You have to try—in the structure of an hour and a half movie—to arrange scenes that appear to follow each other in what seems to be a natural way, but is anything but natural. Because you can choose only forty, forty-five, fifty scenes to tell a story. You have to pick those fifty scenes very carefully if you're going to get a rich story.
> —PAUL SCHRADER

Allan S. Meyers Agency
(WGA)

105 Court St.
Brooklyn, NY 11201

Milestone Literary Agency
(WGA)

247 W. 26th St. #3A
New York, NY 10001
(212) 691-0560 Phone

★ William Morris Agency, Inc. (WGA)

1325 Ave. of the Americas
New York, NY 10019
(212) 586-5100 Phone
Literary agents: Virginia Barber, Mel Berger, Bill Contardi, Joni Evans, Tracy Fisher, Karen Gerwin-Stoopack, Suzanne Gluck, Owen Laster, Jay Mandel, Leora Rosenberg, Jennifer Rudolph Walsh

Henry Morrison, Inc.
(WGA) (Q)

105 S. Bedford Rd. #306A
Mount Kisco, NY 10549
(914) 666-3500 Phone

Omnibus Productions
(WGA) (Q)

184 Thompson St. #1G
New York, NY 10012
(212) 995-2941 Phone

Omnipop, Inc. Talent Agency (WGA)

55 W. Old Country Rd.
Hicksville, NY 11801
(516) 937-6011 Phone
Literary agents: Jamie Ducat, Tom Ingegno

AGENTS

Fifi Oscard Agency, Inc.
(WGA)

. . . .

24 W. 40th St., 17th Fl.
New York, NY 10018
(212) 764-1100 Phone
(212) 840-5019 Fax
E-mail: fifioscard@aol.com
Literary agents: Carme LaVia,
Peter Sawyer, Frances Del Duca,
Adam Chromy, Ivy Fischer-Stone,
Carolyn French, Kevin McShane

Dorothy Palmer Agency
(WGA)

. . . .

235 W. 56th St. #24k
New York, NY 10019
(212) 765-4280 Phone

Paramuse Artists Association (WGA)

. . . .

25 Central Park W. #1B
New York, NY 10023
(212) 758-5055 Phone

Professional Artists Unlimited (WGA)

. . . .

321 W. 44th St. #605
New York, NY 10036
(212) 247-8770 Phone
(212) 977-5686 Fax

Literary agents: Sheldon Lubliner,
Marilynn Scott Murphy, Kevin
Hale

Raines and Raines (WGA)

. . . .

103 Kenyon Rd.
Medusa, NY 12120
(518) 239-8311 Phone
(518) 239-6029 Fax
Literary agents: Joan Raines,
Keith Korman

The Robbins Office (WGA)

. . . .

405 Park Ave., 9th Fl.
New York, NY 10022
(212) 223-0720 Phone

Flora Roberts, Inc. (WGA)

. . . .

393 W. 49th St. #5G
New York, NY 10019
(212) 355-4165 Phone

Rosenstone/Wender

. . . .

38 E. 29th St., 10th Fl.
New York, NY 10016
(212) 725-9445 Phone
(212) 725-9447 Fax
Literary agents: Howard
Rosenstone, Phyllis Wender, Ron
Gwiazda

Victoria Sanders Literary Agency (WGA) (Q)

241 Ave. of the Americas
New York, NY 10014
(212) 633-8811 Phone

Susan Schulman Literary Agency (WGA) (Q)

454 W. 44th St.
New York, NY 10036
(212) 713-1633 Phone
Literary agents: Susan Schulman,
Christine Morin

Laurens R. Schwartz, Esq. (WGA) (Q)

5 E. 22nd St. #15D
New York, NY 10010-5315
(212) 228-2614 Phone
(212) 228-6093 Fax

Robert L. Seigel (WGA)

67-21F 193rd Ln.
Fresh Meadows, NY 11365
(718) 454-7044 Phone

Edythea Ginis Selman Literary Agent (WGA)

14 Washington Pl.
New York, NY 10003
(212) 473-1874 Phone

The Stardust Agency

P.O. Box 610
Lynbrook, NY 11563
(516) 596-0406 Phone
(516) 596-0646 Fax
Literary agents: William Decker,
Albert Ross, Peter Sloan

Lyle Steele & Company, Ltd. (WGA) (Q)

511 E. 73rd #7
New York, NY 10021
(212) 288-2981 Phone

Sterling Lord Literistic, Inc. (WGA) (Q)

65 Bleecker St.
New York, NY 10012
(212) 780-6050 Phone
(212) 780-6095 Fax

In the hands of a free spirit, the cinema is a perilous weapon.
—LUIS BUÑUEL

AGENTS

Miriam Stern, Esq. (WGA)

303 E. 83rd St.
New York, NY 10028
(212) 794-1289 Phone
Literary agent: Miriam Stern

Joan Stewart Agency

800 Third Ave., 34th Fl.
New York, NY 10022
(212) 418-7255 Phone
(212) 888-2953 Fax
Literary agent: Joan Stewart

Marianne Strong
Literary Agency

65 E. 96th St.
New York, NY 10128
(212) 249-1000 Phone
(212) 831-3241 Fax
E-mail: stronglit@aol.com
Literary agents: Marianne Strong,
Craig Kayser, Grace Morgan,
Shannon Schuhmann, Mai-Ding
Wong

Sydra Technique Corp.

998C Old Country Rd. #224
Plainview, NY 11803
(516) 496-0953 Phone
(516) 682-8153 Fax
E-mail: sbuck@sydra-technique.com
Literary agent: Sid Buck

Talent Representatives, Inc.
(WGA) (Q)

20 E. 53rd St.
New York, NY 10022
(212) 752-1835 Phone
Literary agents: Honey Raider,
Jerre Brisky, Richie Kern

The Vines Agency, Inc.

648 Broadway #901
New York, NY 10012
(212) 777-5522 Phone
(212) 777-5978 Fax
Web: www.vinesagency.com
E-mail: jv@vinesagency.com
Literary agents: James C. Vines,
Paul Surdi

Peregrine Whittlesey
Agency (WGA) (Q)

345 E. 80th St.
New York, NY 10021
(212) 737-0153 Phone

Hanns Wolters
International, Inc.

10 W. 37th St., 3rd Fl.
New York, NY 10018

(212) 714-0100 Phone
(212) 643-1412 Fax
E-mail: hannsw@aol.com
Literary agent: Oliver Mahrdt

Ann Wright Representatives (WGA)

165 W. 46th St. #1105
New York, NY 10036-2501
(212) 764-6770 Phone
(212) 764-5125 Fax
Literary agents: Ann Wright, Dan Wright

★ Writers & Artists Agency (WGA)

19 W. 44th St. #1000
New York, NY 10036
(212) 391-1112 Phone
(212) 398-9877 Fax
Literary agents: Nicole Graham, Chris Till

Nick Yellen Creative Agency

Attn: Robin Kaver
1501 Broadway, Ste. 2310
New York, NY 10036
(212) 840-5760 Phone
(212) 840-5776 Fax

▌Ohio

Kick Entertainment (WGA) (Q)

1934 E. 123rd St.
Cleveland, OH 44106
(216) 791-2515 Phone

Le Modeln, Inc. (WGA) (Q)

7536 Market St. #104
Boardman, OH 44512
(330) 758-4417 Phone

A Picture of You (WGA) (Q)

1176 Elizabeth Dr.
Hamilton, OH 45013
(513) 863-1108 Phone
(513) 863-1108 Fax
E-mail: apoy1@aol.com

Tannery Hill Literary Agency (WGA)

6447 Hiram Ave.
Ashtabula, OH 44004
(216) 997-1440 Phone

Universal Talent International

24 W. Daniels
Cincinnati, OH 45219

AGENTS

(513) 369-3398 Phone
(513) 751-5949 Fax
E-mail: talentintellige@webtv.net
Literary agents: Chris Hutchins, Calvin Poole

Qcorp Literary Agency
(WGA) (Q)

4245 S.W. 185th Ave.
Aloha, OR 97007
(503) 649-6038 Phone

▌ Oregon

▌ Pennsylvania

Lois Biggar & Associates
(WGA)

8885 S.W. O'Mara St.
Portland, OR 97223
(503) 639-3686 Phone

Docherty, Inc.

109 Market St.
Pittsburgh, PA 15222
(412) 765-1400 Phone
(412) 765-0403 Fax
E-mail: docherty@sgi.net
Literary agents: Deb Docherty, Theresa Randall, Julie Sciote, Rebecca Thurmer

Creative Communications
(WGA)

6919 S.E. Holgate Blvd.
Portland, OR 97206
(503) 323-4366 Phone

The Good Writers Agency
(WGA) (Q)

Robert Mitnik Agency
(WGA) (Q)

211 N.W. Forest St., Ste. B
Hillsboro, OR 97124
(503) 615-4288 Phone
(503) 640-4776 Fax
Web: www.mitnikagency.com
E-mail: mhobbs@mitnikagency.com
Literary agent: Michael R. Hobbs

113 Henry Hudson Dr.
Delmont, PA 15626
(724) 468-8157 Phone
(724) 468-3420 Fax
E-mail: goodwriters@alltel.net
Literary agents: Sheila Krill, Joseph Krill

Lee Shore Agency

440 Friday Rd.
Pittsburgh, PA 15209
(412) 821-0440 Phone
(412) 821-6099 Fax
Web: www.leeshoreagency.com
E-mail: leeshore1@aol.com
Literary agents: Jennifer Piemme,
Daniel Chiotti

Sister Mania Productions, Inc. (WGA) (Q)

916 Penn St.
Brackenridge, PA 15014
(724) 226-2964 Phone

Toad Hall, Inc. (WGA) (Q)

R.R. 2, Box 2090
Laceyville, PA 18623
(570) 869-2942 Phone

The Winokur Agency (WGA) (Q)

5575 N. Umberland St.
Pittsburgh, PA 15217
(412) 421-9248 Phone

Wordsworth (WGA) (Q)

230 Cherry Ln. Rd.
East Stroudsburg, PA 18301

■ Rhode Island

Hanar Company (WGA)

34 Fairbanks Ave.
Pascoag, RI 02859

Suzanne J. Reynolds Agency (WGA) (Q)

167 Church St.
Tiverton, RI 02878

■ South Carolina

Deuce Talent & Literary Agency (WGA) (Q)

197 Lamplighter Dr. #6C
Winnsboro, SC 29180
(803) 712-0805 Phone

■ Tennessee

Client Fir Phonest Agency (WGA) (Q)

2134 FairFax Ave. #A3
Nashville, TN 37212
(615) 325-4780 Phone

Gil Hayes & Associates
(WGA) (Q)

5125 Barry Rd.
Memphis, TN 38117
(901) 818-0086 Phone

Mirage Enterprises
(WGA) (Q)

5100 Stage Rd. #4
Memphis, TN 38134
(901) 761-9817 Phone

Nash-Angeles

P.O. Box 363
Hendersonville, TN 37077
(615) 347-8258 Phone
E-mail: nafilm1@aol.com
Literary agents: Eddie Reasoner,
Jack Edwards, Rebecca Holden

▌Texas

Philip Adley Agency
(WGA) (Q)

157 Tarmarack Dr.
May, TX 76857-1649
(915) 784-6849 Phone

Bevy Creative Enterprises
(WGA)

7139 Azalea
Dallas, TX 75230
(214) 363-5771 Phone

Thomas D. Boyle (WGA) (Q)

2001 Ross Ave. #3900
Dallas, TX 75201
(214) 661-8913 Phone

▌ *I think our strength, our core, our* dramatis personae, *everything we write about is formed in those early years; and if you forget that person—those early eight to ten years of your life—and become what contemporary success will bring you, it cuts you away from where your strength is as a writer.*

—WILLIAM GOLDMAN, screenwriter, *Butch Cassidy and the Sundance Kid*

The Carolyn Burnam Agency (WGA)

4207 Valleyfield St.
San Antonio, TX 78222-3714
(210) 337-8268 Phone

Farris Literary Agency

P.O. Box 570069
Dallas, TX 75357
(972) 203-8804 Phone
Web: www.farrisliterary.com
E-mail: farris1@airmail.net
Literary agents: Mike Farris,
Susan Morgan Farris

Stanton & Associates Literary Agency (WGA)

4413 Clemson Dr.
Garland, TX 75042
(972) 276-5427 Phone
Web: www.harrypreston.com
E-mail: preston8@onramp.net
Literary agents: Henry Stanton,
Harry Preston

▌Utah

Opfar Literary Agency (WGA)

1357 W., 800 S.
Orem, UT 84058
(801) 224-3836 Phone

Walker Talent Agency, Inc. (WGA) (Q)

1080 S. 1500 E. #98
Clearfield, UT 84015
(801) 725-2118 Phone
(801) 276-0946 Fax
Literary agent: Willie Walker

▌Virginia

The Deiter Literary Agency (WGA) (Q)

6207 Fushsimi Ct.
Burke, VA 22015
(703) 440-8920 Phone

Filmwriters Literary Agency (WGA)

4932 Long Shadow Dr.
Midlothian, VA 23112
(804) 744-1718 Phone
Literary agent: Helene Wagner

Nimbus Production Group, Inc. (WGA)

19999 Ebenezer Church Rd.
Bluemont, VA 20135
(540) 554-8587 Phone

AGENTS

The Cano Agency (WGA) (Q)

8257 Latona Ave., N.E.
Seattle, WA 98115
(206) 522-5974 Phone

Cedar Grove Agency Entertainment

P.O. Box 1692
Issaquah, WA 98027
E-mail: cedargroveagency@juno
.com
Literary agent: Amy B. Taylor

International Creative Management

Oxford House
76 Oxford
London, England W1R1RB

Zebra Agency

Broadlands House
1 Broadlands, Shevington
Lancashire, England WN6 8DH
0794 958 4758 Phone
Web: www.zebragency.co.uk
E-mail: mail@zebraagency.co.uk

Lee Allan Agency (WGA)

7464 N. 107th St.
Milwaukee, WI 53224-3706
(414) 357-7708 Phone

MANAGERS

T HERE IS SOME CROSSOVER in what managers and agents do, but generally an agent sells your script while a manager guides your career. Managers tend to be more approachable than agents and may help you get a better agent than you could on your own. Some management firms have become very powerful in the industry and have moved into production. (While agents are barred from production, managers are barred from negotiating on their clients' behalf. You need an agent or attorney for this.)

A good manager can be very helpful to a writer who is just starting out, but you pay a price: managers typically take 10 to 15 percent of your earnings on top of the 10 percent you'll pay an agent (leaving you with 75 or 80 percent for all the sweat and blood you put into your script).

Never send a script to anyone without permission. Just as with agents and producers, always start with a query letter and self-addressed stamped envelope. Alternatively, you can contact them via e-mail to see if they like your pitch.

In the following listings you'll find the most influential managers denoted by ★ .

It's like carpentry, it's basically putting down some kind of structural form that they can mess around with. And as long as they keep the structural form, whatever I have written is relatively valid; a scene will hold, regardless of the dialogue. It's the thrust of the scene that's kept pure.

—WILLIAM GOLDMAN, screenwriter, *Butch Cassidy and the Sundance Kid*

AEI/Atchity Editorial/Entertainment International

9601 Wilshire Blvd., Box 1202
Beverly Hills, CA 90210
(323) 932-0407 Phone
E-mail: webaei@aol.com

Artist Management Group

9465 Wilshire Blvd.
Beverly Hills, CA 90212
(310) 860-8000 Phone

The Bauer Company

9300 Wilshire Blvd., Penthouse
Beverly Hills, CA 90212
(310) 247-3880 Phone
(310) 247-3881 Fax

Baumgarten/Prophet Entertainment

1640 S. Sepulveda Blvd., Ste. 218
Los Angeles, CA 90025
(310) 445-1601 Phone
(310) 996-1892 Fax

★ Benderspink Management

6735 Yucca St.
Hollywood, CA 90028

(323) 856-5500 Phone
(323) 856-5502 Fax

Michael Black Management

5750 Wilshire Blvd., Ste. 640
Los Angeles, CA 90036
(323) 965-2530 Phone

Blair Silver & Company Entertainment Management

P.O. Box 3188
Manhattan Beach, CA 90266
(310) 546-4669 Phone
E-mail: blairsilver@aol.com

★ Brillstein-Grey Management

9150 Wilshire Blvd., Ste. 350
Beverly Hills, CA 90212
(310) 275-6135 Phone
(310) 275-6180 Fax
Clients include: Brad Pitt,
Adam Sandler, Jennifer Aniston,
Courtney Cox Arquette,
Martin Short, Lorne Michaels,
and Rudolph Giuliani.

Careyes Entertainment

9000 Sunset Blvd., Ste. 800
Los Angeles, CA 90069

(310) 888-1240 Phone
(310) 888-1243 Fax
E-mail: careyesent@aol.com

Celebrity Endeavors

433 N. Camden Dr., Ste. 600
Beverly Hills, CA 90210
(310) 271-5512 Phone

Chic Productions & Management

12228 Venice Blvd., Ste. 499
Los Angeles, CA 90066
(310) 391-2152 Phone

Creative Management Group

301 W. 53rd St., Ste. 4K
New York, NY 10019
(212) 245-3250/(310) 888-0082
   Phone

Crescendo Entertainment Group

407 N. Sycamore Ave., Ste. 3
Los Angeles, CA 90036
(323) 937-9700 Phone
Web: www.crescendoentertainment
   group.com

Edmonds Management

1635 N. Cahuenga Blvd., 5th Fl.
Los Angeles, CA 90028
(323) 769-2444 Phone

Elkins Entertainment Corp.

8306 Wilshire Blvd., Ste. 438
Beverly Hills, CA 90211
(310) 501-9900 Phone
(310) 501-9800 Fax
Web: www.elkinsent.com
E-mail: elkins@elkinsent.com

Energy (Brooklyn Weaver)

10833 Wilshire Blvd., Ste. 219
Los Angeles, CA 90024
(310) 475-0101 Phone
Web: www.energyentertainment.net
E-mail: info@energyentertainment
   .net

Ensemble Entertainment

10474 Santa Monica Blvd., Ste. 380
Los Angeles, CA 90025
(310) 882-8900 Phone

Envision Management

1207 Fourth St., 4th Fl.
Santa Monica, CA 90401
(310) 899-5700 Phone

★ The Firm

9100 Wilshire Blvd., Ste. 400W
Beverly Hills, CA 90212
(310) 246-9000 Phone
Clients include: Leonardo
DiCaprio, Cameron Diaz, Martin
Scorcese, Samuel L. Jackson,
Martin Lawrence, Vin Diesel,
Benicio Del Toro, Ice Cube, Korn,
and Limp Bizkit.

FMA Management

8836 Wonderland Ave.
Los Angeles, CA 90046
(323) 654-1080 Phone
Web: www.fmamanagement.com
E-mail: info@fmamanagement.com

Foundation Management

2121 Ave. of the Stars, Ste. 2900
Los Angeles, CA 90067

Foursight Entertainment

6275 W. Olympic Blvd.
Los Angeles, CA 90048

(323) 549-9899 Phone
Web: www.foursight.com
E-mail: info@foursight.com

Gallagher Literary Management

Attn: Rob Gallagher
8160 Manitoba, Ste. 309
Los Angeles, CA 90293
(310) 822-2070 Phone
Web: www.robgallagher.free
   servers.com

Grade A Entertainment

368 N. La Cienega Blvd.
Los Angeles, CA 90048
E-mail: gradeaprod@aol.com

Handprint Entertainment

1100 Glendon Ave., Ste. 1000
Los Angeles, CA 90024
(310) 481-4400 Phone

▌ **TIP:** Send an e-mail to everyone you know announcing that you've finished your script and you're marketing it yourself. You might be surprised—a friend might have gone to school with someone famous, or be related to a television producer or publicist. Those leads are like gold—use them.

Himber Entertainment, Inc.

211 S. Beverly Dr., Ste. 208
Beverly Hills, CA 90212
(310) 276-2500 Phone

Hofflund/Polone

9465 Wilshire Blvd., Ste. 820
Beverly Hills, CA 90212
(310) 859-1971 Phone

HSI Entertainment

3630 Eastham Dr.
Culver City, CA 90232
(310) 558-7200 Phone

Incognito Management

345 N. Maple Dr., Ste. 348
Beverly Hills, CA 90210
(310) 246-1500 Phone

★ Industry Entertainment

955 S. Carrillo Dr., Ste. 300
Los Angeles, CA 90048
(323) 954-9000 Phone
Clients include: Angelina Jolie,
Billy Bob Thornton, Ted Danson,
Callie Khouri, Tommy Schlamme,
Jeff Goldblum, and Stephen
Hopkins.

Infinity Management International

122 N. Hamilton Dr.
Beverly Hills, CA 90211
(323) 651-3200 Phone

Inneract Entertainment

5410 Wilshire Blvd., Ste. 708
Los Angeles, CA 90036
(323) 965-0967 Phone

International Digital Artists

4223 Glencoe Ave., Ste. C-107
Marina del Rey, CA 90292
(310) 306-4001 Phone

Jaret Entertainment

2017 Pacific Ave., Ste. 2
Venice, CA 90291
(310) 883-8807 Phone

Kaplan/Perrone Entertainment

10202 W. Washington Blvd.
Astaire Bldg., Ste. 3003
Culver City, CA 90232
(310) 244-6681 Phone
(310) 244-2151 Fax

Kritzer Entertainment

275 S. Beverly Dr., Ste. 215
Beverly Hills, CA 90212
(310) 278-3981 Phone
E-mail: krikra@aol.com

Lasalle Management Group, Inc.

1650 Broadway, Ste. 508
New York, NY 10019
(212) 541-4443 Phone
Web: www.lasallemanagement
group.com

Lasher, McManus & Robinson

1964 Westwood Blvd. #400
Los Angeles, CA 90025
(310) 446-1466 Phone
E-mail: lmrla@earthlink.net

Lighthouse Entertainment

409 N. Camden Dr. #202
Beverly Hills, CA 90210
(310) 246-0499 Phone

Lovett Management

1327 Brinkley Ave.
Los Angeles, CA 90049
(310) 451-2536 Phone

Mason Burgess Lifschultz

3311 Barham Blvd.
Los Angeles, CA 90068
(323) 850-7713 Phone
E-mail: burgess.mgmt@usa.net

Mastermind Entertainment

2444 Wilshire Blvd., Ste. 303
Santa Monica, CA 90403
(310) 449-9171 Phone

MBST Entertainment

345 N. Maple Dr., Ste. 200
Beverly Hills, CA 90210
(310) 385-1820 Phone

Messina Baker Entertainment Corp.

955 Carrilo Dr., Ste. 100
Los Angeles, CA 90048
(323) 954-8600 Phone

★ Mosaic Media Group

9200 Sunset Blvd.
Los Angeles, CA 90069
(310) 786-4900 Phone
(310) 777-2173 Fax
Web: www.mosaicla.com
E-mail: erin@mosaicla.com

Clients include: Jim Carrey, Alanis Morrissette, Ellen DeGeneres, Sean Hayes, Damon Wayans, the Wallflowers, Johnny Rzeznik, and Green Day.

Narelle Sheehan Management

P.O. Box 5055
Beverly Hills, CA 90209
(310) 385-0419 Phone

Nine Yards Entertainment

8840 Wilshire Blvd., 1st Fl.
Beverly Hills, CA 90211
(310) 358-3222 Phone
(310) 358-3270 Fax

O/Z Management

c/o Phoenix Pictures
10202 W. Washington Blvd., Ste. 115B
Culver City, CA 90232
(310) 244-6380 Phone

Overland Literary Management

1701 Harvard St., N.W.
Washington, DC 20009
(202) 667-1135 Phone
(310) 205-8998 (Los Angeles)
E-mail: overlandlitmgt@prodigy.net

Phifer Media Management

2420 Hunter Ave., Ste. 20A
Bronx, NY 10475
(718) 671-7474 Phone
Web: www.pmmagency.tripod.com
E-mail: mike-p@chesma.com

Pinch Entertainment

Attn: Shelley Spevakow
7361 Rosewood Ave.
Los Angeles, CA 90036
(323) 782-3815 Phone
Web: www.pinchentertainment.com
E-mail: info@pinchent.com

The Pitt Group

9465 Wilshire Blvd., Ste. 480
Beverly Hills, CA 90212
(310) 246-4800 Phone

Principato-Young Management

The Brill Bldg., 1619 Broadway, 9th Fl.
New York, NY 10019
(212) 603-1843/(310) 274-4474 Phone

Pro And Con Productions Talent Management

P.O. Box 4399
Glendale, CA 91222-0399
(818) 973-2282 Phone
Web: www.geocities.com/proand
  conprods
E-mail: proandconprods@geocities
  .com

Propaganda Management

940 N. Mansfield Ave.
Hollywood, CA 90038
(323) 462-6400 Phone
(323) 962-7192 Fax

The Radmin Company

9201 Wilshire Blvd., Ste. 305
Beverly Hills, CA 90210
(310) 274-9515 Phone

The Rigberg-Roberts-Rugolo Company

1180 S. Beverly Dr., Ste. 608
Los Angeles, CA 90035
(310) 712-0712 Phone

The Roberts Company

3000 W. Olympic Blvd., Bldg. 2, Ste.
  2525
Santa Monica, CA 90404
(310) 264-4238 Phone

Stephanie Rogers & Associates

8737 Carliatas Joy Ct.
Las Vegas, NV 89117
(702) 255-9999 Phone

TIP: Professional writers don't include an SASE and don't request that a script be returned. They just figure it's the cost of doing business.

A movie, I think, is really only four or five moments between two people; the rest of it exists to give those moments their impact and resonance.
—**ROBERT TOWNE**, screenwriter, *Chinatown*

Rogue Pictures

10202 W. Washington Blvd., Gene
  Autry Bldg., Rm. 1019
Culver City, CA 90232
(310) 244-7399 Phone

Shapiro/West & Associates, Inc.

141 El Camino Dr., Ste. 205
Beverly Hills, CA 90212
(310) 278-8896 Phone

The Marion Rosenberg Office

8428 Melrose Pl., Ste. B
Los Angeles, CA 90069
(323) 653-7383 Phone

The Shuman Company

3815 Hughes Ave., 4th Fl.
Culver City, CA 90232
(310) 841-4344 Phone
E-mail: shumanco@aol.com

Rozon/Mercer Management

201 N. Robertson Blvd., Ste. F
Beverly Hills, CA 90211
(310) 777-1100 Phone

Rick Siegel Management

8060 Melrose Ave., 4th Fl.
Los Angeles, CA 90046
(323) 852-1776 Phone

The Sarkes/Kernis Company

315 S. Beverly Dr., Ste. 216
Beverly Hills, CA 90212
(310) 785-0444 Phone

Steinberg Talent Management Group

1600 Broadway, Ste. 410
New York, NY 10019
(212) 582-7589 Phone
Web: www.members.aol.com/
  nycomedy
E-mail: nycomedy@aol.com

Seven Summits Pictures and Management

8447 Wilshire Blvd., Ste. 200
Beverly Hills, CA 90211
(323) 655-0101 Phone

Tavel Entertainment

9171 Wilshire Blvd., Ste. 406
Beverly Hills, CA 90210
(310) 278-6700 Phone

MANAGERS

★ 3 Arts Entertainment

9460 Wilshire Blvd., 7th Fl.
Beverly Hills, CA 90212
(310) 888-3200/(212) 262-6565
  Phone
Clients include: Chris Rock; Cuba Gooding, Jr.; Keanu Reeves; Matthew Broderick; Debra Messing; Frank Muniz; Bernie Mac; Ethan Hawke; and Oliver Platt.

Tudor Management Group

4712 Admiralty Way #560
Marina del Rey, CA 90292
(310) 247-1660 Phone
E-mail: info@tudorgroup.com

Visionary Management

8265 Sunset Blvd., Ste. 203
Los Angeles, CA 90046
(323) 848-9538 Phone
E-mail: tparz@aol.com

Zanuk Entertainment

2155 Verdugo Blvd. #133
Glendale, CA 91020
(818) 624-1630 Phone
(818) 957-7758 Fax
E-mail: dzanuk@aol.com

★ Zide/Perry Management

9100 Wilshire Blvd., Ste.615 E
Beverly Hills, CA 90212
(310) 887-2999 Phone
(310) 887-2995 Fax
Web: www.inzide.com
These are the producers of *American Pie, American Pie 2, Final Destination,* and *Final Destination 2.*

PRODUCERS

IN MOVIEMAKING, the producer is king. He or she is the one who gets the money together and signs the deals. So why can't you just approach a producer with your script? Producers are very hard to approach. They prefer to get their scripts through agents they trust so they won't have to bother with reviewing stacks of scripts. More often than not, however, they *still* have to review stacks of scripts to find something they like. Most producers complain about how hard it is to find material they can feel passionate about (and passion is a requirement if you're going to spend two to three years of your life getting it made). So if you can get through to them and they like your pitch, you may be able to skirt the system and get them to read it.

The lesson here is that there are no hard and fast rules in Hollywood. There is, however, intense competition. Very few screenplays make it to the screen, so you must be (pick any two of the following): *determined, talented,* or *lucky.* Start with a query letter and follow up with a phone call. Give a producer a week to review a query, or six weeks to review a script before following up. Remember, though, that getting a movie made is a struggle for everyone involved. Agents', managers', and producers' jobs are even harder than yours, as they have to convince people to plunk down tens of millions of dollars on your story. For this reason, great writing often isn't what gets movies made, *leverage* is. If a producer brings a studio a beautiful and moving script with Colin Firth and Judy Davis attached, or an insipid teen comedy with Ashton Kutcher, Britney Spears,

---

TIP: Never launch into a major rewrite unless you've heard the same criticism from at least four people.

and Jack Black attached, which one do you think they'll make? If you want to succeed, look at it from Hollywood's point of view. Producers are thinking, how am I going to make money on this? How much publicity will this get? How much of a sure thing is it?

"Attached"? What does that mean? It means that a person has agreed to play the part. It's normally the producer's job to attach talent, but if you have access to anyone famous who might agree to be in your movie, you'll have a much easier time getting a producer's interest. What if you don't know anyone? Pitch the merits of the script; try to make it sound exciting and unique. You probably won't be able to get them on the phone unless they like your query, so start there. Always personalize a query; send it to someone by name rather than just the production company. Hollywood is notorious for rapid turnover so, again, consider buying the *Hollywood Creative Directory* (Lone Eagle Publishing, $64.95) for the most up-to-date addresses and titles of the players at every major production house. (An online edition is also available (www.hcdonline.com) for $19.95 for a one-week trial period, which may be enough time to gather the information you need.)

Don't send it to everyone at once. The first question you'll get when someone's truly interested is, "Who else has seen this?" The movie business revolves around hype—if your script has been all around town it's not going to interest them as much as if you just finished it and haven't breathed a word to anyone. If you don't hear from them, should you follow up? No, absolutely not. And yes, probably. Most agents, managers, and producers will emphatically tell you *not* to call them, they don't want to be pestered. While that's true, it's easy for them to forget about you unless you've connected to them personally. They may like your work but be swamped with more pressing concerns. They may put you into a stack and forget about you. The script is the thing, true, but your personal enthusiasm, drive, and charisma can have a tremendous effect on people's response to your work. If you're friendly, personable, and confident, the phone will be your best friend. Call everyone and keep calling—sooner or later you'll talk your way into an opportunity.

Here's the key to the producer players:

★ Most influential producers

(ANM) Animation producers

A & E Television Networks

235 E. 45th St.
New York, NY 10017
(212) 210-1400 Phone
Web: www.aande.com
Credits: *A&E's Biography,*
American Justice, Investigative
Reports, original movies, Behind
Closed Doors with Joan Lunden,
Cold Case Files, City Confidential

A Band Apart
(**Writer/Director: Quentin Tarantino**)

7966 Beverly Blvd.
Los Angeles, CA 90048
(323) 951-4600 Phone
Credits: *Pulp Fiction, Reservoir*
Dogs, Good Will Hunting, Jackie
Brown, The Mexican

Abandon Entertainment

135 W. 50th St., Ste. 2305
New York, NY 10020
(212) 246-4445 Phone
(212) 397-8361 Fax
Web: www.abandonent.com
Credits: *Oxygen; Pros and Cons;*
Time Shifters; Off the Lip; Mexico
City; Scotland, PA; Glory Days

Acapella Pictures

8271 Melrose Ave., Ste.101
Los Angeles, CA 90046
(323) 782-8200 Phone
(323) 782-8210 Fax
Credits: *The Brave, The House of*
Mirth

Acorn Entertainment (ANM)

5777 W. Century Blvd.
Los Angeles, CA 90045
(818) 340-5272 Phone

Act III Productions
(**Producer: Norman Lear**)

100 N. Crescent Dr., Ste.250
Beverly Hills, CA 90210
(310) 385-4111 Phone
(310) 385-4148 Fax
Credits: *Fried Green Tomatoes, 704*
Hauser, Powers That Be

Adam Productions

11777 San Vincente Blvd., Ste. 880
Los Angeles, CA 90040
(310) 442-3580 Phone

Agamemnon Films Inc.

650 N. Bronson Ave., Ste. B-225
Los Angeles, CA 90004
(323) 960-4066 Phone

Credits: *Treasure Island, Crucifer of Blood, A Man for All Seasons, Mother Lode, Antony and Cleopatra, Alaska, Needful Things, The Bible*

Alcon Entertainment

10390 Santa Monica Blvd., Ste. 250
Los Angeles, CA 90025
(310) 789-3040 Phone
(310) 789-3060 Fax
Credits: *My Dog Skip; Dude, Where's My Car?; The Affair of the Necklace; Lost & Found; Insomnia*

All Girl Productions
(Actress: Bette Midler)

10153 Riverside Dr., Ste. 249
Toluca Lake, CA 91602
(818) 358-4100 Phone
(818) 358-4119 Fax

★ Alliance Atlantis Communications Corporation (Canada)

121 Bloor St. E., Ste. 1500
Toronto, Ont. M4W 3M5 Canada

(416) 967-1174 Phone
(416) 960-0971 Fax
Web: www.allianceatlantis.com
E-mail: info@allianceatlantis.com
Credits: *Life with Judy Garland: Me and My Shadows, When Billie Beat Bobby, Haven, eXistenZ, The Sweet Hereafter, Sunshine, Joan of Arc, Nuremberg, CSI, CSI: Miami, Morvern Callar, Formula 51*

★ Alliance Atlantis Communications Corporation (U.S.)

808 Wilshire Blvd., Ste. 300
Santa Monica, CA 90401
(310) 899-8000 Phone
(310) 899-8100 Fax
Web: www.allianceatlantis.com/
    motionpictures
E-mail: info@allianceatlantis.com
Credits: *Life with Judy Garland: Me and My Shadows, When Billie Beat Bobby, Haven, eXistenZ, The Sweet Hereafter, Sunshine, Joan of Arc, Nuremberg, CSI, CSI: Miami, Morvern Callar, Formula 51*

▌ *The more successful the villain, the more successful the picture.*
—ALFRED HITCHCOCK

Allied Entertainment Group

8899 Beverly Blvd., Ste. 911
West Hollywood, CA 90048
(310) 271-0703 Phone
(310) 271-0706 Fax

Alphaville
(Producers: Sean Daniel/Jim Jacks)

5555 Melrose Ave., DeMille Bldg.
Hollywood, CA 90038
(323) 956-4803 Phone
Credits: *The Hunted, Dark Blue, The Scorpion King, Rat Race, The Mummy, The Mummy Returns, Tombstone, Dazed and Confused, Michael, The Jackal, The Gift, Down to Earth*

Amen Ra (Actor: Wesley Snipes)

520 Washington Blvd., #813
Marina del Rey, CA 90292
(310) 246-6510 Phone
(310) 550-1932 Fax
Credits: *Blade II: The Bloodhunt, Undisputed, FutureSport, The Big Hit, Down in the Delta, Blade, John Henrik Clarke: A Great and Mighty Walk, The Art of War, Disappearing Acts*

American Cinema International

4640 Lankershim Blvd., Ste. 500
N. Hollywood, CA 91602
(818) 985-8500 Phone
(818) 985-4845 Fax

American Empirical Productions
(Writer/Director: Wes Anderson)

36 E. 23rd St., 6th Fl.
New York, NY 10010
(212) 475-1771 Phone

American Entertainment Co. (Actor: Bill Paxton)

5225 Wilshire Blvd. #615
Los Angeles, CA 90036
(323) 939-6746 Phone
(323) 939-6747 Fax

American World Pictures

6355 Topanga Canyon Blvd., Ste. 428
Woodland Hills, CA 91367
(818) 715-1480 Phone
(818) 715-1081 Fax
E-mail: awpics@earthlink.net
Credits: *Instinct to Kill, Devil's Prey, Bad Karma, Mercy Streets, Extreme Days, Beyond the City Limits, Sacrifice, Blowback, Misbegotten, The Base. The Base 2, The Ex-Public Enemy #1, Night of the Running Man, Sex and a Girl, Betrayal, The Wisher, Stealing*

Candy, White Rush, Chopin: Desire for Love, The Wisher, Mail Order Bride, The Anarchist Cookbook, Night at the Golden Eagle, Snow Job

American Zoetrope

(Director/Producer:
Francis Coppola/Fred Fuchs)

. . . .

808 Wilshire Blvd. 3rd Fl.
Santa Monica, CA 90401
(310) 899-8000/(212) 708-0400
  Phone
(310) 899-8135/(212) 708-0475 Fax
Web: www.zoetrope.com
Credits: *Pumpkin, CQ, No Such Thing, Virgin Suicides, Jeepers Creepers*

Amesell Entertainment

. . . .

12001 Ventura Pl., Ste. 404
Studio City, CA 91604
(818) 766-8500 Phone
(818) 766-7873 Fax

AM Productions & Management (Actors: Ann-Margaret/Burt Reynolds)

. . . .

8899 Beverly Blvd., Ste. 713
Los Angeles, CA 90048
(310) 275-9081 Phone
(310) 275-9082 Fax

Credits: *Driven, Blonde, Tempted, Any Given Sunday, Snapshots, A Woman's a Helluva Thing*

Angel Ark Productions

(Actor: Jason Alexander)

. . . .

12711 Ventura Blvd., Ste. 330
Studio City, CA 91604
818-508-3338 Phone
818-508-2009 Fax
Credits: *Bob Patterson, Just Looking, On Edge, For Better or Worse, Shallow Hal, Agent Cody Banks*

Angel/Brown Productions

. . . .

1416 N. La Brea, Bldg. E, 2nd Fl
Hollywood, CA 90028
(323) 802-1535 Phone
(323) 802-1540 Fax
Credits: *Shadow Walkers, Young Blades, Night Visions, Door to Door, X-Files, Goosebumps, Body Bags, The Fearing Mind, Animorphs, Battlestar Galactica*

Angry Dragon Entertainment

(Actor: Dean Cain)

. . . .

10202 Washington Blvd.
Culver City, CA 90232
(310) 244-6996 Phone
Credits: *Ripley's Believe It or Not*

Angry Films, Inc.
(Producer: Don Murphy)

Columbia Pictures
10202 Washington Blvd., Poitier
   Bldg. #3206
Culver City, CA 90232
(310) 244-7590 Phone
(310) 244-2060 Fax
Credits: *Bully, Natural Born Killers, Apt Pupil, Permanent Midnight, From Hell*

Apatow Productions

2900 W. Olympic Blvd., Ste. 141
Santa Monica, CA 90404
(310) 255-7026 Phone
(310) 255-7025 Fax
Credits: *Undeclared, Freaks and Geeks, The Ben Stiller Show, The Larry Sanders Show, The Cable Guy, Celtic Pride, Heavyweights*

Apostle Pictures
(Actor: Denis Leary)

The Ed Sullivan Theater
1697 Broadway, Ste. 906
New York, NY 10019
(212) 541-4323 Phone
E-mail: apostlepix@aol.com
Credits: *Blow, Monument Avenue, The Job*

Appleseed Entertainment, LLC

9801 Amestay Ave.
Los Angeles, CA 91325
(818) 718-6000 Phone
(818) 993-8720 Fax
Web: www.appleseedent
   ertainment.com
Credits: *Nickel & Dime; Good Morning, Vietnam; Without a Clue; What Are We Doing to Our Children; Dying with Dignity; Not a Question of Courage; Hope Ranch; Cupid's Prey*

Arama Entertainment, Inc.

18034 Ventura Blvd., Ste. 435
Encino, CA 91316
(818) 788-6400 Phone
(818) 990-9344 Fax
E-mail: aramaent@aol.com
Credits: *The Heist, Black Eagle, The Last Word, MichaelAngel, Triumph of the Spirit, Eminent Domain, Warriors*

Arlington Entertainment

9200 Sunset Blvd., Ste. 1209
Los Angeles, CA 90069
(310) 247-1863 Phone
(310) 247-1864 Fax
Credits: *Masks of Death, Murder Elite, One-Way Ticket to Hollywood*

Arrow Films International

57 W. 38th St., Ste. 302
New York, NY 10036
(212) 719-4548 Phone
(212) 719-4549 Fax
E-mail: arrowfilmsjmc@aol.com
Credits: *Echoes, Under the Skin, Day at the Beach, Nosferatu, The Titanic Chronicle, The Autumn Heart, 30 Days, Ponette, Restless, My Life's in Turnaround, Dog Run, Maelstrom, See Jane Run, The Independent, The Curse*

Artisan Entertainment

2700 Colorado Ave., 2nd Fl.
Santa Monica, CA 90404
(310) 449-9200 Phone
(310) 255-3840 Fax
Web: www.artisanent.com
Credits: *Amandla! A Revolution in Four-Part Harmony, Roger Dodger, Standing in the Shadows of Motown, National Lampoon's Van Wilder, Jonah-A VeggieTales Movie, Made, Requiem for a Dream, The Blair Witch Project, Dr. T and the Women, The Limey, Stir of Echoes, Buena Vista Social Club, Startup.com , Dirty Dancing 2, Iron Fist*

Artist View Entertainment

12500 Riverside Dr., Ste. 201
North Hollywood, CA 91607

(818) 752-2480 Phone
(818) 752-9339 Fax

The Artists' Colony

256 S. Robertson Blvd., Ste. 1500
Beverly Hills, CA 90211
(310) 720-8300 Phone
Web: www.theartistscolony.com
Credits: *Snow Falling on Cedars; Till the End of Time; Shattered Image; A Girl, Three Guys and a Gun; Heroes*

Asis Productions
(Actor: Jeff Bridges)

200 N. Larchmont Blvd., Ste. 2
Los Angeles, CA 90004
(323) 871-4290 Phone
(323) 871-4847 Fax
Credits: *American Heart, Hidden in America*

Associated Television International

4401 Wilshire Blvd.
Los Angeles, CA 90010
(323) 556-5600 Phone
(323) 556-5610 Fax
E-mail: associatedtv@msn.com

Atelier Pictures

280 S. Beverly Dr. #500
Beverly Hills, CA 90212
(310) 888-7727/805-466-4660
  Phone
Web: www.atelierpix.com
E-mail: webm@atelierpix.com
Credits: *Please Don't Walk Around in the Nude, Starfish, Everyman*

Atlantic Streamline

1323 A Third St.
Santa Monica, CA 90401
(310) 319-9366 Phone
Web: www.atlanticstreamline.com
E-mail: info@atlanticstreamline
  .com
Credits: *Igby Goes Down, The Thirteenth Floor, All the Queen's Men*

Atlas Entertainment

(Producer: Charles Roven)

9169 Sunset Blvd.
Los Angeles, CA 90069
(310) 724-7350 Phone
(310) 724-7345 Fax

Credits: *12 Monkeys, Cool Runnings, City of Angels, Three Kings, Scooby Doo, Bullet Proof Monk*

Atman Entertainment

7966 Beverly Blvd., 3rd Fl.
Los Angeles, CA 90048
(323) 951-4600 Phone
Credits: *Fight Club, Under Suspicion*

Atmosphere Entertainment, Inc.

1828 Broadway, 2nd Fl.
Santa Monica, CA 90404
(310) 449-9220 Phone
(310) 449-9240 Fax
Web: www.atmosphereent.com
E-mail: movies@atmosphereent
  .com

Attract Media

Attn: Paul Lindsey, New Projects
133 Wagstaff Ln.
Jacksdale, Nottingham
England NG16 5JN
E-mail: scripts@attract.co.uk

Films should not address themselves to what people want to see . . . films should try to address themselves to what people need to see.
  —PAUL SCHRADER

PRODUCERS

Aurora Productions

8642 Melrose Ave., Ste. 200
Los Angeles, CA 90069
(310) 854-6900 Phone
(310) 854-0583 Fax
Credits: *The Rock, Eddie & the Cruisers, Heart Like a Wheel*

Automatic Pictures

5225 Wilshire Blvd., Ste. 525
Los Angeles, CA 90036
(323) 935-1800 Phone
(323) 935-8040 Fax
Credits: *There's Something About Mary, Wicked*

Avalanche! Entertainment

506 Santa Monica Blvd., Ste. 322
Santa Monica, CA 90401
(310) 395-3660 Phone
(310) 395-8322 Fax

Avenue Pictures

11111 Santa Monica Blvd., Ste. 525
Los Angeles, CA 90025
(310) 996-6800 Phone
(310) 473-4376 Fax
Credits: *Short Cuts, The Player, Restoration, Drugstore Cowboy, Wayward Son, Wit, Path to War*

Avnet-Kerner Company

3815 Hughes Ave.
Culver City, CA 90232-2715
(310) 838-2500 Phone
(310) 204-4208 Fax

Axial Entertainment

20 W. 21st St., 8th Fl.
New York, NY 10010
Web: www.axialentertainment.com

The Badham Company

(Director: John Badham)

3344 Cleredon Rd.
Beverly Hills, CA 90210
818-990-9495 Phone
Web: www.badhamcompany.com
E-mail: development@badham company.com
Credits: *Nick of Time, Stakeout, Stakeout 2, War Games, Jack Bull*

Baer Animation Company

(ANM)

7743 Woodrow Wilson Dr.
Los Angeles, CA 90046
(323) 874-9122 Phone
Credits: *Roger Rabbit, The Prince & the Pauper, Annabelle's Wish*

Bakula Productions, Inc.
(Actor: Scott Bakula)

. . . .

c/o Paramount Pictures
5555 Melrose Ave.
Los Angeles, CA 90038
(323) 956-3030 Phone
Credits: *What Girls Learn, Papa's Angels, Mr. & Mrs. Smith, The Bachelor's Baby, Prowler, I Do! I Do!, The Importance of Being Wilde*

Ballpark Productions

. . . .

P.O. Box 508
Venice, CA 90294
(310) 827-1328 Phone
(310) 577-9626 Fax
Credits: *The Four Feathers, Crimson Tide, Colors, Lean on Me, The Peacemaker, Very Bad Things, Le Divorce*

Ballyhoo, Inc.

. . . .

6738 Wedgewood Pl.
Los Angeles, CA 90068
(323) 874-3396 Phone
Credits: *Seven Years in Tibet, Bounce, The Opposite of Sex, About Schmidt*

Baltimore/Spring Creek Pictures, LLC
(Director/Producer: Barry Levinson/Paula Weinstein)

. . . .

4000 Warner Blvd.
Burbank, CA 91522-0768
(818) 954-1210 Phone
Web: www.levinson.com
Credits: *Analyze This, Analyze That, Liberty Heights, The Perfect Storm, An Everlasting Piece, Bandits, Possession*

Bandeira Entertainment

. . . .

8447 Wilshire Blvd., Ste. 212
Beverly Hills, CA 90211
(323) 866-3535 Phone

Barnstorm Films
(Director: Tony Bill)

. . . .

73 Market St.
Venice, CA 90291
(310) 396-5937 Phone
Credits: *Taxi Driver, Untamed Heart, My Bodyguard, Five Corners, The Sting*

TIP: You might be better off with a smaller agent when starting out. Big agents have big overhead so they favor clients that are bringing in big money.

PRODUCERS

Barwood Films

(Actress/Director/Producer:
Barbra Streisand)

330 W. 58th St.
New York, NY 10019
(212) 765-7191 Phone
(212) 765-6988 Fax
Credits: *Serving in Silence, Prince of Tides, The Mirror Has Two Faces, Yentl, Reel Models: The 1st Women in Film, Varian's War, What Makes a Family, The Living Century*

Baumgarten/Prophet Entertainment

1640 S. Sepulveda Blvd., Ste. 218
Los Angeles, CA 90025
(310) 455-1601 Phone
(310) 996-1892 Fax

Carol Baum Productions

8899 Beverly Blvd., Ste. 721
Los Angeles, CA 90048
(310) 550-4575 Phone
(310) 550-2088 Fax
Credits: *Fly Away Home, Father of the Bride, Dead Ringers, Kicking and Screaming, My First Mister, IQ, The Good Girl*

Bay Films

(Director: Michael Bay)

2110 Broadway
Santa Monica, CA 90404
(310) 829-7799 Phone
(310) 829-7099 Fax
Credits: *Pearl Harbor, Armageddon, The Rock, Bad Boys*

★ Beacon Communications

120 Broadway #200
Santa Monica, CA 90401
(310) 260-7000 Phone
(310) 260-7050 Fax
Credits: *For Love of the Game, Commitments, Air Force One, A Thousand Acres, End of Days, The Hurricane, Bring It On, Family Man, Thirteen Days, Spy Game, Emperor's Club, Tuck Everlasting*

★ Bedford Falls Company

(Director: Ed Zwick)

409 Santa Monica Blvd., PH
Santa Monica, CA 90401
(310) 394-5022 Phone
(310) 394-5825 Fax
Credits: *Traffic, Once and Again, Dangerous Beauty, Shakespeare in Love, thirtysomething, Legends of the Fall, I Am Sam, The Last Samurai*

Bedlam Pictures

3000 W. Olympic Blvd., Bldg. 4,
Ste. 2204
Santa Monica, CA 90404
(310) 315-4764 Phone
(310) 315-4757 Fax

Beech Hill Films

443 Greenwich St., Ste. 5A
New York, NY 10013
(212) 226-3331 Phone
(212) 226-2179 Fax

Bel-Air Entertainment
(Steve Reuther)

4000 Warner Blvd., Bldg. 66
Burbank, CA 91522
(818) 954-4040 Phone
(818) 954-2838 Fax
Credits: *Rock Star, Message in a Bottle, Chain of Fools, The Replacements, Proof of Life, Pay It Forward, Sweet November, Collateral Damage*

★ Bender-Spink

6735 Yucca St.
Hollywood, CA 90028
(323) 845-1640 Phone
(323) 512-5347 Fax

Credits: *American Pie, American Pie 2, Cats & Dogs, Final Destination, Cheats, The Ring*

Harve Bennett Productions

11766 Wilshire Blvd., Ste. 1610
Los Angeles, CA 90025
(310) 306-7198 Phone
Credits: *Star Trek II–V; Rich Man, Poor Man; A Woman Called Golda; Time Trax; Invasion America*

Berg Entertainment

7421 Beverly Blvd.
Los Angeles, CA 90036
(323) 930-9935 Phone
(323) 930-9934 Fax

Rick Berman Productions

5555 Melrose Ave., Ste.. 232
Los Angeles, CA 90038
(323) 956-5037 Phone
(323) 862-1076 Fax
Credits: *Star Trek: The Next Generation, Star Trek: Insurrection, Star Trek: Deep Space Nine, Star Trek: First Contact, Star Trek: Voyager, Enterprise, Star Trek: Nemesis*

Jay Bernstein Productions

P.O. Box 1148
Beverly Hills, CA 90213
(310) 858-1485 Phone
(310) 858-1607 Fax
Credits: *Come Die with Me,*
Murder Takes All, Mike Hammer,
Sunburn, Diamond Trap, Double
Jeopardy, Houston Knights

Beyond Films, Ltd.

8642 Melrose Ave., Ste. 200
Los Angeles, CA 90069
(310) 358-9494 Phone
(310) 358-9393 Fax
Web: www.beyond.com.au

Big Town Productions
(Actor: Bill Pullman)

6201 Sunset Blvd. #80
Los Angeles, CA 90028
(323) 962-8099 Phone
(323) 962-8029 Fax

Blinding Edge Pictures
(Writer/Director: M. Night
Shyamalan)

100 Four Falls Corporate Center,
Ste. 102
Conshohocken, PA 19428
Credits: *Unbreakable, Signs*

Blue Bay Productions
(Producer: Rod Liber)

1119 Colorado Ave., Ste. 100
Santa Monica, CA 90401
(310) 440-9904 Phone
Credits: *Big Momma's House, Wild*
Things, Dunston Checks In

Blue Relief
(Actress: Diane Keaton)

1438 N. Gower St., Bldg. 35,
Ste. 551
Hollywood, CA 90028
(323) 860-7565 Phone
(310) 860-7497 Fax
Credits: *Hanging Up, Northern*
Lights, Crossed Over, Pasadena,
Heaven

Blue Rider Pictures

2800 28th St., Ste. 105
Santa Monica, CA 90405
(310) 314-8246 Phone
(310) 581-4352 Fax
Web: www.blueriderpictures.com
Credits: *Shergar, Slow Burn,*
Silverwolf, Call of the Wild, My
Five Wives, Hollywood Sign, Hide
and Seek, Wishmaster 3,
Wishmaster 4, Behind the Red
Door, Say Nothing, Kids World,
Holes

Blue Tulip Productions

(Director: Jan De Bont)

1708 Berkeley St.
Santa Monica, CA 90404
(310) 582-1587 Phone
(310) 582-1597 Fax
E-mail: info@bluetulipprod.com
Credits: *Speed, Twister, SLC-Punk, Minority Report, Equilibrium*

Blue Turtle, Inc.

1740 Clear View Dr.
Beverly Hills, CA 90210
(310) 276-4994 Phone
(310) 276-4997 Fax
Credits: *Teknolust, Pontiac Moon, Diggstown*

Bob & Alice Productions

(Actress: Bonnie Hunt)

11693 San Vicente Blvd.
Los Angeles, CA 90049
(310) 449-3858 Phone
Credits: *Return to Me, Life with Bonnie*

Bodega Bay Productions, Inc. (Actor: Michael Murphy)

P.O. Box 17338
Beverly Hills, CA 90209
(310) 273-3157 Phone
(310) 271-5581 Fax

Web: www.bodegabay.net
Credits: *Celebrity Island Videos, The Last Best Sunday, Bill & Ted's Excellent Adventure, Purpose*

Bona Fide Productions

8899 Beverly Blvd., Ste. 804
Los Angeles, CA 90048
(310) 273-6782 Phone
(310) 273-7821 Fax
Credits: *Pumpkin, Crumb, Jack the Bear, King of the Hill, Election, The Wood*

Boxing Cat Productions

(Actor: Tim Allen)

11500 Hart St.
North Hollywood, CA 91605
(818) 765-4870 Phone
(818) 765-4975 Fax
Credits: *Joe Somebody, The Santa Clause, Jungle 2 Jungle*

Boz Productions

(Producer: Bo Zenga)

1632 N. Sierra Bonita Ave.
Los Angeles, CA 90046-2816
(323) 876-3232 Phone
(323) 876-3231 Fax
Credits: *Scary Movie, A Light in the Darkness, Everything's Jake*

Bregman-IAC Productions
(Producer/Director: Martin/
Michael Bregman)

9100 Wilshire Blvd., Ste. 401E
Beverly Hills, CA 90212
(818) 954-9988 Phone

Brillstein-Grey Entertainment

9150 Wilshire Blvd., Ste. 350
Beverly Hills, CA 90212
(310) 275-6135 Phone
(310) 275-6180 Fax
Credits: *Just Shoot Me, The Steve Harvey Show, The Sopranos*

Brooksfilms, Ltd.
(Writer/Director/Producer:
Mel Brooks)

9336 W. Washington Blvd.
Culver City, CA 90232
(310) 202-3292 Phone
(310) 202-3225 Fax
Credits: *The Fly I* and *II, Frances, Elephant Man, My Favorite Year, The Producers*

Brownhouse Productions
(Actress: Whitney Houston)

One William Morris Pl.
Beverly Hills, CA 90212
(323) 650-2670 Phone

★ Jerry Bruckheimer Films

1631 10th St.
Santa Monica, CA 90404
(310) 664-6260 Phone
Credits: *CSI: Miami, Without a Trace, CSI: Crime Scene Investigations, The Amazing Race, Kangaroo Jack, Pearl Harbor, Remember the Titans, Coyote Ugly, Gone in 60 Seconds, Enemy of the State, Armageddon, Crimson Tide, Con Air, Top Gun, The Rock, Black Hawk Down*

The Bubble Factory

8840 Wilshire Blvd., 3rd Fl.
Beverly Hills, CA 90211
(310) 358-3000 Phone
(310) 358-3299 Fax
Credits: *The Pest, A Simple Wish, For Richer or Poorer, Playing Mona Lisa, Flipper, McHale's Navy, Stinkers, That Old Feeling, A Fate Totally Worse Than Death*

Bungalow 78 Productions

5555 Melrose Ave., Lasky Bldg.
  #200
Los Angeles, CA 90038
(323) 956-4440 Phone
(323) 862-2090 Fax
Credits: *Catch Me If You Can, Coach, Romy and Michelle's High School Reunion, Patch Adams*

Bushwood Pictures

320 S. Irving Blvd.
Los Angeles, CA 90020
(323) 936-1659 Phone
(323) 936-1977 Fax

Butchers Run Films

(Actor: Robert Duvall)

8978 Norma Pl.
West Hollywood, CA 90069
(310) 246-4630 Phone
(310) 246-1033 Fax
Credits: *A Family Thing, The Man Who Captured Eichmann, The Apostle, A Shot at Glory*

Calico World Entertainment

(ANM)

10200 Riverside Dr.
North Hollywood, CA 91602
(818) 755-3800 Phone
Web: www.calicoworld.com

Camera Marc

4605 Lankershim Blvd., Ste. 201
North Hollywood, CA 91602
(818) 753-9901 Phone

Canal+ (U.S)

301 N. Canon Dr., Ste. 228
Beverly Hills, CA 90210

(310) 247-0994 Phone
(310) 247-0998 Fax

Cannell Studios

7083 Hollywood Blvd., Ste. 600
Hollywood, CA 90028
(323) 465-5800 Phone
(323) 856-7390 Fax
Credits: *Final Victim, A-Team, King Con, Terror.net, Greatest American Hero, Riding the Snake, 21 Jump Street, The Devil's Workshop, Wiseguy*

The Canton Company

Warner Bros.
4000 Warner Blvd., Bldg. 81, Ste. 200
Burbank, CA 91522
(818) 954-2130 Phone
(818) 954-2967 Fax

Capella International, Inc.

9242 Beverly Blvd., Ste. 280
Beverly Hills, CA 90210-3710
(310) 247-4700 Phone
(310) 247-4701 Fax

Capital Arts Entertainment

23315 Clifton Pl.
Valencia, CA 91354

(310) 581-3020 Phone

(310) 581-3023 Fax

Credits: *Route 9, Casper Meets Wendy, Richie Rich, Addams Family Reunion, Turbulence II, Skipped Parts, Rocket's Red Glare, After the Storm, Au Pair, Au Pair II, Final Ascent, Ice Angel, Oh Baby, Attraction, Rent Control, Comic Book Villains, Ghost Dog, Try 17*

Capstone Pictures

1990 S. Bundy Dr., Ste.370

Hollywood, CA 90025

(310) 571-9211 Phone

(310) 481-6242 Fax

Carlton International Media, Inc.

12711 Ventura Blvd., Ste. 300

Studio City, CA 91604

(818) 753-6363 Phone

(818) 753-6388 Fax

Web: www.carltonint.co.uk

E-mail: enquiries@carltonint.co.uk

Credits: *Danger Beneath the Sea, Rough Air: Danger on Flight 534, Seconds to Spare, Scent of Murder,* *Second Nature, Rush of Fear, Rudy: The Rudy Giuliani Story*

Carlyle Productions & Management

2050 Laurel Canyon Rd.

Los Angeles, CA 90046

(323) 848-4960 Phone

(323) 650-8249 Fax

Credits: *Seven, The Accidental Tourist, Mean Streak*

Carrie Productions

(Actor: Danny Glover)

4444 Riverside Dr., Ste. 110

Burbank, CA 91505

(818) 567-3292 Phone

(818) 567-3296 Fax

Credits: *Buffalo Soldiers, Freedom Song, America's Dream, Just a Dream*

The Thomas Carter Company

3000 W. Olympic Blvd., Bldg. 5, Ste. 1100

Santa Monica, CA 90404

❚ *There should be things in films that only 5 percent of the audience picks up on.*
—PAUL SCHRADER

(310) 586-7600 Phone
(310) 586-7607 Fax
Credits: *Save the Last Dance, Don King: Only in America, Christmas Rush, Five Desperate Hours, The Uninvited, Trapped in a Purple Haze, Ali: An American Hero*

(310) 285-2300 Phone
(310) 285-2345 Fax
Credits: *Miss Congeniality, A Few Good Men, City Slickers, In the Line of Fire, Misery, The Shawshank Redemption, Seinfeld, The Green Mile, When Harry Met Sally*

Cartoon Network (ANM)

1050 Temple Dr.
Atlanta, GA 30318
(404) 885-2263 Phone
Credits: *The Powerpuff Girls Movie*

Cartoon Network Studios (ANM)

300 N. Third St.
Burbank, CA 91502
(818) 729-4000 Phone

Castle Hill Productions Inc./Cinevest

1414 Ave. of the Americas, 15th Fl.
New York, NY 10019
(212) 888-0080 Phone
(212) 644-0956 Fax

★ Castle Rock Entertainment

335 N. Maple Dr., St.. 135
Beverly Hills, CA 90210

Catfish Productions

(Actors: James Keach and Jane Seymour)

23852 Pacific Coast Hwy., Ste. 313
Malibu, CA 90265
(310) 456-7365 Phone
(310) 264-9148 Fax
Credits: *Marriage of Convenience, The Stars Fell on Henrietta, The Absolute Truth, A Passion for Justice, Fanny Kemball, Blackout, Dr. Quinn (The Movie), Murder in the Mirror, Yesterday's Children, Submerged, Moms on Strike!*

Cecchi Gori Group

11990 San Vicente Blvd., Ste. 200
Los Angeles, CA 90049
(310) 442-4777 Phone
(310) 442-9507 Fax
E-mail: msalvo@earthlink.net
Credits: *Il Postino, The Star Maker, Mediterraneo, La Vita Bella (Life Is Beautiful), Il Mostro, Il Ciclone, Johnny Stecchino, Ciao Professore, A Bronx Tale, Dangerous Games, Night and the City, Il Mio West,*

PRODUCERS

House of Cards, Seven, From Dusk Till Dawn, Man Trouble, The Blackout

Chancellor Entertainment

10600 Holman Ave., Ste. 1
Los Angeles, CA 90024
(310) 474-4521 Phone
(310) 470-9273 Fax
Credits: *Idol Maker, The Razor's Edge, Letter to Three Wives, Smilin' Jack*

Chartoff Productions

1250 Sixth St., Ste. 101
Santa Monica, CA 90401
(310) 319-1960 Phone
(310) 319-3469 Fax
Credits: *Rocky* series, *Raging Bull, Straight Talk, The Right Stuff*

Cheyenne Enterprises
(Actor: Bruce Willis)

406 Wilshire Blvd.
Santa Monica, CA 90401
(310) 455-5000 Phone
Credits: *Bandits, Hart's War*

Cine Excel Entertainment

1102 N. Screenland Dr.
Burbank, CA 91505
(818) 848-4478 Phone
(818) 848-1590 Fax
Web: www.cineexcel.com
E-mail: info@cineexcel.com
Credits: *Terminal Velocity, The Jerry FairFax Show, Dead Right, Confessions, Clip Joint*

Cinergi Pictures Entertainment, Inc.

2308 Broadway
Santa Monica, CA 90404-2916
(310) 315-6000 Phone
(310) 828-0443 Fax
Credits: *Die Hard: With a Vengeance, Evita, Tombstone*

Cinetel Films, Inc.

8255 W. Sunset Blvd.
Los Angeles, CA 90046-2432
(323) 654-4000 Phone
(323) 650-6400 Fax
Credits: *Carried Away, Green Sails, A Rumor of Angels*

Cineville International, Inc.

3000 Airport Ave.
Santa Monica, CA 90405
(310) 397-7150 Phone
(310) 397-7155 Fax
Credits: *The Whole Wide World, Drowning on Dry Land, Swimming with Sharks, Gas Food Lodging, Hurlyburly*

Classic Films, Inc.

6427 Sunset Blvd.
Hollywood, CA 90028
(323) 962-7855 Phone
(323) 962-8028 Fax
Credits: *James and the Giant Peach, FernGully I, FernGully II*

Clean Break Productions
(Actor: Tom Arnold)

14046 Aubrey Rd.
Beverly Hills, CA 90210
(818) 995-1221 Phone
(818) 995-0089 Fax
Credits: *The Tom Show*

Cohen Pictures

8439 Sunset Blvd.
Los Angeles, CA 90069
(323) 822-4100 Phone
Credits: *Down to You, Bounce, The Cider House Rules, Rounders, View from the Top*

Collaborative Artists

445 S. Beverly Dr., Ste. 100
Beverly Hills, CA 90212
(310) 274-4800 Phone
(310) 274-4803 Fax

Credits: *The Season: Red Storm Rising*

Collision Entertainment

445 S. Beverly Dr., Ste.310
Beverly Hills, CA 90212
(310) 785-0425 Phone
(310) 785-0463 Fax

Colomby/Keaton Productions

2110 Main St., Ste. 302
Santa Monica, CA 90405
(310) 399-8881 Phone
(310) 392-1323 Fax

Commotion Pictures

301 N. Canon Dr., Ste. 324
Beverly Hills, CA 90210
(310) 432-2000 Phone
(310) 432-2001 Fax

Company Films

2601 Second St.
Santa Monica, CA 90405
(310) 399-2500 Phone
(310) 399-2583 Fax
Credits: *Lord of the Rings, The Matrix, Face/Off, Dick Tracy*

Concorde-New Horizons Corp.

11600 San Vincente Blvd.
Los Angeles, CA 90049
(310) 820-6733 Phone
(310) 207-6816 Fax
Web: www.newconcorde.com

Conquistador Entertainment

131 Green St., Ste. 4A
New York, NY 10012
(212) 353-1496 Phone
(212) 353-1497 Fax

Constantin Film Development, Inc.

9200 Sunset Blvd., Ste. 730
Los Angeles, CA 90069
(310) 247-0305 Phone
(310) 247-0305 Fax
Credits: *Smilla's Sense of Snow, House of the Spirits, Last Exit to Brooklyn, Name of the Rose, Resident Evil*

Contemptible Entertainment

100 N. Crescent Dr., Garden Level
Beverly Hills, CA 90210
(310) 385-6611 Phone
(310) 385-4306 Fax

Conundrum Entertainment

(Writers/Directors: Bobby and Peter Farrelly)

325 Wilshire Blvd., Ste. 201
Santa Monica, CA 90401
(310) 319-2800 Phone
(310) 319-2808 Fax
Credits: *Shallow Hal; Osmosis Jones; Me, Myself & Irene; There's Something About Mary; Dumb & Dumber; Kingpin*

Cornice Entertainment

190 N. Canon Dr. PH
Beverly Hills, CA 90210
(310) 777-0200 Phone
(310) 777-0357 Fax

TIP: When you're cold-calling someone in the industry, it's best to call early in the day (between 9:30 and 10:30 A.M.) before the person's line starts ringing off the hook. Alternatively, if you call after 6 P.M. the receptionists and assistants are often gone but the executives are still there. They may pick up personally.

Cornucopia Pictures

10989 Bluffside Dr., Ste. 3414
Studio City, CA 91604
(818) 985-2720 Phone
Credits: *Race the Sun, The Disappearance of Vonnie, Christmas on Division Street, Rain Man, Switched at Birth, Grosse Point Blank*

The Cort/Madden Company
(Producter: Robert Cort)

5555 Melrose Ave., Marx Bros.
Bldg. #107
Hollywood, CA 90038
(323) 956-5884 Phone
(323) 862-1408 Fax
Credits: *Save the Last Dance, Runaway Bride, Mr. Holland's Opus, The Rats, Harlan County War, Against the Ropes*

Wes Craven Films

11846 Ventura Blvd., Ste. 208
Studio City, CA 91604
(818) 752-0197 Phone
(818) 752-1789 Fax
Credits: *Scream 1–3, Music of the Heart*

Creative Light Worldwide

8383 Wilshire Blvd., Ste. 212
Beverly Hills, CA 90211
(323) 658-9166 Phone
(323) 658-9169 Fax
Web: www.creativelightworldwide.com

Crown International Pictures, Inc.

8701 Wilshire Blvd.
Beverly Hills, CA 90211
(310) 657-6700 Phone
(310) 657-4489 Fax
Web: www.crownintlpictures.com
E-mail: crown@crownintlpictures.com
Credits: *My Mom's a Werewolf, My Tutor, My Chauffeur, Lena's Holiday*

Crusader Entertainment

132-B Lasky Dr.
Beverly Hills, CA 90212
(310) 248-6360 Phone
(310) 248-6370 Fax
Credits: *Sudden Death, The Patriot, Mystery Alaska, Gideon, Resurrection, From the Hip, Spellbinder, Joshua*

Crystal Sky, LLC

1901 Ave. of the Stars #605
Los Angeles, CA 90067
(310) 843-0223 Phone
(310) 553-9895 Fax

PRODUCERS

Credits: *Baby Geniuses I* and *II*, *Murder in a Small Town*, *The Musketeer*, *Unleashed*

C-2 Pictures

2308 Broadway
Santa Monica, CA 90404
(310) 315-6000 Phone
(310) 828-0443 Fax
Credits: *Evita*, *Die Hard 3*, *Star Gate*, *I Spy*

Cunningham Productions, Inc.
(Producer: Sean S. Cunningham)

4420 Hayvenhurst Ave.
Encino, CA 91436
(818) 995-1585 Phone
Credits: *Terminal Invasion*, *Deep Star Six*, *My Boyfriend's Back*, *House*, *Friday the 13th*, *Jason X*, *Extreme Close-Up*

Curb Entertainment International

3907 W. Alameda Ave.
Burbank, CA 91505
(818) 843-8580 Phone
(818) 566-1719 Fax
E-mail: curbfilm@earthlink.net
Credits: *Tough Luck*, *Wendigo*, *Pipe Dream*, *Pressure*, *Mexico City*, *Oxygen*, *The Proposal*, *Wedding Bell Blues*, *Kill Me Later*, *Zoe*, *Out of Line*, *Ring of Fire*, *The Big Day*, *The Operator*, *The Citizen*, *Water's Edge*, *The Untold*, *Coastlines*, *Dummy*

C/W Productions
(Actor: Tom Cruise)

5555 Melrose Ave.
Hollywood, CA 90038
(323) 956-8150 Phone
(323) 862-1250 Fax
Credits: *Mission: Impossible*, *Without Limits*, *Mission: Impossible 2*, *The Others*, *Vanilla Sky*

Danamation Studios (ANM)

1007 Montana Ave., Ste. 404
Santa Monica, CA 90403
(310) 317-517 Phone

Danjaq Inc.

MGM Plaza
2401 Colorado Ave., Ste. 330
Santa Monica, CA 90404
(310) 449-3185 Phone
(310) 449-3189 Fax
Credits: *The James Bond Films*, *Chitty Chitty Bang Bang*

Dark Horse Entertainment

421 S. Beverly Dr.
Beverly Hills, CA 90212
(310) 789-4751 Phone
Credits: *The Mask, Mystery Men, Time Cop*

Darkwoods Productions

(Director: Frank Darabont)

1041 N. Formosa Ave. SME #108
West Hollywood, CA 90046
(323) 850-2497 Phone
(323) 850-2491 Fax
Credits: *The Green Mile, The Shawshank Redemption, Black Cat Run, The Salton Sea, The Majestic*

David Ladd Films

MGM
2450 Broadway St.
Santa Monica, CA 90404
(310) 449-3410 Phone
(310) 586-8272 Fax

Davis Entertainment Co.

(Director: John Davis)

2121 Ave. of the Stars, Ste. 2900
Los Angeles, CA 90067
(310) 556-3550 Phone
Credits: *Behind Enemy Lines, Dr. Doolittle II, Dr. Doolittle, Grumpy*

Old Men I and *II, Out to Sea, Predator I* and *II, The Chamber, Waterworld, The Firm, Asteroid, Heartbreakers, Life or Something Like It*

Dee Gee Entertainment

368 N. La Cienega Blvd.
Los Angeles, CA 90048
(310) 652-0999 Phone
(310) 652-0718 Fax

Deep River Productions

100 N. Crescent Dr., Ste. 350
Beverly Hills, CA 90210
(310) 432-1800 Phone
(310) 432-1801 Fax
Credits: *Dr. Dolittle, Courage Under Fire, Big Momma's House*

Deja View Productions

7603 Atron Ave.
West Hills, CA 91304
(818) 704-9185 Phone
(818) 704-6001 Fax
Credits: *High Crimes, The Flintstones in Viva Rock Vegas, Eraser, Outbreak, Pacific Heights*

Dino De Laurentiis Company

100 Universal City Plaza #5195
Universal City, CA 91608
(818) 777-2111 Phone
(818) 866-5566 Fax
Credits: *Breakdown, Bound, U-571, Hannibal, Red Dragon*

Delaware Pictures

650 N. Brosnan Ave., Ste. 114
Hollywood, CA 90004
(323) 960-4552 Phone
(323) 960-4556 Fax
Credits: *Bad Jim, Pretty Boy Floyd, Hatfield & McCoys, No Drums, Stephanie, Human Error, All Your Children* (Music Video)

De Line Pictures

Paramount Pictures
5555 Melrose Ave.
Los Angeles, CA 90038
(323) 956-3200 Phone
(323) 862-1301 Fax

Dereko Entertainment

9663 Santa Monica Blvd. #722
Beverly Hills, CA 90210
(310) 706-3600 ext. 6280 Phone
Web: www.derekoent.com

Destination Films

1299 Ocean Ave., 5th Fl.
Santa Monica, CA 90401
(310) 434-2700 Phone
(310) 434-2701 Fax

Destiny Force Productions

233 Wilshire Blvd., Ste. 400
Santa Monica, CA 90401
(310) 449-0076 Phone
(310) 734-1822 Fax

DIC Entertainment (ANM)

303 N. Glenoaks Blvd.
Burbank, CA 91502
(818) 955-5400 Phone

★ Dimension Films

c/o Miramax Films
375 Greenwich St.
New York, NY 10013
(212) 941-3800/(323) 951-4200 Phone
(212) 941-3949 Fax
Credits: *The Others, Scream, Scream 2, and Scream 3, Scary Movie, Scary Movie 2, Spy Kids, Spy Kids 2*

Dinamo Entertainment

1537 Pontius Ave., 2nd Fl.
Los Angeles, CA 90025
(310) 473-1311 Phone
(310) 473-8233 Fax
Credits: *Suicide Kings, The Substitute, Bad Influence, Lost & Found*

Di Novi Pictures

(Producer: Denise Di Novi)

3110 Main St. #220
Santa Monica, CA 90405
(310) 581-1355 Phone
(310) 399-0499 Fax
Credits: *Practical Magic, Little Women, Ed Wood, Edward Scissorhands, Batman Returns, A Walk to Remember, The District*

Distant Horizon, Ltd.

8282 Sunset Blvd., Ste. A
Los Angeles, CA 90046
(323) 848-4140 Phone
(323) 848-4144 Fax
Credits: *Sarafina!; Cry, the Beloved Country; Face; Theory of Flight; Get Real; Black Mask; Twin Dragons; The Long Run; The Dish; Happy Now; Zu Warriors; I Capture the Castle*

Diversa Films

7974 Mission Bonita Dr.
San Diego, CA 92120
(619) 286-8384 Phone
(619) 286-8324 Fax
E-mail: karl.kozak@home.com

Maureen Donley Pictures

914 Westwood Blvd., Ste. 591
Los Angeles, CA 90024
(310) 441-0834 Phone
(310) 441-1595 Fax
Credits: *The Little Mermaid, Anastasia*

The Donners Company

Warner Bros. Pictures
4000 Warner Blvd., Bldgs. 102 and 103 #4
Burbank, CA 91522
(818) 954-3611 Phone
(818) 954-4908 Fax
Credits: *Lethal Weapon, Lethal Weapon 2–4, Maverick, Free Willy, Free Willy 2 and 3, Lady Hawke, Dave, Volcano, Conspiracy Theory, You've Got Mail, Any Given Sunday, X-Men*

Double Tree Entertainment

9606 Santa Monica Blvd., 3rd Fl.
Beverly Hills, CA 90210

PRODUCERS

(310) 859-6644 Phone
(310) 859-6650 Fax

Dream Entertainment

8489 W. 3rd St., Ste. 1036
Los Angeles, CA 90048
(323) 655-5501 Phone
(323) 655-5603 Fax
Web: www.diversafilms.com
E-mail: DreamEnter@aol.com
Credits: *According to Spencer, Girl Fever, 100 Girls, More Dogs Than Bones, Never Again, The Journeyman, RSVP, Dahmer*

Dreamworks Animation (ANM)

1000 Flower St.
Glendale, CA 91201
(818) 695-5000 Phone

Dreyfuss/James Productions
(Actor: Richard Dreyfuss)

Warner Hollywood Studios
1041 N. Formosa Ave., Pickford Bldg., Rm. 110
West Hollywood, CA 90046
(323) 850-3140 Phone
(323) 850-3141 Fax
Credits: *Quiz Show, Mr. Holland's Opus, Having Our Say*

Duck Soup Studios (ANM)

2205 Stoner Ave.
Los Angeles, CA 90064
(310) 478-0771 Phone

Eagle Nation Films
(Actor: Levar Burton)

5555 Melrose Ave., Dietrich Bldg., Ste. 207
Los Angeles, CA 90038
(323) 956-5989 Phone
(323) 862-1137 Fax
Credits: *Reading Rainbow*

East West Capital Associates

10900 Wilshire Blvd., Ste. 950
Los Angeles, CA 90024
(310) 209-6155 Phone
(310) 209-6160 Fax

Edmonds Entertainment
(Actor: Kenneth "Babyface" Edmonds)

1635 N. Cahuenga Blvd.
Los Angeles, CA 90028
(323) 860-1550 Phone
(323) 860-1554 Fax

Blake Edwards Productions

10345 W. Olympic Blvd.
Los Angeles, CA 90064

(310) 234-0989 Phone
(310) 207-9305 Fax

Egg Pictures
(Actress: Jodie Foster)

. . . .

5555 Melrose Ave., Jerry Lewis
Bldg.
Los Angeles, CA 90038
(323) 956-8400 Phone
(323) 862-1414 Fax

El Dorado Pictures
(Actor: Alec Baldwin)

. . . .

725 Arizona Ave., Ste. 100
Santa Monica, CA 90401
(310) 458-4800 Phone
(310) 458-4802 Fax
Credits: *The Confession,*
Nuremberg, State and Main

El Norte Productions

. . . .

8701 W. Olympic Blvd.
Los Angeles, CA 90035
(310) 360-1194 Phone

(310) 360-1199 Fax
Credits: *American Tapestry, El*
Norte, Mi Familia, Selena, Why Do
Fools Fall in Love, American Family

Energy
(Producer: Brooklyn Weaver)

. . . .

10833 Wilshire Blvd., Ste. 219
Los Angeles, CA 90024
(310) 475-0101 Phone
Web: www.energyentertainment.net
E-mail: info@energyentertainment
.net
Credits: *The Bachelorette, Prom,*
The Number 23, Rapid, Turn,
Valentine's Day, Kool Herc's
Breakbeat, Wimpy

Equus Entertainment

. . . .

2121 Ave. of the Stars, 29th Fl.
Los Angeles, CA 90067
(310) 551-2262 Phone
(310) 556-3760 Fax
Credits: *Something Wicked, What*
If Guy

▌ *Most people rarely confront things head-on. They're afraid to.*
—ROBERT TOWNE, screenwriter, *Chinatown*

PRODUCERS

Escape Artists

Sony Pictures
10202 W. Washington Blvd., Lean
Bldg., Rm. 333
Culver City, CA 90232
(310) 244-8833 Phone
(310) 244-2151 Fax
Credits: *A Knight's Tale*

Esparaza-Katz Productions

8899 Beverly Blvd., Ste. 506
Los Angeles, CA 90048
(310) 281-3770 Phone
(310) 281-3777 Fax
Credits: *Gods and Generals,*
Avenging Angel, Selena,
Gettysburg, Rough Riders, The
Cisco Kid, Milagro Beanfield War,
The Disappearance of Garcia
Lorca, Introducing Dorothy
Dandridge

The Robert Evans Company

Paramount Pictures
5555 Melrose Ave., Lubitsch #117
Los Angeles, CA 90038
(323) 956-8800 Phone
(323) 862-0070 Fax
Credits: *Chinatown, The Saint,*
The Godfather, Sliver, The Out-of-
Towners, How to Lose a Guy in 10
Days

Everyman Pictures

(Director: Jay Roach)

10202 W. Washington Blvd., Gene
Autry Rm. 1043
Culver City, CA 90232
(310) 244-1686 Phone
(310) 244-1315 Fax
Credits: *Austin Powers in*
Goldmember, Mystery, Alaska,
Meet the Parents, Austin Powers:
International Man of Mystery,
Austin Powers: The Spy Who
Shagged Me

Evil Twin Productions, LLC

5201 Fulton Ave.
Sherman Oaks, CA 91401
(818) 986-8551 Phone
(818) 986-8582 Fax

Evolution Entertainment

7720 Sunset Blvd.
Los Angeles, CA 90046
(323) 850-3232 Phone
(323) 850-0521 Fax
Credits: *Bull Durham, Set It Off,*
John Q, Good Advice

Face Productions

(Actor: Billy Crystal)

Castle Rock Entertainment
335 N. Maple Dr., Ste. 135

Beverly Hills, CA 90210
(310) 285-2300 Phone
(310) 285-2386 Fax
Credits: *Analyze That, America's Sweethearts, 61*, Forget Paris, Analyze This, Mr. Saturday Night, City Slickers, City Slickers II, My Giant*

Fair Dinkum Productions
(Actor: Henry Winkler)

2500 Broadway St., Bldg. E-5018
Santa Monica, CA 90404
(310) 586-8471 Phone
(310) 586-8469 Fax

Farrell/Minoff Productions
(Actor: Mike Farrell)

14011 Ventura Blvd., Ste. 401
Sherman Oaks, CA 91423
(818) 789-5766 Phone
(818) 789-7459 Fax
Credits: *Dominick and Eugene, Sins of the Mind, Patch Adams*

Edward S. Feldman Company

520 Evelyn Pl.
Beverly Hills, CA 90210
416-761-0123 Phone
416-761-0040 Fax

Credits: *K-19: The Widowmaker, 101 Dalmatians, 102 Dalmatians, The Truman Show, The Doctor, Witness, Green Card, Forever Young*

FGM Entertainment
(Producer: Frank Mancuso, Jr.)

8670 Wilshire Blvd., Ste. 301
Beverly Hills, CA 90211
(310) 358-1370 Phone
(310) 358-1380 Fax
Credits: *Stigmata, Species, Internal Affairs, Ronin*

Adam Fields Productions

10390 Santa Monica Blvd., Ste. 350
Los Angeles, CA 90025
(310) 552-8244 Phone
(310) 552-8247 Fax
Credits: *Donnie Darko, Brokedown Palace, Ravenous, Money Train, Great Balls of Fire, Johnny Be Good, Vision Quest, Whoopee Boys*

Fifty Cannon Entertainment, LLC
(Director: Mike Newell)

10390 Santa Monica Blvd., Ste. 350
Los Angeles, CA 90025
(310) 552-1518 Phone
(310) 552-2310 Fax
Credits: *Traffic*

Filmcolony, Ltd.

7966 Beverly Blvd., 3rd Fl.
Los Angeles, CA 90048
(323) 951-4650 Phone
(323) 951-4660 Fax
Credits: *Bourne Identity, The Cider House Rules, She's All That, Hurlyburly, Jackie Brown, Pulp Fiction, Reservoir Dogs*

Filmfour International

76–78 Charlotte St.
London, W1P 1LX United Kingdom
44-207-868-7700 Phone
44-207-868-7766 Fax
Web: www.filmfour.com
E-mail: filmfourintl@
  channel4.co.uk

Film Roman (ANM)

12020 Chandler Blvd., Ste. 300
North Hollywood, CA 91607
(818) 761-2544 Phone
(818) 752-1317 Fax
Credits: *Motocrossed, The Simpsons, King of the Hill, Johnny Tsunami, Mission Hill, Doomsday, The Oblongs, My First Mister, X-Men*

Filmworld, Inc

304 N. Edinburgh Ave.
Los Angeles, CA 90048
(323) 655-7705 Phone
(323) 655-7706 Fax

Fine Line Features

116 N. Robertson Blvd., Ste. 200
Los Angeles, CA 90048
(212) 649-4800/(310) 854-5811
  Phone
(310) 659-1453 Fax
Credits: *The Anniversary Party, Before Night Falls, Pecker, Shine, The Sweet Hereafter, Filth and Fury, Tumbleweeds, Dancer in the Dark, State and Main, Saving Grace, Lord of the Rings, Hedwig and the Angry Inch, Ripley's Game*

Wendy Finerman Productions

10201 W. Pico Blvd.
Los Angeles, CA 90035
(310) 369-8800 Phone
(310) 369-8808 Fax
Credits: *Fairy Tale . . . A True Story, Stepmom, Forrest Gump, The Fan, Sugar & Spice, Drumline*

★ Fireworks Pictures

421 S. Beverly Dr., Ste. 700
Beverly Hills, CA 90212
(310) 789-4700 Phone
(310) 789-4747 Fax
Web: www.watchfireworks.com

E-mail: info@fireworkspix.com
Credits: *Mutant X, Relic Hunter, Queen of Swords, Gene Roddenberry's Andromeda, La Femme Nikita, Highlander: The Raven, FX: The Series, 18 Wheels of Justice, 100 Deeds for Eddie McDowd, Caitlin's Way, Being Eve, Real Kids: Real Adventures, Black Top, The Girl Next Door, Robocop: Prime Directives, A Wrinkle in Time, Poison, Blonde, Rat Race, Hardball, Who Is Cletis Tout?, Interstate 60, Onegin, An American Rhapsody, The Believer, Adventure Inc., Black Hole High, The Man from Elysian Fields, Greenfingers, Innocence, Better Than Sex, Simon Magus, Me Without You*

First Kiss Productions
(Actress: Alicia Silverstone)

468 N. Camden Dr., Ste. 200
Beverly Hills, CA 90210
(310) 860-5611 Phone
Credits: *Braceface, Excess Baggage*

First Look Media

8800 Sunset Blvd. #302
Los Angeles, CA 90069
(310) 855-1199 Phone
(310) 855-0719 Fax
Credits: *Lawless Heart, Map of the World, Waking Ned Devine, Mrs. Dalloway, Ratcatcher, Me & Isaac*

Newton, Chopper, Bread and Tulips, Skins

First Street
(Producer: Bill Borden)

120 Broadway Ave., 2nd Fl.
Santa Monica, CA 90401
(310) 393-9150 Phone
(310) 393-1430 Fax
Credits: *La Bamba, End of Days, Get on the Bus, Desperado, Excess Baggage, Ready to Run, Midnight Clear*

Flatiron Films

830 17th St., Ste.2
Santa Monica, CA 90403
(310) 315-2726 Phone
(310) 315-1906 Fax
Credits: *Pay It Forward*

Fleischer Studios (ANM)

10160 Cielo Dr.
Beverly Hills, CA 90210
(310) 276-7503 Phone

Florida Straits Productions

312 Sixth St.
Venice, CA 90291
(310) 399-0114 Phone
(310) 496-3181 Fax

PRODUCERS

Flower Films, Inc.
(Actress: Drew Barrymore)

9220 Sunset Blvd. #309
Los Angeles, CA 90069
(310) 285-0200 Phone
(310) 285-0827 Fax
Credits: *Charlie's Angels, Charlie's Angels: Full Throttle, Duplex, Never Been Kissed, Olive, the Other Reindeer, Donnie Darko*

Flying Freehold Productions
(Actor: Patrick Stewart)

5555 Melrose Ave., Dreire Bldg. #216
Los Angeles, CA 90038
(310) 459-8142 Phone
(310) 230-3572 Fax
Credits: *King of Texas, A Christmas Carol*

Focus Features

65 Bleecker St., 2nd Fl.
New York, NY 10012
(212) 539-4000 Phone
(310) 385-4400 Phone (L.A.)
(212) 539-4099 Fax
Credits: *8 Women, Far from Heaven, The Pianist, The Guys, The Shape of Things, Untitled Sylvia Plath Feature, 21 Grams, Gosford Park, The Man Who Wasn't There, Monsoon Wedding, Maybe Baby, One Night at McCool's*

Fortis Films
(Actress: Sandra Bullock)

8581 Santa Monica Blvd., Ste. 1
West Hollywood, CA 90069
(310) 659-4533 Phone
(310) 659-4373 Fax
Credits: *Practical Magic, Hope Floats, Making Sandwiches, Trespasses, Gun Shy, Miss Congeniality, Two Weeks' Notice, The George Lopez Show*

40 Acres & A Mule Filmworks, Inc.
(Writer/Director: Spike Lee)

75 S. Elliot Place, 3rd Fl.
Brooklyn, NY 11217
(718) 624-3703/(310) 276-2116 Phone

Forward Pass
(Director: Michael Mann)

12233 Olympic Blvd., Ste. 224
Los Angeles, CA 90064
(310) 571-3443 Phone
Credits: *Ali, Last of the Mohicans, Manhunter, Thief, Drug Wars, Heat, Jericho Mile, The Insider*

> I don't write 'close-up' or any of that. There are code words you can use in writing that indicate shots, visual things. You can write, 'From a distance he is only a figure among the cars, but seen up close, anxiety covers his face.' Well, that's one sentence, but to a director it's a long shot and a close-up.
>
> —PAUL SCHRADER

David Foster Productions

5555 Melrose Ave., Clara Bow Bldg., Ste. 224
Los Angeles, CA 90038
(323) 956-5226 Phone
(323) 862-2589 Fax
Credits: *Running Scared, Short Circuit, Short Circuit 2, The Mask of Zorro, The River Wild, The Getaway, The Thing, Collateral Damage, Hart's War, The Core*

Foundation Entertainment

8800 Venice Blvd., Ste. 217
Los Angeles, CA 90034
(310) 204-4686 Phone
(310) 204-4603 Fax
Credits: *The Umbilical Brothers' THWAK!, The Basketball Diaries, Daybreak, Swing Kids, Foxfire, Tortilla Soup*

Foundry Capital
(Producer: Robert Greenhut)

140 W. 57th St.

New York, NY 10019
(212) 977-9597 Phone
(212) 977-9525 Fax

4 Kids Entertainment (ANM)

1414 Ave. of the Americas
New York, NY 10019
(212) 758-7666 Phone
Web: www.4kidsent.com

1492 Pictures
(Director: Chris Columbus)

c/o Warner Brothers
4000 Warner Blvd., Bldg. 139, Rm. 118
Burbank, CA 91522
(818) 954-4924 Phone

Fox Family Channel/Fox Family Television Studios

10960 Wilshire Blvd.
Los Angeles, CA 90024
(310) 235-9700 Phone
(310) 235-5102 Fax

PRODUCERS

F.R. Productions
(Producer: Fred Roos)

2980 Beverly Glen Circle, Ste. 200
Los Angeles, CA 90077
(310) 470-9212 Phone
(310) 470-4905 Fax
Credits: *Black Stallion, Barfly, Godfather II, The Godfather III, Apocalypse Now, The Secret Garden, Town and Country, The Virgin Suicides, The Conversation, The Outsiders*

Franchise Pictures LLC

8228 Sunset Blvd., Ste. 311
Los Angeles, CA 90046
(323) 822-0730 Phone
(323) 822-2165 Fax
E-mail: npielak@franchisepictures
.com
Credits: *Heist, The Whole Nine Yards, The Pledge, Angel Eyes, Get Carter, Ballistic: Ecks vs. Sever, City by the Sea*

Fried Films
(Producer: Robert Fried)

4503 Glencoe Ave., 2nd Fl.
Marina del Rey, CA 90292
(310) 754-2676 Phone
(310) 778-9596 Fax

Furthur Films
(Actor: Michael Douglas)

100 Universal City Plaza, Bldg. 1320
Universal City, CA 91608
(818) 777-6700 Phone
(818) 866-1278 Fax
Credits: *It Runs in the Family, The In-Laws, Swimfan, Don't Say a Word, One Night at McCool's*

Gaylord Films

4000 Warner Blvd., Bldg. 148
Burbank, CA 91522
(818) 954-3500 Phone
Credits: *Divine Secrets of the Ya-Ya Sisterhood, What a Girl Wants*

Geisler/Roberdeau

511 Ave. of the Americas #368
New York, NY 10011
(212) 475-7472 Phone

George Street Pictures
(Actor: Chris O'Donnell)

3815 Hughes Ave., Ste. 3
Culver City, CA 90232
(310) 841-4361 Phone
(310) 204-6310 Fax

Gerber Pictures

9465 Wilshire Blvd., Ste. 318
Beverly Hills, CA 90212
(310) 385-8219 Phone
(310) 385-5881 Fax
Credits: *Juwanna Man, James Dean, Queen of the Damned*

Giants Entertainment

1800 Ave. of the Stars, Ste. 480
Los Angeles, CA 90067
(310) 652-5400 Phone
(310) 569-4000 Fax
E-mail: giantsfilms@aol.com

Gillen & Price

7425 Oakwood Ave.
Los Angeles, CA 90036
(323) 655-8047 Phone
(323) 655-8047 Fax
Credits: *Fried Green Tomatoes, Mercy Point*

Girlie Girl Productions

6700 Hillpark Dr., Ste. 302
Los Angeles, CA 90068
(323) 851-1206 Phone
(323) 851-1263 Fax
Web: www.girliegirlproductions.com
E-mail: info@girliegirlproductions
.com

Gitlin Productions

1741 Ivar Ave.
Hollywood, CA 90028
(323) 802-6950 Phone
(323) 802-6951 Fax

Gittes, Inc.

10202 W. Washington Blvd. Poitier
#1200
Culver City, CA 90232-3195
(310) 244-4333 Phone
(310) 244-1711 Fax
Credits: *Little Nikita, Breaking In, Goin' South, About Schmidt*

Given Films

28 Warren St., 5th Fl.
New York, NY 10007
(212) 962-9375 Phone
(212) 962-9666 Fax

Global Network Pictures

244 Fifth Ave., 2nd Fl., Ste. A215
New York, NY 10001
(212) 802-9357 Phone
Web: www.chezrisque.com

Goat Cay Productions

(Actress: Sigourney Weaver)

P.O. Box 38
New York, NY 10150

PRODUCERS

(212) 421-8293 Phone
(212) 421-8294 Fax

The Goatsingers
(Actor: Harvey Keitel)

179 Franklin St., 6th Fl.
New York, NY 10013
(212) 966-3045 Phone
(212) 966-4362 Fax
Credits: *The Grey Zone, Three Seasons*

Godsick Entertainment

8701 Old Dominion Dr.
McLean, VA 22102
(703) 442-3445 Phone
(703) 442-3446 Fax

Goepp Circle Productions
(Actor: Jonathan Frakes)

Paramount Pictures
5555 Melrose Ave., Cooper #116
Los Angeles, CA 90038
(323) 956-4620 Phone
(323) 862-1119 Fax

Credits: *Clockstoppers, Dying to Live, Roswell, Star Trek: Insurrection, Star Trek: First Contact*

Goldcrest Films International, Ltd.

1240 Olive Dr.
Los Angeles, CA 90069
(323) 650-4551 Phone
(323) 650-3581 Fax
Credits: *To End All Wars, Space Truckers, No Way Home, Rock-A-Doodle, Black Rainbow, Clockwatchers*

Golden Harvest Entertainment Co.

9891 Santa Monica Blvd., Ste. 209
Beverly Hills, CA 90212

Golden Quill
(Director: Arthur Hiller)

8899 Beverly Blvd., Ste. 702
Los Angeles, CA 90048
(310) 274-5016 Phone

▌ *Robert Towne has made the comment, and I agree with him, 'An audience will forgive a lot at the beginning but very little at the end.' If the story is constructed properly, then the ending should be inevitable, but not predictable.*
    —**LAWRENCE KONNER**, screenwriter, *Jewel of the Nile*

(310) 274-5028 Fax
Credits: *The In-Laws, Love Story, The Babe, Outrageous Fortune*

The Goldstein Company

1644 Courtney Ave.
Los Angeles, CA 90046
(310) 659-9511 Phone
(310) 659-8779 Fax
Credits: *The Mothman Prophecies, Ringmaster, Under Siege, Pretty Woman, The Hunted*

Gone Fishin' Productions

3000 W. Olympic Blvd., Bldg. 2,
 Ste. 1509
Santa Monica, CA 90404
(310) 315-4737 Phone
(310) 315-4715 Fax

Good Machine International, Inc.

417 Canal St., 4th Fl.
New York, NY 10013
(212) 343-9230 Phone
(212) 343-7412 Fax
Web: www.goodmachine.com
E-mail: info@goodmachine.com

Dan Gordon Productions

2060-D Ave. Los Arboles #256
Thousand Oaks, CA 91362

(805) 496-2566 Phone
Credits: *Gotcha, Passenger 57, Wyatt Earp, Murder in the First, The Assignment, The Hurricane*

Gracie Films
(Producer/Director: James L. Brooks)

Sony Pictures
10202 W. Washington Blvd.,
 Poitier Bldg.
Los Angeles, CA 90232
(310) 244-4222 Phone
(310) 244-1530 Fax
Credits: *Riding in Cars with Boys, What About Joan, As Good As It Gets, Big, Bottle Rocket, Broadcast News, Jerry Maguire, The Simpsons*

Grade A Entertainment

368 N. La Cienega Blvd.
Los Angeles, CA 90048
E-mail: gradeaprod@aol.com
Credits: *Captain Ron, It Takes Two, A Chance of Snow*

Graham/Rosenzweig Films

6399 Wilshire Blvd., Ste.510
Los Angeles, CA 90048
(323) 782-6888 Phone
(323) 782-6967 Fax
Credits: *Windtalkers, Phoenix, Dumb and Dumber, The War at Home, Threesome*

Grainy Pictures

75 Main St.
Cold Spring, NY 10516
(845) 265-2241 Phone
(845) 265-2543 Fax
Credits: *How's Your News?, Split Screen, Chasing Amy*

Grammnet Productions
(Actor: Kelsey Grammer)

5555 Melrose Ave.,
   Lucy Bldg. #206 (TV)
   Bob Hope Bldg. #202 (film)
Los Angeles, CA 90038-3197
(323) 956-5547/(323) 956-5840
   Phone
(323) 862-1433 Fax
Credits: *Kelsey Grammer Salutes Jack Benny, Fired Up, The Innocent, Girlfriends, Gary the Rat, In-Laws*

Granada Film

5225 Wilshire Blvd., Ste. 603
Los Angeles, CA 90036
(323) 692-9940 Phone
(323) 692-9944 Fax
Credits: *The Great Gatsby, Cracker, Dash & Lilly, The John Denver Story, The Warden, Princess of Thieves, Beggars and Choosers, Strange Relations, The Lady in Question, Murder in a Small Town, Skinwalkers, Second Nature*

Green Communications

303 N. Glenoaks Blvd., Ste. 605
Burbank, CA 91502
(818) 557-0050 Phone
(818) 557-0056 Fax
Web: www.greenfilms.com
E-mail: info@greenfilms.com
Credits: *Ground Control, Living in Peril, Space Marines, The Time of Her Time, Dark Prince, The Last Producer, Sordid, Mambo Cafe, G-men from Hell, Outpatient, Lucky Town*

Green Moon Productions
(Actors: Antonio Banderas and Melanie Griffith)

3110 Main St., Ste. 205
Santa Monica, CA 90405
(310) 450-6111 Phone
(310) 450-1333 Fax
Credits: *Crazy in Alabama, The Body, Along for the Ride, Tart*

Greenstreet Films, Inc.

9 Desbrosses St., 2nd Fl.
New York, NY 10013
(212) 343-1049 Phone
(212) 343-0774 Fax
Credits: *Pinero, Just a Kiss, The Chateau, A Price Above Rubies, Illuminata, Company Man, I'm Not*

Rappaport, Lisa Picard Is Famous,
In the Bedroom, Swimfan

The Alan Greisman Company

335 N. Maple Dr., Ste. 135
Beverly Hills, CA 90210
(310) 205-2766 Phone
(310) 285-2345 Fax

Merv Griffin Entertainment

9860 Wilshire Blvd.
Beverly Hills, CA 90210
(310) 385-3160 Phone
(310) 385-3162 Fax
Credits: *The Ainsley Harriott*
Show; The Christmas List; Click!;
Men Are from Mars, Women Are
from Venus; Murder at the Cannes
Film Festival; Inside the Osmonds;
Gilda Radner: It's Always
Something

Matt Groening Productions
(ANM)

10201 W. Pico Blvd., Bldg. 208,
   Ste. 28
Los Angeles, CA 90035
(310) 369-3872 Phone

Randa Haines Company

11693 San Vincente Blvd., Ste. 389
Los Angeles, CA 90049
(310) 889-1843 Phone
(310) 472-7951 Fax
Credits: *Children of a Lesser God,*
The Doctor, Wrestling Ernest
Hemingway, A Family Thing,
Dance with Me, The Antwone
Fisher Story

Hallway Pictures

4929 Wilshire Blvd., Ste. 830
Los Angeles, CA 90010
(323) 937-9210 Phone
(323) 937-9222 Fax

Halsted Pictures

15 Brooks Ave., Unit B
Venice, CA 90291
(310) 450-7804 Phone
(310) 450-8174 Fax

Hamzeh Mystique Films

61 Blaney St.
Swampscott, MA 01907-2546
781-596-1281 Phone
781-599-2424 Fax
E-mail: ziad@hamzehmystique
   films.com

PRODUCERS

Handprint Entertainment

1100 Glendon Ave., Ste.1000
Los Angeles, CA 90024
(310) 481-4400 Phone
(310) 481-4419 Fax
Credits: *Fresh Prince of Bel Air,
Above the Rim, Booty Call*

Harpo Films, Inc.
(Actress/Producer: Oprah Winfrey)

345 N. Maple Dr., Ste. 315
Beverly Hills, CA 90210
(310) 278-5559 Phone
Credits: *Beloved, Before Women
Had Wings, The Wedding, David &
Lisa, Tuesdays with Morrie, Amy
& Isabelle*

Hart-Sharp Entertainment

380 Lafayette St., Ste. 304
New York, NY 10003
(212) 475-7555 Phone
(212) 475-1717 Fax
Credits: *Boys Don't Cry, You Can
Count on Me, Lift, Nicholas
Nickleby*

Harvey Entertainment Company

11835 W. Olympic Blvd. #550E
Los Angeles, CA 90064

(310) 444-4100 Phone
(310) 444-4101 Fax

HBO Original Movies

2049 Century Park E., Ste. 4200
Los Angeles, CA 90067
(310) 201-9200 Phone
Credits: *Six Feet Under, Curb Your
Enthusiasm, Oz, Sex and the City,
The Sopranos, The Wire*

Heel & Toe Films
(Producer: Paul Attanasio)

650 N. Bronson Ave., Bronson Bldg.
200
Hollywood, CA 90293
(323) 960-4591 Phone
(323) 960-4592 Fax
Credits: *Quiz Show, Donnie Brasco,
Homicide: Life on the Street,
Gideon's Crossing, Sum of All Fears*

Jim Henson Company

Raleigh Studios
5358 Melrose Ave., Ste. 300 W.
Hollywood, CA 90038
(323) 960-4096 Phone
(212) 794-2400 (NYC)

Vicky Herman Productions

8001 Highland Trail
Los Angeles, CA 90046
(323) 656-4207 Phone
Credits: *Dirty Pictures, A Dangerous Affair, Trial by Fire, Holiday Affair, The Baby Dance, All She Ever Wanted*

Hero Entertainment

P.O. Box 50811
Santa Barbara, CA 93150
805-695-0757 Phone
805-695-0757 Fax
Credits: *Blank Check, Roger Ramjet: Hero of Our Nation*

Debra Hill Productions

1250 6th St., Ste. 205
Santa Monica, CA 90401
(310) 319-0052 Phone
(310) 260-8502 Fax
Credits: *The Fisher King, Crazy in Alabama, Escape from LA, Halloween*

Hit & Run Productions

150 W. 56th St., Ste. 5606
New York, NY 10019
(212) 974-8400 Phone
(212) 974-8443 Fax
Credits: *Eye of the Beholder, Beautopia*

Hofflund/Polone

9465 Wilshire Blvd., Ste. 820
Beverly Hills, CA 90212
(310) 859-1971 Phone
(310) 859-7250 Fax

Hogan Moorhouse Pictures

1250 6th St., Ste. 305
Santa Monica, CA 90401
(310) 319-9299 Phone

Horizon Entertainment, Inc.

1040 Hamilton St., Ste. 205
Vancouver, BC V6B 2R9 Canada
(604) 632-1707 Phone
(604) 632-1607 Fax
Web: www.filmhorizon.com
E-mail: rhs@filmhorizon.com

The minute you see the sweat on a word you're aware of it being a joke.
—NEIL SIMON

PRODUCERS

Horseshoe Bay Productions

500 S. Buena Vista St.,
Animation 1G
Burbank, CA 91521
(818) 560-3229 Phone
(818) 848-6832 Fax

HRD Productions

1041 N. Formosa Ave.
West Hollywood, CA 90046
(323) 850-3595 Phone
(323) 850-3596 Fax
Credits: *The Replacements, Odd Couple II, Pretty in Pink, Article 99, Grumpier Old Men, Gleason*

Hungry Man Films

428 Broadway, 6th Fl.
New York, NY 10013
(212) 625-5600 Phone
(212) 625-5699 Fax

Hunt-Tavel Productions
(Actress: Helen Hunt)

10202 W. Washington Blvd., Astaire
Bldg. #2410
Culver City, CA 90232
(310) 244-3144 Phone
(310) 244-0164 Fax

Peter Hyams Productions, Inc.

1453 Third St., Ste. 315
Santa Moncia, CA 90401
(310) 393-1553 Phone
(310) 393-1554 Fax
Credits: *The Musketeer, Sudden Death, Running Scared, The Relic, Timecop, Narrow Margin, End of Days*

Hyde Park Entertainment

2500 Broadway St.
Santa Monica, CA 90404
(310) 449-3191 Phone
(310) 449-3356 Fax
Credits: *Bringing Down the House, Moonlight Mile, Bandits, Original Sin, Antitrust*

Icon Productions, Inc.
(Actor: Mel Gibson)

5555 Melrose Ave.
Los Angeles, CA 90038
(323) 956-2100 Phone
(323) 862-2121 Fax
Credits: *Maverick, Hamlet, Braveheart, Payback, The Three Stooges, What Women Want, We Were Soldiers*

IFM Film Associates, Inc.

1328 E. Palmer Ave.
Glendale, CA 91205
(818) 243-4976 Phone
(818) 550-9728 Fax
E-mail: ifmfilm@aol.com
Credits: *Sally Marshall Is Not an Alien, The Whole of the Moon, The Hit*

Imagemovers
(Director: Robert Zemeckis)

100 Universal City Plaza, Bldg. 484
Universal City, CA 91608
(818) 733-8313 Phone
(818) 733-8333 Fax
Credits: *Romancing the Stone, Used Cars, Forrest Gump, Back to the Future, Back to the Future 2 and 3, Who Framed Roger Rabbit, Death Becomes Her, Contact, 1941, What Lies Beneath, Cast Away*

★ Imagine Entertainment
(Director/Producer: Ron Howard/ Brian Grazer)

9465 Wilshire Blvd., 7th Fl.
Beverly Hills, CA 90212
(310) 858-2000 Phone
(310) 858-2020 Fax
Credits: *A Beautiful Mind, 8 Mile, Blue Crush, How the Grinch Stole Christmas*

Incognito Entertainment

9440 Santa Monica Blvd., Ste. 302
Beverly Hills, CA 90210
(310) 246-1500 Phone
(310) 246-0469 Fax
Credits: *Three to Tango, Morning, Freeway II*

Indican Productions
(Actress: Julia Ormond)

2565 Broadway, Ste. 138
New York, NY 10025
(212) 666-1500 Phone
(212) 666-9588 Fax
Credits: *Calling the Ghosts*

Industry Entertainment
(Producers: Keith Addis and Nich Wechsler)

955 S. Carrilo Dr., 3rd Fl.
Los Angeles, CA 90048
(323) 954-9000 Phone
(323) 954-0990 Fax
Credits: *25th Hour; The Player; sex, lies, and videotape; Drugstore Cowboy; The Yards; Fifteen Minutes; Requiem for a Dream; Quills; Antitrust; Only Joking; The Education of Max Bickford; Becker; Live from Baghdad; Going to California*

PRODUCERS

Initial Entertainment Group, Inc.

3000 W. Olympic Blvd., Ste. 1550
Santa Monica, CA 90404
(310) 315-1722 Phone
(310) 315-1723 Fax
Web: www.initial-ent.com
Credits: *Gangs of New York, Ali,
The Dangerous Lives of Altar Boys,
Traffic, Dr. T & the Women, Desert
Saints, Joe the King, Savior, Little
City, Montana*

Interlight

8981 Sunset Blvd., Ste. 101
West Hollywood, CA 90069
(310) 248-4477 Phone
(310) 248-4494 Fax
E-mail: contact@interlightusa.com

Intermedia

9350 Civic Center Dr., Ste. 100
Beverly Hills, CA 90210
(310) 777-0007 Phone
(310) 777-0008 Fax
Web: www.intermediafilm.com
Credits: *Adaptation, Dark Blue,
The Life of David Gale, K-PAX, K-
19: The Widowmaker, Nurse Betty,
The Wedding Planner, Iris, Sliding
Doors, Playing by Heart, Hilary
and Jackie, Terminator 3: The Rise
of the Machines*

International Film Group

7910 Ivanhoe Ave., Ste. 529
La Jolla, CA 92037
(858) 551-7310 Phone
(858) 551-7611 Fax
E-mail: ifg@ifgfilms.com

Irish Dreamtime

(Actor: Pierce Brosnan)

2450 Broadway, Ste. E-5021
Santa Monica, CA 90404
(310) 449-3411 Phone
(310) 586-8138 Fax
Credits: *Evelyn, The Nephew, The
Thomas Crown Affair, The Match*

Ixtlan Productions

(Writer/Director/Producer:
Oliver Stone)

201 Santa Monica Blvd., Ste. 610
Santa Monica, CA 90401
(310) 395-0525 Phone
(310) 395-1536 Fax

The Jacobson Company

(Producer: Tom Jacobson)

500 S. Buena Vista St.
Burbank, CA 91521
(818) 560-1600 Phone
(818) 655-8746 Fax

Jaffilms

152 W. 57th St., 52nd Fl
New York, NY 10019
(212) 262-4700 Phone
(212) 262-4729 Fax
Credits: *Four Feathers, I Dreamed of Africa, Madeline, The Accused, Fatal Attraction, Kramer vs. Kramer, Taps*

Jaret Entertainment

2017 Pacific Ave., Ste.2
Venice, CA 90291
(310) 883-8807 Phone
(310) 822-0916 Fax
Credits: *10 Things I Hate About You*

Jersey Films

(Actor/Director: Danny De Vito)

P.O. Box 491246
Los Angeles, CA 90049
(310) 550-3200 Phone
(310) 550-3210 Fax
Credits: *Erin Brockovich, Man on the Moon, Living Out Loud, Out of Sight, Gattaca, Feeling Minnesota, Sunset Park, Get Shorty, Reality Bites, Pulp Fiction, Hoffa, 8 Seconds*

The Jinks/Cohen Company

100 Universal City Plaza, Bldg. 5171
Universal City, CA 91608
(818) 733-9880 Phone
(818) 733-9843 Fax
Credits: *American Beauty, Down with Love*

Jonesing Pictures

4502 Jouster Ct. #306
Orlando, FL 32817
Web: www.jonesingpictures.com
E-mail: jonesing@jonesingpictures
.com

Jovy Junior Enterprises Ltd

31 Kingly St.
London W1R 5LA United Kingdom

Jump Rope Productions

10932 Morrison St. #108
Studio City, CA 91601
(818) 752-2229 Phone

Junction Entertainment

(Director: Jon Turtletaub)

. . . .

500 S. Buena Vista St.,
  Animation 1-B
Burbank, CA 91521
(818) 560-2800 Phone
(818) 841-3176 Fax
Credits: *Instinct, Phenomenon,
While You Were Sleeping, The Kid*

Kaplan/Perrone Entertainment

(Producers: Aaron Kaplan
and Sean Perrone)

. . . .

10202 W. Washington Blvd., Astaire
  Bldg., Ste. 3003
Culver City, CA 90232
(310) 244-6681 Phone
(310) 244-2151 Fax

Kareem Productions

(Actor: Kareem Abdul-Jabbar)

. . . .

5458 Wilshire Blvd.
Los Angeles, CA 90036
(310) 201-7960 Phone
(310) 201-7964 Fax

Marty Katz Productions

. . . .

1250 6th St., Ste. 205
Santa Monica, CA 90401
(310) 260-8501 Phone

(310) 260-8502 Fax
Credits: *Man of the House, Lost
in America, Mr. Wrong, Reindeer
Games, Impostor, The Four
Feathers*

Keller Entertainment Group

. . . .

14225 Ventura Blvd.
Sherman Oaks, CA 91423
(818) 981-4950 Phone
(818) 501-6224 Fax
E-mail: jimperi105@aol.com
Credits: *Conan, Tarzan, Acapulco
Heat, Summer of Fear*

David E. Kelley Productions

. . . .

Raleigh Manhattan Beach Studios
1600 Rosecrans Ave., Bldg. 4B
Manhattan Beach, CA 90266
(310) 727-2200 Phone
Credits: *Picket Fences, Chicago
Hope, The Practice, Lake Placid,
Ally McBeal, Mystery, Alaska,
Snoops, Boston Public, Girls Club*

Kennedy/Marshall Company

. . . .

3000 W. Olympic Blvd., Bldg. 5,
  Ste. 1250
Santa Monica, CA 90404
(310) 656-8400 Phone
(310) 656-8430 Fax

Killer Films, Inc.

380 Layfayette St. #302
New York, NY 10003
(212) 473-3950 Phone
(212) 473-6152 Fax
Credits: *Far from Heaven, One Hour Photo, The Grey Zone, Hedwig and the Angry Inch, Storytelling, Safety of Objects, Safe, I Shot Andy Warhol, Kids, Velvet Goldmine, Happiness, Boys Don't Cry, Series 7, Crime and Punishment in Suburbia, Women in Film, Chelsea Walls*

Kingsgate Films, Inc. (Actor: Nick Nolte)

18954 W. Pico, 2nd Fl.
Los Angeles, CA 90035
(310) 281-5880 Phone
(310) 281-2633 Fax
Credits: *Affliction, Simpatico, Investigating Sex, Rules of Attraction*

Kinowelt Film Production UK

38-42 Whitfield St.

London W1T 2AP United Kingdom
+44 207 916 0157

Klasky-Csupo (ANM)

6353 Sunset Blvd.
Hollywood, CA 90028
(323) 463-0145 Phone
Web: www.cooltoons.com
Credits: *Stressed Eric, Rugrats, The Wild Thornberrys, Rocket Power, As Told by Ginger, Aaahh! Real Monsters, Santo Bugito, Duckman, The Simpsons, The Rugrats Movie, Rugrats in Paris: The Movie, Ronald McDonald's Wacky Adventures*

Randal Kleiser Productions

3050 Runyon Canyon Rd.
Los Angeles, CA 90046
(323) 850-5511 Phone
(323) 850-1074 Fax

The Koch Company

2791 Ellison Dr.
Beverly Hills, CA 90210
(310) 271-0466 Phone

❚ **TIP:** When getting notes on your writing, try to avoid being defensive. Sometimes they're just testing you to see how easy you are to work with. Everybody gets notes—no matter how famous they are.

P R O D U C E R S

Konrad Pictures

Columbia Pictures
10202 W. Washington Blvd., TriStar
 Bldg. #222
Culver City, CA 90232
(310) 244-3555 Phone
(310) 244-0555 Fax
Credits: *Scream; Scream 2;,
Scream 3; Citizen Ruth; Beautiful
Girls; Kids; Girl, Interrupted;
Teaching Mrs. Tingle; The Sweetest
Thing; Kate & Leopold*

Kopelson Entertainment

(Producers: Arnold and Anne
Kopelson)

8490 Sunset Blvd., 2nd Fl.
Los Angeles, CA 90069
(310) 360-3200 Phone
(310) 360-3201 Fax
Credits: *Don't Say a Word, A
Perfect Murder, U.S. Marshals,
Devil's Advocate, Eraser, Seven,
Outbreak, The Fugitive, Falling
Down, Platoon*

Robert Kosberg
Productions

c/o Merv Griffin Entertainment
9860 Wilshire Blvd.
Beverly Hills, CA 90210
(310) 385-3165 Phone
(310) 385-3162 Fax

Credits: *Commando, In the Mood,
Man's Best Friend, Twelve Monkeys*

Kouf-Bigelow Productions

(Producers: Jim Kouf and Lynn
Bigelow-Kouf)

10061 Riverside Dr. #1024
Toluca Lake, CA 91602
(818) 508-1010 Phone

The Jonathan Krane Group

8033 Sunset Blvd., Ste. 6750
Los Angeles, CA 90046
(310) 278-0142 Phone
(310) 278-0925 Fax
Credits: *Look Who's Talking,
Chocolate War, Michael, Blind
Date, Face/Off, The General's
Daughter, Swordfish, Domestic
Disturbance*

Kushner-Locke Company

11601 Wilshire Blvd., 21st. Fl.
Los Angeles, CA 90025
(310) 445-1111 Phone
(310) 445-1191 Fax
Web: www.kushner-locke.com
Credits: *Pinocchio, Andre, Brave
Little Toaster, Brave Little Toaster
2, Brave Little Toaster 3, Gun ,
Freeway, Freeway 2, Harvard Man,
Basil, Whole Wide World, Picking*

Up the Pieces, Ringmaster, Harts of the West

The Ladd Company

(Producer: Alan Ladd, Jr.)

9465 Wilshire Blvd., Ste. 910
Beverly Hills, CA 90212
(310) 777-2060 Phone
(310) 777-2061 Fax
Credits: *Chariots of Fire, Blade Runner, The Right Stuff, Police Academy, Braveheart*

Lakeshore International

5555 Melrose Ave., Gloria Swanson
    Bldg., 4th Fl.
Hollywood, CA 90038
(323) 956-4222 Phone
(323) 862-1456 Fax
Web: www.lakeshoreentertainment
    .com
Credits: *The Mothman Prophecies, The Gift, Autumn in New York, Runaway Bride, Arlington Road*

La Luna Films

335 N. Maple Dr., Ste. 235
Beverly Hills, CA 90210
(310) 285-9696 Phone
(310) 285-9691 Fax
Credits: *Mermaids, The Butcher's Wife, Drop Zone, Dream Lover, Fires Within, Shadow Ops, 6 Days/7 Nights*

La-Mont Communications, Inc.

13323 Washington Blvd., Ste. 306
Los Angeles, CA 90066
(310) 577-6725 Phone
(310) 577-6727 Fax

Larger Than Life Productions

100 Universal City Plaza, Bldg. 6111
Universal City, CA 91608
(818) 777-4004 Phone
(818) 866-5677 Fax
Credits: *Pleasantville*

Largo Entertainment

2029 Century Park E., Ste. 4125
Los Angeles, CA 90067
(310) 203-0055 Phone
(310) 203-0254 Fax

Cyd Levin & Associates

Attn: Rob Gallagher
8919 Harrat St., Ste. 305
Los Angeles, CA 90069
(310) 271-6484 Phone
Web: www.robgallagher.freeservers
    .com

Licht/Mueller Film Corporation

132 S. Lasky Dr., Ste. 200
Beverly Hills, CA 90212
(310) 205-5500 Phone
(310) 205-5590 Fax
Credits: *Idle Hands, The Cable Guy, Waterworld*

Lighthouse Productions

120 El Camino Dr., Ste. 212
Beverly Hills, CA 90212
(310) 859-4923 Phone
(310) 859-7511 Fax
Credits: *Impostor, The Flamingo Kid, The Sting, Close Encounters, Taxi Driver, Mimic*

Lightstorm Entertainment
(Writer/Director: James Cameron)

919 Santa Monica Blvd.
Santa Monica, CA 90401
(310) 656-6100 Phone
(310) 656-6102 Fax
Credits: *Strange Days, Titanic, Aliens, Abyss, Terminator, T2, True Lies*

Lion Rock Productions
(Producers: John Woo
And Terence Chang)

2500 Broadway St., Ste. E590

Santa Monica, CA 90404
(310) 449-3205 Phone
(310) 449-3512 Fax
Credits: *The Big Hit, Face/Off, Broken Arrow, Windtalkers*

Lions Gate Films International

4553 Glencoe Ave., Ste. 200
Marina del Rey, CA 90292
(310) 314-2000 Phone
(310) 392-0252 Fax
Credits: *Monster's Ball, O, Lovely & Amazing, Secretary, Frailty, Rules of Attraction, The Wash, Amores Perros, Lantana, The Grey Zone*

Little Studio Films

270 N. Canon Dr. #1861
Beverly Hills, CA 90210
(310) 652-5385 Phone

Live Planet

2950 31st St., 3rd Fl.
Santa Monica, CA 90405
(310) 664-2400 Phone
Credits: *Project Greenlight, Push, Nevada*

Lobell Productions

335 N. Maple Dr., Ste. 130
Beverly Hills, CA 90210
(310) 285-2383 Phone
(310) 205-2767 Fax
Credits: *Striptease, It Could Happen to You, The Freshman, Honeymoon in Vegas, White Fang, Journey of Natty Gann, Tears of the Sun*

Longbow Productions

4181 Sunswept Dr., Ste. 100
Studio City, CA 91604
(818) 762-6600 Phone
Credits: *Secret Cutting, The Summer of Ben Tyler, A Private Matter, A League of Their Own, The Last Brickmaker In America, Forever & Always*

Love Spell Entertainment

(Actress: Jennifer Love Hewitt)

(818) 754-5453 Phone
(818) 754-5463 Fax
Credits: *Bunny, My Romance, Secrets, 13 Seconds*

Lower East Side Films

(Actor: John Leguizamo)

302A W. 12th St. #218
New York, NY 10014
(212) 966-0111 Phone

Lucid Film

(Actor: Ryan Phillippe)

8490 Sunset Blvd., Ste. 700
Los Angeles, CA 90069
(310) 777-0007 Phone
(310) 360-8613 Fax
Credits: *Drive It Like You Stole It, Found, Honey West, What the World Needs Now, The White Boy Shuffle*

Lumiere Films Inc.

8079 Selma Ave.
Los Angeles, CA 90046
(323) 650-6773 Phone
(323) 650-7339 Fax

Lyles Productions, Inc.

Paramount Pictures
5555 Melrose Ave.
Los Angeles, CA 90038-3197
(323) 956-5819 Phone
(323) 862-0256 Fax
Credits: *Conversations with the President, The Last Day, Dear Mr. President, Here's Boomer*

Mad Chance

4000 Warner Blvd. #3
Burbank, CA 91522
(818) 954-3803 Phone
(818) 954-3447 Fax

Credits: *Confessions of a Dangerous Mind, Death to Smoochy, Cats and Dogs, Panic, Space Cowboys, Lucky Numbers, Ten Things I Hate About You, Bound, Assassins, The Astronaut's Wife*

Mainline Releasing

1801 Ave. of the Stars, Ste. 1035
Los Angeles, CA 90067
(310) 286-1001 Phone
(310) 286-0530 Fax
Web: www.mainlinereleasing.com
E-mail: info@mainlinereleasing
.com
Credits: *Indiscreet, Hangman, Spider's Web*

Malpaso Productions

(Actor/Director: Clint Eastwood)

c/o Warner Bros.
4000 Warner Blvd., Bldg. 81
Burbank, CA 91522-0811
(818) 954-3367 Phone
(818) 954-4803 Fax
Credits: *The Bridges of Madison County, Bird, Unforgiven, Space Cowboys, Blood Work*

Mandalay Pictures

c/o Paramount Pictures
5555 Melrose Ave., Lewis Bldg.
Hollywood, CA 90038
(323) 956-2400 Phone
(323) 862-2266 Fax

Mandolin Entertainment

1741 Ivar Ave.
Hollywood, CA 90028
(323) 802-6950 Phone
(323) 802-6951 Fax
Credits: *Trapped, Angel Eyes, Thelma and Louise, White Squall, When a Man Loves a Woman*

Mandy Films, Inc.

9201 Wilshire Blvd. #206
Beverly Hills, CA 90210
(310) 246-0500 Phone
(310) 246-0350 Fax
Credits: *Sleeping with the Enemy, War Games, Distinguished Gentleman, Double Jeopardy, Charlie's Angels, Ground Zero, Charlie's Angels 2*

You miss 100 percent of the shots you never take.
—WAYNE GRETZKY

The Manhattan Project Ltd.

1775 Broadway, Ste. 410
New York, NY 10019-1903
(212) 258-2541 Phone
(212) 258-2546 Fax
Credits: *Jaws, The Verdict, The Player, Deep Impact, Chocolat, Along Came a Spider, A Few Good Men, Sweet Smell of Success, Mr. Goldwyn*

Manifest Film Company

(Producers: Lisa Henson and Janet Wang)

1247 Euclid St.
Santa Monica, CA 90404
(310) 899-5554 Phone
(310) 899-5553 Fax
Credits: *High Crimes, The People vs. Larry Flynt, The Joy Luck Club, Zero Effect, The Weight of Water*

Laurence Mark Productions

10202 W. Washington Blvd., Poitier Bldg., Ste. 3111
Culver City, CA 90232
(310) 244-5239 Phone
Credits: *Riding in Cars with Boys, Romy and Michele, As Good As It Gets, The Object of My Affection, Simon Birch, Working*

Girl, Jerry Maguire, Center Stage, Anywhere But Here, Hanging Up, Finding Forrester

Marmont Productions, Inc.

1022 Palm Ave., Ste. 3
Los Angeles, CA 90069
(310) 659-0768 Phone
Credits: *Mountains of the Moon, Blood & Wine, Poodle Springs, The Postman Always Rings Twice, Porn.com*

Marstar Productions

8840 Wilshire Blvd. #102
Beverly Hills, CA 90211
(310) 358-3210 Phone
(310) 820-1850 Fax
Credits: *Mask, Sophie's Choice, Escape from Sobibor, Love Letters, On Golden Pond*

Marvel Studios Inc.

10474 Santa Monica Blvd., Ste. 206
Los Angeles, CA 90025
(310) 234-8991 Phone
(310) 234-8481 Fax
Credits: *Spider-Man, X-Men, Blade, Hulk, Iron Man, Fantastic Four*

Material

(Producer: Jorge Saralegui)

4000 Warner Blvd., 139/27
Burbank, CA 91522
(818) 954-1551 Phone
(818) 954-5299 Fax
Credits: *Queen of the Damned, Red Planet, Showtime, Time Machine*

The Matthau Company

(Actor/Director: Charles Matthau)

11661 San Vicente Blvd. #609
Los Angeles, CA 90049
(310) 454-3300 Phone
Credits: *Hanging Up, Mrs. Lambert Remembers Love, The Grass Harp, Grumpier Old Men, The Marriage Fool, Dennis the Menace, Doin' Time on Planet Earth*

Maverick Films

(Actress: Madonna)

9348 Civic Center Dr., 1st Fl.
Beverly Hills, CA 90210
(310) 276-6177 Phone
(310) 276-9477 Fax
Credits: *Turn It Up, Agent Cody Banks*

MDP Worldwide

1875 Century Park E., Ste. 2000
Los Angeles, CA 90067

(310) 226-8300 Phone
(310) 226-8350 Fax
Credits: *Eye of the Beholder, Jungle Book, The Body, Extreme Ops , Feardotcom, The Musketeer*

Meerson-Krikes

427 N. Canon Dr., Ste. 216
Beverly Hills, CA 90210
(310) 858-0552 Phone
(310) 858-0554 Fax
Credits: *Anna and the King, Star Trek IV, Back to the Beach, Double Impact*

Barry Mendel Productions

100 Universal City Plaza #5163
Universal City, CA 91608
(818) 733-3076 Phone
(818) 733-4070 Fax
Credits: *The Royal Tenenbaums, The Sixth Sense, Rushmore, Flora Plum, Unbreakable*

Merchant-Ivory

(Director/Producer: Ismail Merchant and James Ivory)

250 W. 57th St., Ste. 1825
New York, NY 10107
(212) 582-8049 Phone
(212) 459-9201 Fax

Credits: *The Mystic Masseur, The Golden Bowl, A Soldier's Daughter Never Cries, Howards End, A Room with a View, Surviving Picasso, The Remains of the Day, The Bostonians, Jefferson in Paris, Mr. & Mrs. Bridge, Slaves of New York, Cotton Mary*

Ricardo Mestres Productions

500 S. Buena Vista St.
Burbank, CA 91521
(818) 560-1000 Phone
(818) 953-4238 Fax
Credits: *101 Dalmatians, Jack, Flubber, Just Visiting, The Hunted*

Metafilmics, Inc.

4250 Wilshire Blvd.
Los Angeles, CA 90010
(818) 734-9320 Phone
Credits: *What Dreams May Come, Quantum Project, The Linda McCartney Story, Homeless to Harvard*

Middle Fork Productions

10877 Wilshire Blvd., Ste. 1810
Los Angeles, CA 90024
(310) 271-4200 Phone
(310) 271-8200 Fax

Credits: *Anaconda, Vacuums, Who's Your Daddy?*

Mike's Movies
(Producer: Michael Peyser)

627 N. Las Palmas
Los Angeles, CA 90004
(323) 462-4690 Phone
(323) 462-4699 Fax
Credits: *Haiku Tunnel, Honest, SLC Punk!, Speed 2, Matilda, The Distinguished Gentleman, Big Business, Ruthless People, FX, Desperately Seeking Susan, The Purple Rose of Cairo*

Millar/Gough Ink

3800 Barham Blvd., Ste. 503
Los Angeles, CA 90068
(323) 882-1307 Phone
(323) 851-6045 Fax

Mindfire Entertainment

3740 Overland Ave.
Los Angeles, CA 90034
(310) 204-4481 Phone
(310) 204-5882 Fax
Credits: *Free Enterprise, The Specials, The House of the Dead*

PRODUCERS

Minervision

8000 Sunset Blvd., Ste. 301A
Los Angeles, CA 90046
(323) 848-3080 Phone
(323) 848-3085 Fax

Miracle Pictures
(Producer: A. Kidman Ho)

11301 W. Olympic Blvd. #600
Los Angeles, CA 90064
(310) 828-1127 Phone
(310) 392-2021 Fax
Credits: *Ali, The Weight of Water, The Ghost and the Darkness, JFK, Born on the Fourth of July, Platoon, Brokedown Palace, The Doors, Wall Street, Heaven & Earth, On Deadly Ground, Talk Radio*

Mirage Enterprises
(Directors: Sydney Pollack and Anthony Kinchella)

233 S. Beverly Dr., Ste. 200
Beverly Hills, CA 90212
(310) 888-2830 Phone
(310) 888-2820 Fax
Credits: *Sliding Doors, The Talented Mr. Ripley, Random Hearts, Up at the Villa, Heaven, Blow Dry, Iris, Birthday Girl, The Quiet American*

Modern Entertainment

16255 Ventura Blvd., Ste. 1100
Encino, CA 91436
(818) 386-0444 Phone
(818) 728-8294 Fax

Mojo Films
(Producer: Gary Fleder)

9021 Melrose Ave., Ste. 302
Los Angels, CA 90069
(310) 248-6070 Phone
(310) 385-0475 Fax

The Montecito Picture Company (Director: Ivan Rittman)

1482 E. Valley Rd., Ste. 477
Montecito, CA 93108
(805) 565-8590 Phone
(805) 565-1893 Fax
Credits: *Beethoven, Ghostbusters, Dave, Space Jam, 6 Days/7 Nights, Private Parts, Road Trip, Evolution, Old School, Killing Me Softly*

Moonstone Entertainment

P.O. Box 7400
Studio City, CA 91614
(818) 985-3003 Phone
(818) 985-3009 Fax
Credits: *Hotel, Dancing at the Blue Iguana, Pandemonium, Twin Falls Idaho, Miss Julie, Cookie's Fortune,*

Afterglow, Digging to China, The Only Thrill

Morgan Creek Productions

4000 Warner Blvd., Bldg. 76
Burbank, CA 91522
(818) 954-4800 Phone
(818) 954-4811 Fax
Credits: *Robin Hood, Ace Ventura, Ace Ventura II, Major League, Major League II, Diabolique, Wild America, Chill Factor, American Outlaws, Juwanna Mann, I'll Be There, Exorcist Sequel*

Mostow/Lieberman

Universal Pictures
100 Universal City Plaza #4111
Universal City, CA 91608
(818) 777-4444 Phone
(818) 866-1328 Fax
Credits: *Breakdown, The Jackal, The Game, Flight of Black Angel, U-571, Terminator 3: Rise of the Machines, Around the World in 80 Days*

Motion Picture Corporation of America

1401 Ocean Ave., Ste. 301
Santa Monica, CA 90401
(310) 319-9500 Phone
(310) 319-9501 Fax

Credits: *Pavement, Consequence, Borderline, Undisputed, Boat Trip, Joe and Max, Dumb and Dumber, B.H. Ninja, Kingpin, Annie, The Breed*

MPCA/2K Media

1401 Ocean Ave., Ste. 301
Santa Monica, CA 90401
(310) 319-9500 Phone
(310) 319-9501 Fax

Mr. Mudd

(Actor: John Malkovich)

5225 Wilshire Blvd., Ste. 604
Los Angeles, CA 90036
(323) 932-5656 Phone
(323) 932-5666 Fax
Credits: *Crumb, Man in the Iron Mask, Ghost World, The Dancer Upstairs, Kill the Poor, How to Draw a Bunny*

Mutant Enemy, Inc.

(Producer: Joss Whedon)

P.O. Box 900
Beverly Hills, CA 90213-0900
(310) 579-5180 Phone
(310) 579-5380 Fax
Credits: *Buffy the Vampire Slayer, Alien Resurrection, Angel, Toy Story, Titan A.E., Firefly, Buffy the Animated Series*

Mutual Film Company
(Producers: Mark Gordon and Gary Levinsohn)

650 N. Bronson Ave., Clinton Bldg.
Hollywood, CA 90004
(323) 871-5690 Phone
(323) 871-5689 Fax
Credits: *Paulie, Tomb Raider, Saving Private Ryan, 12 Monkeys, The Patriot, Primary Colors, The Jackal, A Simple Plan, Man on the Moon, Wonder Boys, Virus, Isn't She Great, Hard Rain*

Myriad Pictures

421 S. Beverly Dr., 5th Fl.
Beverly Hills, CA 90212
(310) 789-4500 Phone
(310) 789-4545 Fax
Web: www.myriadpictures.com
E-mail: info@myriadpictures.com
Credits: *Jeepers Creepers 2, The Good Girl, National Lampoon's Van Wilder, Imagining Argentina*

Mace Neufeld Productions

10202 W. Washington Blvd.
Culver City, CA 90232
(310) 244-2555 Phone
(310) 244-0255 Fax
Credits: *The Saint, Clear and Present Danger, Patriot Games, Hunt for Red October, The*

General's Daughter, Sum of All Fears

New Amsterdam Entertainment, Inc.

675 Third Ave., Ste. 2521
New York, NY 10017
(212) 922-1930 Phone
(212) 922-0674 Fax
Credits: *Pet Sematary, The Stand, The Vernon Johns Story, Frank Herbert's Dune, Dawn of the Dead, Martin*

New Crime Productions
(Actor: John Cusack)

555 Rose Ave.
Venice, CA 90291
(310) 396-2199 Phone
(310) 396-4249 Fax
Credits: *Grosse Pointe Blank, The Jack Bull, High Fidelity*

★ New Regency Productions
(Producer: Arnon Milchan)

10201 W. Pico Blvd., Bldg. 12
Los Angeles, CA 90035
(310) 369-8300 Phone
(310) 369-0470 Fax
Credits: *L.A. Confidential, Entrapment, A Time to Kill, The Negotiator, Fight Club, City of*

Angels, Heat, Big Momma's House, Don't Say a Word, High Crimes, Unfaithful, Daredevil, Down with Love

Nickelodeon Animation Studios (ANM)

231 W. Olive Ave.
Burbank, CA 91502
(818) 736-3000 Phone
Web: www.nick.com
Credits: *Clockstoppers, Jimmy Neutron: Boy Genius, Harriet the Spy, Good Burger, Rugrats: The Movie, Snow Day, Rugrats in Paris, Hey Arnold, Wild Thornberrys: The Movie*

Nite Owl Productions, Ltd.

Attention: Sonia Satra
1409 Armacost Ave., Ste. 6
Los Angeles, CA 90025
Web: www.niteowlproductionsltd.com
E-mail: upbeatmag@aol.com

No Hands Productions

375 Greenwich St., 7th Fl.
New York, NY 10013
(212) 941-4081 Phone
(212) 941-4082 Fax
Web: www.nohandsproductions.com
Credits: *Blue's Clues*

Nuance Productions
(Actor: Paul Reiser)

345 N. Maple Dr., Ste. 208
Beverly Hills, CA 90210
(310) 247-1870 Phone
(310) 247-8150 Fax
Credits: *Mad About You*

Numenorean Films

P.O. Box 11409
Beverly Hills, CA 90210
Web: www.numenoreanfilms.com
E-mail: info@NumenoreanFilms.com
Credits: *Point Blank, TNT, The Immortal, Race Against Time, HBO Creature Features: The Spider*

If I have anything to say to young writers, it's stop thinking of writing as art. Think of it as work.
—PADDY CHAYEFSKY, screenwriter, *Network*

PRODUCERS

★ **Lynda Obst Productions**

Paramount Pictures
5555 Melrose Ave., Bldg. 210
Hollywood, CA 90038
(323) 956-8744 Phone
(323) 862-2287 Fax
Credits: *Sleepless in Seattle, The Fisher King, One Fine Day, Contact, Hope Floats, The Siege, The 60's, Someone Like You, Abandon, How to Lose a Guy in 10 Days*

Ocean Pictures
(Actor: Harold Ramis)

10201 W. Pico Blvd., Bldg. 12, Rm. 123
Los Angeles, CA 90035
(310) 369-0093 Phone
(310) 369-7742 Fax
Credits: *Analyze That, Analyze This, Bedazzled, Groundhog Day, Caddyshack, Multiplicity, National Lampoon's Vacation*

Offroad Entertainment

Paramount Pictures
5555 Melrose Ave., Bldg. 209
Hollywood, CA 90038
(323) 956-4425 Phone
(323) 862-1120 Fax

Credits: *3 Ninjas Kick Back, Jury Duty, 200 Cigarettes*

Olmos Productions, Inc.
(Actor: Edward James Olmos)

500 S. Buena Vista St.
Old Animation Bldg. 3A6, Code 1803
Burbank, CA 91521
(818) 560-8651 Phone
(818) 560-8655 Fax
Credits: *Roosters, American Me, It Ain't Love, Americanos, Stand and Deliver, Lives in Hazard*

Omega Entertainment, Ltd.

8760 Shoreham Dr.
Los Angeles, CA 90069
(310) 855-0516 Phone
(310) 652-2044 Fax
Web: www.omegapic.com/ home.htm
Credits: *.com for Murder, Hired to Kill, In the Cold of the Night, The Naked Truth*

Open City Films

44 Hudson St.
New York, NY 10013
(212) 587-8800 Phone
(212) 587-1950 Fax

★ Original Film

(Producer: Neal Moritz)

2045 S. Barrington Ave.
Los Angeles, CA 90025
(310) 445-9000 Phone
(310) 445-9191 Fax
Credits: *Greg the Bunny, Not a Teen Movie, The Fast and the Furious, Cruel Intentions, I Know What You Did Last Summer, I Know What You Did Last Summer II, Blue Streak, The Glass House, The Skulls, The Rat Pack, Saving Silverman, Urban Legend, Urban Legend II, Juice, Volcano, Sweet Home Alabama, XXX, The Skulls II, The Skulls III, Cruel*

Original Voices, Inc.

2617 3rd St.
Santa Monica, CA 90405-4108
(310) 392-3479 Phone
(310) 392-3480 Fax

Outasite New Media Studios

1099 Gainard St.
Crescent City, CA 95531
(707) 465-1556/(888) 975-8889
  Phone
(707) 465-1556 Fax
Web: http://www.outasite.com
E-mail: admin@outasite.com

Outerbanks Entertainment

(Producer: Kevin Williamson)

8000 Sunset Blvd., 3rd Fl.
Los Angeles, CA 90046
(323) 654-3700 Phone
(323) 654-3797 Fax
Credits: *Scream, Scream 2, Dawson's Creek, I Know What You Did Last Summer, Glory Days, Halloween H20*

The Outfit Management/ Noci Pictures

Web: www.nocipictures.com
E-mail: moviegossfilms@aol.com

Outlaw Productions

9155 Sunset Blvd.
West Hollywood, CA 90069
(310) 777-2000 Phone
(310) 777-2010 Fax
Credits: *National Security; Santa Clause II; Training Day; Gossip; Ready to Rumble; Three to Tango; Addicted to Love; Don Juan deMarco; The Santa Clause; sex, lies, and videotape; The Opposite Sex*

Out of the Blue . . . Entertainment

10202 W. Washington Blvd., Astaire
Bldg. #1200
Culver City, CA 90232
(310) 244-7811 Phone
(310) 244-1539 Fax
Credits: *Mr. Deeds, Master of Disguise, Big Daddy, Deuce Bigalow*

Overbrook Entertainment
(Actor: Will Smith)

450 N. Roxbury Dr., 4th Fl.
Beverly Hills, CA 90210
(310) 432-2400 Phone
Credits: *Wild Wild West* (soundtrack), *Love & Basketball* (soundtrack), *Ali*

Overseas Filmgroup/ First Look Pictures

8800 Sunset Blvd., Ste. 302
Los Angeles, CA 90069
(310) 855-1199 Phone
(310) 855-0719 Fax
Web: www.ofg.com
E-mail: info@ofg.com

Oxygen Media

75 Ninth Ave.
New York, NY 10011
(212) 651-2000 Phone
(212) 651-2099 Fax

Credits: *Pure Oxygen, The Issac Mizrahi Show, Real Families, Oprah: After the Show, Conversations from the Edge with Carrie Fisher, Girls Behaving Badly*

Pacifica Entertainment, Inc.

335 N. Maple Dr., Ste. 235
Beverly Hills, CA 90210
(310) 285-9696 Phone
(310) 285-9691 Fax
Credits: *Nurse Betty, Clay Pigeons, Where the Money Is, The Wedding Planner, K-Pax, K-19: The Widowmaker, The Quiet American*

Pandora Cinema (U.S. Office)

400 Warner Blvd., Ste. 81
Burbank, CA 91522
(818) 560-6790 Phone
(818) 841-3186 Fax
Credits: *Donnie Darko, Shine, Kolya, Like Water for Chocolate, A Walk to Remember, White Oleander, Welcome to Collinwood*

Panoptic Pictures

6888 Alta Loma Terrace
Los Angeles, CA 90068
(323) 874-3060 Phone
(323) 876-3290 Fax

Parkway Productions

(Director: Penny Marshall)

10202 W. Washington Blvd., Astaire
Bldg. 2210
Culver City, CA 90232
(310) 244-4040 Phone
(310) 244-0240 Fax
Credits: *Riding in Cars with Boys,
The Preacher's Wife, Awakenings,
Renaissance Man, A League of
Their Own, Big*

Zak Penn's Company

Twentieth Century Fox
10201 W. Pico, Bldg. 31, Rm. 303
Los Angeles, CA 90035
(310) 369-7360 Phone
(310) 969-0249 Fax
Credits: *Inspector Gadget, PCU,
Osmosis Jones, Behind Enemy
Lines, Last Action Hero, Antz*

Permut Presentations

(Actor: David Permut)

9150 Wilshire Blvd., Ste. 247
Beverly Hills, CA 90212
(310) 248-2792 Phone
(310) 248-2797 Fax
Credits: *Face/Off, Eddie, Dragnet,
Blind Date, Double Take,
Consenting Adults, Three of Hearts,
Richard Pryor Live in Concert*

Pfeffer Film

Walt Disney Studios
500 S. Buena Vista Blvd., Animation
Bldg. 2F-8
Burbank, CA 91521
(818) 560-3177 Phone
(818) 843-7485 Fax
Credits: *Crazy/Beautiful, Malice,
Grand Avenue, A Civil Action, The
Horse Whisperer, A Few Good Men*

Phase I Productions

(Producer: Joe Wizan)

3210 Club Dr.
Los Angeles, CA 90064
(310) 842-8401 Phone
(310) 280-0415 Fax

Phoenix Pictures

10125 W. Washington Blvd.,
Frankovich Bldg.
Culver City, CA 90232
(310) 244-6100 Phone
(310) 839-8915 Fax
Credits: *Werewolf, Damnation
Game, Bad News, Zodiac, Yeager,
All The King's Men, Shanghai,
Hardcourt, Destination Unknown,
Dangerous Waters, Black Autumn,
Flower Girl*

PRODUCERS

Marc Platt Productions

Universal Studios
100 Universal City Plaza #5184
Universal City, CA 91608
(818) 777-1122 Phone
(818) 866-6353 Fax
Credits: *Josie and the Pussycats, Legally Blonde*

Playhouse Pictures (ANM)

1401 N. La Brea Ave.
Hollywood, CA 90028
(323) 851-2112 Phone

+Entertainment

468 N. Camden Dr., Ste. 250
Beverly Hills, CA 90210
(310) 860-5604 Phone
(310) 860-5194 Fax
Web: www.plusent.com
E-mail: mail@plusent.com
Credits: *Blood Dancers, Good Neighbor, Sweet Nightmare, Future Shock Vol. 1, Tons Do Brasil, Zoo Safari, Three Cultures of Appalachia: Women of These Hills II*

Edward R. Pressman Film Corporation

130 El Camino Dr.
Beverly Hills, CA 90212
(310) 271-8383 Phone
(310) 271-9497 Fax
Credits: *Owning Mahowny, City Hall, The Crow, Conan, Reversal of Fortune, Wall Street, Two Girls and a Guy, Black & White, American Psycho*

Promark Entertainment Group

3599 Cahuenga Blvd., Ste. 300
Los Angeles, CA 90068
(323) 878-0404 Phone
(323) 878-0486 Fax
E-mail: sales@promarkgroup.com
Credits: *Pilgrim, After Alice, Contaminated Man, Styx, The Enemy, Last Run, The Shipment, The Stick-Up, Greenmail, One Way Out, Miami Sands, Lone Hero, Black Point, Federal Protection*

Propaganda Films

1741 N. Ivar Ave.
Los Angeles, CA 90028
(323) 462-6400 Phone
(323) 802-7001 Fax

Prufrock Pictures

(Actress: Meg Ryan)

335 N. Maple Dr., Ste. 315
Beverly Hills, CA 90210
(310) 285-2360 Phone

Punch Productions

(Actor: Dustin Hoffman)

1926 Broadway #305
New York, NY 10023
(212) 595-8800/(310) 442-4888
  Phone
(310) 442-4884 Fax
Credits: *Tootsie, Mad City, Wag
the Dog, Walk on the Moon, Devil's
Arithmatic, Outbreak, Death of a
Salesman, American Buffalo, Boys
and Girls, Clubland*

Radar Pictures, Inc.

10900 Wilshire Blvd., Ste. 1400
Los Angeles, CA 90024
(310) 208-8525 Phone
(310) 208-1764 Fax
Credits: *They, Pitch Black,
Runaway Bride, Jumanji, Mr.
Holland's Opus*

Radiant Pictures

(Director/Producer: Wolfgang
Peterson and Gail Katz)

914 Montana Ave., 2nd Fl.

Santa Monica, CA 90403
(310) 656-1400 Phone
(310) 656-1408 Fax
Credits: *Troy, The Perfect Storm,
Air Force One, Outbreak, In the
Line of Fire, Das Boot, The Agency*

Radical Media

435 Hudson St.
New York, NY 10014
(212) 462-1500/(310) 664-4500
  Phone

Raffaella Productions, Inc.

100 Universal City Plaza #5162
Universal City, CA 91608-1085
(310) 841-4355 Phone
(310) 815-9849 Fax
Credits: *Prancer Returns, Daylight,
Dragonheart, Dragon: Bruce Lee
Story, Dragonheart: A New
Beginning, Uprising, The World of
Tomorrow*

Rainmaker Productions, Inc.

7255 Santa Monica Blvd.
Hollywood, CA 90046
(323) 874-6770 Phone
(800) 858-0520 Fax

Martin Ranshohoff Productions, Inc.

400 S. Beverly Dr., Ste. 308
Beverly Hills, CA 90212
(310) 551-2680 Phone
(310) 551-2094 Fax
Credits: *Guilty as Sin, Jagged Edge, Switching Channels, Class*

Rastar Productions

10202 W. Washington Blvd.,
Lean Bldg., Rm. 430
Culver City, CA 90232
(310) 244-7874 Phone
(310) 244-2331 Fax
Credits: *To Gillian on Her 37th Birthday, Steel Magnolias, Harriet the Spy, Random Hearts, Brighton Beach Memoirs, Chapter Two, Lost in Yonkers, Mr. Jones, Nothing in Common, Peggy Sue Got Married, Revenge, The Slugger's Wife, Sylvester, Violets Are Blue*

Rat Entertainment
(Director: Brett Ratner)

9255 Sunset Blvd., Ste. 310
Los Angeles, CA 90069
(310) 228-5000 Phone
(310) 860-9251 Fax
Credits: *Red Dragon, Rush Hour, Rush Hour 2, The Family Man, Money Talks*

Recorded Picture Company

7001 Melrose Ave.
Los Angeles, CA 90038
(323) 937-0733 Phone
(323) 936-4913 Fax
Credits: *Sexy Beast, The Last Emperor, Rabbit-Proof Fence, Stealing Beauty, The Brave, Crash, Besieged, All the Little Animals, Brother, The Cup, The Triumph of Love*

Red Bird Productions
(Producer: Debbie Allen)

3623 Hayden Ave.
Culver City, CA 90203
(310) 202-1711 Phone
Credits: *Amistad, Out of Sync, Cool Women*

Redeemable Features

381 Park Ave., S. PH
New York, NY 10016
(212) 685-8585 Phone
(212) 685-1455 Fax

Red Hen Productions
(Producer: Stuart Gordon)

13500 Crewe St.
Valley Glen, CA 91405
(818) 787-6600 Phone
(818) 787-6637 Fax

Credits: *Deathbed; Dagon; Space Truckers; Ice Cream Suit; Honey, I Shrunk the Kids; Honey, I Blew Up the Kid; Re-Animator; Fortress*

Red Hour Films
(Actor: Ben Stiller)

193 N. Robertson Blvd.
Beverly Hills, CA 90211
(310) 289-2565 Phone
(310) 289-5988 Fax
Credits: *Duplex, Zoolander, The Ben Stiller Show, Reality Bites, The Cable Guy*

Red Mullet, Inc.
(Director: Mike Figgis)

1532 N. Hayworth Ave. #9
Los Angeles, CA 90046
(323) 874-3372 Phone
(323) 874-3372 Fax

Red Strokes Entertainment
(Actor: Garth Brooks)

9465 Wilshire Blvd., Ste. 319
Beverly Hills, CA 90212
(310) 786-7887 Phone
(310) 786-7827 Fax
Credits: *Call Me Claus*

★ Red Wagon Productions
(Producer: Doug Wick)

10202 W. Washington Blvd.,
Hepburn West
Culver City, CA 90232
(310) 244-4466 Phone
(310) 244-1480 Fax
Credits: *Wolf; Working Girl; The Craft; Hollow Man; Girl, Interrupted; Gladiator; Stuart Little; Stuart Little 2; Spy Game*

Rehme Productions
(Producer: Robert Rehme)

1145 Gayley Ave., Ste. 301
Los Angeles, CA 90024
(310) 824-3371 Phone
(310) 824-5459 Fax
Credits: *Gettysburg, Patriot Games, Clear & Present Danger, Deacons for Defense, Gods and Generals*

Renaissance Films, Ltd.

34–35 Berwick St.
London W1V 8RP United Kingdom
44-207-287-5190 Phone
44-207-287-5100 Fax

Art is a lie that tells the truth.
—PABLO PICASSO

Web: www.renaissance-films.com
E-mail: info@renaissance-films.com

Credits: *Gremlins, Gremlins 2, Innerspace, Deceived, Matinee, 2nd Civil War, Small Soldiers*

Renaissance Pictures

(Director: Sam Raimi)

- -

100 Universal City Plaza,
Bldg. 5166, 3rd Fl.
Universal City, CA 91608
(818) 777-0088 Phone
(818) 866-0223 Fax
Credits: *Evil Dead, Hard Target, A Simple Plan, The Gift, Hercules, Xena, Cleopatra 2525, Jack of All Trades, Spider-Man*

Renegade Animation (ANM)

- -

204 N. San Fernando Blvd.
Burbank, CA 91502
Web: www.renegadecartoons.com
Credits: *Captain Sturdy in Back in Action, Captain Sturdy in The Originals*

Renfield Productions

(Director: Joe Dante)

- -

1041 N. Formosa Ave, Writers
Bldg. 321
West Hollywood, CA 90046
(323) 850-3905 Phone
(323) 850-3907 Fax

Reperage

- -

8530 Wilshire Blvd., Ste. 400
Beverly Hills, CA 90211
(310) 360-8499 Phone
(310) 360-9865 Fax
Credits: *Enemy at the Gates, Seven Years in Tibet, Wings of Courage, The Lover, The Bear*

Reveal Entertainment

- -

Dreamworks, SKG
100 Universal Plaza, Bldg. 5171
Universal City, CA 91608
(818) 733-9818 Phone
(818) 733-9808 Fax
Credits: *Moonlight Mile, City of Angels, Casper*

Revelations Entertainment

(Actor: Morgan Freeman)

- -

301 Arizona Ave., Ste. 303
Santa Monica, CA 90401
(310) 394-3131 Phone
(310) 394-3133 Fax
Credits: *Along Came a Spider, Bopha!, Mutiny, Under Suspicion*

Revolution Studios

(Producer: Joe Roth)

2900 W. Olympic Blvd.
Santa Monica, CA 90404
(310) 255-7000 Phone

RKO Pictures, Inc.

1875 Century Park E., Ste. 2140
Los Angeles, CA 90067
(310) 277-0707 Phone
(310) 226-2490 Fax
Credits: *Mighty Joe Young, The Magnificent Ambersons, Milk & Money, A Holiday Affair*

Roadside Attractions

427 N. Canon Dr., Ste. 216
Beverly Hills, CA 90210
(310) 860-1692 Phone
(310) 860-1693 Fax
Credits: *Lovely & Amazing, Lifetime Guarantee: Phranc's Adventures in Plastic, Trick, The Shoe, They Nest*

Rockfish Films

5514 Wilshire Blvd., 6th Fl.
Los Angeles, CA 90036
(323) 937-9060 Phone
(323) 937-9361 Fax

Rogue Pictures

(Producer: Lauren Lloyd)

10202 W. Washington Blvd.
Culver City, CA 90232
(310) 244-7399 Phone
(310) 244-0800 Fax

Roscoe Enterprises, Inc.

3000 W. Olympic Blvd., Ste. 2276
Santa Monica, CA 90404
(310) 449-4066 Phone
(310) 264-4158 Fax
Credits: *The Usual Suspects, Hard Eight, Serpent's Kiss*

Alex Rose Productions, Inc.

8291 Presson Pl.
Los Angeles, CA 90069
(323) 654-8662 Phone
(323) 654-0196 Fax

Howard Rosenman Productions

635A Westbourne Dr.
Los Angeles, CA 90069
(310) 659-2100 Phone
Credits: *Eagle's Wings, Foul Play, Ten Good Men, Park Avenue Ghost, Life of an Honest Man, Gloria & Doria Gray, Trapped, You & Me and You, Fenwick's Suit, Fairhope,*

GhettoFabulous, Extended Family Christmas, Hypotheticals

Herbert Ross

c/o F. Altman & Co.
9255 Sunset Blvd., Ste. 901
Los Angeles, CA 90069
(310) 278-4201 Phone
(310) 278-5330 Fax

Roundtable Ink

6161 Santa Monica Blvd., Ste. 202
Hollywood, CA 90038
(323) 466-4646 Phone
(323) 466-4640 Fax
Credits: *What Women Want, The Chronicle, Urban Legend, Urban Legend 2, Summer's End, The Wishing Tree, Popular*

Ruby-Spears Productions
(ANM)

213 W. Alameda Ave., Ste. 102
Burbank, CA 91502
(818) 840-1234 Phone
Web: www.rubyspears.com
Credits: *Rumpelstiltskin, Jirimpimbira, Slammin' Sammy: The Sammy Sosa Story*

The Ruddy Morgan Organization, Inc.

9300 Wilshire Blvd., Ste. 508
Beverly Hills, CA 90212
(310) 271-7698 Phone
(310) 278-9978 Fax
Credits: *Farewell to the King, Bad Girls, Impulse, Lady Bugs, The Godfather, Cannonball Run, The Scout, Heaven's Prisoners, Mr. Magoo, Walker: Texas Ranger, Martial Law, Running Mates*

Scott Rudin Productions

5555 Melrose Ave., DeMille Bldg.
#200
Los Angeles, CA 90038
(323) 956-4600 Phone
(323) 862-0262 Fax
Credits: *Iris; The Royal Tenenbaums; The Hours; Changing Lanes; Zoolander; First Wives Club; Clueless; The Firm; In and Out; The Truman Show; Sleepy Hollow; Wonder Boys; Shaft; South Park: Bigger, Longer & Uncut; Ransom*

Rysher Entertainment

2425 Olympic Blvd., Ste. 6040 W.
Santa Monica, CA 90404
(310) 309-5200 Phone
(310) 309-5205 Fax

Saban Entertainment

10960 Wilshire Blvd.
Los Angeles, CA 90024
(310) 235-5100 Phone
(310) 235-5102 Fax

(310) 385-1486 Phone
(310) 936-2800 Fax
Credits: *Rush Hour, Rush Hour 2,
Last Man Standing, While You Were
Sleeping, Wanted Dead or Alive*

Samuel Goldwyn Films

9750 W. Pico Blvd., Ste. 400
Los Angeles, CA 90035
(310) 860-3100 Phone
(310) 860-3195 Fax
Credits: *He Loves Me, He Loves Me
Not; Raising Victor Vargas; Man
from Elysian Fields; Das
Experiment; Little Secrets; Me
Without You; Tortilla Soup*

Samuelson Productions

10401 Wyton Dr.
Los Angeles, CA 90024-2527
(310) 208-1000 Phone
(310) 208-2809 Fax
Credits: *Wilde, Revenge of the
Nerds, Tom & Viv, Turk 182,
Arlington Road, Dog's Best Friend,
The Commissioner, Gabriel and
Me, Playmaker*

Arthur Sarkissian Productions

5455 Wilshire Blvd., Ste. 1515
Los Angeles, CA 90036

Saturn Films

(Actor: Nicolas Cage)

9000 Sunset Blvd. #911
West Hollywood, CA 90069
(310) 887-0900 Phone
(310) 248-2965 Fax
Credits: *Sonny, Shadow of the
Vampire, The Life of David Gale*

Paul Schiff Productions

1741 Ivar Ave.
Hollywood, CA 90028
(323) 462-6400 Phone
(323) 852-1640 Fax
Credits: *Maid in Manhattan, My
Cousin Vinny, Young Guns, Young
Guns II, Rushmore, Black Knight*

Schindler Weissman Company

1710 N. Vermont Ave.
Los Angeles, CA 90027
(323) 666-5566 Phone
(323) 666-5565 Fax

PRODUCERS

Adam Schroeder Productions

4000 Warner Blvd.
Burbank, CA 91522
(818) 954-6000 Phone
Credits: *The Truman Show; Sleepy Hollow; A Simple Plan;, South Park: Bigger, Longer & Uncut; The First Wives Club; Wonder Boys; Clueless*

Joel Schumacher Productions

10201 W. Pico Blvd., Bldg. 50
Los Angeles, CA 90035
(310) 369-2300 Phone
(310) 969-1102 Fax
Credits: *Batman & Robin, A Time to Kill, Batman Forever, Flawless, Tigerland, Bad Company, Phone Booth*

Scott Free Productions
(Directors: Ridley and Tony Scott)

634 N. La Peer Dr.
West Hollywood, CA 90069
(310) 360-2250 Phone
(310) 360-2251 Fax
Credits: *Black Hawk Down, The Gathering Storm, Crimson Tide, Thelma & Louise, Enemy of the State, Gladiator*

★ Screen Gems

10202 W. Washington Blvd.
Culver City, CA 90232
(310) 244-4000 Phone
Credits: *Snatch, Arlington Road, Ghosts of Mars, Forsaken, The Mothman Prophesies, Resident Evil, Swept Away, Formula 51, Half Past Dead, Resident Evil 2*

Screen Media Ventures, LLC

757 Third Ave., 2nd Fl.
New York, NY 10017
(212) 308-1790 Phone
(212) 308-1791 Fax

Section Eight
(Actor/Director: George Clooney and Steven Soderbergh)

4000 Warner Bros., Bldg. 81 #117
Burbank, CA 91522
(818) 954-4860 Phone
Credits: *Oceans 11, Welcome to Collinwood, Insomnia, Far from Heaven, Solaris, Confessions of a Dangerous Mind*

Senator Film International

8666 Wilshire Blvd.
Beverly Hills, CA 90211
(310) 360-1441 Phone
(310) 360-1447 Fax
Credits: *Trapped, Das Experiment*

Seraphim Films

(Writer: Clive Barker)

9326 Readcrest Dr.
Beverly Hills, CA 90210
(310) 246-0050 Phone
(310) 246-0051 Fax
Credits: *Saint Sinner, Salome, The Forbidden, Nightbreed, Candyman, Candyman: Farewell to the Flesh, Lord of Illusions, Hellraiser* series, *Gods and Monsters*

Seven Arts Pictures

9051 Oriole Way
Los Angeles, CA 90069
(310) 887-3830 Phone
(310) 887-3840 Fax
Credits: *An American Rhapsody, The Believer, Johnny Mnemonic, Never Talk to Strangers, Shattered Image, Duets, 9 ½ Weeks II, Rules of Engagement*

★ Shady Acres Entertainment

100 Universal City Plaza, Bldg.
 5225, 2nd Fl.
Universal City, CA 91608
(818) 777-4446 Phone
(818) 866-6612 Fax
Credits: *Liar Liar, Patch Adams, The Nutty Professor, Dragonfly, 8 Simple Rules for Dating My Teenage Daughter*

Shoelace Productions, Inc.

(Actress: Julia Roberts)

16 W. 19th St. 12th Fl.
New York, NY 10011
(212) 243-2900 Phone
(212) 243-2973 Fax

Shonkyte Productions, Inc.

(Actress: Sean Young)

11935 Kling St. #10
Valley Village, CA 91607
(818) 505-1332 Phone
(818) 505-1411 Fax
Credits: *Mirage, Men*

Shooting Gallery, Inc.

3000 Olympic Blvd., Bldg. 3, Ste.
 1464
Santa Monica, CA 90404
(310) 315-4880 Phone
Web: www.shootinggallery.com

Shoreline Entertainment, Inc.

1875 Century Park E., Ste. 600
Los Angeles, CA 90067
(310) 551-2060 Phone
(310) 201-0729 Fax
Credits: *The Godson, Detour, Flight of Fancy, The Continued Adventures of Reptile Man, The Man from Elysian Fields, A Crack*

PRODUCERS

in the Floor, Clubland, Dark Asylum, Beeper, Tail Sting, The Visit, The King's Guard, A Matter of Trust

Showcase Entertainment, Inc.

Warner Center
21800 Oxnard St., Ste. 150
Woodland Hills, CA 91367
(818) 715-7005 Phone
(818) 715-7009 Fax

Charles Shyer, Inc.

12210 Nebraska, Ste. 8
Los Angeles, CA 90025
(310) 826-0314 Phone
(310) 826-2752 Fax

Signature Films/ Millennium Dance Complex

5113 Lankershim Blvd.
North Hollywood, CA 91601
(818) 752-2991 Phone
(818) 752-8386 Fax
Credits: *Double Jeopardy, Payback, A Stolen Life, Your Chance to Dance, Millennium Dance Complex Instructional Series*

★ Silver Pictures
(Producer: Joel Silver)

4000 Warner Blvd., Bldg. 90
Burbank, CA 91522-0001
(818) 954-4490 Phone
(818) 954-3237 Fax
Credits: *Predator, Predator 2, The Matrix, The Matrix Reloaded, The Matrix Revolutions, Die Hard, Die Hard 2, Lethal Weapon* series, *Action, Tales from the Crypt, Cradle 2 the Grave*

Simian Films (Actors: Hugh Grant and Elizabeth Hurley)

13741 Mulholland Dr.
Beverly Hills, CA 90210
(818) 789-1613 Phone
(818) 789-1277 Fax
Credits: *Extreme Measures, Mickey Blue Eyes*

The Gene Simmons Company

P.O. Box 16075
Beverly Hills, CA 90210
(310) 859-1694 Phone
(310) 859-2631 Fax
Credits: *Detroit Rock City*

Randy Simon Productions

1113 N. Hillcrest Rd.
Beverly Hills, CA 90210
(310) 274-7440 Phone
(310) 274-9809 Fax
Credits: *Pi, Requiem for a Dream, Lover's Knot, Jump, The Mao Game, End of Innocence, Intern, In the Weeds, Get Well Soon*

The Robert Simonds Company

500 S. Buena Vista St.
Animation Bldg. #2G
Burbank, CA 91521-1775
(818) 560-8900 Phone
(818) 842-2078 Fax
Credits: *Just Married, The Water Boy, Big Daddy, Happy Gilmore, Problem Child, Problem Child II, Billy Madison, The Wedding Singer, Half Baked, Corky Romano, See Spot Run*

Single Cell Pictures

(Producer: Michael Stipe)

1016 N. Palm Ave.
West Hollywood, CA 90069
(310) 360-7600 Phone
(310) 360-7011 Fax
Credits: *Velvet Goldmine, Being John Malkovich, Freak City, 13 Conversations About One Thing*

Sirk Productions

2460 Lemoine Ave., 3rd Fl.
Fort Lee, NJ 07024
(201) 944-0982 Phone
Web: www.sirkproductions.com
E-mail: sirkprod@yahoo.com

Skylark Entertainment/R&R Films

12405 Venice Blvd., Ste. 237
Los Angeles, CA 90066
(310) 390-2659 Phone
(310) 402-3223 Fax
Credits: *Steal This Movie, Orgazmo, Ace Ventura: When Nature Calls, Election, Linda McCartney, Deadlocked, Blonde, Super Fire, Blood Crime*

Skylark Films

1123 Pacific St., Ste. G
Santa Monica, CA 90405-1525
(310) 396-5753 Phone
Credits: *Terminal Justice, The Styx, Chasing Justice, Coal of the Heart*

Daniel Sladek Entertainment Corporation

(Producer: Daniel Sladek)

8306 Wilshire Blvd. #510
Beverly Hills, CA 90211
(323) 934-9268 Phone
(323) 934-7362 Fax

SNL Studios (L.A.)

5555 Melrose Ave., Rm. #105
Los Angeles, CA 90038-3197
(323) 956-5729 Phone
(323) 862-8605 Fax

Solaris

(Greg and Gavin O'Connor)

144 Franklin St., Ste. 1
New York, NY 10013
Credits: *Tumbleweeds, The Slaughter Rule, The Specimen, Mule Skinner Blues, My Generation, Murphy's Dozen*

Sonnenfeld/Josephson Worldwide Entertainment

(Barry Sonnenfeld and Barry Josephson)

10202 W. Washington Blvd., Stewart Bldg. #205
Culver City, CA 90232
(310) 244-8777 Phone
(310) 244-1977 Fax

South Fork Pictures

(Actor/Director: Robert Redford)

1101 Montana Ave., Ste. B
Santa Monica, CA 90403
(310) 395-7779 Phone
(310) 395-2575 Fax

Credits: *Quiz Show, A River Runs Through It, Ordinary People*

Southern Skies, Inc.

1104 S. Holt Ave., Ste. 302
Los Angeles, CA 90035
(310) 855-9833 Phone
(310) 855-0220 Fax
Credits: *For the Boys, Major League, Major League 2, City Slickers, Alien 3, The Great Santini*

Spelling Films

5700 Wilshire Blvd., Ste. 375
Los Angeles, CA 90036
(323) 965-5700 Phone
Credits: *7th Heaven, Charmed, Any Day Now*

Spyglass Entertainment Group

(Producer: Roger Birnbaum)

500 S. Buena Vista St.
Burbank, CA 91521-1855
(818) 560-3458 Phone
(818) 563-1967 Fax
Credits: *The Recruit, Shanghai Knights, The Count of Monte Cristo, Instinct, The Sixth Sense, The Insider, Keeping the Faith, Shanghai Noon, Unbreakable, Reign of Fire, Miracles*

Stampede Entertainment

(Producer: Ron Underwood)

3000 W. Olympic Blvd., Bldg. 2
Santa Monica, CA 90404
(310) 264-4229 Phone
(310) 264-4227 Fax
Credits: *City Slickers, Heart and Souls, Tremors* series

Stan Lee Media, Inc.

15821 Ventura Blvd., Ste. 675
Encino, CA 91436
(818) 461-1757 Phone

Starway International

12021 Wilshire Blvd., Ste. 661
Los Angeles, CA 90025
(310) 458-6202 Phone
(310) 458-6102 Fax
E-mail: starwayint@yahoo.com

Stone vs. Stone

189 Franklin St., 3rd Fl
New York, NY 10013
(212) 941-1200 Phone
Credits: *Citizen X, The Negotiator, Gone in 60 Seconds*

Stone Village Productions

(Producer: Scott Steindorff)

1033 Carol Dr., Ste. 302
West Hollywood, CA 90069
(310) 205-6339 Phone
Credits: *Empire Falls, Fire, Jake & Mimi, Untitled Howard Hughes Project, Coincidence, Straight Man, Prizonaz of War, Junior Police Academy*

Storm Entertainment

127 Broadway, Ste. 200
Santa Monica, CA 90401
(310) 656-2500 Phone
(310) 656-2510 Fax
Credits: *Modern Vampires, Hurlyburly, The Criminal, Fast Sofa, Kart Racer*

Storyline Entertainment

10202 W. Washington Blvd.
Culver City, CA 90232
(310) 244-3222 Phone
(310) 244-0322 Fax

Studiocanal France

301 N. Canon Dr., Ste. 207
Beverly Hills, CA 90210
(310) 247-0994 Phone
(310) 247-0998 Fax

Studios USA

8800 Sunset Blvd.
West Hollywood, CA 90069
(310) 360-2300 Phone
(310) 360-2517 Fax

Sudden Storm Productions

1 Deer Park Crescent, Ste. 703
Toronto, ONT M4V 3C4
(416) 927-9342 Phone
Web: www.suddenstorm.ca
E-mail: info@suddenstorm.ca

Summit Entertainment

1630 Stewart St., Ste. 120
Santa Monica, CA 90404
(310) 309-8400 Phone
(310) 828-4132 Fax
Credits: *The Alibi, Mr. & Mrs. Smith, Locked & Upright, Action!, Postmortem*

Sundance Institute

8857 W. Olympic Blvd.
Beverly Hills, CA 90211
(310) 360-1981 Phone
(310) 360-1969 Fax

Tall Trees Productions

7758 Sunset Blvd.
Los Angeles, CA 90046
(323) 378-1111 Phone
Credits: *Private Parts, The Brady Bunch Movie, Dr. Dolittle, The Late Shift, 28 Days, Can't Hardly Wait, Charlie's Angels, I Spy*

Tapestry Films, Inc.

9328 Civic Center Dr.
Beverly Hills, CA 90210
(310) 275-1191 Phone
(310) 275-1266 Fax
Credits: *Point Break, A Kid in King Arthur's Court, She's All That, The Wedding Planner, Pay It Forward, Serendipity, National Lampoon's Van Wilder*

Taurus Entertainment Company

5831 Sunset Blvd.
Hollywood, CA 90028
(323) 860-0807 Phone
(323) 860-0834 Fax
Web: www.taurus-entertainment.com
E-mail: taurusec@aol.com
Credits: *Killing Point, Mastermind, Morella, Creepshow, Hot Springs Hotel, Horror 101, Lesson of an Assassin, Girls Fight Tonight*

Taylor Made Films

225 Santa Monica Blvd., Ste. 610
Santa Monica, CA 90401
(310) 899-6739 Phone
(310) 899-5715 Fax
Credits: *Moscow on the Hudson,
Down and Out in Beverly Hills, The
Tempest, Taking Care of Business,
Moon Over Parador, Faithful*

Team Todd

9021 Melrose Ave., Ste. 301
Los Angeles, CA 90069
(310) 248-6001 Phone
(310) 385-8072 Fax
Credits: *Austin Powers* series, *If
These Walls Could Talk, If These
Walls Could Talk 2, Boiler Room,
Memento*

Ten Thirteen Productions

(Producer: Chris Carter)

P.O. Box 900
Beverly Hills, CA 90213
(310) 369-1100 Phone
Credits: *The X-Files, The Lone
Gunmen, Millennium, Harsh Realm*

3am Pictures

P.O. Box 639
San Gabriel, CA 91778
(626) 285-0005 Phone

(309) 416-8924 Fax
Web: www.3ampictures.com
E-mail: query@3ampictures.com

3 Arts Entertainment

9460 Wilshire Blvd., 7th Fl.
Beverly Hills, CA 90212
(310) 888-3200 Phone
(310) 888-3210 Fax

3 Ring Circus Films

3699 Wilshire Blvd., Ste. 12000
Los Angeles, CA 90010
(213) 251-3300 Phone
(213) 251-3350 Fax

Three Strange Angels, Inc.

2450 Broadway St.
Santa Monica, CA 90404
(310) 449-3425 Phone
(310) 449-8858 Fax

Threshold Entertainment

(ANM)

1649 11th St.
Santa Monica, CA 90404
(310) 452-8899 Phone
Web: www.thethreshold.com
Credits: *Mortal Kombat, Mortal
Kombat Annihilation, Mortal
Kombat Conquest, Beowulf*

TIG Productions, Inc.

100 Universal City Plaza
Universal City, CA 91608
(818) 777-2737 Phone
(818) 733-5616 Fax
Credits: *Thirteen Days, Dances with Wolves, The Bodyguard, Wyatt Earp, Message in a Bottle, Head Above Water*

The Steve Tisch Company

3815 Hughes Ave.
Culver City, CA 90232-2715
(310) 838-2500 Phone
(310) 204-2713 Fax
Credits: *Long Kiss Goodnight; Forrest Gump; The Postman; American History X; Corrina, Corrina; Lock, Stock and Two Smoking Barrels; Snatch*

Tomorrow Film Corporation

9250 Wilshire Blvd.
Beverly Hills, CA 90212
(310) 385-7900 Phone
(310) 385-7990 Fax
E-mail: admin@tomorrowfilms.com
Credits: *The Third Wheel, Double Bang, Just the Ticket*

Totem Productions
(Director: Tony Scott)

8009 Santa Monica Blvd.
Los Angeles, CA 90046
(323) 650-4994 Phone
(323) 650-1961 Fax
Credits: *Spy Game, True Romance, Days of Thunder, Crimson Tide, Top Gun, Enemy of the State*

Tribeca Productions
(Actor: Robert De Niro)

375 Greenwich St., 8th Fl.
New York, NY 10013
(212) 941-4000 Phone
(212) 941-4044 Fax
Credits: *A Bronx Tale, Wag the Dog, Analyze This, Marvin's Room, Thunderheart, Rocky & Bullwinkle, Meet the Parents, About a Boy, Showtime*

Trilogy Entertainment Group

2450 Broadway St., Penthouse
 Ste. 675
Santa Monica, CA 90404-3061
(310) 449-3095 Phone
(310) 449-3195 Fax
Credits: *Moll Flanders, Poltergeist: The Legacy, The Magnificent Seven, Outer Limits, Robin Hood: Prince of Thieves, Backdraft, Blown Away, Breaking News, The Dangerous*

Lives of Altar Boys, Twilight Zone 2002, Brother's Keeper

Troma Entertainment, Inc.

The Troma Building
733 Ninth Ave.
New York, NY 10019
(212) 757-4555 Phone
(212) 399-9885 Fax
Web: www.troma.com
Credits: *Toxic Avenger, Citizen Toxie: The Toxic Avenger Part 4, Terror Firmer, Sgt. Kabukiman NYPD, Tromeo & Juliet, Cannibal! The Musical, Rowdy Girls, Def by Temptation, Decampitated, Bloodsucking Freaks, All the Love You Cannes, Apocalypse Soon*

True Blue Productions
(Actress: Kirstie Alley)

P.O. Box 27127
Los Angeles, CA 90027
(323) 661-9191 Phone
(323) 661-9190 Fax

The Turman-Morrissey Company

12220 Dunoon Ln.
Los Angeles, CA 90049
(213) 740-3307 Phone
(213) 745-6652 Fax

Credits: *American History X, What's the Worst That Could Happen?, Kingdom Come, Booty Call*

Ufland Productions

534 21st St.
Santa Monica, CA 90402
(310) 656-3031 Phone
(310) 656-3073 Fax
Credits: *Night and the City, The Last Temptation of Christ, Not Without My Daughter, Snow Falling on Cedars, One True Thing, Crazy/Beautiful*

Universal Cartoon Studios
(ANM)

100 Universal City Plaza, Ste. 1320-03-M
Universal City, CA 91608
(818) 777-1213 Phone
Web: www.unistudios.com

Upfront Productions

12841 S. Hawthorne Blvd. #297
Hawthorne, CA 90250
Web: www.upfrontproductions.com
E-mail: filmnu@yahoo.com

PRODUCERS

USA Films

65 Bleecker St., 2nd Fl.
New York, NY 10012
(212) 539-4000 Phone
(212) 539-4099 Fax
Web: www.usafilms.com
Credits: *Traffic, Gosford Park, The Man Who Wasn't There, Monsoon Wedding*

Valhalla Motion Pictures
(Producer: Gale Anne Hurd)

8530 Wilshire Blvd., Ste. 400
Beverly Hills, CA 90211
(310) 360-8530 Phone
(310) 360-8531 Fax
Credits: *Dick, Terminator, Terminator 2, Aliens, Armageddon, Tremors, Dante's Peak, Clockstoppers, Water Dance, No Escape, Abyss, Safe Passage, Virus*

Vanguard Films

1230 La Collina Dr.
Beverly Hills, CA 90210
(310) 888-8020 Phone
(310) 888-8012 Fax
Credits: *7 Years in Tibet, Sarafina, Thin Blue Line, Shrek, The Tuxedo*

The Vault Inc.

1831 Centinela Ave., 2nd Fl.
Santa Monica, CA 90404

(310) 315-0012 Phone
(310) 315-9322 Fax
Credits: *The Last Supper, Campfire Tales, Panic*

Vertigo Entertainment

9348 Civic Center Dr., Mezzanine
Beverly Hills, CA 90210
(310) 288-5170 Phone
(310) 278-5295 Fax
Credits: *The Ring*

View Askew Productions, Inc.

3 Harding Rd.
Red Bank, NJ 07701
(732) 842-6933 Phone
(732) 842-3772 Fax
Credits: *Jay and Silent Bob Strike Back, Dogma, Clerks, Mallrats, Chasing Amy*

★ Village Roadshow Pictures International

3400 Riverside Dr., Ste. 900
Burbank, CA 91505
(818) 260-6000 Phone
(818) 260-6001 Fax
Web: www.village.com.au
Credits: *The Matrix, Analyze This, Practical Magic, Deep Blue Sea, Three Kings, Space Cowboys, Miss Congeniality, Swordfish, Cats &*

Dogs, Don't Say a Word, Training Day, Oceans 11, Two Weeks Notice, Analyze That, The Matrix Reloaded, Dreamcatcher

Will Vinton Studios (ANM)

1400 N.W. 22nd Ave.
Portland, OR 97210
(503) 225-1130 Phone
Web: www.vinton.com

The Robert D. Wachs Company

345 N. Maple Dr., Ste. 179
Beverly Hills, CA 90210
(310) 276-1123 Phone
(310) 276-5572 Fax
Credits: *Another 48 Hours, Beverly Hills Cop II, Raw, Coming to America*

Walking Bear Entertainment

284 Cross Country Loop
Westerville, OH 43081
(614) 899-3169 Phone
Web: www.wbei.com
E-mail: postmaster@wbei.com

Vincent Ward Films, Inc.

1134 N. Gardner St.
West Hollywood, CA 90046

(323) 850-5703 Phone
(323) 850-5743 Fax

Warner Brothers Animation (ANM)

15303 Ventura Blvd., Ste. 1200
Sherman Oaks, CA 91403
(818) 977-0333 Phone

Weed Road Pictures
(Writer/Director: Akiva Goldsman)

4000 Warner Blvd., Bldg. 81,
  Ste. 115
Burbank, CA 91522
(818) 954-3371 Phone
(818) 954-3061 Fax
Credits: *Deep Blue Sea, Starsky & Hutch*

Jerry Weintraub Productions

4000 Warner Blvd. #1
Burbank, CA 91522-0001
(818) 954-2500 Phone
(818) 954-1399 Fax
Credits: *Ocean's 11, Vegas Vacation, The Specialist, Diner, Nashville, Karate Kid* series, *Avengers, Soldier*

PRODUCERS

Weitz Brothers

(Writer/Director: Chris Weitz)

300 TV Plaza, Bldg. 136, Ste. 234
Burbank, CA 91505
(818) 954-6485 Phone

Wheelhouse

(Writer/Director: Randall Wallace)

15464 Ventura Blvd.
Sherman Oaks, CA 91403-3002
(818) 461-3599 Phone
(818) 907-0819 Fax
Credits: *Braveheart, The Man in
the Iron Mask, Pearl Harbor, We
Were Soldiers*

White Wolf Productions

2932 Wilshire Blvd., Ste. 201
Santa Monica, CA 90403
(310) 829-7500 Phone
(310) 586-0717 Fax

Winkler Films

(Producer/Director: Irwin Winkler)

211 S. Beverly Dr., Ste. 200
Beverly Hills, CA 90212
(310) 858-5780 Phone
(310) 858-5799 Fax

Credits: *Rocky, Goodfellas, Raging
Bull, The Right Stuff, The Net, At
First Sight, Life as a House, The
Shipping News, Enough*

Ralph Winter
Productions, Inc.

1201 W. Fifth St., Maryland Bldg.,
Rm. M230
Los Angeles, CA 90017
(213) 534-3654 Phone
(213) 534-3078 Fax
Credits: *X-Men 2, Planet of the
Apes, X-Men, Inspector Gadget,
Left Behind: The Movie, Mighty Joe
Young, Hackers, Star Trek IV-VI,
Shoot or Be Shot*

Witt-Thomas Films

4000 Warner Blvd., Producers 3,
Rm. 20
Burbank, CA 91522
(818) 954-2545 Phone
(818) 954-2660 Fax
Credits: *Insomnia, Three Kings,
Final Analysis, Dead Poets Society*

Wolper Organization, Inc.

c/o Warner Bros.
4000 Warner Blvd., Bldg. 14

Burbank, CA 91522

(818) 954-1421 Phone

(818) 954-1593 Fax

Credits: *L.A. Confidential, Murder in the 1st, Surviving Picasso, The Thornbirds, Roots, Mists of Avalon*

Mother's Testimony, Touched by a Killer, She's No Angel, Living with Fear, Seduced by a Thief, Redemption of the Ghost, Cloverbend, Perilous, Above and Beyond, Spirit

★ Working Title Films

9720 Wilshire Blvd., 4th Fl.

Beverly Hills, CA 90212

(310) 777-3100 Phone

(310) 777-5243 Fax

Credits: *Bean; Dead Man Walking; Fargo; Four Weddings and a Funeral; Notting Hill; Elizabeth; Bridget Jones's Diary; About a Boy; O Brother, Where Art Thou?; 40 Days and 40 Nights; The Big Lebowski; The Man Who Wasn't There; The Guru; Billy Elliot; High Fidelity*

World International Network, LLC

301 N. Canon Dr., Ste. 300

Beverly Hills, CA 90210

(310) 859-2500 Phone

(310) 859-7500 Fax

Credits: *The Perfect Nanny, The Perfect Wife, Yesterday's Children, Blind Obsession, Rain, Determination of Death, A*

Worldwide Entertainment

280 S. Beverly Dr., Ste. 208

Beverly Hills, CA 90212

(310) 205-9324 Phone

(310) 205-9325 Fax

Wychwood Productions

c/o Propaganda Films

1741 Ivar Ave.

Hollywood, CA 90038

(323) 802-7000 Phone

(323) 802-7131 Fax

The Wyle/Katz Company

(Actor: Noah Wyle)

c/o Warner Bros.

4000 Warner Blvd., Bldg. 138

Burbank, CA 91522

(818) 954-7440 Phone

(818) 954-1846 Fax

Yak Yak Pictures

c/o Warner Bros.
4000 Warner Blvd., Bldg. 138
Burbank, CA 91522
(818) 954-3861 Phone
(818) 954-1614 Fax
Credits: *The Peacemaker, Deep Impact, Pay It Forward, The Beast, John Doe*

Bud Yorkin Productions

345 N. Maple Dr., Ste. 206
Beverly Hills, CA 90210
(310) 274-8111 Phone
(310) 274-8112 Fax
Credits: *Intersection, Twice in a Lifetime, Blade Runner, All in the Family*

Yorktown Productions, Inc.
(Producer/Director: Norman Jewison)

3000 W. Olympic Blvd., Bldg. 2, Ste. 2465
Santa Monica, CA 90404
(310) 264-4155 Phone
(310) 264-4167 Fax
Credits: *Moonstruck, The Hurricane, A Soldier's Story*

The Saul Zaentz Company

2600 Tenth St.
Berkeley, CA 94710
(510) 549-1528 Phone
Credits: *One Flew Over the Cuckoo's Nest, Amadeus, The English Patient*

★ The Zanuck Company
(Producers: Richard and Lili Fini Zanuck)

9465 Wilshire Blvd., Ste. 930
Beverly Hills, CA 90212
(310) 274-0261 Phone
(310) 273-9217 Fax
Credits: *Deep Impact, The Verdict, Cocoon, The Sting, Driving Miss Daisy, Jaws, Rush, True Crime, Rules of Engagement, Academy Awards 2000, Planet of the Apes, Road to Perdition, Reign of Fire*

★ Zide/Perry Entertainment
(Producers: Warren Zide and Chris Perry)

9100 Wilshire Blvd., Ste. 615 E.
Beverly Hills, CA 90212
(310) 887-2999 Phone
(310) 887-2995 Fax

Credits: *The Big Hit, Final Destination, Cats and Dogs, Repli-Kate, American Pie, American Pie 2, Final Destination, Final Destination 2*

Laura Ziskin Productions

10202 W. Washington Blvd.
Culver City, CA 90232
(310) 244-7373 Phone
(310) 244-0073 Fax
Credits: *Dinner with Friends, Pretty Woman, To Die For, As Good As It Gets, Fail Safe, Spider-Man*

Zollo Productions, Inc.

257 W. 52nd St., 2nd Fl.
New York, NY 10019
(212) 957-1300 Phone
(212) 957-1315 Fax
Credits: *The Paper, Quiz Show, In the Gloaming, Mississippi Burning, Hurlyburly, Ghosts of Mississippi,*

Lansky, Naked in New York, Could Be Worse

Zucker Productions

1351 4th St., 3rd Fl.
Santa Monica, CA 90401
(310) 656-9202 Phone
(310) 656-9220 Fax
Credits: *Rat Race, Unconditional Love, My Best Friend's Wedding, My Life, Ghost, Ruthless People, Airplane!, First Knight*

Zucker/Netter Productions

1411 5th St., Ste. 402
Santa Monica, CA 90401
(310) 394-1644 Phone
(310) 899-6722 Fax
Credits: *The Guest; Dude, Where's My Car?; Phone Booth*

ACT 3

RESOURCES

COPYRIGHT and SCRIPT REGISTRATION

S CREENWRITERS PROTECT their completed work in one of two ways: by registering it with the Writer's Guild of America (WGA) or by copyrighting it. A copyright offers you more legal protection than Writer's Guild registration but costs more (a copyright costs $30; registration costs $10 for guild members and $20 for nonmembers). However, when you file with the U.S. Copyright Office your registration serves as notice to everyone else that you created the work and affords you additional legal rights of enforcement. Although the WGA's registration service does not provide legally binding protection, it offers certifiable proof of date of origin and is adequate protection for most writers. It is also instantaneous if you apply over the Internet. You don't even have to wait until the script is finished—you can register the idea, treatment, or synopsis.

Copyright, on the other hand, is the legal right to "control the display, publication, reproduction, and creation of derivative works or original works of authorship which are fixed in a tangible medium." The U.S. Constitution speaks to the subject at Article I, Section 8 as follows: "To promote the Progress of Science and useful Arts, by securing for limited Times to Authors and Inventors the exclusive Right to their respective Writings and Discoveries."

Copyrights spring into existence the moment an original work of creative authorship is fixed in a tangible medium of expression. Although a copyright may be registered to give notice to the world of the rights of the copyright owner, registration is theoretically not necessary and nothing further needs to be done to obtain ownership of the copyright. The author of the work owns the copyright unless the individual author either produced the work in the course and scope of his employment or pursuant to a written agreement that the work is a work-made-for-hire, in which case the copyright belongs to the employer. A copyright may be assigned or transferred just like other types of property.

What this means is that your work is protected the moment you write it. You can register it over the Internet with the Writer's Guild but it is the inherent copyright that legally protects it from plagiarism. If you register the work with the Copyright Office, do you need to register it with the Writer's Guild? No. Thirty dollars for a copyright is money well spent and it offers you the maximum protection. Registration is a prerequisite to the right to recover damages if you have to sue for infringement. So even if your Writer's Guild registration is adequate proof the work is yours, you would *still* have to register it with the Copyright Office before you could take action. Why not just do it now and forget about it?

You may be surprised to discover that it is relatively simple and painless to secure a copyright. You can download the application off the Internet. (Download Form PA for a screenplay; if you are the only author you can use Short Form PA.) You fill out the information, sign it, enclose a copy of the work and a check for $30, and mail it off. Your work is immediately protected, but it may be a few months before you receive an official registration and copyright number. You should place the © notation on the cover or title page of your script and follow it with the year you completed it. e.g., "©2006."

Once you have registered your copyright you do not need to worry about copyrighting revisions and additions to your script unless they are extensive. (If they *are* extensive, submit a new Form PA—the regular, not the short version—and reference the original copyright number by writing it in the space provided).

Library of Congress

Copyright Office
Publications Section, LM-455
101 Independence Ave. S.E.
Washington, DC 20559

(202) 707-3000 Phone
Web: www.copyright.gov
You can also call (202) 707-9100 and key in your fax number to receive forms via fax.

Writers Guild of America East (WGAE)

555 W. 57th St., Ste. 1230
New York, NY 10019
(212) 767-7800 Phone
(212) 582-1909 Fax
Web: www.wgaeast.org

Writers Guild of America West (WGAW)

7000 W. Third St.
Los Angeles, CA 90048-4329
(323) 951-4000 Phone
(323) 782-4502 Agency Listing
(323) 782-4800 Fax
Web: www.wga.org
The WGA provides a collective bargaining agreement that protects writers' financial and creative rights in all work contracts with WGA signatories (virtually all mainstream providers in the entertainment business are signatories). The WGA also provides pension, health, credit union, and other benefits to its members. Please note: you cannot join the Writer's Guild until you have sold a script to a Writers Guild signatory. Once you are eligible, the cost to join is $2,500 and the dues are $100 a year plus 1.5 percent of your gross earnings. (Writers living west of the Mississippi may join the WGA-West, those living east of the Mississippi are advised to contact the WGA-East.)

NOTE: Titles, concepts, and ideas cannot be copyrighted.

EMERGENCY FUNDS

THE PEN FUND provides assistance to writers experiencing financial hardships. These funds are notoriously difficult to get, so be sure you request or download the submission guidelines and follow them carefully if you want a decent shot at success. Alternatively, check out the Fellowships and Grants Section in this book or log onto the Writers Grants listings at www.nyfa.org.

The PEN Writers Fund is an emergency fund for professional (published or produced) writers with serious financial difficulties. Depending on the situation, the fund gives grants or loans of up to $1,000. The maximum amount is given only under especially dire circumstances and when monies are available.

Getting the audience to cry for the Terminator at the end of T2, for me that was the whole purpose of making that film. If you can get the audience to feel emotion for a character that in the previous film you despised utterly and were terrified by, then that's a cinematic arc.

—JAMES CAMERON, director, The Terminator and Terminator 2: Judgment Day

---

TIP: Avoid similar names for characters, e.g., Jason and Julia, Skeen and Meeks. The more different the names, the easier it is to remember them. Give each character a unique and dynamic one-sentence description when he or she first appears. That way each character will make a strong impression. You know them a lot better than we do.

PEN Writers Fund

PEN American Center
568 Broadway
New York, NY 10012
(212) 334-1660 Phone
(212) 334-2181 Fax
Web: www.pen.org
E-mail: motika@pen.org
Deadline: Ongoing
Application Fee: None

PEN Fund for Writers and Editors with AIDS

PEN American Center
568 Broadway
New York, NY 10012
(212) 334-1660 Phone
(212) 334-2181 Fax
Web: www.pen.org
E-mail: motika@pen.org
The PEN Fund for Writers and Editors with HIV/AIDS, administered under the PEN Writers Fund, gives grants of up to $1,000 to professional writers and editors who face serious financial difficulties because of HIV- or AIDS-related illness.
Deadline: Ongoing
Application Fee: None

COLONIES, RETREATS, AND RESIDENCIES

SOMETIMES the best thing writers can do is get away from the pressures of everyday life to concentrate on their work. Poet Maya Angelou holes up in a hotel with a bottle of bourbon and a Bible when she wants to do some serious writing. Most writers find the words come easier when they're not faced with their normal distractions of ringing telephones and bills to pay. It may be just what you need to get past a stumbling block or to complete a rewrite.

Colonies, retreats, and residencies also offer the company of fellow writers and artists, often in a pastoral setting. You can bounce ideas off other writers or simply enjoy the camaraderie of people who understand your struggles. Although some colonies offer monk-like solitude, others allow you to bring family members and pets, so be sure to check out each Web site to find one that's right for you.

For new listings and updated information, consult www.artistcom munities.org.

> *You sit at the board and suddenly your heart leaps. Your hand trembles to pick up the piece and move it. But what chess teaches you is that you must sit there calmly and think about whether it's really a good idea and whether there are other, better ideas.*
>
> —STANLEY KUBRICK

Alden B. Dow Creative Center

Northwood University
4000 Whiting Dr.
Midland, MI 48640
(517) 837-4478 Phone
(517) 837-4468 Fax
Web: www.northwood.edu/abd
E-mail: creativity@northwood.edu

Four creativity fellowships are provided each year for playwrights, translators, composers, librettists, lyricists, or screenwriters. The ten-week summer residency covers travel, room, and board at Northwood University, which provides an environment for intense independent study. The program includes interaction among fellows and formal presentation of work at the end of the program, and offers a $750 stipend for project costs.

Deadline: December 31
Application Fee: $10

Altos De Chavon

c/o Parsons School of Design
2 W. 13th St., Rm. 707
New York, NY 10011
(212) 229-5370 Phone
(212) 229-8988 Fax
Web: www.altosdechavon.com
E-mail: altos@spacelab.net

Residencies of three and a half months are available for fifteen artists a year, one or two of whom may be writers or composers, at an arts center located in tropical Caribbean surroundings eight miles from the town of La Romana in the Dominican Republic. Resident pays rent of $350 per month and provides his or her own meals (at an estimated cost of $20 a day). The program prefers Spanish-speaking artists whose work relates to a Dominican or Latin American context. Residents may teach workshops and are expected to contribute to a group exhibition/performance at the end of their stay.

Deadline: Committee reviews materials in July
Application Fee: None

Byrdcliffe Art Colony

The Woodstock Guild
34 Tinker St.
Woodstock, NY 12498
(914) 679-2079 Phone
(914) 679-4529 Fax
Web: www.woodstockguild.org
E-mail: wguild@ulster.net

The Byrdcliffe Arts Colony is located in the Catskill Mountains, one-and-a-half miles from the center of Woodstock, New York. Founded as an arts and crafts community in 1902, it has been a haven for visual artists, writers, craftspeople, musicians, and theater artists for almost a century. Past artists have included sculptor Eva Hesse, poet Wallace

Stevens, painter Milton Avery, and dancer Isadora Duncan. In 1976, The Woodstock Guild inherited Byrdcliffe's current thirty buildings and 300 forested acres. Five years later, the Villetta Inn and surrounding cottages were once again designated as a summer artists' colony. The Artist in Residence Program offers writers, visual artists, and composers one-month residencies from June through September. The program's goal is to provide solitude in community and undisturbed time in which to concentrate on independent, creative work in the company of follow artists.

Deadline: April 1
Application Fee: None

Centrum Creative Residencies Program

Fort Worden State Park
Box 1158
Port Townsend, WA 98368
(360) 385-3102 Phone
(360) 385-2470 Fax
Web: www.centrum.org
E-mail: sally@centrum.org
Creative residencies are available for writers, composers, poets, visual artists, and choreographers at this center near a Victorian seaport in 440-acre Fort Worden State Park. Writers must show clear direction and some accomplishment in their field.

Deadline: October 1
Application Fee: $20

Djerassi Resident Artists Program

2325 Bear Gulch Rd.
Woodside, CA 94062-4405
(650) 747-1250 Phone
(650) 747-0105 Fax
Web: www.djerassi.org
E-mail: drap@djerassi.org
One-month residencies for writers; choreographers; composers; media, visual, and interdisciplinary artists; and performers are offered at 600-acre ranch in Santa Cruz Mountains one hour south of San Francisco. Interdisciplinary projects are encouraged and collaborative projects are considered. Room and board are included as part of the residency.

Deadline: February 15
Application Fee: $25

The Gell Writers Center

c/o Writers & Books
740 University Ave.
Rochester, NY 14607-1259
(716) 473-2590 Phone
(716) 442-9333 Fax
Web: www.wab.org/gell
E-mail: wab@wab.org
Playwrights, translators, librettists, lyricists, solo performers, screenwriters, and television writers are invited to apply for a residency to

work on specific projects. There are two private bedrooms available in the house, which is surrounded by twenty-three acres of woodlands. Workshops on creative writing are sometimes available at extra cost. Residents provide their own meals and pay $35 a day.

Deadline: Ongoing
Application Fee: None

Headlands Center for the Arts

944 Fort Barry
Sausalito, CA 94965
(415) 331-2787 Phone
(415) 331-3857 Fax
Web: www.headlands.org
E-mail: staff@headlands.org

Residencies of one to three months are available for artists in all disciplines at this center in a national park on 13,000 acres of coastal wilderness across the bay from San Francisco. Accommodation is in a four-bedroom house with communal kitchen; evening meals are provided in mess hall. Eleven-month live-out residencies are available for Bay Area artists only, providing studio space, two meals a week, and access to the center's facilities but no housing. All residents are encouraged to interact with fellow artists in other media and with the environment. Travel, housing, and a stipend of $500 a month are offered to artists from outside Bay Area; a $2,500 stipend and studio space are offered to Bay Area artists. This residency is open to California, North Carolina, New Jersey, and Ohio residents only; students are ineligible.

Deadline: April 2
Application Fee: None

Helene Wurlitzer Foundation of New Mexico

Box 1891
Taos, NM 87571
(505) 758-2413 Phone
(505) 758-2559 Fax

Eleven studio/apartments are available to writers, composers, and poets. The length of residency is flexible, but is usually three months. Housing and utilities are free, but residents must provide their own meals.

Deadline: January 18
Application Fee: None

Make visible what, without you, might perhaps never have been seen.
—ROBERT BRESSON, director, *A Man Escaped*

RESIDENCIES AND RETREATS, REUNIONS, AND COLONIES

Kalani Oceanside Eco-Resort Institute For Culture and Fitness

RR2 Box 4500
Pahoa-Beach Rd., HI 96778
(808) 965-7828 Phone
(808) 965-0527 Fax
Web: www.kalani.com
E-mail: kalani@kalani.com

Up to twenty artists and writers share four large studio spaces for two-week to two-month residencies at this 113-acre coastal resort spa with private rooms, communal kitchen facilities, and shared or private baths. Artists are eligible for a 50 percent discount on regular daily room rates of $75 to $135, and have the option of preparing their own food or paying an additional $27 per day for resort's meals.
Deadline: Ongoing
Application Fee: None

Ledig House International Writers' Colony

55 Fifth Ave., 15th Fl.
New York, NY 10003
(212) 206-6114 Info
(518) 392-7656 Phone
(518) 392-2848 Fax
Web: www.artomi.org/ao/
    ledig.htm
E-mail: artomi55@aol.com

Residencies of one week to two months are available for up to ten writers of all genres at this 150-acre farm in upstate New York. Facilities include a library, computer access, sleep space, workspace, communal living, and meals.
Deadline: November 30
Application Fee: None

The MacDowell Colony

100 High St.
Peterborough, NH 03458-2485
(603) 924-3886/(212) 535-9690
    Phone
(603) 924-9142 Fax
Web: www.macdowellcolony.org
E-mail: info@macdowellcolony.org

The MacDowell Colony offers residencies of up to two months for composers, visual artists, video/filmmakers, architects, and interdisciplinary artists at a 450-acre estate. Studios and common areas are accessible for those with mobility impairments. Travel grants are available, and writers in need of financial assistance are eligible for grants of up to $1,000.
Deadlines: September 15; January 15; April 15
Application Fee: $20

The Millay Colony for the Arts

454 E. Hill Rd., Box 3
Austerlitz, NY 12017-0003

> *Filmmaking is a chance to live many lifetimes.*
> —ROBERT ALTMAN, director

(518) 392-3103 Phone
E-mail: application@millay
colony.org
Web: www.millaycolony.org
One-month residencies are available for up to six writers, composers, and visual artists at this 600-acre estate in upstate New York. Residencies include free room, board, and studio space.
Deadline: November 1
Application Fee: None

Montana Artists Refuge

Box 8
Basin, MT 59631
(406) 225-3500 Phone
Web: www.montanaartists
refuge.org
E-mail: mar@mt.net
Three-month to one-year residencies are available for four to five artists of all disciplines. Montana Artists Refuge is located in a former gold camp in the midst of the Rocky Mountains, approximately twelve miles from the Continental Divide. The town of Basin has 250 residents, two restaurant/bars, a production pottery outlet, post office, and town park. Artists are housed in three fully equipped apartments and one studio apartment, all with kitchens and private phones. Residents pay $400 to $600 per month and provide their own meals. Financial aid is available for up to the full amount of rent.
Deadlines: January 15; May 15; August 15
Application Fee: None

New York Mills Arts Retreat

24 N. Main Ave.
Box 246
New York Mills, MN 56567
(218) 385-3339 Phone
(218) 385-3366 Fax
Web: www.kulcher.org/html/
artsretreat.html
E-mail: nymills@kulcher.org
One writer or artist at a time is housed for two to four weeks at this retreat located in a small farming community in north central Minnesota. The resident provides his or her own meals and receives a $750 stipend for two weeks or a $1,500 stipend for four weeks. Resident must donate eight hours per week during residency to community outreach.
Deadlines: April 1; October 1
Application Fee: None

RESIDENCIES AND ARTS, RETREATS, AND COLONIES

Norcroft

Box 218
Lutsen, MN 55612
(800) 770-0058 Phone
(218) 663-7605 Fax
Web: www.norcroft.org
E-mail: info@norcroft.org

Four concurrent residencies of one to four weeks are available for women writers in all genres at a remote lodge on the shores of Lake Superior. Writers have private bedrooms and individual writing sheds. Groceries are provided but residents do their own cooking. The writer's work must demonstrate an understanding of and commitment to feminist change.
Deadline: October 1
Application Fee: None

Shenandoah International Playwrights Retreat

Pennyroyal Farm
717 Quick Mills Rd.
Staunton, VA 24401
(540) 248-1868 Phone
(540) 248-7728 Fax
Web: www.shenanarts.org
E-mail: theatre@shenanarts.org

This program offers residences of six weeks to two months for selected writers to test new work in a challenging environment. Room, board, and transportation are provided. Writers must be eager to explore new styles, seek input and constructive criticism from other writers, and as a result push their writing in new directions.
Deadline: February 1
Application Fee: None

Studio for Creative Inquiry

Carnegie Mellon University
College of Fine Arts, Rm. 111
5000 Forbes Ave.
Pittsburgh, PA 15213-3890
(412) 268-3454 Phone
(412) 268-2829 Fax
Web: www.cmu.edu/studio
E-mail: studio-info@andrew.cmu
.edu

Residencies of six months to three years are offered to artists in all disciplines. Residency provides a studio facility located in Carnegie Mellon's College of Fine Arts building, including office and meeting space, work area, computer, and sound and video editing equipment. Fel-

---

The only reason for being a professional writer is that you can't help it.
—LEO ROSTEN

> ❚ *All great work is preparing yourself for the accident to happen.*
> —SIDNEY LUMET, director, *Serpico*

lows may also use university resources, including the library.

There is a stipend as well as assistance in finding housing in the community.

Deadline: Ongoing
Application Fee: None

The Tyrone Guthrie Centre

Annaghmakerrig
Newbliss
County Monaghan, Ireland
353-47-54003 Phone
353-47-54380 Fax
Web: www.tyroneguthrie.ie
E-mail: thetgc@indigo.ie

Artists in all disciplines are welcome to apply for residencies of one week to one year at a 450-acre forested estate overlooking a large lake in Ireland that was once the country home of Tyrone Guthrie. Facilities include private apartments, music room, rehearsal/performance space, and an extensive library. Non-Irish artists pay about $2,400 a month for housing and meals; fees may be negotiable depending on factors such as the length of stay, the nature of the project, and involvement with Irish artists or institutions.

Deadline: Ongoing
Application Fee: None

The U.S./Japan Creative Artists' Program

Japan-U.S. Friendship Commission
1120 Vermont Ave. N.W., Ste. 925
Washington, DC 20005
(202) 275-7712 Phone
(202) 275-7413 Fax
Web: www.jusfc.gov
E-mail: jusfc@jusfc.gov

Residencies of six continuous months are offered for three to five artists each year. Residents must find their own housing in the location of their choice in Japan. A monthly stipend of $3,700 is provided, plus $925 for housing and $925 for professional expenses, travel, and predeparture Japanese language instruction.

Deadline: June 26
Application Fee: None

Virginia Center for the Creative Arts

154 San Angelo Dr.
Amherst Briar, VA 24521
(804) 946-7236 Phone

(804) 946-7239 Fax

Web: www.vcca.com

E-mail: vcca@vcca.com

Writers, composers, and visual and performance artists are welcome to apply for residencies of two weeks to two months at this 450-acre estate in the Blue Ridge Mountains. Separate studios and all meals are provided. Each resident pays a suggested minimum of $30 a day for room and board (or as means allow). Financial status is not a factor in the selection process.

Deadlines: May 15; September 15; January 15

Application Fee: None

William Flanagan Memorial Creative Persons Center

Edward F. Albee Foundation

14 Harrison St.

New York, NY 10013

(212) 226-2020 Phone

One-month residencies are available for up to five writers, com-posers, and visual artists concurrently at "The Barn" in Montauk, Long Island. Housing is provided.

Deadline: April 1

Application Fee: None

Yaddo

Box 395

Saratoga Springs, NY 12866-0395

(518) 584-0746 Phone

(518) 584-1312 Fax

Web: www.yaddo.org

E-mail: yaddo@yaddo.org

Residencies of two weeks to two months are provided for artists in all genres, working individually or as collaborative teams of up to three persons, at a nineteenth-century estate on 400 acres. About 200 residents a year receive free room, board, and studio space.

Deadlines: January 15; August 1

Application Fee: None

Fortunately, somewhere between chance and mystery lies imagination, the only thing that protects our freedom, despite the fact that people keep trying to reduce it or kill it off altogether.

—LUIS BUÑUEL

ENTERTAINMENT INDUSTRY RESOURCE GUIDE

▌ Guilds, Unions, and Professional Associations

T HE FOLLOWING LISTINGS are organizations and unions that cater specifically to the entertainment industry. Even though you may not be eligible to join, their Web sites are well worth looking over as they contain a wealth of information. It's good to learn as much as you can about the professional aspects of the business, so be sure to look at the big three unions: the DGA (Director's Guild of America), SAG (Screen Actor's Guild), and WGA (Writer's Guild of America).

Many sites let you sign up for e-mail newsletters that can provide tips, advice, and leads in marketing your screenplay. In addition there are numerous articles that will help you understand the trends and ever-changing tastes of Hollywood.

Say all you have to say in the fewest possible words, or your reader will be sure to skip them; and in the plainest possible words or he will certainly misunderstand them.

—JOHN RUSKIN

Academy of Motion Picture Arts and Sciences (AMPAS)

8949 Wilshire Blvd.
Beverly Hills, CA 90211-1972
(310) 247-3000 Phone
(310) 271-3395 Fax
Web: www.oscars.org
E-mail: ampas@oscars.org

This is the "Academy" in the Academy Awards. Its Web site features a searchable database of all previous Oscar winners as well as extensive film credits. AMPAS also administers the academy film archive, film scholars program, Nicholl Fellowship (see the "Fellowships and Grants" section of this text) and Margaret Herrick Library (see "Libraries and Museums").

Academy of Television Arts and Sciences (ATAS)

5220 Lankershim Blvd.
North Hollywood, CA 91601
(818) 754-2800 Phone
(818) 761-2827 Fax
Web: www.emmys.tv
E-mail: webmaster@emmys.org

This is the organization that gives out the Emmy Awards every year. In addition ATAS administers the Emmy Hall of Fame, offers educational programs and services, and publishes *Emmy* magazine.

Academy Players Directory

1313 N. Vine St.
Hollywood, CA 90028
(310) 247-3058 Phone
(310) 550-5034 Fax
Web: www.playersdirectory.com
E-mail: players@oscars.org

The Hollywood casting agent's bible, the *Academy Players Directory* has headshots and contact information for more than 16,000 featured stars and extras. Don't expect to find home addresses—this lists agents, managers, and lawyers who officially represent actors.

Actors Equity Association (AEA–Chicago)

203 N. Wabash Ave., Ste. 1700
Chicago, IL 60601
(312) 641-0393 Phone
(312) 641-0418 Audition Hotline
(312) 641-6365 Fax
Web: www.actorsequity.org
E-mail: info@actorsequity.org

The secret to film is that it's an illusion.
—GEORGE LUCAS

Actors Equity Association (AEA–L.A.)

Museum Square
5757 Wilshire Blvd., Ste. 1
Los Angeles, CA 90036
(323) 634-1750 Phone
(323) 634-1776 Audition Hotline
(323) 634-1777 Fax
Web: www.actorsequity.org
E-mail: info@actorsequity.org

Actors Equity Association (AEA–New York)

165 W. 46th St., 15th Fl.
New York, NY 10036
(212) 869-8530 Phone
(212) 869-1242 Audition Hotline
(212) 719-9815 Fax
Web: www.actorsequity.org
E-mail: info@actorsequity.org

Actors Equity Association (AEA–San Francisco)

350 Sansome St., Ste. 900
San Francisco, CA 94104
(415) 913-3838 Phone
(415) 434-8007 Audition Hotline
(415) 391-0102 Fax
Web: www.actorsequity.org
E-mail: info@actorsequity.org

Actors' Equity Association is a labor union that represents more than 45,000 American actors and stage managers working in the pro- fessional theater. Equity negotiates minimum wages and working con- ditions, administers contracts, and enforces the provisions of various agreements with theatrical employ- ers across the country. Here are telephone listings for AEA offices around the country:

Atlanta	(404) 257-2575
Austin/	
San Antonio	(512) 326-7648
Baltimore/D.C.	(202) 722-7350
Boston	(617) 720-6048
Buffalo/Rochester	(716) 883-1767
Chicago	(312) 641-0393
Cleveland	(440) 779-2001
Dallas/Ft. Worth	(214) 922-7843
Denver	(720) 377-0072
Detroit	(248) 788-6118
Florida–Central	(407) 345-9322
Florida–South	(305) 460-5880
Houston	(713) 917-4564
Kansas City	(816) 926-9293
Las Vegas	(702) 452-4200
Milwaukee/	
Madison	(414) 963-4023
Minneapolis/	
St. Paul	(612) 924-4044
Philadelphia	(215) 966-1895
Phoenix/Tucson	(602) 265-7117
Pittsburgh	(412) 481-0816
San Diego	(619) 858-0055
Seattle	(425) 637-7332
St. Louis	(314) 851-0906

Actors' Fund of America

Chicago
203 N. Wabash Ave., Ste. 2104
Chicago, IL 60601
(312) 372-0989 Phone
(312) 372-0272 Fax
Web: www.actorsfund.org
E-mail: dtowne@actorsfund.org

L.A.
5757 Wilshire Blvd., Ste. 400
Los Angeles, CA 90036
(323) 933-9244 Phone
(323) 933-7615 Fax
Web: www.actorsfund.org
E-mail: bmcdonald@actorsfund.org

New York
729 Seventh Ave., 10th Fl.
New York, NY 10019
(212) 221-7300 Phone
(212) 764-0238 Fax
Web: www.actorsfund.org
E-mail: bdavis@actorsfund.org

The Actors' Fund of America is a national nonprofit organization serving all entertainment professionals through comprehensive services and programs. In addition to providing emergency grants for essentials such as food, rent, and medical care, the Actors' Fund provides counseling, substance abuse and mental health services, senior and disabled care, nursing home and assisted living care, an AIDS initiative, the Actors' Work Program, the Phyllis Newman Women's Health Initiative, the Artists' Health Insurance Resource Center, and supportive housing on both coasts.

American Cinematheque

1800 N. Highland Ave., Ste. 717
Hollywood, CA 90028
(323) 461-2020 Phone
(323) 461-9737 Fax
Web: www.egyptiantheatre.com
E-mail: info@egyptiantheatre.com
The American Cinematheque is a cultural organization created to honor and promote America's indigenous art form—the moving picture. The organization aims to present the full range of film and video not otherwise available to the widest possible audience, to establish a forum for an ongoing dialogue between filmmakers and filmgoers, to provide a high-profile exhibition facility for other inde-

A hunch is creativity trying to tell you something.
—FRANK CAPRA

pendent film and video organizations, and to encourage and support new talent by creating a showcase for their work.

Big Bird, Jay Leno to Susan Lucci, Larry David to Howard Stern, Dan Rather to Cedric the Entertainer, and Bill Cosby to Ryan Seacrest.

American Federation of Television and Radio Artists (AFTRA–L.A.)

5757 Wilshire Blvd., Ste. 900
Los Angeles, CA 90036
(323) 634-8100 Phone
(323) 634-8194 Fax
Web: www.aftra.org
E-mail: info@aftra.org
The American Federation of Television and Radio Artists (AFTRA) is a national labor union that represents nearly 80,000 performers, journalists, and other artists working in the entertainment and news media. AFTRA's scope of representation covers broadcast, public, and cable television (news, sports, weather, drama, comedy, soap operas, talk and variety shows, documentaries, children's programming, reality and game shows); radio (news, commercials, hosted programs); sound recordings (CDs, singles, Broadway cast albums, audio books); nonbroadcast and industrial material as well as Internet and digital programming. AFTRA's membership includes an array of talent currently working in AFTRA-covered programming, ranging from Walter Cronkite to

American Film Institute (AFI–L.A.)

2021 N. Western Ave.
Los Angeles, CA 90027
(323) 856-7600 Phone
(323) 467-4578 Fax
Web: www.afi.com
E-mail: info@afi.com
The American Film Institute (AFI) is the preeminent national organization dedicated to advancing and preserving film, television, and other forms of the moving image. AFI's programs promote innovation and excellence through teaching, presenting, preserving, and redefining this art form.

American Film Marketing Association (AFMA)

10850 Wilshire Blvd., 9th Fl.
Los Angeles, CA 90024-4321
(310) 446-1000 Phone
(310) 446-1600 Fax
Web: www.afma.com
E-mail: info@afma.com
AFMA is the trade association for the independent film and television industry. AFMA's global membership distributes and often pro-

duces the films and programs made apart from the seven major studios. Artisan Entertainment, Discovery Communications, Franchise Pictures, Focus, Intermedia, Lions Gate, MDP Worldwide, Miramax, New Line, and 130 other leading independent film and television companies comprise AFMA. The American Film Market, held in Los Angeles annually, is the world's largest film market; it attracts more than 7,000 film and television industry professionals from around the globe.

American Screenwriters Association

269 S. Beverly Dr., Ste. 2600
Beverly Hills, CA 90212-3807
(866) 265-9091 Phone
(866) 265-9091 Fax
Web: www.asascreenwriters
.com
E-mail: asa@goasa.com
The American Screenwriters Association (ASA) is organized for educational purposes, including the promotion and encouragement of the art of screenwriting. ASA exists to serve the needs of the largest and most under-represented writers population today—the emerging screenwriter. The ASA seeks to establish favorable relations and ties between writers in the United States and foreign countries by encourag-

ing and enabling the sharing of information concerning screenwriting. Today, the American Screenwriters Association has an international membership of more than 1,200 members located throughout the United States, Europe, the Pacific, and the Middle East.

Association of Independent Video and Filmmakers (AIVF)

304 Hudson St., 6th Fl.
New York, NY 10013
(212) 807-1400 Phone
(212) 463-8519 Fax
Web: www.aivf.org
E-mail: info@aivf.org
The Association of Independent Video and Filmmakers (AIVF) is the membership organization of the Foundation for Independent Video and Film. Its mission is to increase the creative and professional opportunities for independent video and filmmakers and to enhance the growth of independent media by providing services and information such as health and production insurance, networking seminars and events, a resource library, and publication of books and directories, as well as the *Independent Film & Video Monthly*. AIVF's membership consists of media artists working in all genres, including documentary, an-

imation, experimental, narrative, interactive, and multimedia.

Association of Talent Agents

9255 Sunset Blvd., Ste. 930
Los Angeles, CA 90069
310-274-0628 Phone
310-274-5063 Fax
Web: www.agentassociation.com
E-mail: shellie@agentassociation
.com

The Association of Talent Agents is an advocacy group that represents talent agencies. ATA's member agencies are dedicated to the uncompromised representation of the clients they serve. ATA's foundation provides the bedrock for perpetual growth, educational output, and activity.

Black Filmmaker Foundation (BFF)

670 Broadway, Ste. 300
New York, NY 10012
(212) 253-1690 Phone
(212) 253-1689 Fax
Web: www.dvrepublic.com
E-mail: hudlin@dvrepublic.com

Established in 1978, the Black Filmmaker Foundation (BFF) is a nonprofit organization that develops and administers programs that assist emerging filmmakers and build audiences for their work. For more than two decades, BFF has played a pivotal role in the emergence of the contemporary black film movement. BFF administers dvRepublic.com, an online community that hosts public discussion and political critiques of film and television programming. The dvRepublic.com domain is the home of the BFF DV Lab, which partners with filmmakers of color to develop, market, distribute, and Webcast socially concerned, entertainment-driven digital films.

Caucus for Television Producers, Writers, and Directors

P.O. Box 11236
Burbank, CA 91510-1236
(818) 843-7572 Phone
(818) 846-2159 Fax
Web: www.caucus.org
E-mail: info@caucus.org

For the past twenty-five years in network television (and now in cable and satellite television as well), the Caucus for Television Producers, Writers, and Directors has provided a forum for the best creative talent in Hollywood to network together as the creative conscience of the television industry. As the leader of the creative television community, the

Caucus has always stood for better and more meaningful television. That means television programs produced, written, and directed in a working environment that supports the best product for the audience.

Cinestory

University of Chicago
Gleacher Center, Ste. 36
450 N. Cityfront Plaza Dr.
Chicago, IL 60611
(312) 464-8725 Phone
(312) 464-8724 Fax
Web: www.cinestory.com
E-mail: info@cinestory.com

CineStory works with emerging screenwriters to hone their craft and help them find alternative access to the screen. CineStory's mission has always been to create a sustaining, nurturing community of writers that understand the professional demands of the craft, can express their own voices through the medium, and are trained to be true collaborators with other filmmakers.

CineWomen

CineWomen (L.A.)
9903 Santa Monica Blvd., Ste. 461
Beverly Hills, CA 90212
(310) 288-1160 Phone
Web: www.cinewomen.org
E-mail: info@cinewomen.org

CineWomen (New York)
P.O. Box 1477, Cooper Station
New York, NY 10276
(212) 604-4264 Phone
Web: www.cinewomen.org
E-mail: info@cinewomenny.org

CineWomen is a nonprofit organization of professionals in the entertainment industry whose purpose is to support the advancement of women and their career goals in a noncompetitive environment. CineWomen is dedicated to developing the number and range of opportunities available to women in the industry, fostering a strong, independent spirit, interpersonal relationships and career building, and creating outreach projects which benefit other nonprofits and the larger community.

▌ *A film is—or should be—more like music than like fiction. It should be a progression of moods and feelings. The theme, what's behind the emotion, the meaning, all that comes later.*

—STANLEY KUBRICK

Clear, Inc.

P.O. Box 628
Burbank, CA 91503-0628
(413) 647-3380 Fax
Web: www.clearinc.org
E-mail: info@clearinc.org

Clear, Inc. is an organization of clearance and research professionals who work in the film, television and multimedia industries. It serves as an educational and networking resource for television and film research and clearance professionals in the Los Angeles area.

Directors Guild of America (DGA)

7920 Sunset Blvd.
Los Angeles, CA 90046
(310) 289-2000 Phone
(323) 851-3671 Agency Listing
(310) 289-2029 Fax
Web: www.dga.org
E-mail: info@dga.org

The Directors Guild of America is the trade union for professional directors. It represents more than 12,000 members working in U.S. cities and abroad. Their creative work is represented in theatrical, industrial, educational and documentary films and television, as well as videos and commercials. There are branches in Chicago, New York, and Los Angeles.

Dramatists Guild of America, Inc.

1501 Broadway, Ste. 701
New York, NY 10036
(212) 398-9366 Phone
(212) 944-0420 Fax
Web: www.dramaguild.com
E-mail: igor@dramaguild.com

The Dramatists Guild of America is the only professional association for playwrights, composers, and lyricists. Any writer who has completed a dramatic script may become a member of the Dramatists Guild of America and receive a wide range of benefits: business affairs advice; contract review; a subscription to the Guild's bimonthly magazine, *The Dramatist; The Dramatists Guild Newsletter,* and the *Resource Directory.*

Members also have access to complimentary or discounted tickets to New York productions; national hotel and travel discounts; access to the Guild's Frederick Loewe Room in the heart of the theater district for use in readings and auditions (for a discounted fee).

Filmmakers Alliance

4470 Sunset Blvd., Ste. 716
Los Angeles, CA 90027
(323) 876-0241 Phone
(310) 281-6093 Hotline
(323) 876-9393 Fax

Web: www.filmmakersalliance.com

E-mail: membership@filmmakers
alliance.com

Filmmakers Alliance (FA) is a collective of filmmakers, film and digital artists, technicians, and craftspeople dedicated to empowering, educating, and supporting fellow filmmakers through active participation and shared resources. FA offers support, experience, and education to emerging filmmakers, in addition to producing low-budget features, shorts, commercials, music videos, corporate videos, training videos, television shows, and infomercials.

Hispanic Organization of Latin Actors (HOLA)

107 Suffolk St., Ste. 302

New York, NY 10002

(212) 253-1015 Phone

(212) 253-9651 Fax

Web: www.hellohola.org

E-mail: holagram@hellohola.org

The Hispanic Organization of Latin Actors is an arts service organization founded in 1976 to expand the presence of Hispanic actors in both the Latino and mainstream entertainment and communications media by facilitating industry access to professional and emerging Hispanic actors. HOLA members represent the full spectrum of Latino cultures, reflecting the nation's growing Hispanic population.

Horror Writers Association (HWA)

P.O. Box 50577

Palo Alto, CA 94303

(650) 322-4610 Phone

Web: www.horror.org

E-mail: hwa@horror.org

The Horror Writers Association is a worldwide organization of writers and publishing professionals dedicated to promoting occult literature and the interests of those who write it. HWA was formed in the late 1980s with the help of many of the field's greats, including Dean Koontz, Robert McCammon, and Joe Lansdale. Today, with more than 1,000 members around the globe, it is the oldest and most respected professional organization for the much-loved writers who bring you the most enjoyable sleepless nights of your life.

Independent Feature Project (IFP–L.A.)

1964 Westwood Blvd., Ste. 205

Los Angeles, CA 90025

(310) 475-4379 Phone

(310) 441-5676 Fax

Web: www.ifp.org

Independent Feature Project (IFP-New York)

104 W. 29th St., 12th Fl.
New York, NY 10001-5310
(212) 465-8200 Phone
(212) 465-8525 Fax

The Independent Feature Project (IFP), a not-for-profit, membership-supported organization, was founded in 1979 to encourage creativity and diversity in films produced outside the established studio system. The IFP produces the IFP Market, which features 300 American independent features, shorts, works-in-progress, documentaries, and feature scripts. The IFP and IFP/West publish *Filmmaker,* a quarterly magazine. IFP also sponsors a series of screenings, professional seminars, and industry showcases, including a conference on screenplay development. Group health insurance, production insurance, discounts, a resource program, publications, and a series of transcripts of previous seminars and workshops are available to members. Membership dues start at $100 a year ($65 for students). IFP has branches in Chicago, Los Angeles, Miami, New York, Minneapolis, and Seattle.

International Press Academy (IPA)

468 N. Camden Dr., Ste. 334
Beverly Hills, CA 90210
(310) 285-1756 Phone
(310) 530-0420 Fax
Web: www.pressacademy.com
E-mail: info@pressacademy.com

Founded in 1996 by Mirjana Van Blaricom, the IPA has grown to be both the largest and most diverse association of professional entertainment journalists in the world. With a membership of more than 200 working press representing both domestic and foreign markets, the IPA reaches more than 500 million people globally via major print, television, radio, cable, and new media outlets and the Internet. IPA's primary mission is to find common ground and equitable competition among all artists throughout the world whose aim is to entertain, enrich, and enlighten, regardless of their chosen medium.

The International Women's Writing Guild

Box 810, Gracie Station

> *The only safe thing is to take a chance.*
> —MIKE NICHOLS

New York, NY 10028-0082
(212) 737-7536 Phone
(212) 737-9469 Fax
Web: www.iwwg.com
E-mail: iwwg@iwwg.com
The International Women's Writing Guild, founded in 1976, is a network of international women writers. Playwrights, television and film writers, songwriters, producers, and other women involved in the performing arts are included in its membership. Workshops are offered throughout the United States and annually at a weeklong writing conference/retreat at Skidmore College in Saratoga Springs, New York. Members may also submit play scripts to theaters that have offered to read, critique, and produce FWWG members' works. *Network,* a 32-page newsletter published six times a year, provides a forum for members to share views and to learn about playwriting contests and awards, and theater- and TV-related opportunities. The guild offers contacts with literary agents, group health insurance, and other services to its members. Annual dues are $35 ($45 for foreign membership).

Motion Picture Association of America (MPAA)

15503 Ventura Blvd.
Encino, CA 91436
(818) 995-6600 Phone
(818) 382-1799 Fax
Web: www.mpaa.org
E-mail: hotline@mpaa.org
The Motion Picture Association of America and its international counterpart, the Motion Picture Association (MPA), serve as the voice and advocate of the American motion picture, home video, and television industries. Today, these associations not only represent the world of theatrical film, but also serve as leader and advocate for major producers and distributors of entertainment programming for television, cable, home video and future delivery systems not yet imagined. Founded in 1922 as the trade association of the American film industry, the MPAA has broadened its mandate over the years to reflect the diversity of an expanding industry. The initial task assigned to the association was to stem the waves of criticism of American movies, then silent—

▌ *I've got a peculiar weakness for criminals and artists—neither takes life as it is. Any tragic story has to be in conflict with things as they are.*
—STANLEY KUBRICK

though sometimes rambunctious and rowdy—and to restore a more favorable public image for the motion picture industry. The MPAA has offices in Los Angeles and Washington, D.C.

Multicultural Motion Picture Association (MMPA)

9244 Wilshire Blvd.

Beverly Hills, CA 90212

(310) 285-9743 Phone

(310) 285-9770 Fax

Web: www.diversityawards.org

E-mail: diversitymmpa@cs.com

The purpose of the MMPA is to honor outstanding and inspiring individuals in the entertainment industry for their contribution to diverse perspectives in film and television, to promote and enhance even greater opportunities for all cultures to bring their stories and perspectives to the screen, and to bring people together from all arenas in the entertainment community to celebrate positive contributions and diversity.

National Association of Television Program Executives (NATPE)

2425 Olympic Blvd., Ste. 600E

Santa Monica, CA 90404

(310) 453-4440 Phone

(310) 453-5258 Fax

Web: www.natpe.org

E-mail: info@natpe.org

NATPE is known throughout the global television industry as the leading association for television-content professionals. At the core of NATPE's mission is a commitment to furthering the quality and quantity of content, which means offering the wealth of our resources and experience to every content creator, no matter the medium.

National Conference of Personal Managers (NCOPM)

P.O. Box 609

Palm Desert, CA 92261-0609

(818) 762-NCPM Phone

(760) 341-7830 Fax

Web: www.ncopm.com

E-mail: askncopm@ncopm.com

The NCOPM is the trade organization of personal managers. A personal manager advises and counsels talent and personalities in the entertainment industry. Personal managers have the expertise to find and develop new talent and create opportunities for the artists they represent. Personal managers act as liaisons between their clients, the public, and entertainment industry professionals such as theatrical agents, publicists, attorneys, and business managers who provide services to their clients. NCOPM has branches in California and New York.

New Playwrights Foundation (NPF)

c/o 608 San Vicente Blvd, #18
Santa Monica, CA 90402
(310) 393-3682
Web: www.newplaywrights.org

Founded in 1968, New Playwrights Foundation is a service organization for writers working in theater, film, television, and video. The foundation runs developmental workshops, holds readings, occasionally coproduces video and film projects, and assists members in furthering their careers. Membership in NPF is limited to twenty-five writers who must be able to attend meetings in Santa Monica every other Monday. Candidates for membership attend meetings before submitting materials to be reviewed by the group. Annual membership dues are $25.

New York Foundation for the Arts (NYFA)

155 Ave. of the Americas, 14th Fl.
New York, NY 10013-1507
(212) 366-6900 Phone
(212) 366-1778 Fax
Web: www.nyfa.org
E-mail: info@nyfa.org

The New York Foundation for the Arts is a statewide arts-service organization that provides a free national information resource for artists in all disciplines and for those who support the arts in any way. The organization features a searchable nationwide database of more than 2,800 grants, residencies, and apprenticeships; 3,100 arts organizations; and more, including listings of emerging-artist grants of up to $7,000.

Organization of Black Screenwriters, Inc. (OBS)

1968 W. Adams Blvd.
Los Angeles, CA 90018
(323) 735-2050 Phone

People in Hollywood are not showmen, they're maintenance men, pandering to what they think their audiences want.
—TERRY GILLIAM

(323) 735-2051 Fax

Web: www.obswriter.com

E-mail: obswriter@sbcglobal.com

The Organization of Black Screenwriters, Inc., began in 1988 to address the lack of black writers represented within the entertainment industry. The organization's primary function is to assist screenwriters in the creation of works for film and television and to help them present their work to the industry.

Philadelphia Dramatists Center (PDC)

1516 South St.

Philadelphia, PA 19146

(215) 735-1441

Web: www.libertynet.org/pdc

E-mail: pdc@libertynet.org

Philadelphia Dramatists Center is a service organization for professional playwrights, screenwriters, and musical theater writers. Programs and services include developmental readings, writers' circles, chats with area artistic directors and literary managers, craft development workshops, access to actor/director files, discounted tickets to participating theaters, rehearsal space, a telephone hotline listing upcoming events, and the bimonthly newsletter *First Draft*. Annual membership dues are $15 for students and $25 for individuals, which includes a subscription to *First Draft*.

Producers Guild of America (PGA)

6363 Sunset Blvd., 9th Fl.

Los Angeles, CA 90028

(323) 960-2590 Phone

(323) 960-2591 Fax

Web: www.producersguild.com

E-mail: info@producersguild.com

The Producers Guild of America represents, protects, and promotes the interests of all members of the producing team for motion pictures and television. Primary PGA goals are to combat producer credit proliferation, expand health benefits, and represent the entire producing team.

Screen Actors Guild

SAG–L.A.

5757 Wilshire Blvd.

Los Angeles, CA 90036

(323) 954-1600 Phone

(323) 549-6850 Fax

SAG–New York

1515 Broadway, 44th Fl.

New York, NY 10036

(212) 944-1030 Phone

(212) 944-6774 Fax

Web: www.sag.org

E-mail: info@sag.org

The Screen Actors Guild is the trade union of professional actors for motion picture work. SAG administers health insurance, pension benefits, contract negotiation, and other employment-related matters for its members. SAG also sponsors the annual Screen Actors Guild Awards and the SAG Foundation.

The Screenwriters Guild of America (SGA)

4337 Marina City Dr., Ste. 1141
Marina del Rey, CA 90292
Web: www.screenwritersguild.com
E-mail: generalinfo@screenwriters guild.com

The Screenwriters Guild of America is a proactive confederation of industry professionals united for the mutual aid and promotion of common interests. SGA's experience and expertise is derived from the cooperative, collective wisdom of industry screenwriters, directors, producers, literary agents, managers, educators, authors, and studio executives who share their years and, in many cases, lifetimes of priceless knowledge, experience, insight, and wisdom.

Scriptwriters Network

11684 Ventura Blvd., Ste. 508
Studio City, CA 91604
(323) 848-9477 Phone
Web: www.scriptwritersnetwork .com
E-mail: info@scriptwritersnetwork .com

The Scriptwriters Network, founded in 1986, is a group of affiliated film, television, and corporate/ industrial writers. Meetings feature guest speakers; developmental feedback on scripts is available; and staged readings may be arranged in conjunction with other groups. The network sponsors members-only contests and publishes a newsletter. Prospective members submit a professionally formatted script and a completed application; membership is not based on the quality of the script. There is a $15 initiation fee, and dues are $50 a year for nonlocal members, $60 for Southern California residents.

In the future, everybody is going to be a director. Somebody's got to live a real life so we have something to make a movie about.
—CAMERON CROWE

Society for Theatrical Artists' Guidance and Enhancement (STAGE)

Box 214820
Dallas, TX 75221
(214) 630-7722 Phone
(214) 630-4468 Fax
Web: www.stage-online.org
E-mail: stage-tx@swbell.net

Founded in 1981, STAGE is a non-profit membership organization based in Dallas/Fort Worth that serves as an information clearing-house and provides training and education for the theater, broadcast television, and film industries in north central Texas. The society maintains a library of plays, theater texts, and resource information; offers counseling on agents, unions, personal marketing, and other career-related matters; posts job opportunities; maintains a callboard for regional auditions in theater and film; and sponsors an actor's show-case called *Noon Preview*. Members of STAGE receive audition postings via e-mail and a monthly publication, *Centerstage*. Annual dues are $65; $45 for volunteers.

Talent Managers Association (TMA)

4804 Laurel Canyon Blvd., Ste. 611
Valley Village, CA 91607
(310) 205-8495 Phone
(818) 765-2903 Fax
Web: www.talentmanagers.org
E-mail: info@talentmanagers.org

The Talent Managers Association (founded in 1954) is an association of professional talent managers who have shown themselves to be ethical, knowledgeable, and skilled as talent/artist/literary managers. The association exists for the benefit of its members, the talent represented by the members, and the profession of talent management.

Women's Image Network (WIN)

P.O. Box 69-1774
Los Angeles, CA 90069
(310) 229-5365 Phone
Web: www.winfemme.com
E-mail: info@winfemme.com

Women's Image Network celebrates and promotes the role of women in the entertainment industry through the annual Women's Image Network award and the WinFemme Month-lies screenwriting awards.

Women in Film (WIF)

8857 W. Olympic Blvd., Ste. 201
Beverly Hills, CA 90211
(310) 657-5144 Phone
(310) 657-5154 Fax
Web: www.wif.org
E-mail: info@wif.org

The purpose of Women in Film is to empower, promote, nurture, and mentor women in the industry through a network of valuable contacts, events, and programs including the Women In Film Mentor Program, the Public Service Announcement Production Program, and the Internship Program in association with the Fulfillment Fund. Please take some time to view our mission statement, reel news, and upcoming events, and find out about membership and sponsorship.

grievances and arbitrations under those agreements. The guild gives annual awards and sponsors a foundation, which currently teaches film writing to disadvantaged high school students. WGAE participates in reciprocal arrangements with the International Affiliation of Writers Guilds and with its sister union, Writers Guild of America West. The guild publishes a monthly newsletter, which is available to nonmembers by subscription; and a quarterly journal called *On Writing.*

Writers Guild of America East (WGAE)

555 W. 57th St., Ste. 1230
New York, NY 10019
(212) 767-7800 Phone
(212) 582-1909 Fax
Web: www.wgaeast.org
E-mail: info@wgaeast.org
WGAE is the union for freelance writers in the fields of motion pictures, television, and radio who reside east of the Mississippi River (regardless of where they work). The union negotiates collective bargaining agreements for its members and represents them in

Writers Guild of America West (WGAW)

7000 W. Third St.
Los Angeles, CA 90048-4329
(323) 951-4000 Phone
(323) 782-4502 Agency Listing
(323) 782-4800 Fax
Web: www.wga.org
E-mail: info@wga.org
WGAW is the union for writers in the fields of motion pictures, television, radio, and new media who write both entertainment and news programming and who reside west of the Mississippi River. It

If it can be written, or thought, it can be filmed.
—STANLEY KUBRICK

represents its members in collective bargaining and other labor matters. It publishes a monthly magazine called *Written By*. The library is open to the public Monday through Friday (see the "Motion Picture Libraries and Museums" section of this text).

Writers Guild of Canada

366 Adelaide St. W., Ste. 401
Toronto, Ontario
M5V 1R9 Canada
(416) 979-7907 Phone
(800) 567-9974 Toll-Free
(416) 979-9273 Fax
Web: www.wrgc.ca
E-mail: info@wgc.ca

The Writers Guild of Canada is a national association representing more than 1,700 screenwriters working in film, television, radio, and multimedia production in Canada. Members of the guild are professionals who write dramatic TV series, MOWs, feature films, miniseries, documentaries, animation, comedy and variety series, children's and educational programming, and radio drama, as well as corporate videos and multimedia productions. On behalf of its members, the guild negotiates, administers, and enforces collective agreements setting out minimum rates, terms, and working conditions within its jurisdiction (all English-language production in Canada). The central collective agreement, the Independent Production Agreement, is negotiated between the guild and the Canadian Film and Television Production Association, the association representing independent producers in Canada. The Guild also has agreements in place with CBC Radio, CBC-TV, CTV, NFB, and TVOntario.

▌ Motion Picture Libraries and Museums

MOTION PICTURE LIBRARIES and museums contain information about the history of cinema and television along with extensive archives of past productions. Many have information lines that are manned by film experts that can often answer obscure trivia questions without having to look up the answer. Libraries and museums have voluminous statistics regarding the entertainment industry, such as audience demographics, viewership numbers, box office rankings, credits, and award winners.

They also maintain extensive collections of scripts, stills, promotional materials, biographical notes, and cinema history.

Academy of Motion Picture Arts and Sciences (AMPAS)

. . . .

Margaret Herrick Library
333 S. La Cienega Blvd.
Beverly Hills, CA 90211
(310) 247-3035 Phone
(310) 247-3020 Reference
(310) 657-5193 Fax
Web: www.oscars.org

This organization's library attempts to collect every English-language book on motion pictures (histories, biographies, the film industry around the world, genre studies, technical aspects, etc.), as well as important foreign reference sources and selected books in allied fields such as television, radio, theater, and music. There are many rare items in the collection, such as the first edition of Eadweard Muybridge's 1881 *Attitudes of Animals in Motion,* the *Moving Picture Annual and Yearbook* for 1912, and a copy of the novel *Gone with the Wind,* autographed by all of the film's principal cast members as well as its producer and director.

The library also maintains its Core Collection Files, which contain articles clipped from a wide range of newspapers and magazines, studio press releases, and advertising material along with photographs, programs, pressbooks, synopses, cast and credit sheets, lobby cards, reviews, production notes and other articles. The Biography Files include photographs, articles, and press releases on performers as well as those who work behind the scenes. The large poster collection contains items dating back to 1905 through current releases, and includes feature films, shorts, and documentaries. The majority of the library's photographs are original black-and-white prints. In addition, there are both black-and-white and color negatives, color slides and transparencies, motion picture film frames, glass negatives, and glass slides. The photographs include scene stills from films, portraits or publicity stills of individuals, set reference stills; wardrobe and make-up test pho-

---

❚ *The writer, when he is also an artist, is someone who admits what others don't dare reveal.*

—ELIA KAZAN

tos; research photos; location reference stills; premiere photos; advertising stills; behind-the-scenes production shots; candid and informal photos; and images of studios, theaters, cameras, residences, and Hollywood landmarks. The Turner/MGM Script Collection comprises more than 50,000 script items documenting nearly 1,900 productions from 1918 to 1986. The Paramount Pictures Corporation Collection includes scripts and pressbooks relating to more than 2,200 Paramount films spanning the years 1912 to 1965.

American Museum of Moving Images

35th Ave. at 36th St.
Astoria, NY 11106
(718) 784-4520 Phone
(718) 784-4681 Fax
Web: www.ammi.org

The American Museum of the Moving Image is dedicated to educating the public about the art, history, technique, and technology of film, television, and digital media and to examining their impact on culture and society. It achieves these goals by maintaining the nation's largest permanent collection of moving image artifacts and by offering exhibitions, film screenings, lectures, seminars, and other educational programs.

Museum of Television and Radio (L.A.)

465 N. Beverly Dr.
Beverly Hills, CA 90210
(310) 786-1000 Phone
(310) 786-1086 Fax
Web: www.mtr.org

This museum presents a wide variety of programs from the collection in two screening rooms and two main theaters. Also available are complete schedules for exhibitions and screening series that have been organized by the curatorial department. The Ahmanson Radio Listening Room, with its five preprogrammed listening series, offers a unique way for visitors to experience the radio collection. The museum also offers live and taped radio broadcasts throughout the year, where stations from across the country come to the Ralph Guild Radio Studio to broadcast their shows. These events are usually open to the public. Throughout the year, performers, critics, writers, directors, producers, and journalists come to the museum to discuss topics ranging from the collaborative process behind programming to significant events in the media industry. The seminars include television and radio clips from the museum's collection, and time for the audience members to ask questions.

Museum of Television and Radio (New York)

25 W. 52nd St.
New York, NY 10019
(212) 621-6600 Phone
(212) 621-6700 Fax
Web: www.mtr.org

This museum, like its sister institution in Los Angeles, presents a wide variety of programs from the collection in two screening rooms and two main theaters. Also available in the lobby are complete schedules for exhibitions and screening series that have been organized by the curatorial department. The Ralph Guild Radio Listening Room, with its five preprogrammed listening series, offers a unique way for visitors to experience the radio collection. The Museum also offers live and taped radio broadcasts throughout the year, where stations from across the country come to the Ralph Guild Radio Studio to broadcast their shows. These events are usually open to the public. The Library offers easy access to information on the museum's vast collection. You can search the database for the television or radio program of your choice. When you find a program you want, you reserve it and then go to a console room, where you watch or listen to the program at a monitor with headphones. Throughout the year, performers, critics, writers, directors,

producers, and journalists visit the museum to discuss topics ranging from the collaborative process behind programming to significant events in the media industry. The seminars include television and radio clips from the museum's collection, and time for the audience members to ask questions.

New York Public Library for the Performing Arts

At the Annex–Dance, Theater,
Music, Recorded Sound
Archive–Research
521 W. 43rd St.
New York, NY 10036-4396
(212) 870-1630 Phone
(212) 870-1663 Recordings
(212) 870-1639 Theater
(212) 870-1657 Dance
(212) 870-1650 Music
Web: www.nypl.org

The New York Public Library for the Performing Arts houses one of the world's most extensive combined collections of circulating, reference, and rare archival materials in the field. These materials are available free of charge, along with a wide range of special programs, including exhibitions, seminars, and performances. An essential resource for everyone with an interest in the arts—whether professional or amateur—the library is known particularly for its prodigious collections of nontext materials, such as historic recordings, videotapes, autograph manuscripts, correspondence, sheet music, stage designs, press clippings, programs, posters, and photographs.

Writers Guild Foundation
James R. Webb
Memorial Library
. . . .
7000 W. Third St.
Los Angeles, CA 90048-4329

(323) 782-4544 Phone
(323) 782-4695 Fax
Web: www.wga.org

The James R. Webb Memorial Library is dedicated to the art, craft, and history of writing for motion pictures, television, radio, and the new interactive media. In addition to providing a central archive of scripts recognized for excellence in their fields, it also operates as a clearinghouse and resource center for information about writers and writing in these collaborative media.

▮ Networks and Cable Channels

THESE WEB SITES are only for fans, but they are fun to peruse and contain a wealth of information about your favorite television shows. They don't have much information for anyone looking to break into the business, but they provide some idea of the way each network positions itself (drama-oriented, comedy-oriented, and so on) and how they approach marketing new series. Pay close attention to what new shows are being touted the most as they will give you some indication of the direction the industry is going.

ABC
. . . .
500 S. Buena Vista St.
Burbank, CA 91521
(818) 460-7777 Phone
Web: www.abc.com

CBS
. . . .
7800 Beverly Blvd.
Los Angeles, CA 90036-2188
(323) 575-2345 Phone
Web: www.cbs.com

Comedy Central

1775 Broadway, 10th Fl.
New York, NY 10019
(212) 767-8600 Phone
Web: www.comedycentral.com

Fox

10201 W. Pico Blvd.
Los Angeles, CA 90035
(310) 369-1000 Phone
Web: www.fox.com

HBO

1100 Ave. of the Americas
New York, NY 10036
(212) 512-1000 Phone
Web: www.hbo.com

NBC

3000 W. Alameda Ave.
Burbank, CA 91523-0001
(818) 840-4444 Phone
Web: www.nbc.com

PBS

1320 Braddock Park
Alexandria, VA 22314-1698
(703) 739-5000 Phone
Web: www.pbs.org

Showtime

1633 Broadway
New York, NY 10019
(212) 708-1600 Phone
Web: www.sho.com

UPN

11800 Wilshire Blvd.
Los Angeles, CA 90025
(310) 575-7000 Phone
Web: www.upn.com

WB Television Network

4000 Warner Blvd., Bldg. 34-R
Burbank, CA 91522-0001
(818) 977-5000 Phone
Web: www.thewb.com

You exist only in what you do.
—FEDERICO FELLINI

▌ THE DISTRIBUTOR'S PERSPECTIVE ▌

Scripts fall into one of three categories:

1. Scripts that are submitted to the major studios
2. Scripts that are submitted to smaller independents
3. Scripts that are self-produced by the screenwriter where the screenwriter may end up being the financier, director, and/or producer as well

The marketability of the script comes into play at different points for each possibility.

For Number 1: If the major studios see some potential in it, they will pick it up and rewrite it. The screenwriter only needs to meet the basic marketability threshold, i.e., an exciting and novel concept.

For Number 2: Independent producers want something that is mainstream (horror, thriller, action) and ready to go. They do not want to spend much time or effort on rewrites, so the script must be nearly perfect or they'll pass.

For Number 3: The independent distributors want a completed feature that is mainstream (horror, thriller, action) and is easily sellable.

With numbers 2 and 3, it is crucial for the screenwriter to solicit the advice of a sales agent/distributor on the marketability of a feature before going forward. For Number 2, this improves the chances that an independent producer will pick up the script; and for Number 3, this improves the odds that the feature will be picked up and enjoy good sales. So what kind of advice can the sales agent/distributors give? Well, it depends on what genre is hot at the moment and why.

Sales agent/distributors are on the front lines of the market and they know what sells. These are the key elements I look for in a project:

- The story has to have a significant hook—usually something memorable, catchy, shocking, unthinkable, and so on (because it helps with marketing). Something eye-catching should happen in the story in the first five minutes.
- It should be marketable to the lowest common denominator (not too high-brow).
- It should have at least one recognizable actor in a key role (again, this helps with marketing).
- Script must be smooth, no holes, no lag in the action or suspense.
- Cinematography has to be crisp and sexy (think *CSI* or *Alias*).

Moreover, the following are the genres I would be very interested in right now: horror films, thrillers, and urban genre films (the industry currently seeks smarter scripts, a cross between *Barbershop* and a gangster script). Latin genre is in vogue (hot/spicy action-romantic films such as *Y Tu Mama Tambien* or gangster), and finally, high concept is always popular (usually in the thriller genre). What will I be looking for next year? It could be a whole different list; you need to stay in touch with the business to know what's hot.

I know this takes some of the creativity out of the screenwriting process, but marketing is key in the entertainment business. We can't just buy films we like, we have to buy films we know we can sell.

—Pejman Partiyeli
+ENTERTAINMENT
468 N. Camden Dr., Ste. 250, Beverly Hills, CA 90210
(310) 860-5604 Phone
(310) 860-5194 Fax
Web: www.plusent.com
E-mail: mail@plusent.com

A director makes only one movie in his life. Then he breaks it into pieces and makes it again.

—JEAN RENOIR, director, *La Règle du jeu*

▌ Studios

THE MAJOR STUDIOS are listed here solely for research, as you cannot call them to get someone to read your script. Their legal departments don't allow them to accept submissions from writers, so if you send them a script you will get it returned unopened—no exceptions. Their Web sites are interesting to peruse, however, as they contain a wealth of information on the studio's production history and upcoming releases.

You can glean some information about what Hollywood is looking for by paying close attention to their production slate. Look at the artwork, the logline, the teaser, and the approach to the movie's marketing and you will get insight into each studio's target audience and what it considers to be the hottest genres.

Columbia Pictures

10202 W. Washington Blvd.
Culver City, CA 90232-3195
(310) 244-4000 Phone
Web: www.spe.sony.com

DreamWorks SKG

1000 Flower St.
Glendale, CA 91201
(818) 695-5000 Phone
Web: www.dreamworks.com

Fox Searchlight

10201 W. Pico Blvd.
Los Angeles, CA 90035
(310) 369-2359 Phone
Web: www.fox.com

Hollywood Pictures

500 S. Buena Vista St.
Burbank, CA 91521
(818) 560-1000 Phone

Metro-Goldwyn-Mayer Pictures

2500 Broadway St.
Santa Monica, CA 90404-3061

(310) 449-3000 Phone
Web: www.mgm.com

Miramax Films (New York)

c/o Tribeca Film Center
375 Greenwich St.
New York, NY 10013-2338

Miramax Films (L.A.)

8439 Sunset Blvd.
West Hollywood, CA 90069-1921
(323) 822-4200 Phone
Web: www.miramax.com

New Line Cinema

116 N. Robertson Blvd., Ste. 200
Los Angeles, CA 90048
(310) 854-5811 Phone
Web: www.newline.com

Paramount Pictures

5555 Melrose Ave.
Los Angeles, CA 90038
(323) 956-5000 Phone
Web: www.paramount.com

RKO Pictures

1875 Century Park E., Ste. 2140
Los Angeles, CA 90067
(310) 277-0707 Phone
Web: www.rko.com

Twentieth Century Fox

10201 W. Pico Blvd.
Los Angeles, CA 90035
(310) 369-1000 Phone
Web: www.fox.com

Universal Pictures

100 Universal City Plaza
Universal City, CA 91608-1085
(818) 777-1000 Phone
Web: www.universalpictures.com

Walt Disney Pictures/Touchstone

500 S. Buena Vista St.
Burbank, CA 91521-0001
(818) 560-1000 Phone
Web: www.disney.com

Warner Brothers Pictures

4000 Warner Blvd.
Burbank, CA 91522-0001
(818) 954-6000 Phone
Web: www.warnerbros.com

Sometimes you have to lie. One often has to distort a thing to catch its true spirit.
—**ROBERT FLAHERTY,** director, *Nanook of the North*

PUBLIC AGENCIES

▮ State Arts Agencies

STATE ARTS AGENCIES have information about writers' residencies, development opportunities, grants, education, and programs of special interest to artists and writers. Eligibility is not always restricted to current residents, so you might also contact the state you were born in or in which you attended school. Additionally, if the project you're working on is set in another state you might contact the arts agency there.

They are different from film commissions (next section) in that they cover all the arts, not just filmmaking. In many cases, though, a state arts agency will have more to offer an aspiring filmmaker or screenwriter, as its mission statement is simply to support the arts in any form. Film commissions are funded by economic development agencies and are thus mostly focused on fostering film production in the state.

> ▮ *You must keep sending work out; you must never let a manuscript do nothing but eat its head off in a drawer. You send that work out again and again, while you're working on another one. If you have talent, you will receive some measure of success—but only if you persist.*
> —ISAAC ASIMOV

Alabama State Council on the Arts

201 Monroe St.
Montgomery, AL 36130-1800
(334) 242-4076 Phone
(334) 240-3269 Fax
Web: www.arts.state.al.us
E-mail: staff@arts.state.al.us

Alaska State Council on the Arts

411 W. 4th Ave., Ste. 1E
Anchorage,, AK 99501-2343
(907) 269-6610 Phone
(907) 269-6601 Fax
Web: www.aksca.org
E-mail: info@aksca.org

American Samoa Council on Culture

Arts and Humanities
Office of the Governor, Box 1540
Pago Pago, AS 96799
011-684-633-4347 Phone
011-684-633-2059 Fax
Web: www.nasaa-arts.org/new/
    nasaa/gateway/AS.html

Arizona Commission of the Arts

41 7 W. Roosevelt St.
Phoenix, AZ 85003
(602) 255-5882 Phone
(602) 256-0282 Fax
Web: www.arizonaarts.org
E-mail: general@ArizonaArts.org

Arkansas Arts Council

1500 Tower Bldg., 323 Center St.
Little Rock, CO 72201
(501) 324-9766 Phone
(501) 324-9154 Fax
Web: www.arkansasarts.com
E-mail: info@arkansasarts.com

California Arts Council

1300 I St., Ste. 930
Sacramento, CA 95814
(916) 322-6555 Phone
(916) 322-6575 Fax
Web: www.cac.ca.gov
E-mail: cac@cwo.com

▌ *All you need for a movie is a gun and a girl.*
　　—JEAN-LUC GODARD

> *Art depends on luck and talent.*
> —FRANCIS FORD COPPOLA

> *All art is autobiographical. The pearl is the oyster's autobiography.*
> —FEDERICO FELLINI

Colorado Council on the Arts

750 Pennsylvania St.
Denver, CO 80203
(303) 894-2617 Phone
(303) 894-2615 Fax
Web: www.coloarts.state.co.us
E-mail: coloarts@artswire.org

Connecticut Commission on the Arts

755 Main St., 1 Financial Plaza
Hartford, CT 06103
(860) 566-4770 Phone
(860) 566-6462 Fax
Web: www.ctarts.org
E-mail: kdemeo@ctarts.org

Delaware Division of the Arts

Carvel State Office Bldg.
820 N. French St., 4th Fl.
Wilmington, DE 19801

(302) 577-8278 Phone
(302) 577-6561 Fax
Web: www.artswire.org
E-mail: delarts@artswire.org

District of Columbia Commission on the Arts and Humanities

410 8th St. N.W., 5th Fl.
Washington, DC 20004
(202) 724-5613 Phone
(202) 727-4135 Fax
Web: www.capaccess.org/ane/
   dccah
E-mail: dccah@erols.com

Florida Division of Cultural Affairs

1001 DeSoto Park Dr.
Tallahassee, FL 32301
(850) 245-6470 Phone
(850) 245-6497 Fax
Web: www.florida-arts.org
E-mail: info@florida-arts.org

PUBLIC AGENCIES

Georgia Council for the Arts

260 14th St. N.W., Ste. 401
Atlanta, GA 30318
(404) 685-2787 Phone
(404) 685-2788 Fax
Web: www.gaarts.org

Guam Council on the Arts and Humanities Agency

Box 2950
Agana, Guam 96910
(671) 475-2242 Phone
(671) 472-2781 Fax
Web: www.guam.net/gov/kaha

State Foundation on Culture and the Arts (Hawaii)

44 Merchant St.
Honolulu, HI 96813
(808) 586-0300 Phone
(808) 586-0308 Fax
Web: www.state.hi.us/sfca
E-mail: sfca@sfca.state.hi.us

Idaho Commission on the Arts

Box 83720
Boise, ID 83720-0008
(208) 334-2119 Phone
(208) 334-2488 Fax

Web: www.state.id.us/arts
E-mail: cconley@ica.state.id.us

Illinois Arts Council

James R. Thompson Center
100 W. Randolph St., Ste. 10-500
Chicago, IL 60601
(312) 814-6750 Phone
(312) 814-1471 Fax
Web: www.state.il.us/agency/iac
E-mail: info@arts.state.il.us

Indiana Arts Commission

402 W. Washington St., Rm. W072
Indianapolis, IN 46204-2741
(317) 232-1268 Phone
(317) 232-5595 Fax
Web: www.state.in.us/iac
E-mail: arts@state.in.us

Iowa Arts Council

Capitol Complex
600 E. Locust
Des Moines, IA 50319-0290
(515) 281-4451 Phone
(515) 242-6492 Fax
Web: www.culturalaffairs.org/iac/
   index.html
E-mail: jhenke@max.state.ia.us

Kansas Arts Commission

700 S.W. Jackson, Ste. 1004
Topeka, KS 66603-3761

(785) 296-3335 Phone
(785) 296-4989 Fax
Web: www.arts.state.ks.us
E-mail: kac@arts.state.ks.us

Kentucky Arts Council

Old Capitol Annex
300 W. Broadway
Frankfort, KY 40601
(502) 564-3757 Phone
(502) 564-2839 Fax
Web: www.kyarts.org
E-mail: kyarts@mail.state.ky.us

Louisiana Division of the Arts

Box 44247
Baton Rouge, LA 70804
(225) 342-8180 Phone
(225) 342-8173 Fax
Web: www.crt.state.la.us/arts/
    index.htm
E-mail: arts@crt.state.la.us

Maine Arts Commission

55 Capitol St.
25 State House Station
Augusta, ME 04333-0025
(207) 287-2724 Phone
(207) 287-2335 Fax
Web: www.mainearts.com/vendors
    /meet-vendors/default.asp
E-mail: jan.poulin@state.me.us

Maryland State Arts Council

175 W. Ostend St., Ste. E
Baltimore, MD 21230
(410) 767-6555 Phone
(410) 333-1062 Fax
Web: www.msac.org
E-mail: moliver@mdbusiness.state
    .md.us

Massachusetts Cultural Council

120 Boylston St., 2nd Fl.
Boston, MA 02116-4600
(617) 727-3668 Phone
(617) 727-0044 Fax
Web: www.massculturalcouncil.org
E-mail: web@art.state.ma.us

Michigan Council for the Arts and Cultural Affairs

702 West Kalamazoo
P.O. Box 30705
Lansing, MI 48909-8205
(517) 241-4011 Phone
(517) 241-3979 Fax
Web: www.michigan.gov/hal/0,
    1607,7-160-17445_19272---,00.html
E-mail: artsinfo@michigan.gov

PUBLIC AGENCIES

Minnesota State Arts Board

Park Square Ct.
400 Sibley St., Ste. 200
St. Paul, MN 55101-1928
(651) 215-1600 Phone
(651) 215-1602 Fax
Web: www.arts.state.mn.us
E-mail: msab@arts.state.mn.us

Mississippi Arts Commission

239 N. Lamar St., Ste. 207
Jackson, MS 39201
(601) 359-6030 Phone
(601) 359-6008 Fax
Web: www.arts.state.ms.us
E-mail: vlindsay@arts.state.ms.us

Missouri Arts Council

111 N. 7th St., Ste. 105
St. Louis, MO 63101
(314) 340-6845 Phone
(314) 340-7215 Fax
Web: www.missouriartscouncil.org
E-mail: moarts@mail.state.mo.us

Montana Arts Council

Box 202201
Helena, MT 59620-2201
(406) 444-6430 Phone
(406) 444-6548 Fax
Web: www.arts.state.mt.us
E-mail: mac@state.mt.us

Nebraska Arts Council

Joslyn Carriage House
3838 Davenport St.
Omaha, NE 68131-2329
(402) 595-2122 Phone
(402) 595-2334 Fax
Web: www.nebraskaartscouncil.org
E-mail: cmaiioy@nebraskaarts
council.org

Nevada Arts Council

602 N. Curry St.
Carson City, NV 89703
(775) 687-6680 Phone
(775) 687-6688 Fax
Web: www.dmla.clan.lib.nv.us/
docs/arts

▌ **TIP:** Don't send out a script based on a true story or a published work unless you own the adaptation rights. Never assume it can be taken care of later.

New Hampshire State Council on the Arts

. . . .

40 N. Main St.
Concord, NH 03301-4974
(603) 271-2789 Phone
(603) 271-3584 Fax
Web: www.state.nh.us/nharts

New Jersey State Council on the Arts

. . . .

225 W. State St., Box 306
Trenton, NJ 08625-0306
(609) 292-6130 Phone
(609) 989-1440 Fax
Web: www.njartscouncil.org
E-mail: njsca@arts.sos.state.nj.us

New Mexico Arts

. . . .

Box 1450
Santa Fe, NM 87504-1450
(505) 827-6490 Phone
(505) 827-6043 Fax
Web: www.nmarts.org

New York State Council on the Arts

. . . .

915 Broadway, 8th Fl.
New York, NY 10010
(212) 387-7000 Phone
(212) 387-7164 Fax
Web: www.nysca.org

North Carolina Arts Council

. . . .

Department of Cultural Resources
Raleigh, NC 27699-4632
(919) 733-2111 Phone
(919) 733-4834 Fax
Web: www.ncarts.org/home.html
E-mail: ncarts@ncmail.net

North Dakota Council on the Arts

. . . .

418 E. Broadway, Ste. 70
Bismarck, ND 58501-4086
(701) 328-3954 Phone
(701) 328-3963 Fax
Web: www.state.nd.us/arts
E-mail: comserv@state.nd.us

Northern Mariana Islands Commonwealth Council for Arts and Culture

. . . .

Box 5553, CHRB
Saipan, MP 96950
(670) 322-9982 Phone
(670) 322-9028 Fax
Web: www.geocities.com/ccacarts/
ccacwebsite.html
E-mail: galaidi@gtepacifica.net

Ohio Arts Council

. . . .

727 E. Main St.
Columbus, OH 43205-1796
(614) 466-2613 Phone
(614) 466-4494 Fax
Web: www.oac.state.oh.us

PUBLIC AGENCIES

Oklahoma Arts Council

Box 52001-2001
Oklahoma City, OK 73152-2001
(405) 521-2931 Phone
(405) 521-6418 Fax
Web: www.arts.state.ok.us
E-mail: okarts@arts.state.ok.us

Oregon Arts Commission

775 Summer St. N.E., Ste. 350
Salem, OR 97301-1284
(503) 986-0082 Phone
(503) 986-0260 Fax
Web: www.art.econ.state.or.us
E-mail: oregon.artscomm@state.
   or.us

Pennsylvania Council on the Arts

Finance Bldg., Rm. 216
Harrisburg, PA 17120
(717) 787-6883 Phone
(717) 783-2538 Fax
Web: www.artsnet.org/pca

Institute of Puerto Rican Culture

Box 9024184
San Juan, PR 00902-4184
(787) 725-5137 Phone
(787) 724-8393 Fax
Web: www.nasaa-arts.org/new/
   nasaa/gateway/PR.html

Rhode Island State Council on the Arts

95 Cedar St., Ste. 103
Providence, RI 02903-1062
(401) 222-3880 Phone
(401) 521-1351 Fax
Web: www.risca.state.ri.us
E-mail: info@risca.state.ri.us

South Carolina Arts Commission

1800 Gervais St.
Columbia, SC 29201
(803) 734-8696 Phone
(803) 734-8526 Fax
Web: www.state.sc.us/arts

You have to show violence the way it is. If you don't show it realistically, then that's immoral and harmful. If you don't upset people, then that's obscenity.
—ROMAN POLANSKI

South Dakota Arts Council

Office of the Arts; Dept. of
Education and Cultural Affairs
800 Governors Dr.
Pierre, SD 57501-2294
(605) 773-3131 Phone
(605) 773-6962 Fax
Web: www.state.sd.us/state/
executive/deca/sdarts/sdarts.htm
E-mail: sdac@stlib.state.sd.us

Tennessee Arts Commission

401 Charlotte Ave.
Nashville, TN 37243-0780
(615) 741-1701 Phone
(615) 741-8559 Fax
Web: www.arts.state.tn.us
E-mail: dadkins@mail.state.tn.us

Texas Commission on the Arts

Box 13406
Austin, TX 78711-3406
(512) 463-5535 Phone
(512) 475-2699 Fax
Web: www.arts.state.tx.us
E-mail: front.desk@arts.state.tx.us

Utah Arts Council

617 E. South Temple
Salt Lake City, UT 84102-1177
(801) 236-7555 Phone
(801) 236-7556 Fax
Web: http://arts.utah.gov

Vermont Arts Council

136 State St., Drawer 33
Montpelier, VT 05633-6001
(802) 828-3291 Phone
(802) 828-3363 Fax
Web: www.vermontartscouncil.org
E-mail: info@arts.vca.state.vt.us

Virginia Commission for the Arts

Lewis House, 2nd Fl.
223 Governor St.
Richmond, VA 23219-2010
(804) 225-3132 Phone
(804) 225-4327 Fax
Web: www.arts.state.va.us
E-mail: vacomm@artswire.org

PUBLIC AGENCIES

Virgin Islands Council on the Arts

41-42 Norre Gade
St. Thomas, VI 00802
(340) 774-5984 Phone
(340) 774-6206 Fax
Web: www.vicouncilonarts.org
E-mail: vicouncil@islands.vi

Washington State Arts Commission

234 E. 8th Ave., Box 42675
Olympia, WA 98504-2675
(360) 753-3860 Phone
(360) 586-5351 Fax
Web: www.arts.wa.gov
E-mail: pamm@wsac.wa.gov

West Virginia Commission on the Arts

1900 Kanawha Blvd. E.
Charleston, WV 25305-0300

(304) 558-0240 Phone
(304) 558-2779 Fax
Web: www.wvculture.org
E-mail: ressmeyr@wvlc.wvnet.edu

Wisconsin Arts Board

101 E. Wilson St., 1st Fl.
Madison, WI 53702
(608) 266-0190 Phone
(608) 267-0380 Fax
Web: www.arts.state.wi.us/static
E-mail: artsboard@arts.state.wi.us

Wyoming Arts Council

2320 Capitol Ave.
Cheyenne, WY 82002
(307) 777-7742 Phone
(307) 777-5499 Fax
Web: www.commerce.state.wy.us/
   cr/arts/index.htm

▌ State Film Commissions

THOUGH FILM COMMISSIONS are typically biased toward helping large-scale productions, they maintain databases of information on locations, upcoming productions, equipment providers, experienced crew members, film festivals, organizations, and student shoots. They may be able to help an aspiring screenwriter get his or her script into hands of local producers who are trying to establish a filmmaking community.

Alabama Film Office

Alabama Center for Commerce
401 Adams Ave., Ste. 630
Montgomery, AL 36104
(334) 242-4195/(800)-633-5898
  Phone
(334) 242-2077 Fax
Web: www.alabamafilm.org

Alaska Film Program

550 W. Seventh Ave., Ste. 1770
Anchorage, AK 99501-3510
(907) 269-8110 Phone
(907) 269-8125 Fax
Web: www.alaskafilm.org

Arizona Film Commission

3800 N. Central Ave., Bldg. D
Phoenix, AZ 85012
(602) 280-1380/(800)-523-6695
  Phone
(602) 280-1384 Fax
Web: www.azcommerce.com

Arkansas Department of Economic Development

Film Office
One Capitol Mall, Rm. 4B-505
Little Rock, AR 72201
(501) 682-7326 Phone
(501) 682-3456 Fax
Web: www.1800arkansas.com/film

California Film Commission

7080 Hollywood Blvd., Ste. 900
Hollywood, CA 90028
(323) 860-2960/(800) 858-4749
  Phone
(323) 860-2972 Fax
Web: www.film.ca.gov
Web: www.cinemascout.com
Web: www.filmcafirst.com

Colorado Film Commission

1625 Broadway, Ste. 1700
Denver, CO 80202
(303) 620-4500/(800) 726-8887
  Phone
(303) 620-4545 Fax
Web: www.coloradofilm.org

Connecticut Film, Video, and Media Office

805 Brook St., Bldg. 4
Rocky Hill, CT 06067
(860) 571-7136/(800) 392-2122
  Phone
(860) 571-7150 Fax
Web: www.cffilm.com

Delaware Film Office

99 Kings Highway
Dover, DE 19901
(302) 739-4271/(800) 441-8846
  Phone

PUBLIC AGENCIES

(302) 739-5749 Fax
Web: www.state.de.us

(404) 656-3565 Fax
Web: www.georgia.org/film/
index.html

District of Columbia Office of Motion Picture and TV

410 Eighth St. N.W., 6th Fl.
Washington, DC 20004
(202) 727-6608 Phone
(202) 727-3787 Fax
Web: www.filmdctv.com

Hawaii Film Office

P.O. Box 2359
Honolulu, HI 96804
(808) 586-2570 Phone
(808) 586-2572 Fax
Web: www.hawaiifilmoffice.com

Florida Office of Film and Entertainment

Executive Office of the Governor
2001 The Capitol
Tallahassee, FL 32399-0001
(850) 410-4765/(877) 352-3456
  Phone
(850) 410-4770 Fax
Web: www.filminflorida.com

Idaho Film Bureau

700 W. State St., P.O. Box 83720
Boise, ID 83720-0093
(208) 334-2470/(800) 842-5858
  Phone
(208) 334-2631 Fax
Web: www.filmidaho.org

Illinois Film Office

100 W. Randolph, Ste. 3-400
Chicago, IL 60601
(312) 814-7179 Phone
(312) 814-8874 Fax
Web: www.filmillinois.state.il.us

Georgia Film and Videotape Office

285 Peachtree Center Ave. #1000
Atlanta, GA 30303
(404) 656-3591 Phone

❚ *Trust your own instinct. Your mistakes might as well be your own, instead of someone else's.*

  —BILLY WILDER

I dream for a living.
—STEVEN SPIELBERG

Indiana Film Commission

Indiana Dept. of Commerce
1 N. Capitol Ave., Ste. 700
Indianapolis, IN 46204-2288
(317) 232-8829 Phone
(317) 232-6887 Fax
Web: www.filmindiana.com

Iowa Film Office

200 E. Grand Ave.
Des Moines, IA 50309
(515) 242-4726 Phone
(515) 242-4809 Fax
Web: www.state.ia.us/film

Kansas Film Commission

700 S.W. Jackson, Ste. 100
Topeka, KS 66612
(785) 296-4927 Phone
(785) 296-6988 Fax
Web: www.kansascommerce.com

Kentucky Film Commission

500 Mero St., 2200 Capitol Plaza
  Tower
Frankfort, KY 40601

(502) 464-3456/(800) 345-6591
  Phone
(502) 564-7588 Fax
Web: www.kyfilmoffice.com

Louisiana Film Commission

P.O. Box 94185
Baton Rouge, LA 70804
(225) 342-8150 Phone
(225) 342-5389 Fax
Web: www.lafilm.org

Maine Film Office

59 State House Station
Augusta, ME 04333
(207) 624-7631 Phone
(207) 287-8070 Fax
Web: www.filminmaine.com

Maryland Film Office

217 E. Redwood St., 9th Fl.
Baltimore, MD 21202
(410) 767-6340/(800) 333-6632
  Phone
(410) 333-0044 Fax
Web: www.marylandfilm.org

PUBLIC AGENCIES

Massachusetts Film Office

10 Park Plaza, Ste. 2310
Boston, MA 02116
(617) 973-8800 Phone
(617) 973-8810 Fax
Web: www.state.ma.us/film

Michigan Film Office

717 W. Allegan, P.O. Box 30739
Lansing, MI 48909
(517) 373-0638/(800) 477-3456
   Phone
(517) 241-2930 Fax
Web: www.michigan.org

Minnesota Film and TV Board

401 N. Third St., Ste. 460
Minneapolis, MN 55401
(612) 332-6493 Phone
(612) 332-3735 Fax
Web: www.mnfilm.org

Mississippi Film Office

P.O. Box 849
Jackson, MS 39205
(601) 359-3297 Phone
(601) 359-5757 Fax
Web: www.mississippi.org

Missouri Film Commission

301 W. High St., Rm. 720,
   P.O. Box 118
Jefferson City, MO 65102
(573) 751-9050 Phone
(573) 522-1719 Fax
Web: www.showmemissouri.org/
   film

Montana Film Office

1424 Ninth Ave.
Helena, MT 59620
(406) 444-3762/(800) 553-4563
   Phone
(406) 444-4191 Fax
Web: www.montanafilm.com

Nebraska Film Office

P.O. Box 98907
Lincoln, NE 68509-8907
(402) 471-3680/(800) 228-4307
   Phone
(402) 471-3026 Fax
Web: www.filmnebraska.org

Nevada Film Office

555 E. Washington Ave., Ste. 5400
Las Vegas, NV 89101
(702) 486-2711 Phone
(702) 486-2712 Fax
Web: www.nevadafilm.com

New Hampshire Film and Television Office

....

P.O. Box 1856, 172 Pembroke Rd.
Concord, NH 03302-1856
(603) 271-2665 Phone
(603) 271-6870 Fax
Web: www.filmnh.org

New Jersey Motion Picture and Television Commission

....

153 Halsey St., 5th Fl.
Newark, NJ 07101
(973) 648-6279 Phone
(973) 648-7350 Fax
Web: www.nj.com/njfilm

New Mexico Film Office

....

P.O. Box 20003
Santa Fe, NM 87504-5003
(505) 827-9871/(800) 545-9871
  Phone
(505) 827-9799 Fax
Web: www.nmfilm.com

New York City Mayor's Office of Film, Theater, and Broadcasting

....

1697 Broadway, Ste. 602
New York, NY 10019
(212) 489-6710 Phone
(212) 307-6237 Fax
Web: www.ci.nyc.ny.us/html/
film.com

New York State Governor's Film Office

....

633 Third Ave., 33rd Fl.
New York, NY 10017
(212) 803-2330 Phone
(212) 803-2339 Fax
E-mail: nyfilm@empire.state.ny.us

North Carolina Film Commission

....

301 N. Wilmington St.
Raleigh, NC 27601
(919) 733-9900/(800) 232-9227
  Phone
(919) 715-0151 Fax
Web: www.ncfilm.com

PUBLIC AGENCIES

▌ *I'd love to sell out completely. It's just that nobody has been willing to buy.*
  —JOHN WATERS

North Dakota Film Commission

400 E. Broadway, Ste. 50
Bismarck, ND 58502
(701) 328-2874/(800) 328-2871
    Phone
(701) 328-4878 Fax
Web: www.ndtourism.com

Ohio Film Commission

77 S. High St., 29th Fl.
Columbus, OH 43215
(614) 466-2284/(800) 230-3523
    Phone
(614) 466-6744 Fax
Web: www.ohiofilm.com

Oklahoma Film Commission

15 N. Robinson, Ste. 802
Oklahoma City, OK 73102
(405) 522-6760/(800) 766-3456
    Phone
(405) 522-0656 Fax
Web: www.otrd.state.ok.us/
    filmcommission

Oregon Film and Video Office

One World Trade Center
121 S.W. Salmon St., Ste. 1205
Portland, OR 97204

(503) 229-5832 Phone
(503) 229.6869 Fax
Web: www.oregonfilm.org

Pennsylvania Film Office

Commonwealth Keystone Bldg.,
    4th Fl.
Harrisburg, PA 17120-0225
(717) 783-3456 Phone
(717) 787-0687 Fax
Web: www.filminpa.com

Puerto Rico Film Commission

P.O. Box 362350
San Juan, PR 00936
(787) 754-7110 Phone
(787) 756-5706 Fax
E-mail: lavelez@preda.com

Rhode Island Film and TV Office

One W. Exchange St.
Providence, RI 02903
(401) 222-2601 Phone
(401) 273-8270 Fax
Web: www.rifilm.com

South Carolina Film Office

P.O. Box 7367
Columbia, SC 29202

(803) 737-0490 Phone
(803) 737-3104 Fax
Web: www.scfilmoffice.com

Web: www.governor.state.tx.us/
film

South Dakota Film Office

711 E. Wells Ave.
Pierre, SD 57501
(605) 773-3301/(800) 952-3625
  Phone
(605) 773-3256 Fax
Web: www.media.sd.com

Tennessee Film and Music Commission

312 Eighth Ave. N., Tennessee
  Tower, 9th Fl.
Nashville, TN 37243
(615) 741-3456/(877) 818-3456
  Phone
(615) 741-5554 Fax
Web: www.state.tn.us/film

Texas Film Commission

P.O. Box 13246
Austin, TX 78711
(512) 463-9200 Phone
(512) 463-4114 Fax

Utah Film Commission

American Plaza III
47 W. 200 S., Ste. 600
Salt Lake City, UT 84101
(801) 741-4540/(800) 453-8824
  Phone
(801) 741-4549 Fax
Web: www.film.utah.org

Vermont Film Commission

P.O. Box 129
Montpelier, VT 05601
(802) 828-3618 Phone
(802) 828-2221 Fax
Web: www.vermontfilm.com

Virginia Film Office

901 E. Byrd St.
Richmond, VA 23219-4048
(804) 371-8204/(800) 854-6233
  Phone
(804) 371-8177 Fax
Web: www.film.virginia.org

PUBLIC AGENCIES

You have to have a dream so you can get up in the morning.
—BILLY WILDER

Washington State Film Office

2001 Sixth Ave., Ste. 2600
Seattle, WA 98121
(206) 956-3200 Phone
(206) 956-3205 Fax
Web: www.wafilm.wa.gov

West Virginia Film Office

Capitol Complex, Bldg. 6, Rm. 620
Charleston, WV 25305-0311
(304) 558-2234/(800) 982-3386
  Phone
(304) 558-0362 Fax
Web: www.wvdo.org

Wisconsin Film Office

201 W. Washington Ave., 2nd Fl.
Madison, WI 53703
(800) 345-6947 Phone
(608) 266-3403 Fax
Web: www.filmwisconsin.org

Wyoming Film Office

214 W. 15th St.
Cheyenne, WY 82002
(307) 777-3400/(800) 458-6657
  Phone
(307) 777-2838 Fax
Web: www.wyoming film.org

I steal from every movie ever made.
  —QUENTIN TARANTINO

Drama is life with the dull bits cut out.
  —ALFRED HITCHCOCK

ONLINE RESOURCES

THE WEB PROVIDES a tremendous amount of information and support to aspiring screenwriters. From writing groups to advice to employment opportunities to legal help, there is almost no end to what you can learn if you spend the time to research the sites in this section carefully.

Many have articles with up-to-date information and leads, and there are dozens of periodicals and newsletters that can help you keep up with the ever-changing Hollywood dynamics. When it comes to getting an idea of what professional screenwriting is all about, there is no better resource than your computer. By the time you read most books on the subject, the information is already out of date whereas changes and updates on the Internet are instantaneous.

Networking is at the center of the entertainment business and the Internet may be the most efficient way to do it these days. Many friendships have begun in newsgroups. Other writers can be instrumental in sharing contacts that could help you get your start.

For instance, if you know a producer looking for a good romantic comedy and you don't have one but a friend of yours does, wouldn't you call that person? It's better to have a friend get the deal than a stranger; after all, next time that friend might help *you*. It's that sort of business, so by all means meet as many writers as you can. You might also end up with a writing partner, a good sounding board, or at least a shoulder to cry on—all of which a writer needs sometimes.

> Myths are public dreams; dreams are private myths.
> —JOSEPH CAMPBELL

The Pauper

Web: www.thepauper.com

"Helping artists with the art of survival," reads The Pauper's motto. This organization provides advice on issues such as financial planning and health insurance, and offers a community for artists and writers. Publications include *The Starving Artist's Guide to Survival,* a *Career Planning Guide,* and a monthly newsletter called *The Newspauper.*

PEN American Center

Web: www.pen.org

PEN calls itself "A fellowship of writers working for more than eighty years to advance literature, to promote a culture of reading, and to defend free expression." The organization provides grants and awards, promotes writing programs, publishes a literary journal, and provides an open forum for discussion.

Screenwriters Utopia

Web: www.screenwritersutopia.com

Site for aspiring writers features discussion groups, articles, writing tips, interviews, and links. Screen-

writers Utopia also publishes *Screenwriters Monthly.*

A Story Is a Promise

Web: www.storyispromise.com

This site offers writers of all levels new ideas on the essential elements of storytelling. It includes reviews of popular novels, plays, and screenplays that highlight those aspects of storytelling essential to fulfilling a writer's promise to the reader.

Wordplay

Web: www.wordplayer.com

Wordplay features essays covering all facets of screenwriting, written by working screenwriters. It also offers a full course in writing screenplays from an insider's perspective, letters, columns, advice, and a writer's forum.

Writing for Film

Web: http://www.online-communicator.com/writfilm.html

This Web site offers helpful advice and lots of links for the aspiring screenwriter or TV writer.

▮ Copyright Clearance

Copyright Clearance Center

Web: www.copyright.com

Here you can get permission to reproduce copyrighted content such as articles and book chapters in your journals, photocopies, course packs, library reserves, Web sites, e-mail, and more.

The Copyright Website

Web: www.benedict.com

This portal provides relevant, real-world copyright information for anyone navigating the Internet. It contains interesting anecdotes, historic copyright battles, and even media snippets of content that has been subject to contentious copyright debate.

Motion Picture Licensing Corp.

Web: www.mplc.com/index2.htm

This is an independent copyright licensing service exclusively authorized by major Hollywood motion picture studios and independent producers to grant umbrella licenses to nonprofit groups, businesses, and government organizations for the public performances of home videocassettes and DVDs. The Web site contains a primer on copyright law and links to other copyright sites.

National Creative Registry (NCR)

Web: www.ncronline.com

NCR processes thousands of online registrations each year from writers, screenwriters, attorneys, songwriters, advertising agencies, Internet and software developers, inventors, scientists, and corporations worldwide. Registration here is not necessary if you copyright your work.

Scriptfly

Web: www.scriptfly.com

This site contains screenwriting articles, scene study, spec market updates, contests, interviews, legal information, resources, tips, and screenplays of recently released movies.

ONLINE RESOURCES

▋ SOME SCREENWRITING STATISTICS

Varieties of screenwriting software available from the Writers Store in West Hollywood (www.writerstore.com): 26

Average annual income of the 9,000 members of the Writers Guild of America West: $90,000

Number of new members admitted to the Writers Guild each month: 45

Number of books, DVDs, software, and more that Amazon.com lists in a search for screenwriting: 2,130

Number of classes on screenwriting offered by UCLA Extension: 46

Number of literary properties bought by entertainment companies last year: 270

Number of movies made in the United States last year: 340

Number of scripts, treatments, and pitches registered last year with the Writers Guild West: 50,000

▋ Entertainment Business

Baseline/Filmtracker

Web: www.baseline.com
This site plays a vital part in how Hollywood keeps track of what everyone else is doing. This fee-based, searchable database contains 1.5 million records on projects tracked from development to release, offering cast and crew credits, box office grosses, celebrity biographies, talent contact information, company directories, and industry news.

Showbizdata

Web: www.showbizdata.com
This is an entertainment industry site geared to the business side, featuring box office grosses, news, market guides, development news, literary sales, and distribution graphs.

Association of Authors' Representatives (AAR)

Web: www.aar-online.org

The AAR keeps agents informed about conditions in publishing, theater, the motion picture and television industries, and related fields. It encourages cooperation among literary organizations, and assists agents in representing their author-clients' interests.

Authorassist

Web: www.authorassist.com

This site's fee-based services offers script consulting services and help with writing proposals and queries, text editing, securing an agent, marketing your script, and strategizing your promotion efforts.

Hollywood Creative Directory (HCD)

Web: www.hcdonline.com

Known as the phone book to Hollywood, the HCD contains the most reliable, up-to-date contact information for producers. Published three times a year, it contains phone numbers, fax numbers, Web sites, e-mail addresses, credits, and names of office staff members and their titles. Separate guides are available for distributors, agents and managers, film buyers, music industry players, and more. It's available in print or online.

Screenwriters 101

Web: www.screenwriters101.com

"How to Get an Agent . . . Tips and Guidance" contains a list of fifty-six tips about how to get an agent to look at your work.

▌**TIP:** Don't ever sign anything without talking to an attorney that specializes in entertainment law. For a referral, call the Los Angeles County Bar Association at (213) 243-1525 (www.lacba.org) or the Beverly Hills Bar Association at (310) 553-4022 (www.bhba.org).

ONLINE RESOURCES

Writers Guild of America (WGA)

Web: www.wga.org/agentinfo.html

The Writers Guild of America maintains a list of franchised agents that are signatories to an agreement that mandates certain protections for writers. The list identifies those agencies that will accept unsolicited material. Also included is a primer for new writers about how to get their work read and considered by busy agents, and a list of agents that have agreed to review queries from new writers.

■ Independent Filmmaking

Film Threat

Web: www.filmthreat.com

Film Threat is a magazine with an emphasis on independent, underground, and low-budget films. It offers reviews, interviews, updates on film festivals, and box-office stats. It also features a free e-mail newsletter.

Movie Partners

Web: www.moviepartners.com

Movie Partners offers resources, industry tools, networking opportunities, news, and an events calendar to aspiring writers and filmmakers.

Underground Film

Web: www.undergroundfilm.com

This resource for guerrilla filmmakers features articles, reviews, career advice, top ten lists, a screenplay library, and downloadable films.

Webcinema

Web: www.webcinema.org

Subscriber-based site allows the independent filmmaker to use Internet media technologies to finance, create, produce, distribute, and market independent film.

▮ Job Opportunities

Entertainment Careers

Web: www.entertainmentcareers
.net

This site contains an education center; research related to careers in the motion picture and television industries; lists of studio, network, and production company job lines; and links to other entertainment employment sites and resources.

Entertainment Jobs and Internships

Web: www.eej.com/featuredjobs/
jobinfo.html

Here you'll find lists of jobs and internships, advertising, marketing, finance, graphic arts, etc. The site also offers articles targeted to finding work, notices on upcoming competitions (screenplay contests, film festivals, fellowships, etc.), and an up-to-date calendar of industry events.

Hollywood Creative Directory

Web: www.hcdonline.com/
jobboard/default.asp

HCD maintains a comprehensive listing of employment positions available in the entertainment industry. Categories include creative, casting, agents and managers, new media, distributors, production/post-production, support, internships, film crews, technical, and music.

Surfview Entertainment

Web: www.surfview.com/
seindlst.htm

This site is designed to help filmmakers connect with potential financing and legal information sources.

> ▮ *I write entirely to find out what I'm thinking, what I'm looking at, what I see and what it means, what I want, and what I fear.*
> —JOAN DIDION

ONLINE RESOURCES

International Entertainment, Multimedia and Intellectual Property Law and Business Network

Web: www.medialawyer.com/
home.html

This site is designed as a central reference point for helpful information to entertainment, multimedia, intellectual property, and online professionals along with international links to professional, legal, and business services.

Mark Litwak, Entertainment and Multimedia Attorney

Web: www.marklitwak.com

Mark Litwak is a veteran entertainment lawyer and an author. His Web site contains general information concerning copyrights, trademarks, contracts, multimedia law, intellectual property, book publishing, and film financing.

The Publishing Law Center

Web: www.publaw.com

The Publishing Law Center offers legal information for the publishing community including publishers, authors, editors, Web masters, and freelancers. This site contains a searchable database of articles and links.

Paul D. Supnik Law Offices

Web: www.supnik.com

This site offers information on copyright, trademark, and entertainment law, as well as a database of entertainment law links and resources.

Creativity is the act of forgetting, for just a moment, what you know.
–THOMAS EDISON

Writing is not necessarily something to be ashamed of, but do it in private and wash your hands afterwards.
–ROBERT HEINLEIN

▮ Miscellaneous

Alliance of Artist Communities

Web: www.artistscommunities.org

This site features a well-maintained database of communities where writers can work in peace—or at least seek the commiseration of other crazy, starving nonconformists.

Cinema Now

Web: www.cinemanow.com

This site allows you to watch full-screen DVD-quality movies on your desktop or laptop computer or your TV.

FilmFestivals.com

Web: www.filmfestivals.com

This Web site features a searchable database of film festivals all over the world. It contains news, a calendar, a bulletin board, a checklist, and interviews.

The Greatest Films

Web: www.filmsite.org

This site is for movie buffs; it contains lists of the greatest films ever made, plus information on stars, directors, quotes, scenes, etc.

IFILM

Web: www.ifilm.com

This is a site where any independent filmmaker can make his or her short film available to the public for free. IFILM offers thousands of short films, clips, trailers, and interviews that viewers can download for free.

Movie Clichés

Web: www.moviecliches.com

This fun site lists thousands of movie moments you never realized were clichés, categorized by subject.

Trailervision

Web: www.trailervision.com

This site promotes the movie trailer as the medium of the future when our attention span no longer lasts beyond two minutes. It offers movie trailer parodies and trailers for films that (thankfully) never existed.

Absolute Write

Web: www.absolutewrite.com

This site features articles, an agent report, writers' markets guide, writers' directory, market listings, and a newsletter.

Ain't It Cool News

Web: www.aint-it-cool-news.com

This site features reviews of unreleased movies, live chats, a forum, and breaking news that Hollywood doesn't want you to know (the studios hate this Web site).

American Cinematographer

Web: www.cinematographer.com

This is the official site of the American Society of Cinematographers and *American Cinematographer* magazine. It features information, news, reviews, articles, and interviews with cinematographers.

American Zoetrope

Web: www.zoetrope.com

Francis Ford Coppola's company provides a voice for the independent film community with news, articles, a screenplay contest, chat rooms, and new technology such as the Zoetrope Virtual Studio, a complete motion picture production studio on the Web offering collaborative tools for writers, directors, producers, and other film artists.

Animation World Network

Web: www.awn.com

This site contains breaking news, reviews, interviews, and articles about animation production around the world.

Backstage

Web: www.backstage.com

This is one of the entertainment industry's leading trade papers, but its emphasis is on theater. It contains casting opportunities, production news, a show guide, and a calendar. It publishes editions in Los Angeles, New York, Chicago, Florida, and Las Vegas editions.

Black Talent News

Web: www.blacktalentnews.com

This is a news publication that targets African American professionals within the entertainment business.

Creative Screenwriting Magazine

Web: www.creativescreen
writing.com

This publication offers interviews and information for aspiring and established screenwriters.

Dark Horizons

Web: www.darkhorizons.com

This site contains film news, film index, trailers, interviews, release dates, film reviews, DVD reviews, and script reviews for films in release.

Done Deal

Web: www.scriptsales.com

This is a news resource for screenplay, pitch, treatment, and book sales in the film industry. It features interviews, software and book reviews, advice, agency and production company listings, contests, news, and more.

Fade In Magazine

Web: www.fadeinonline.com

Fade In offers interviews, reviews, and articles covering all aspects of the movie business. It also features a free e-mail newsletter.

Film & Video Magazine

Web: www.filmandvideo
magazine.com

The online version of *Film & Video* magazine offers articles, interviews, news, and reviews of releases and new products, with an emphasis on digital filmmaking.

Hollywood Lit Sales

Web: www.hollywoodlitsales.com

This is a fee-based forum for writers to sell their material to Hollywood. It includes spec sales charts, writing tips, online seminars, interviews, columns, reviews, message board, and contest information.

Hollywoodnetwork.com

Web: www.hollywoodnetwork.com

Hollywoodnetwork.com is the sponsor of the Hollywood Film Festival. It also offers seminars and conferences.

ONLINE RESOURCES

The Hollywood Reporter

Web: www.hollywoodreporter.com

This is the online version of one of the industry's leading trade papers. It features news about the latest film, television, and music deals. It covers the entire entertainment business, with information on box-office receipts, international news, piracy issues, new media, and films in production.

Hollywood Scriptwriter

Web: www.hollywoodscript
writer.com

This trade newspaper features articles on screenwriting, profiles, and question-and-answer sessions with industry professionals, news, commentary, tips, and resources.

Movie Bytes

Web: www.moviebytes.com

This searchable database of literary agents and screenplay contests also offers news, advice, a writers' bulletin board, and a free e-mail newsletter.

MovieMaker

Web: www.moviemaker.com

This online version of *MovieMaker* magazine contains news, articles,

interviews, reviews, trailers, and helpful links.

Scr(i)pt Magazine

Web: www.scriptmag.com

Scr(i)pt lists multiple screenplay contests and festivals, interviews with acclaimed Hollywood writers, and features on upcoming releases. Online courses are offered through the magazine's classes page.

Variety

Web: www.variety.com

The online version of the entertainment industry's premiere trade publication features film industry articles, interviews, breaking news, box office receipts, festival information, film reviews, an event calendar, and listings of films in production.

Zoetrope All Story

Web: www.all-story.com

This is the online site for *Zoetrope: All-Story* magazine, which was created by Francis Ford Coppola to explore the intersection of story and art, fiction and film. It also offers news, events, and screenwriting courses.

▌ Online Screenwriting Courses

Alpha Scripts

Web: www.rivalquest.com/
alphascripts

This is a guide to the basic tenets of screenwriting. It covers character traits, character creation, scenes, locations, and the pitch.

E-Script Courses and Workshops for Screen and TV Writers

Web: www.singlelane.com/escript/
escreen.htm

This site offers five- and ten-week intensives in playwriting, screenwriting, and television writing in both course and workshop form.

From Script to Screen

Web: www.fromscripttoscreen.com

This site offers advice and tips to beginning writers as well as a forum that allows writers to submit their own ideas and scripts to Praxis Film Company. There is also a free e-mail newsletter.

John Truby's Writer's Studio

Web: www.truby.com

Well-known screenwriting teacher John Truby offers online courses, audio courses, software, books, and advice for a fee.

UCLA Extension

Web: www.uclaextension.com

This UCLA-sponsored lifelong learning center offers a full array of courses in screenwriting and film production. Many courses are available online; the program awards a certificate.

Virtual Script Workshop

Web: www.xerif.com

This Europe-based site contains information about screenwriting, listings for online screenwriting

---

▌ *I don't think anyone should write their autobiography until after they're dead.*
   —SAMUEL GOLDWYN

ONLINE RESOURCES

workshops, and the *Scriptunities* newsletter.

Writers Guild of America Mentor Service

Web: www.wga.org/mentors
This online mentoring service is provided by professional Hollywood-based Writers Guild members to aspiring writers for no charge. WGA members that have agreed to share their time and expertise are from a variety of fields including theatrical films, television, animation, and interactive games.

Writers Write University

Web: http://www.writerswrite .com/screenwriting
This online education center offers screenwriting courses as well as news, advice; tips; lists of recommended books, periodicals, software, and other resources; and a discussion board.

Writing Classes

Web: www.writingclasses.com
Offers online ten-week screenwriting workshops for beginning and advanced writers. The site also offers classes in writing dialogue, film analysis, TV sitcom writing, TV drama writing, and how to sell a screenplay.

Writingschool.com

Web: www.writingschool.com/ scren201.htm
Writingschool.com offers a comprehensive online ten-week class in screenwriting for $245, as well as fee-based mentoring and an advanced class.

Thus, in a real sense, I am constantly writing autobiography, but I have to turn it into fiction in order to give it credibility.
—**KATHERINE PATERSON**, *The Spying Heart*

About the most originality that any writer can hope to achieve honestly is to steal with good judgment.
—**JOSH BILLINGS**

■ Research

All-Movie Guide

Web: www.allmovie.com

This fun site contains a searchable movie database, film finder, people finder, glossary, essays, DVD reviews, and factoids. It also offers the All-Music Guide and All-Game Guide.

Bartlett's *Familiar Quotations*

Web: www.bartleby.com/100

This site offers more than 11,000 quotations and a concordance index with more than 52,000 entries searchable by keyword.

Doctor Dictionary

Web: www.dictionary.com

This site offers a voluminous online dictionary, thesaurus, and translator. It also contains foreign dictionaries and language resources. You can sign up for a free e-mail word of the day.

Encyclopedia.com

Web: www.encyclopedia.com

This site contains a comprehensive online encyclopedia and includes illustrations, graphs, and photographs.

Highbeam Research

Web: www.highbeam.com/library

This extensive archive has more than 28 million documents from 2,600 sources—a vast collection of articles from leading publications. It is updated daily and goes back twenty years.

Internet Movie Database

Web: www.imdb.com

This is the site everyone in Hollywood uses to track down credits, year of release, award history, production notes, plot details, and so forth, for the more than 180,000 movies in release. The site also contains daily news and newsletters, articles, trailers, and trivia.

Library of Congress

Web: www.loc.gov

Official government repository lists major categories of American Memory, Global Getaways, America's Library, Exhibitions, Wise Guide, and Legislative Information.

ONLINE RESOURCES

The Margaret Herrick Library

Web: www.oscars.org/mhl/
index.html
This is the research library of the Academy of Motion Picture Arts and Sciences. (See this text's "Libraries and Museums" section for more details.)

MAX FilmPro

Web: www.maxfilmpro.com
This global resource guide for film, television, commercial, and video production offers production resource listings, location scouting information, and film and television production activity.

▌ Screenwriting Software

Character Pro

Web: www.characterpro.com
This software helps writers develop their characters by creating a "Character Spine" and assessing each character's behavioral traits. It retails for $59.99, but a free demo is available.

Final Draft

Web: www.finaldraft.com
Final Draft is the industry standard for screenwriting software (but at $199.95—$149 for students—do you really *need* the industry standard?). The newest edition allows you to print your scripts to .pdf (Acrobat Reader) format for submitting online. The Web site features updates, add-ons, and software. In addition, you can download the demo for free.

IdeaFisher

Web: www.ideacenter.com
IdeaFisher is story creation software that guides you in a brainstorming session as you work out the basic el-

▌ *I believe more in the scissors than I do in the pencil.*
—TRUMAN CAPOTE

ements of your idea. It costs $147, but a free demo is available.

Page 2 Stage

Web: www.page2stage.com

This word processing software is designed for playwrights and screenwriters. It works well in a Windows environment, is easy to learn, and, at $79.95, is less than half the cost of Final Draft. You can check out the demo before you buy.

Screenplay Systems

Web: www.screenplay.com

Movie Magic is a screenwriting program almost as well-known in the industry as Final Draft (in fact, many people prefer it), but at $249 it's even more expensive. This company also makes Dramatica Pro and Story View, two respected programs that assist in the writing process. Free download demos are available for all.

Sophocles Screenwriting Software

Web: www.sophocles.net

Sophocles is a new screenplay software program that emphasizes the

writing process. It allows writers to navigate and manipulate story elements as they create the script. It costs $120, but a trial version is free.

StoryWeaver

Web: www.storymind.com

StoryWeaver guides you through the story-development process by cross-referencing story cards you create along the way. The software is $29.95, but a free demo is available.

Writers DreamKit

Web: www.store.write-bros.com

This story software takes you from initial story idea through to completed narrative treatment. It costs $59.95, but a free demo is available.

Writer's Software Companion

Web: www.writers-software.com

This is a multimedia learning system for fiction writers that assists in composing the plot and building structure.

The Daily Script

Web: www.dailyscript.com

This collection of movie scripts and screenplays is a great resource for writers and actors and those who simply enjoy reading movie scripts, any of which you can download for free.

Drew's Script-O-Rama

Web: www.script-o-rama.com

This is a comprehensive index of movie and television scripts on the Internet. You'll find more than 600 screenplays, transcripts, and television scripts, any of which you can download for free.

Iscriptdb.com

Web: www.iscriptdb.com

This is a searchable database of movie scripts from many different Web sites, any of which you can download for free.

MovieCentre

Web: www.moviecentre.net

MovieCentre lists more than 1,600 movie scripts, any of which you can download for free.

Movie Page

Web: www.movie-page.com

This is an online magazine with news, articles, clips, posters, trailers, DVD release information, and a long list of movie scripts, any of which you can download for free.

Script Crawler

Web: www.scriptcrawler.net

This search engine allows you to look through multiple resources listing thousands of movie and TV scripts. Some providers charge a fee.

Simply Scripts

Web: www.simplyscripts.com

This fee-based service is a searchable index of screenplays and transcripts for television, radio, movies, anime, and foreign films.

❚ Stores

Larry Edmund's Cinema Bookstore

Web: www.larryedmunds.com

Located in Hollywood, this store caters to film aficionados and collectors, with more than 500,000 movie photographs, 6,000 original posters, and 20,000 motion picture and theater books for sale.

Samuel French Bookstore

Web: www.samuelfrench.com

Samuel French is primarily a theater-related resource with stores in New York, Los Angeles, Toronto, and London. Titles include plays, monologues, audition material, and classroom guides, but the Los Angeles store also features an extensive collection of film-related material.

Screenstyle.com

Web: www.screenstyle.com

This Web site sells screenwriting software, books, magazines, instructional DVDs, and audiotapes.

The Writers Store

Web: www.writersstore.com

This is where the professionals go. Located in West Los Angeles, The Writers Store specializes in screenwriting books, software, and supplies. Its staff is quite knowledgeable. The Web site keeps track of the store's most popular products, which will give you some insight into what working writers are buying.

❙ *I am a galley slave to pen and ink.*

−HONORE DE BALZAC

❙ *Better to write for yourself and have no public, than to write for the public and have no self.*

−CYRIL CONNOLLY

Hollywood Digest

Web: www.hollywooddigest.com

The HollywoodNet Screenwriters List gives you a great way to communicate and network with fellow writers. It's free to subscribe, but you must have written at least one screenplay, book manuscript, or play.

Keepwriting

Web: www.davetrottier.com/ allwriters/index.htm

Contains a list of screenwriters' groups all over the country and offers tips on how to start, run, and maintain a writer's group.

Venice Arts Screenwriters Workshop

Web: www.venicearts.com/work shopframe.htm

Venice Arts offers Web-based screenwriters' groups classed by genre, which allow members to read and critique each others' work.

A writer is a person for whom writing is more difficult than it is for other people.
   —THOMAS MANN

GLOSSARY OF IMPORTANT TERMS

Action | The description of the moving pictures within a scene, as opposed to dialogue, which is formatted differently. Action includes sounds that are particularly notable in the scene, such as when a CAR EXPLODES (important sounds are often capitalized).

Ad lib | In a script, this instructs the actors to fill in the dialogue with incidental lines.

Agent | A contractually retained representative of a writer, director, actor, cinematographer, composer, or other artist. Agents are licensed by the state and are legally prohibited from producing.

Angle | Directs the camera to a particular person or object as in "Angle on Tree" or "Angle on Lisa."

Angles (or Shots) | In a screenplay, the camera angle should be designated only when absolutely necessary: *wide, low, tight, close, high, bird's eye,* and so on.

Arbitration | A binding committee determination by members of the Writers Guild of America regarding which writers should receive screen credit on a completed film.

Attached | Term designating that a well-known actor and/or director agreed to make a movie from a particular script.

Back end | To receive payment after a project is fully funded and/or sold is to receive it at the back end.

Bankable | Designation given to movie stars or directors who can get a project financed if their name is attached.

Brad | An industry-standard brass fastener used to hold a three-hole punched screenplay together.

CGI | Computer-generated images. They are seen more and more in big-budget films such as *Lord of the Rings* and *The Matrix*. They are very expensive to achieve professionally.

Character | Any person appearing in a screenplay.

Character arc | The progress of the emotional development of a character over the course of the script.

Cinematographer | The person who puts the story on film by overseeing the camerawork and lighting. Also known as the director of photography (DP).

Close-up | A very close camera angle on a character or object.

Committed | Term designating that an actor, director, producer, production company, or studio has agreed in writing to be involved in a project.

Compress | To adjust a word-processing or screenplay-formatting program so that it compresses the distance between lines on a page, allowing a writer to squeeze a 125-page document into 120 pages or less. It's hard to fool knowledgeable professionals with compressing.

Coverage | Two- to three-page synopsis and assessment of a script written by a staff reader. Most executives don't read scripts; they only read coverage.

Crane shot | A moving shot from a camera on a lift.

Development | What happens to a script after it is acquired, usually referring to the process of rewriting it after repeated rounds of notes. When the process drags on, it is often referred to as "development hell." Often other writers are brought in during this process.

Dialogue | The words exchanged between characters.

Digital | A film made entirely with a digital video camera.

Director | The person with the overall creative power on a film. Directors usually choose or have approval over the rest of the creative staff, i.e., cast, cinematographer, production designer, and composer. They are responsible for seeing the script brought to life in the shooting process, and the movie's success or failure ultimately rests on their shoulders.

Dissolve | An editing direction in which one scene melts into another, one fading out while the next fades in.

Fade out | The image fades to black.

Feature | A film approximately two hours long made to be exhibited in movie theaters.

Flashback | A scene from the past that interrupts the action.

Freeze frame | The image freezes on the screen and becomes a still shot.

Greenlight | The go-ahead to proceed into production once financing is secured.

Headshot | An eight- by ten-inch photograph of an actor used for audition and casting purposes.

Heat | When a script becomes "hot," it means a lot of people are talking about it.

Hip pocket | An unofficial relationship with an established agent in which the agent will represent you even though you haven't signed with them, as in, "After Writers and Artists hip pocketed me I got a meeting with New Line and pitched my script." You have to do all the work; the agent's name simply gives you some cachet.

Hook | A catchy phrase that makes you want to see a movie, even though it doesn't tell you what it's about.

Indies | Motion pictures financed and produced independently, that is, outside of the major studios.

Logline | A one- or two-sentence description of your story.

Manager | A representative of a writer, director, actor, cinematographer, composer, or other artist who may or may not be contractually retained. Managers are not licensed by the state. Unlike agents, they are allowed to produce their client's projects. They are prohibited, however, from negotiating their clients' contracts so artists who have a manager but do not have an agent must retain an attorney.

Miniseries | Three hours or more of the same movie, shown on successive nights or weeks on television.

MOS | Without sound. Originated with German technicians in the early days of film, i.e., "Ve'll shoot dis *mit out sound.*"

MOW | Movie of the week. A film made primarily for airing on television.

Notes | Creative input about a script from a director, producer, agent, or film or TV executive.

Option | The right to buy a property for a set amount of time for a set amount of money. If the option expires without being exercised, all rights return to the writer. Commonly used by independent producers reluctant to buy a script without knowing for sure that they can get it financed.

Package | To put together the elements necessary to secure financing for a film, i.e., a script, a director, and some name talent.

Pass | A rejection of your script. "We're going to pass" is Hollywood's way of saying "We didn't like it."

Pinks | From the expression "we'll fix it in the pinks." Revisions of shooting scripts are usually done on colored paper. Multiple revisions, all on different colors, are keyed on the title page so everyone in the cast and crew can make sure they're working from a fully updated script.

Pitch | The attempt to sell a project to someone capable of giving you a deal.

Points | Percentage profit participation. One point equals 1 percent.

Polish | A minor rewrite intended to be final.

Preproduction | After a project's financing comes through, it moves into preproduction, or preparation for shooting.

Producer | The head honcho in the movie hierarchy. The producer is the individual who gets the film made. The producer finds the script, attaches talent, finds a director, and secures financing. The director is the creative boss on a film set, but the producer is the director's boss. The producer can fire anyone, including the director, although when the director or actors are well known, their power often overrides the producer's.

Production script | A script that is considered final; the script that will be used in preparation for shooting.

Property | Any story or idea that might form the basis of a movie.

Reader | A person who reads screenplays for a production company and writes a synopsis and assessment.

Release | A legal document that absolves the company reading your material from legal liability in the event that they have already acquired material similar or identical to your story.

Rewrite | The process of implementing story notes offered by an agent or producer.

Script consultant | Someone in the business who reads and critiques a writer's script for a fee. This rarely leads to a script sale, but it can help the writer focus on problems in the writing. This service costs anywhere from $150 to $1,000 so it should truly be a writer's last resort. Instead, writers should try to find other screenwriters or a writing group, as other writers' notes are often just as helpful.

Script doctor | A screenwriter whose specialty is fixing story or dialogue problems. Many working writers fall into this category because it is often more lucrative. Subsequently some well-known script doctors have worked for decades without earning a 'written by' credit.

Script reader | Same as a story analyst. Someone who works for agents, producers, and executives by reading, analyzing, and critiquing scripts. The script reader's report is referred to as coverage, and unless it is highly complimentary no one else in that company will read the script. Each company uses its own script readers, so bad coverage in one place won't hurt you in another.

Shooting script | The final version of the screenplay from which the movie is made. At this stage the script is locked, so any changes are designated by different-colored pages, i.e. pinks.

Short script | A story meant to be made into a short film from one to thirty minutes in length.

Signatory | If a producer, production company, or agent is a signatory of the Writers Guild of America, he or she has signed an agreement to abide by WGA rules. A new screenwriter who has sold a script cannot join the WGA unless the entity that purchased the script is a WGA signatory.

Smash cut | A sudden cut from one scene to another.

Spec ⏐ A script the writer creates speculatively, without being hired or commissioned, on the hope that it can be sold.

Step deal ⏐ A typical script deal in which the writer can be removed from the project at several different junctures. The writer will only get the full purchase price if the producer is happy with the rewrite. If he or she is not happy with the rewrite, the writer will get a percentage of the money, and the producer will hire someone else to finish. It's not what most writers want, but they don't have a choice on their first sale.

Story analyst ⏐ Same as a script reader. Someone who works for agents, producers, and executives by reading, analyzing, and critiquing scripts. The story analyst's report is referred to as coverage, and unless it is highly complimentary no one else in that company will read the script. Each company uses its own story analysts so bad coverage in one place won't hurt the writer's chances in another.

Sublim ⏐ A shot lasting a fraction of a second.

Super ⏐ A superimposition—one image (usually words) overlaid on another.

Synopsis ⏐ A one- to two-page description of a script.

Trades ⏐ The major newspapers (*Variety* and the *Hollywood Reporter*) that cover the entertainment business.

Trailer ⏐ A two- to four-minute preview of a finished movie.

Treatment ⏐ A scene-by-scene description of all the action of an entire script written in prose form, generally five to ten pages long.

Turnaround ⏐ When a script has been developed but the decision is made not to produce it, the writer or producer in control is given the chance to get it produced elsewhere.

Tweak ⏐ To make minor changes to a script.

Zip pan ⏐ A superfast pan, creating a blurred image and a sense of quick movement.

Zoom ⏐ A stationary camera with a zoom lens enlarges or diminishes the image.

SUGGESTED READING

Argentini, Paul. *Elements of Style for Screenwriters.* Lone Eagle, 1998. This is a good nuts-and-bolts introduction to the terminology of filmmaking and a step-by-step guide to making sure your story is properly formatted. The author starts with a short sample screenplay, which is then peppered with helpful annotations. The book also contains an extensive glossary.

Blacker, Irwin W. *The Elements of Screenwriting.* Longman, 1996. In the tradition of Strunk and White's classic *The Elements of Style,* this reference work offers screenwriters an easily searchable index that is particularly useful for specific formatting or style questions.

Brady, John. *The Craft of the Screenwriter.* Simon & Schuster, 1981. This enjoyable book features interviews with an impressive roster of well-known screenwriters such as Robert Towne, William Goldman, Paul Schrader, and Paddy Chayefsky. All the big screenwriters from the seventies are here; the author seems to have gotten to them before they got sick of telling the same stories over and over.

Cole, Hillis R., Jr., and Judith H. Haag. *The Complete Guide to Standard Script Formats.* CMC Publishing, 1999. This book is an excellent resource for understanding the format component of writing a screenplay. It does not address the art of writing or the literary aspects of how to construct a story suitable for making into a film; instead it offers all you need to know to format your story properly.

Cowgill, Linda J. *Secrets of Screenplay Structure: How to Recognize and Emulate the Structural Frameworks of Great Films.* Lone Eagle, 1999. This book leads writers through the principles and fundamentals of screenwriting and teaches what to look for when analyzing a movie. Many finished films differ from the final shooting script; the author uses examples to help illuminate why changes were made and how they improved the story.

Field, Syd. *Selling a Screenplay: the Screenwriter's Guide to Hollywood*. Dell, 1989. ▌ Syd Field is the best-known author of screenwriting books in Hollywood and his first book, *Screenplay,* is considered a classic. Here, he shares his wealth of knowledge about how Hollywood works, and discusses the best way for a new screenwriter to break in on the strength of his or her writing.

Flinn, Denny Martin. *How Not to Write a Screenplay: 101 Common Mistakes Most Screenwriters Make*. Lone Eagle, 1999. ▌ This book carefully identifies and examines the common mistakes screenwriters invariably make when writing a screenplay. The author offers practical advice on formatting, content, structure, pacing, plot resolution, and dialogue, illustrating his points with excerpts from screenplays both good and bad. In Hollywood, it's often said you can learn more from reading bad scripts than good ones. This book shows you why.

Frensham, Raymond G. *Teach Yourself Screenwriting*. McGraw-Hill, 1997. ▌ This volume teaches the fundamentals of translating creative ideas into script format. Among the topics covered are writing effective dialogue, the basics of plot structure, expressing ideas in visual language, and presenting a finished work to its best advantage.

Hicks, Neill D. *Screenwriting 101: The Essential Craft of Feature Film Writing*. Michael Wiese Productions, 1999. ▌ If you want to understand the basics of screenwriting, this book covers them all: format, structure, character, and dialogue. It also offers exercises for writers to work on as they progress. It is one of the most comprehensive guides to getting a first script written.

Howard, David. *The Tools of Screenwriting: A Writer's Guide to the Craft and Elements of a Screenplay*. St. Martin's Press, 1995. ▌ This book illuminates the essential elements of cinematic storytelling and reveals the central principles that all good screenplays share. The author addresses questions of dramatic structure, plot, dialogue, character development, setting, imagery, and other crucial topics as they apply to the special art of filmmaking.

SUGGESTED READING

Keane, Christopher. *How to Write a Selling Screenplay.* Broadway Books, 1998. This book takes writers through the entire writing process from developing a story to finding the best agent. Using an annotated version of his own screenplay and citing examples from *Casablanca, Lethal Weapon, Sling Blade, The English Patient,* and other films, the author discusses how to create three-dimensional characters, find a compelling story, build an airtight plot structure, and fine-tune dialogue.

Lerch, Jennifer. *500 Ways to Beat the Hollywood Script Reader: Writing the Screenplay the Reader Will Recommend.* Fireside, 1999. If anyone important in Hollywood reads your story, it will most likely come to them in the form of coverage, a brief report reducing your screenplay to a two-page synopsis and offering an assessment of your characters, dialogue, and plot. This book, written by a Hollywood script reader, offers you 500 tips on what the industry is looking for, what to avoid, and how to turn a "pass" into a "recommend."

McKee, Robert. *Story: Substance, Structure, Style, and the Principles of Screenwriting.* Regan Books, 1997. McKee is one of the best-known screenwriting teachers and is very respected in Hollywood. In *Story,* McKee puts into book form what he has been teaching screenwriters for years in his seminar on story structure, which is considered by many to be a prerequisite to the film biz. McKee is passionate about the art of screenwriting. "No one needs yet another recipe book on how to reheat Hollywood leftovers," he writes. "We need a rediscovery of the underlying tenets of our art, the guiding principles that liberate talent."

Rosenthal, Lisa (editor). *The Writing Group Book: Creating and Sustaining a Successful Writing Group.* Chicago Review Press, 2003. Marketing your script is a useless and expensive endeavor unless your story is truly spectacular before you begin. Without access to professional script consultants or an armload of film school professors, you would be strongly advised to seek the input, expertise, and objectivity of fellow writers to help you hone your story until it's as close to perfect as you can get it. This useful book tells you how to find, start, or maintain a writing group and have a lot of fun in the process.

Seger, Linda. *Creating Unforgettable Characters.* Henry Holt & Co., 1990. Linda Seger is another well-known and highly respected screenwriting teacher; you can find her most famous book, *How to Make a Good Script Great,* on almost every shelf in Hollywood. Here, she shows how to create strong, multidimensional characters, covering everything from research to character. This book also contains great interviews with today's top writers.

Seger, Linda. *Making a Good Writer Great: A Creativity Workbook for Screenwriters*. Silman-James Press, 1999. ▌Designed not just to awaken creativity but to teach the writer the process of being a creative thinker within the context of screenwriting, this unique book combines current theories of creativity with the practices of screenwriting, focusing on ways in which screenwriters can learn to think and work more creatively.

Trottier, David. *The Screenwriter's Bible*. Silman-James Press, 1998. ▌This is six books in one: (1) A screenwriting primer that provides a concise presentation of screenwriting basics; (2) a workbook that walks the writer through the writing process, from nascent ideas through revisions; (3) a guide to correct formats for both screenplays and TV scripts; (4) a spec-writing guide that demonstrates today's spec style through sample scenes and analysis; (5) a sales and marketing guide that presents proven strategies to help you create a marketing plan; and (6) a resource guide that provides addresses and contacts for industry organizations, schools, publications, support groups, services, contests, etc.

Wharton, Brooke A. *The Writer Got Screwed (But Didn't Have To)*. Harper Resource, 1999. ▌An authoritative and entertaining primer for the beginning writer, this book takes on not just the legal and business issues of writing, but also how to get a career jump-started. The first section covers copyright, libel, and contracts; the next section covers the differences between agents, lawyers, and managers. The third section is a series of interviews with writers, agents, and producers; and the final section offers lists of competitions, fellowships, internships, and agencies.

CONTEST SUBMISSION CALENDAR

All dates listed in this calendar denote *final* entry deadlines. Please refer to individual entries for early deadlines, where appropreate.

January

10 Broadcast Education Association (BEA) National Juried Faculty Script Writing Competition, 17

23 UCLA Extension/Diane Thomas Screenwriting Awards, 58

30 Christian Screenwrite Contest, 21

31 Applause Screenwriting Competition, 13

31 AudioScript CD Contest, 15

31 *Filmmakers* Magazine/The Radmin Company Screenwriting Competition, 25

31 Key West IndieFest, 34

31 PEN Center USA West Literary Awards, 41

February

6 CinemaSpoke Screenplay Competition, 84

13 CAPE Foundation New Writer Awards, 82

14 All Student Screenplay Contest, 7

May

June

July

SUBMISSION CALENDAR

CONTEST

15 Cape Fear Independent Film Network (CFIFN) Sometime in October Film Festival and Screenplay Competition, 84
16 Walt Disney Studios/ABC Writers Fellowship, 79
23 A.K.A Shriekfest Horror/Science Fiction Screenwriting Contest, 6
25 Drawn Productions Short Script Writing Contest, 23
25 POWER UP Movie Making Grant, 77
31 Blue Sky International Film Festival's Screenplay Competition, 81

August

1 Tennessee Screenwriting Association Script Competition, 55
16 Mania Fest, 35
20 20/20 Screenwriting Contest, 58
31 Organization of Black Screenwriters Script Competition, 39
31 Set in Texas Screenwriting Competition, 49

September

1 American Zoetrope Screenplay Contest, 11
1 Screenplay Festival, 46
3 WriteMovies.com Writing Contest, 62
21 Thanks Be to Grandmother Winifred Foundation, 79
23 America's Best Writing Competition, 12
30 Screenwriters Forum Annual Screenplay Contest, 46

October

15 American Screenwriters Association International Screenplay Competition, 10
15 Guy A. Hanks and Marvin Miller Screenwriting Program, 73
30 The Fade In Awards, 24
31 Independent Black Film Festival Screenwriting Contest, 31

November

5 Screen Arts Foundation $5,000 Prize for Screenwriting, 45
13 American Accolades/TV and Shorts Competition, 9

December

Open Submission

CALENDAR

CONTEST SUBMISSION

INDEX OF CONTESTS BY GENRE

Note: Contests that are not listed here accept all genres.

ALPHABETICAL INDEX

ALPHABETICAL INDEX

ALPHABETICAL INDEX

▮ About the Author

M ICHAEL HADDAD is a professional story analyst for Paramount Classics with more than twenty years' experience in the movie business. He has also done story analysis for Initial Entertainment Group, Unapix Films, Capella International, Little Studio Pictures, American Filmworks, and Karlin Green Media. He earned a B.A. in Drama from Bennington College and has studied film at the American Film Institute, UCLA Extension, and the Art Center School of Design. He has read and analyzed thousands of scripts, and his ability to pinpoint story strengths and weaknesses, and assess character development, plotting, narrative, dialogue, marketability, and audience demographics has helped him advise many producers and distributors with regard to acquiring material.

The Film Festival Guide

For Filmmakers, Film Buffs, and Industry Professionals

Revised and Updated

Adam Langer

"It's good at last to have all this material gathered in the same place, since it is otherwise so hard to find."

—ROGER EBERT, film critic

"Everything's here, from the big and famous (Cannes) to the small and specialized (Insect Fear Film Festival). . . . Any library with travel or film reference collections will want to consider adding this guide."

—BOOKLIST

"More detailed and personal than Internet festival sites, this work is well worth the price."

—LIBRARY JOURNAL

Breaking into films is tough, finding the scoop on each festival is even tougher . . . until now. The best film festival guide just got better with more festivals, more insider information, and great new additions including

- Tips for first-time filmmakers
- Submission calendar so you'll never miss a deadline
- Over 500 newly updated festivals
- Interviews with top festival directors
- More than 100 film houses around the world for film buffs

Paper, $16.95 (CAN $25.95)

6 × 9, 1-55652-415-3

 CHICAGO REVIEW PRESS

Distributed by Independent Publishers Group

www.ipgbook.com

Available at your local bookstore, or call 1-800-888-4741.

The Writing Group Book

Creating and Sustaining a Successful Writing Group

Edited by Lisa Rosenthal

"This book's cheer is write on! Read it and you will."
—RITA MAE BROWN

"This is a book for all of us. Write. It will make the sun shine and the rain bring flowers. Write. For the love of the future. And for the future of love."
—NIKKI GIOVANNI, poet

"This book anticipates many of the reefs that bedevil the launching of a group and wise counsel on how to navigate them. Both useful and cheering."
—JEFFREY SWEET, playwright

"*The Writing Group Book* brims with useful information and anecdotes that are anything but dry."
—*WRITER'S DIGEST*

"The collection succeeds by providing how-to information and inspiration."
—*THE WRITER MAGAZINE*

In this insightful guide, more than 30 members of writing groups explain how and why they found a group to join or started one from scratch; how they have kept their group going; and what it has enabled them to accomplish, from simple self-expression to a lifetime of published work. Poets, playwrights, screenwriters, fiction and nonfiction writers, memoirists, children's writers, and others share their tips on how to give constructive critiques, manage difficult members, delegate responsibility for maintaining the group, and keep meetings productive. A resource section details ways to market and sell finished work.

Paper, $14.95 (CAN $22.95)

5½ × 8½, 1-55652-498-6

Distributed by Independent Publishers Group
www.ipgbook.com
Available at your local bookstore, or call 1-800-888-4741.